Fruits Basket™

Volume 11

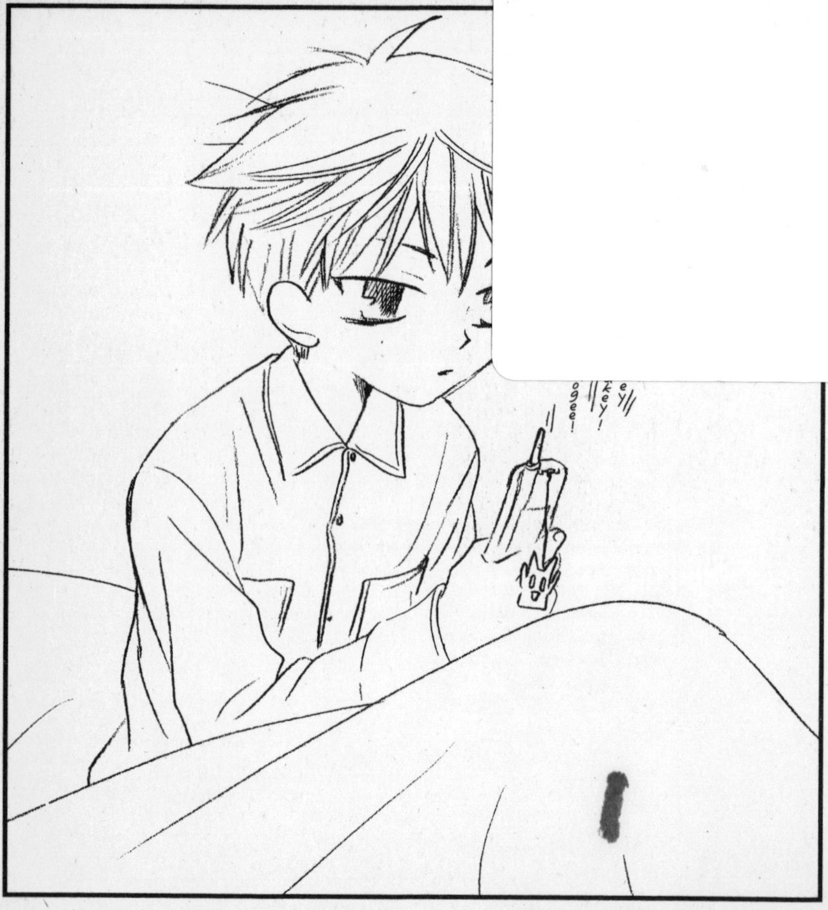

Natsuki Takaya

Fruits Basket Vol. 11
Created by Natsuki Takaya

Translation - Alethea Nibley and Athena Nibley
English Adaptation - Jake Forbes
Contributing Writer - Adam Arnold
Associate Editor - Peter Ahlstrom
Retouch and Lettering - Deron Bennett
Production Artist - Adriana Rivera
Cover Design - Christian Lownds

Editor - Paul Morrissey
Digital Imaging Manager - Chris Buford
Production Managers - Jennifer Miller and Mutsumi Miyazaki
Managing Editor - Jill Freshney
VP of Production - Ron Klamert
Publisher and E.I.C. - Mike Kiley
President and C.O.O. - John Parker
C.E.O. - Stuart Levy

A  Manga

TOKYOPOP Inc.
5900 Wilshire Blvd. Suite 2000
Los Angeles, CA 90036

E-mail: info@TOKYOPOP.com
Come visit us online at www.TOKYOPOP.com

ISBN: 1-59532-406-2

First TOKYOPOP printing: August 2005
10 9 8 7 6 5 4 3 2 1
Printed in the USA

Fruits Basket™

Volume 11

By
Natsuki Takaya

HAMBURG // LONDON // LOS ANGELES // TOKYO

Fruits Basket™

Table of Contents

STORY SO FAR...

Hello, I'm Tohru Honda and I have come to know a terrible secret. After the death of my mother, I was living by myself in a tent, when the Sohma family took me in. I soon learned that the Sohma family lives with a curse! Each family member is possessed by the vengeful spirit of an animal from the Chinese Zodiac. Whenever one of them becomes weak or is hugged by a member of the opposite sex, they change into their Zodiac animal!

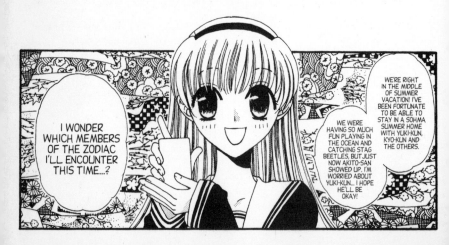

WE'RE RIGHT IN THE MIDDLE OF SUMMER VACATION! I'VE BEEN FORTUNATE TO BE ABLE TO STAY IN A SOHMA SUMMER HOME WITH YUKI-KUN, KYO-KUN AND THE OTHERS.
WE WERE HAVING SO MUCH FUN PLAYING IN THE OCEAN AND CATCHING STAG BEETLES, BUT JUST NOW AKITO-SAN SHOWED UP. I'M WORRIED ABOUT YUKI-KUN... I HOPE HE'LL BE OKAY!
I WONDER WHICH MEMBERS OF THE ZODIAC I'LL ENCOUNTER THIS TIME...?

Tohru Honda

The ever-optimistic hero of our story. An orphan, she now lives in Shigure's house, along with Yuki and Kyo, and is the only person outside of the family who knows the Sohma family's curse.

Yuki Sohma, the Rat

Soft-spoken. Self-esteem issues. At school he's called "Prince Yuki."

Kyo Sohma, the Cat

The Cat who was left out of the Zodiac. Hates Yuki, leeks and miso. But mostly Yuki.

Kagura Sohma, the Boar

Bashful, yet headstrong. Determined to marry Kyo, even if it kills him.

Fruits Basket Characters

Mabudachi Trio

Shigure Sohma, the Dog

Enigmatic, mischievous and a little perverted. A popular novelist.

Hatori Sohma, the Dragon

Family doctor to the Sohmas. Only thing he can't cure is his broken heart.

Ayame Sohma, the Snake

Yuki's older brother. A proud and playful drama queen...er, king. Runs a costume shop.

Saki Hanajima

"Hana-chan." Can sense people's "waves." Goth demeanor scares her classmates.

Arisa Uotani

"Uo-chan." A tough-talking "Yankee" who looks out for her friends.

Tohru's Best Friends

Momiji Sohma, the Rabbit

Half-German. He's older than he looks. Mother rejected him because of the Sohma curse.

Hatsuharu Sohma, the Ox

The nicest of guys, except when he goes "Black." Then you'd better watch out.

Kisa Sohma, the Tiger

Kisa became shy and self-conscious due to constant teasing by her classmates. Yuki, who has similar insecurities, feels particularly close to Kisa.

Fruits Basket Characters

Hiro Sohma, the Ram (or sheep)

This caustic tyke is skilled at throwing verbal barbs, but he has a soft spot for Kisa.

Ritsu Sohma, the Monkey

This shy kimono-wearing member of the Sohma family is gorgeous. But this "she" is really a he!! Crossdressing calms his nerves.

Akito Sohma

The head of the Sohma clan. A dark figure of many secrets. Treated with fear and reverence.

Filler sketch

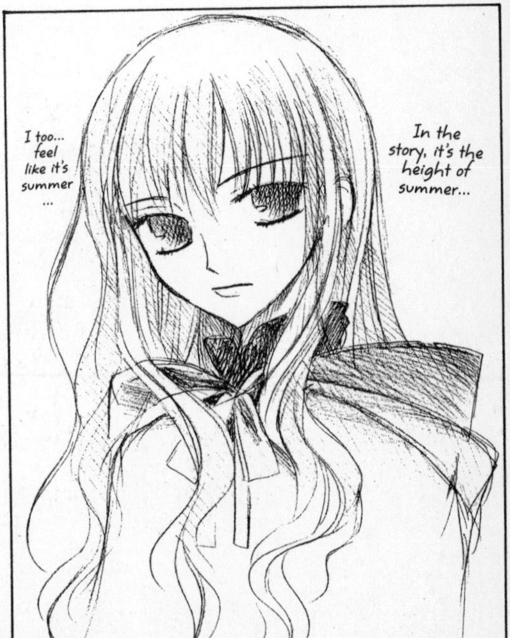
In the story, it's the height of summer...
I too... feel like it's summer ...

We get hot just looking at you, Hana-chan!

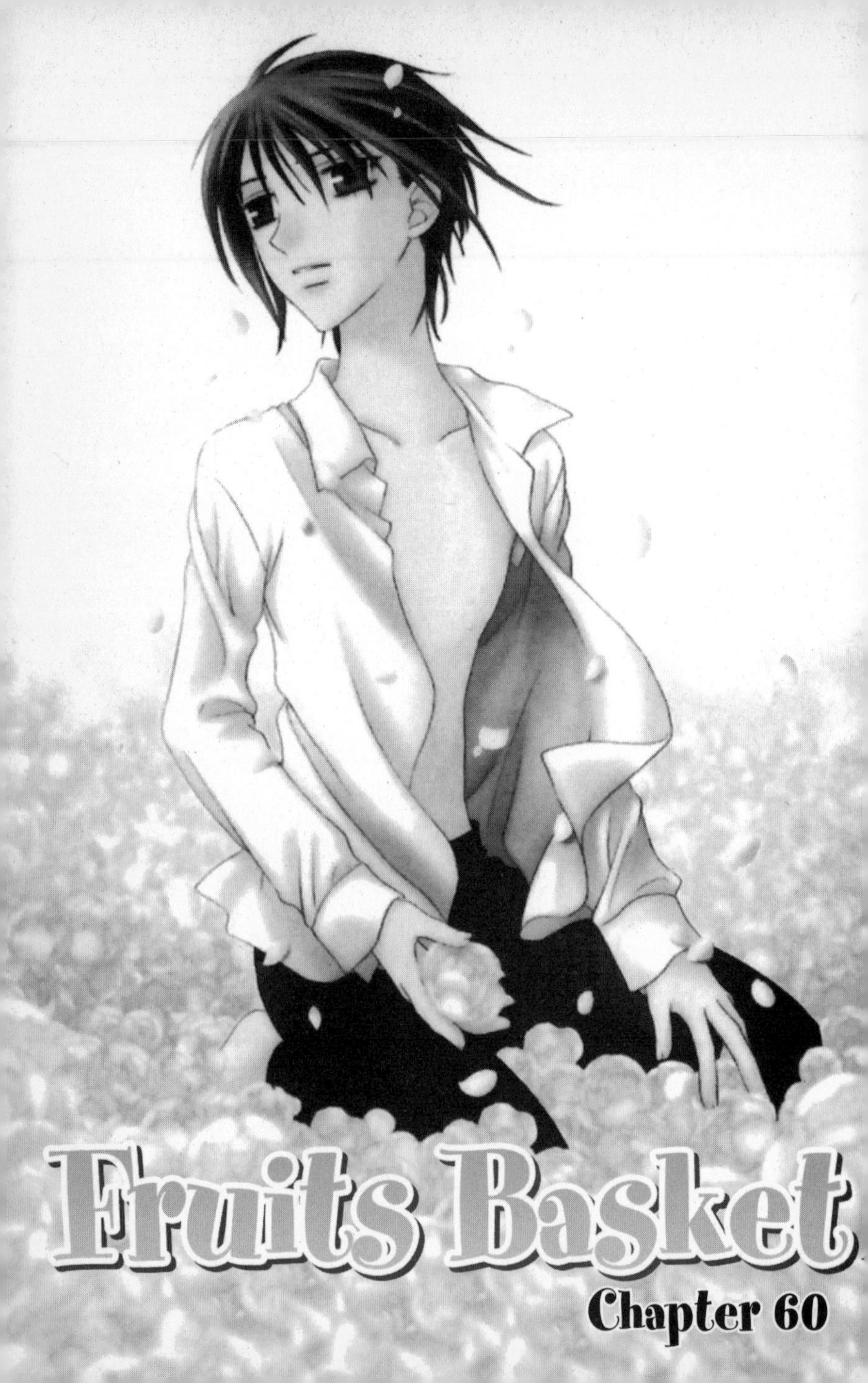
Fruits Basket
Chapter 60

Filler sketch

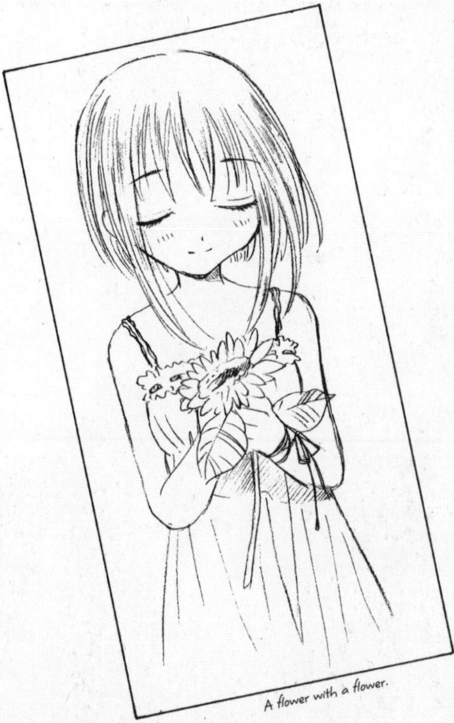

A flower with a flower.

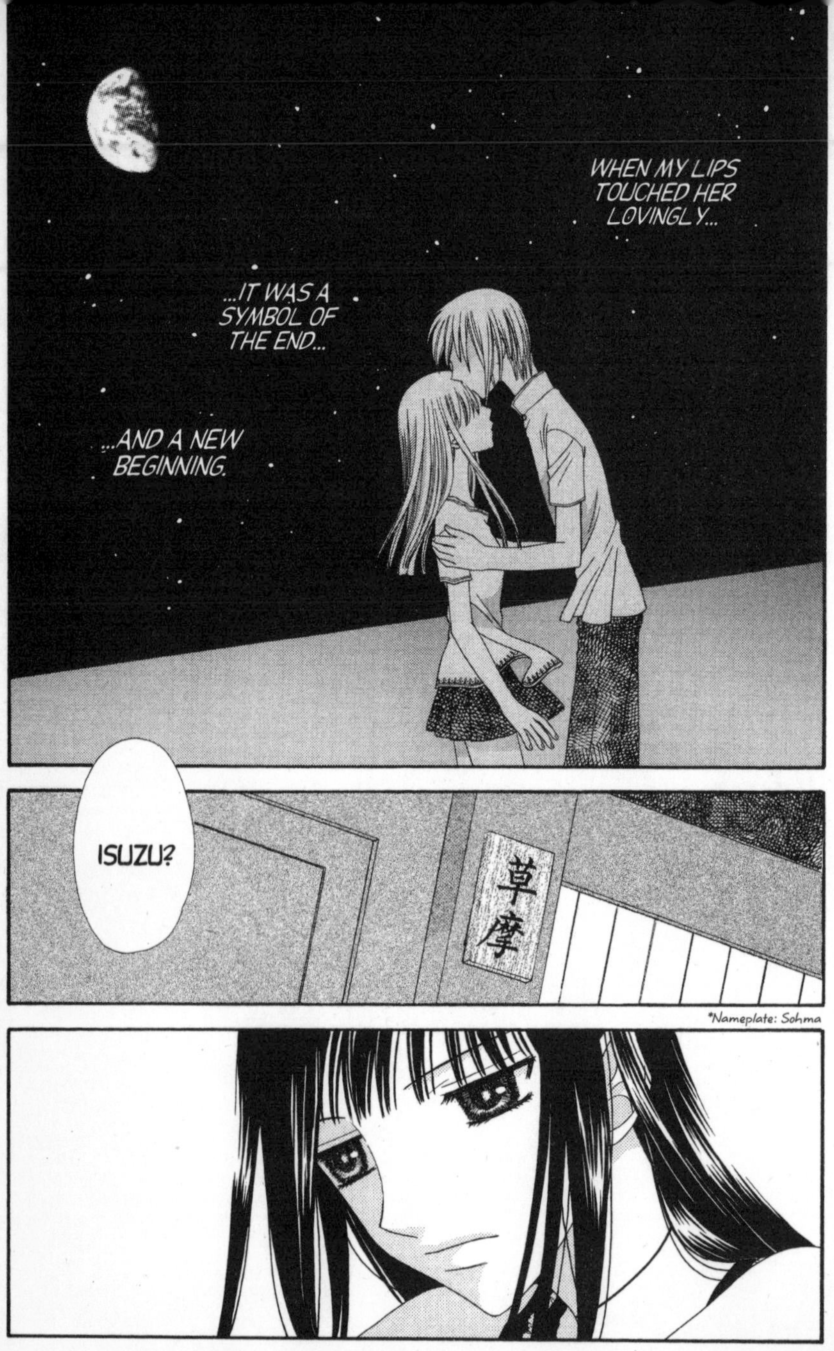
WHEN MY LIPS TOUCHED HER LOVINGLY...
...IT WAS A SYMBOL OF THE END...
...AND A NEW BEGINNING.
ISUZU?
草摩
*Nameplate: Sohma

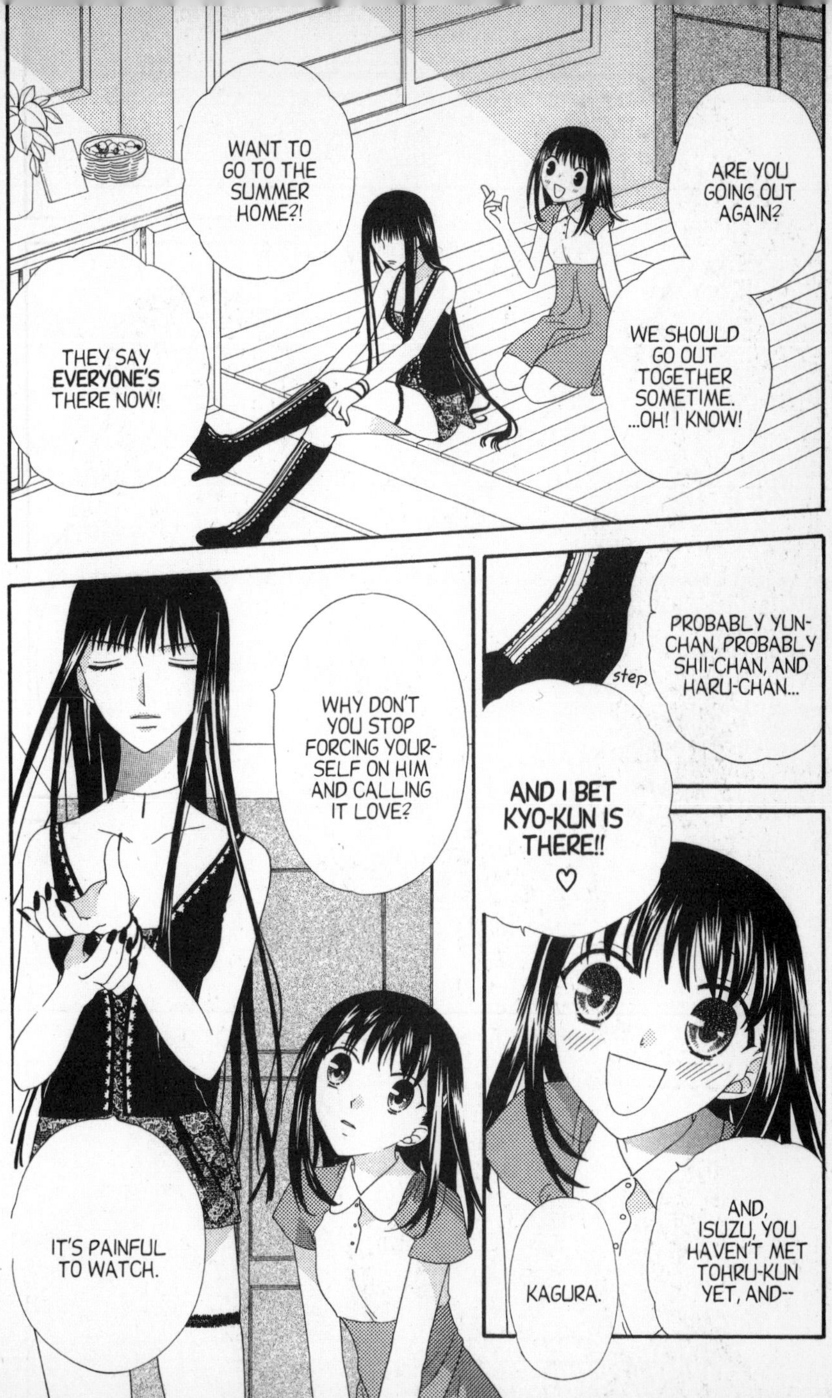
ARE YOU GOING OUT AGAIN?
WE SHOULD GO OUT TOGETHER SOMETIME. ...OH! I KNOW!
WANT TO GO TO THE SUMMER HOME?!
THEY SAY **EVERYONE'S** THERE NOW!
PROBABLY YUN-CHAN, PROBABLY SHII-CHAN, AND HARU-CHAN...
step
AND I BET KYO-KUN IS THERE!! ♡
AND, ISUZU, YOU HAVEN'T MET TOHRU-KUN YET, AND--
KAGURA.
WHY DON'T YOU STOP FORCING YOUR-SELF ON HIM AND CALLING IT LOVE?
IT'S PAINFUL TO WATCH.

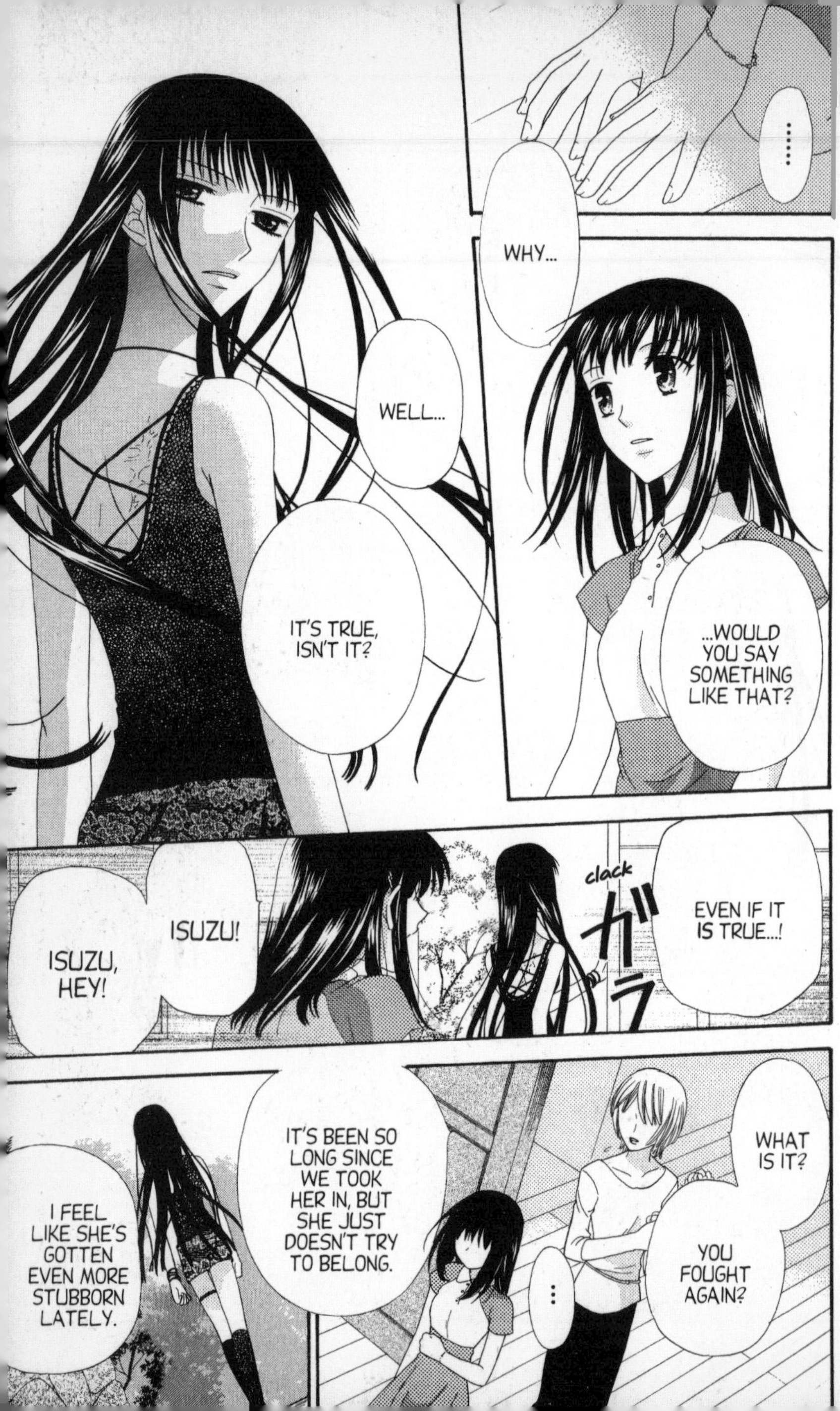
......
WHY...
...WOULD YOU SAY SOMETHING LIKE THAT?
WELL...
IT'S TRUE, ISN'T IT?
EVEN IF IT IS TRUE...!
clack
ガラ
ISUZU!
ISUZU, HEY!
WHAT IS IT?
YOU FOUGHT AGAIN?
...
IT'S BEEN SO LONG SINCE WE TOOK HER IN, BUT SHE JUST DOESN'T TRY TO BELONG.
I FEEL LIKE SHE'S GOTTEN EVEN MORE STUBBORN LATELY.

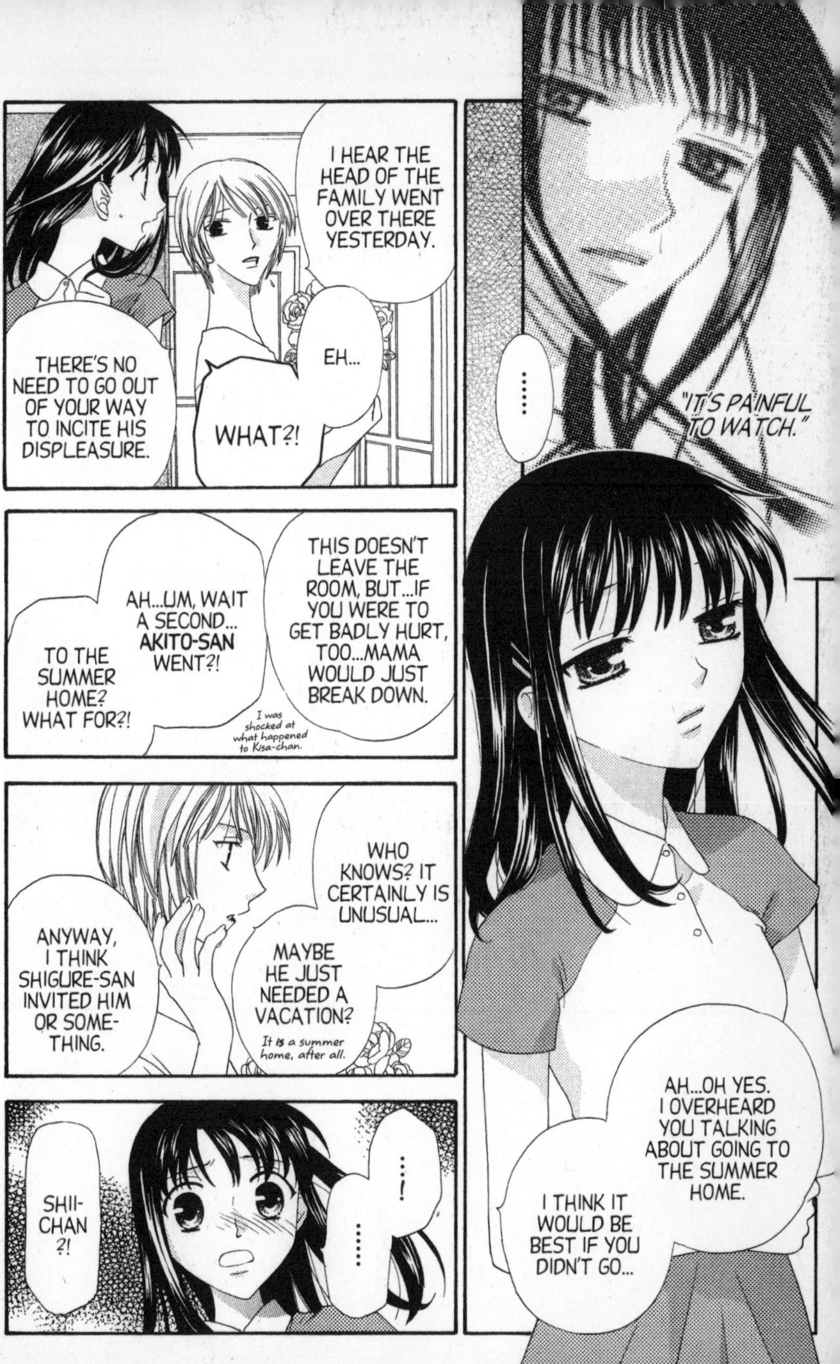
......
"IT'S PAINFUL TO WATCH."
AH...OH YES. I OVERHEARD YOU TALKING ABOUT GOING TO THE SUMMER HOME.
I THINK IT WOULD BE BEST IF YOU DIDN'T GO...
I HEAR THE HEAD OF THE FAMILY WENT OVER THERE YESTERDAY.
EH...
WHAT?!
THERE'S NO NEED TO GO OUT OF YOUR WAY TO INCITE HIS DISPLEASURE.
THIS DOESN'T LEAVE THE ROOM, BUT...IF YOU WERE TO GET BADLY HURT, TOO...MAMA WOULD JUST BREAK DOWN.
I was shocked at what happened to Kisa-chan.
AH...UM, WAIT A SECOND... AKITO-SAN WENT?!
TO THE SUMMER HOME? WHAT FOR?!
WHO KNOWS? IT CERTAINLY IS UNUSUAL...
MAYBE HE JUST NEEDED A VACATION?
It is a summer home, after all.
ANYWAY, I THINK SHIGURE-SAN INVITED HIM OR SOMETHING.
...!
......
SHII-CHAN?!

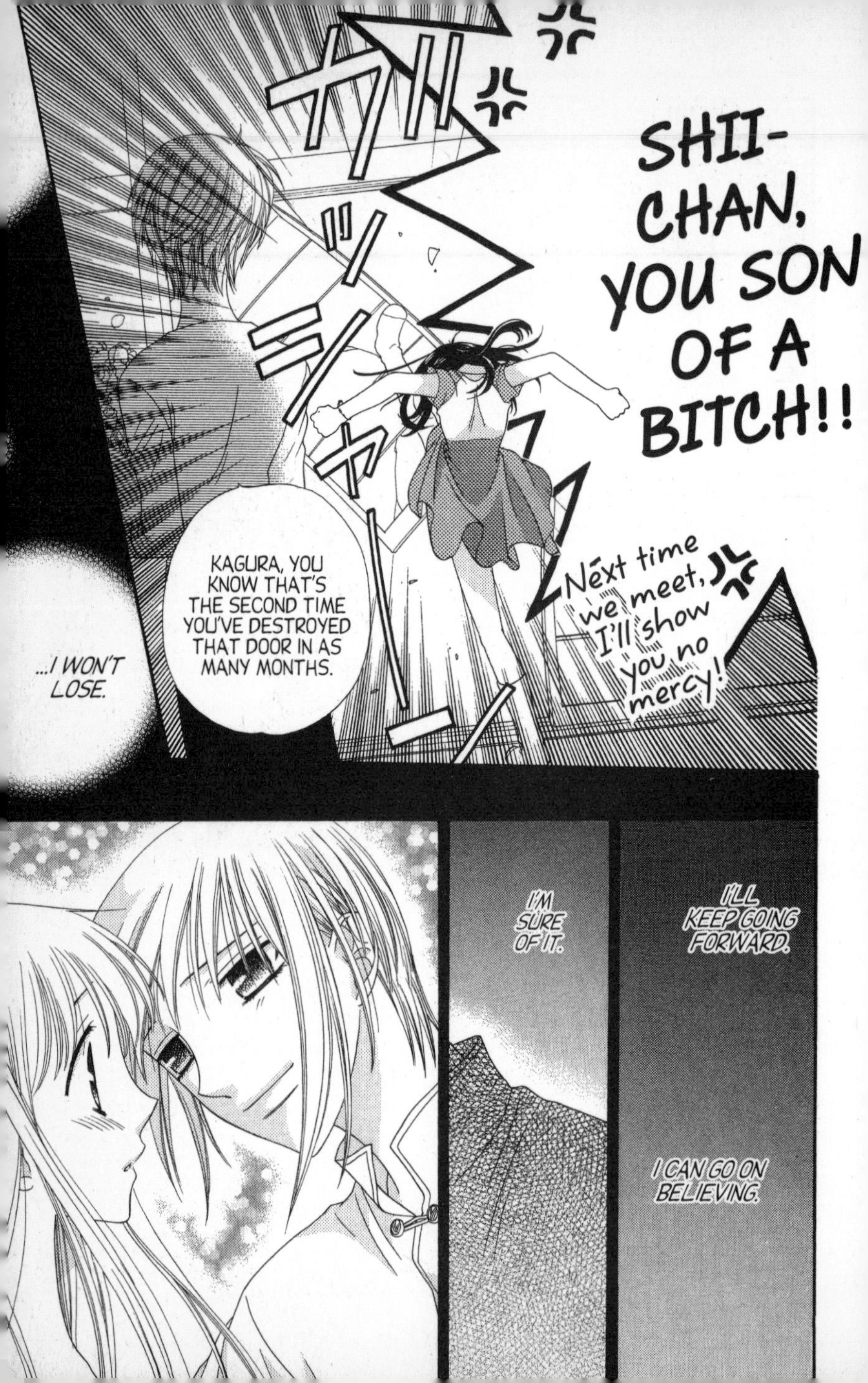
SHII-CHAN, YOU SON OF A BITCH!!
Next time we meet, I'll show you no mercy!
KAGURA, YOU KNOW THAT'S THE SECOND TIME YOU'VE DESTROYED THAT DOOR IN AS MANY MONTHS.
...I WON'T LOSE.
I'LL KEEP GOING FORWARD.
I CAN GO ON BELIEVING.
I'M SURE OF IT.

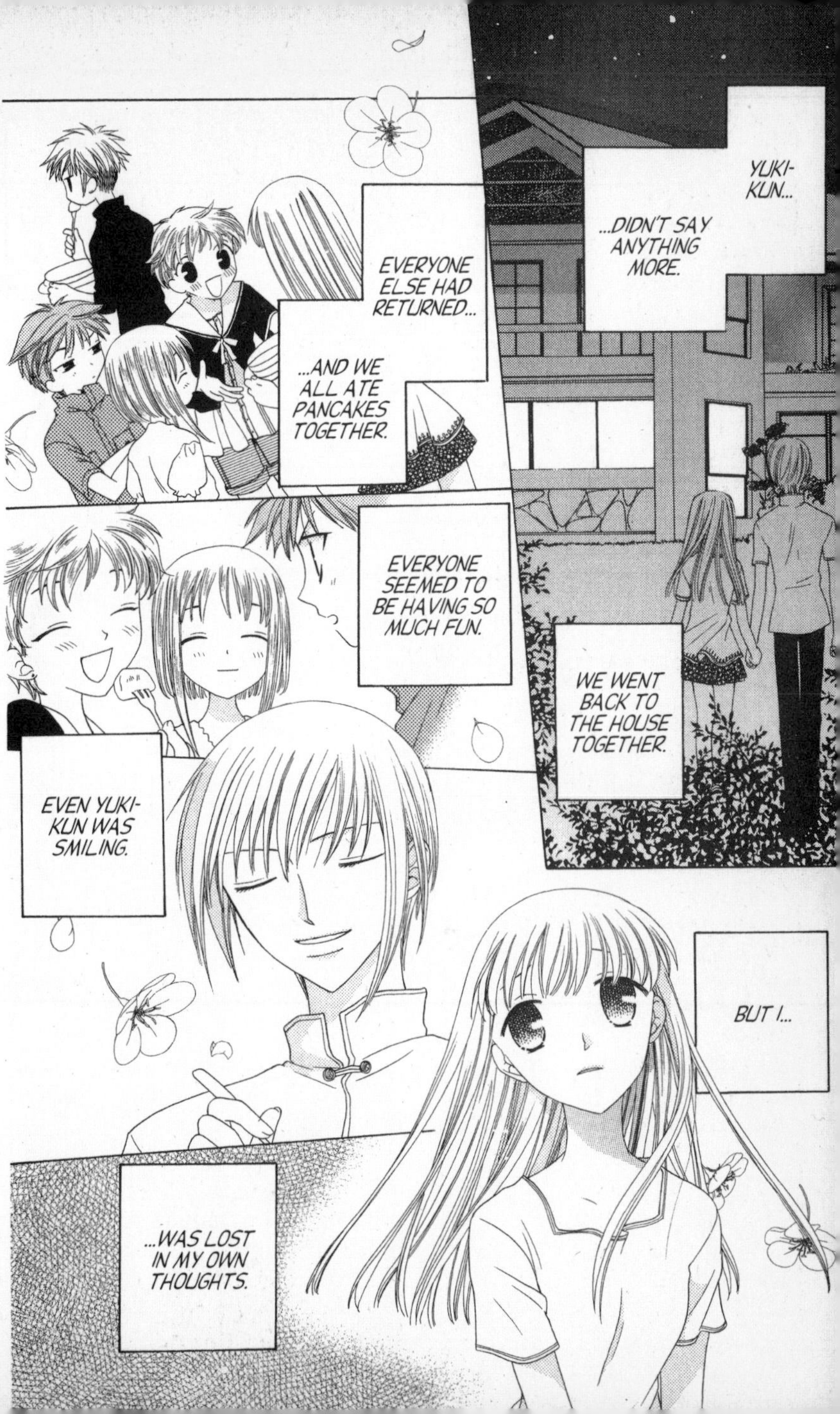

YUKI-KUN...
...DIDN'T SAY ANYTHING MORE.
WE WENT BACK TO THE HOUSE TOGETHER.
EVERYONE ELSE HAD RETURNED...
...AND WE ALL ATE PANCAKES TOGETHER.
EVERYONE SEEMED TO BE HAVING SO MUCH FUN.
EVEN YUKI-KUN WAS SMILING.
BUT I...
...WAS LOST IN MY OWN THOUGHTS.

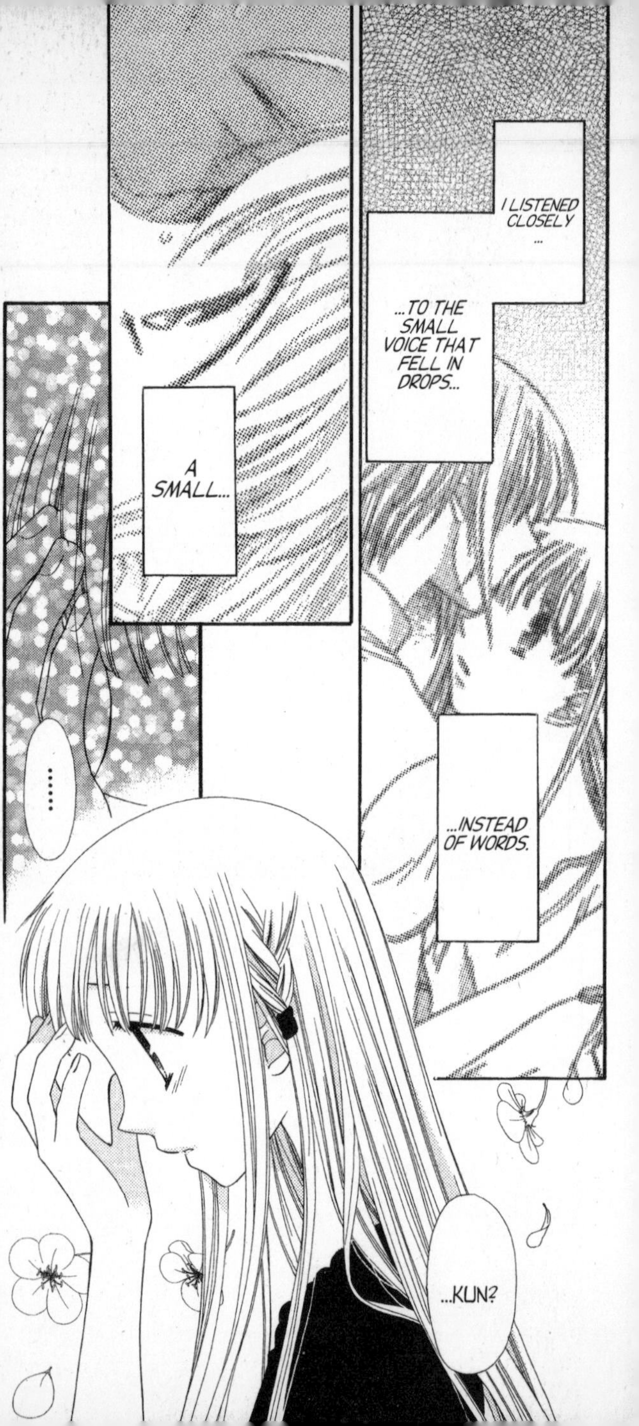
I LISTENED CLOSELY ...
...TO THE SMALL VOICE THAT FELL IN DROPS...
...INSTEAD OF WORDS.
A SMALL...
......
...KUN?

Fruits Basket 11 Part 1:

Hajimemashite and konnichiwa! Takaya, here! I'm pleased to present Furuba volume 11! Eleven is Hiro-kun. Could it be that his desire to be an adult is the basis for his recent decline in his smart-aleck comments, and that he's about to grow? You never know... He might shoot up like a weed. I hope it's not too much of a shock, but, starting with Volume 11, the "Ultra-Special Blah Blah Blah" columns are gone. Not to worry, though. These side columns are still going strong, so you'll still hear plenty of me going on about whatever crosses my mind. Well, please enjoy Furuba.

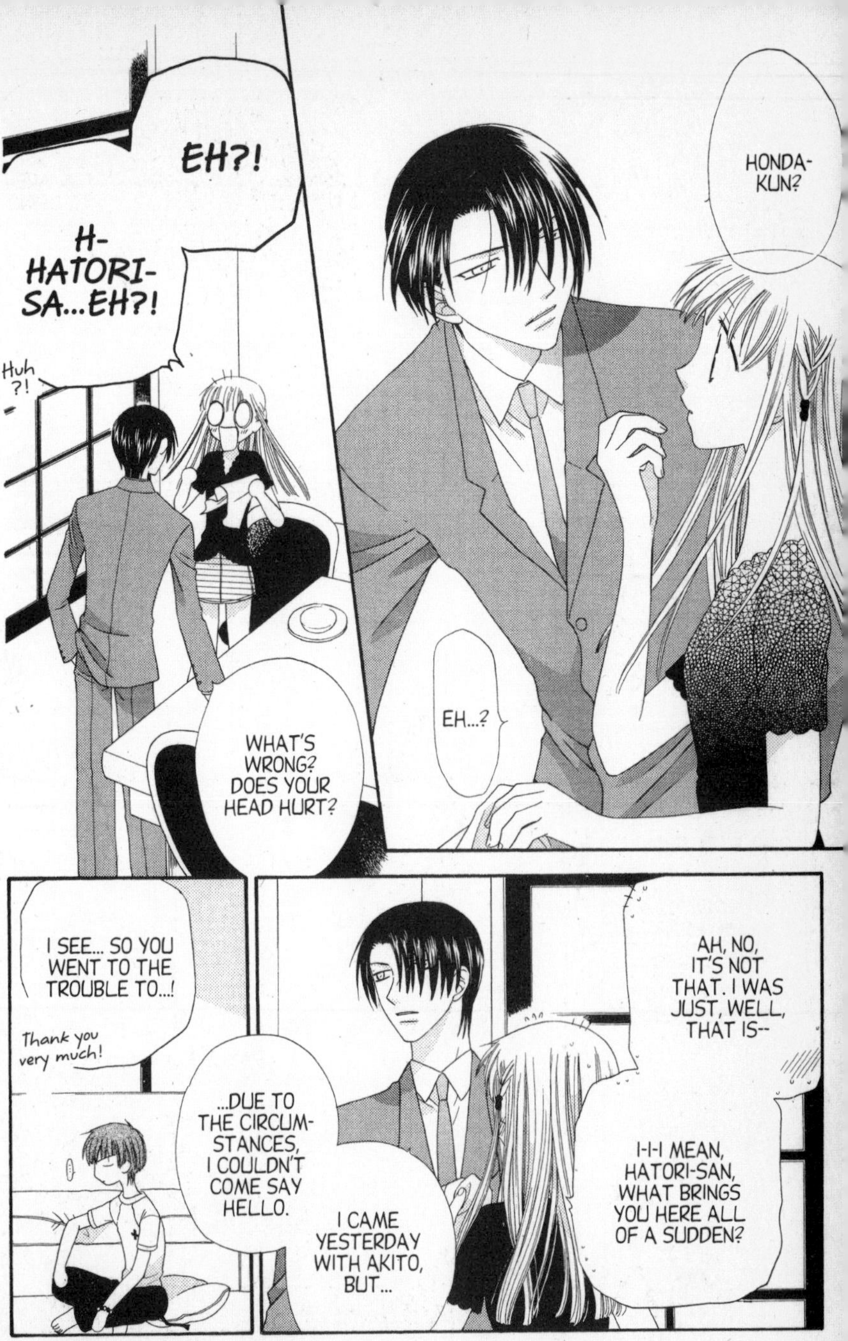
HONDA-KUN?
EH...?
EH?!
H-HATORI-SA...EH?!
Huh ?!
WHAT'S WRONG? DOES YOUR HEAD HURT?
AH, NO, IT'S NOT THAT. I WAS JUST, WELL, THAT IS--
I-I-I MEAN, HATORI-SAN, WHAT BRINGS YOU HERE ALL OF A SUDDEN?
I CAME YESTERDAY WITH AKITO, BUT...
...DUE TO THE CIRCUM-STANCES, I COULDN'T COME SAY HELLO.
I SEE... SO YOU WENT TO THE TROUBLE TO...!
Thank you very much!

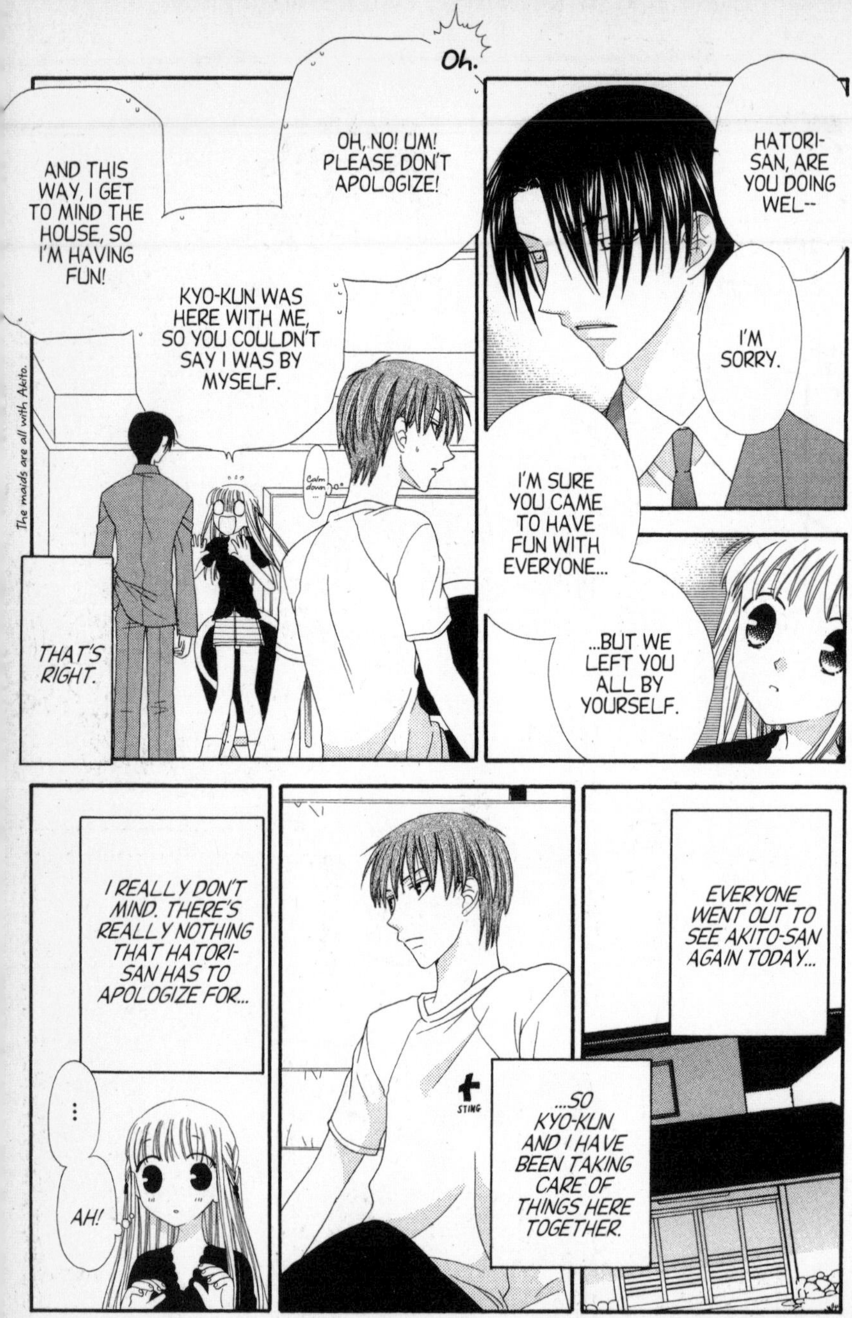
HATORI-SAN, ARE YOU DOING WEL--
Oh.
I'M SORRY.
I'M SURE YOU CAME TO HAVE FUN WITH EVERYONE...
...BUT WE LEFT YOU ALL BY YOURSELF.
OH, NO! UM! PLEASE DON'T APOLOGIZE!
AND THIS WAY, I GET TO MIND THE HOUSE, SO I'M HAVING FUN!
KYO-KUN WAS HERE WITH ME, SO YOU COULDN'T SAY I WAS BY MYSELF.
Calm down...
THAT'S RIGHT.
The maids are all with Akito.
EVERYONE WENT OUT TO SEE AKITO-SAN AGAIN TODAY...
...SO KYO-KUN AND I HAVE BEEN TAKING CARE OF THINGS HERE TOGETHER.
STING
I REALLY DON'T MIND. THERE'S REALLY NOTHING THAT HATORI-SAN HAS TO APOLOGIZE FOR...
...
AH!

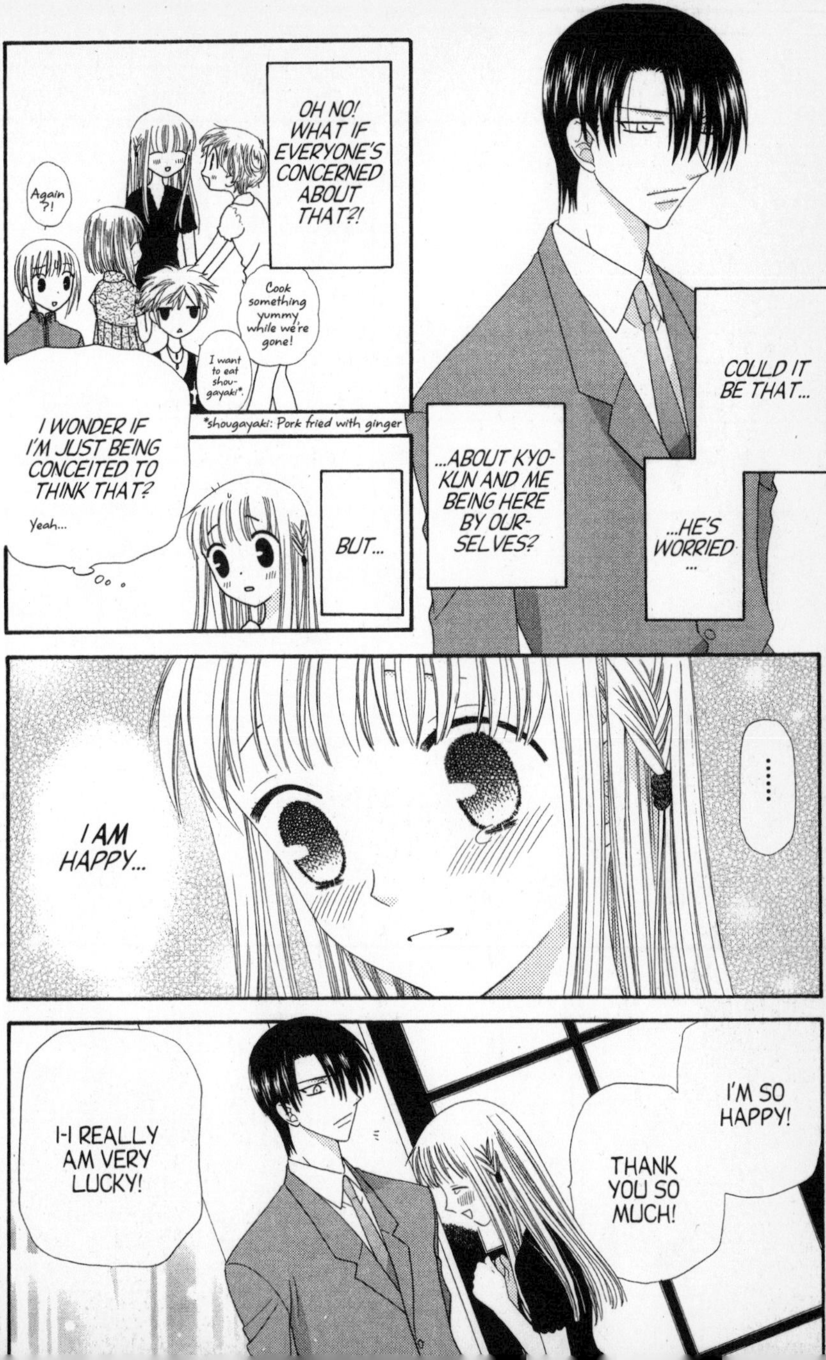
COULD IT BE THAT...
...HE'S WORRIED...
...ABOUT KYO-KUN AND ME BEING HERE BY OURSELVES?
OH NO! WHAT IF EVERYONE'S CONCERNED ABOUT THAT?!
Again?!
Cook something yummy while we're gone!
I want to eat shougayaki*.
*shougayaki: Pork fried with ginger
BUT...
I WONDER IF I'M JUST BEING CONCEITED TO THINK THAT?
Yeah...
......
I AM HAPPY...
I'M SO HAPPY!
THANK YOU SO MUCH!
I-I REALLY AM VERY LUCKY!

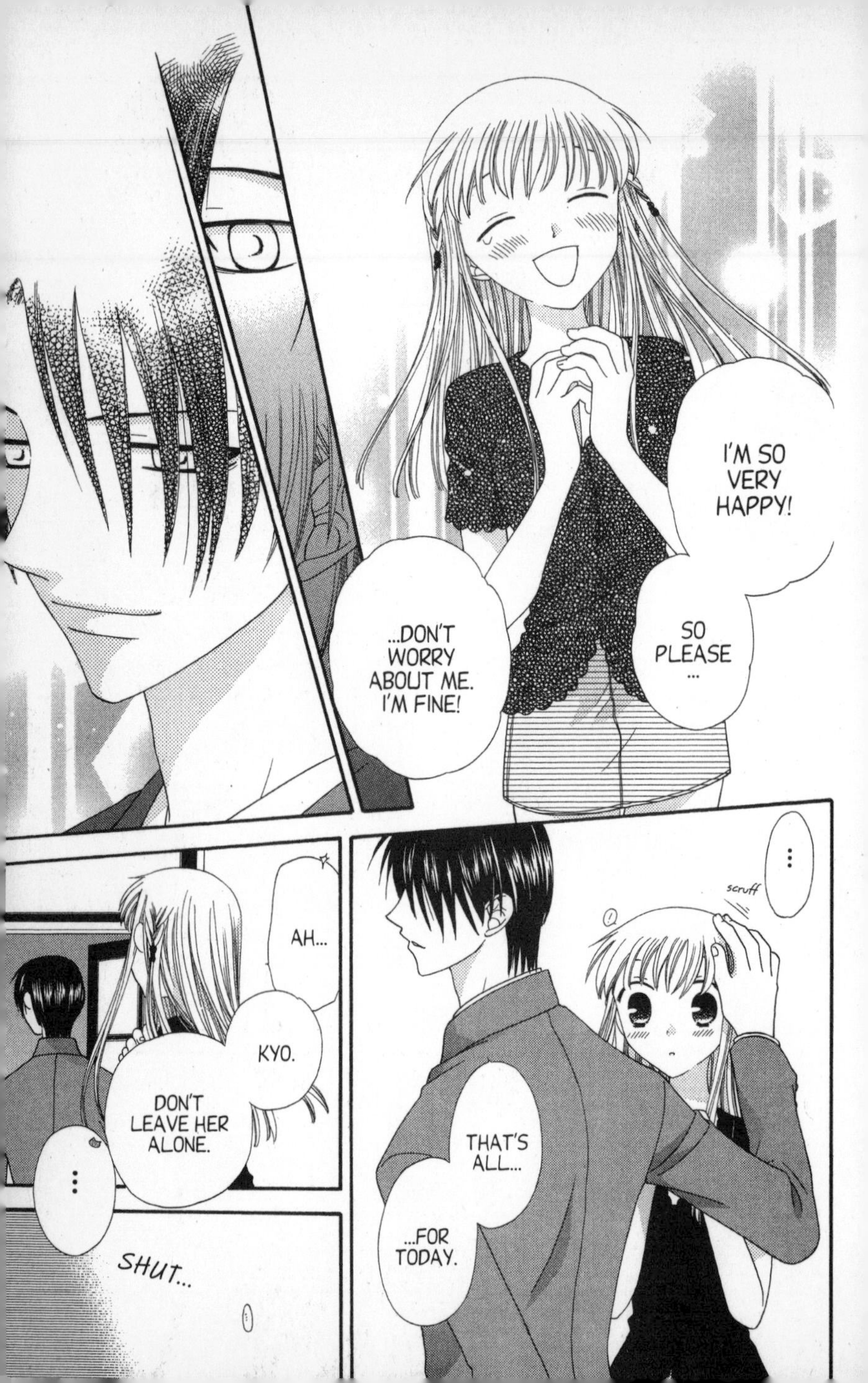
I'M SO VERY HAPPY!
SO PLEASE ...
...DON'T WORRY ABOUT ME. I'M FINE!
...
scruff
!
THAT'S ALL...
...FOR TODAY.
AH...
KYO.
DON'T LEAVE HER ALONE.
...
SHUT...

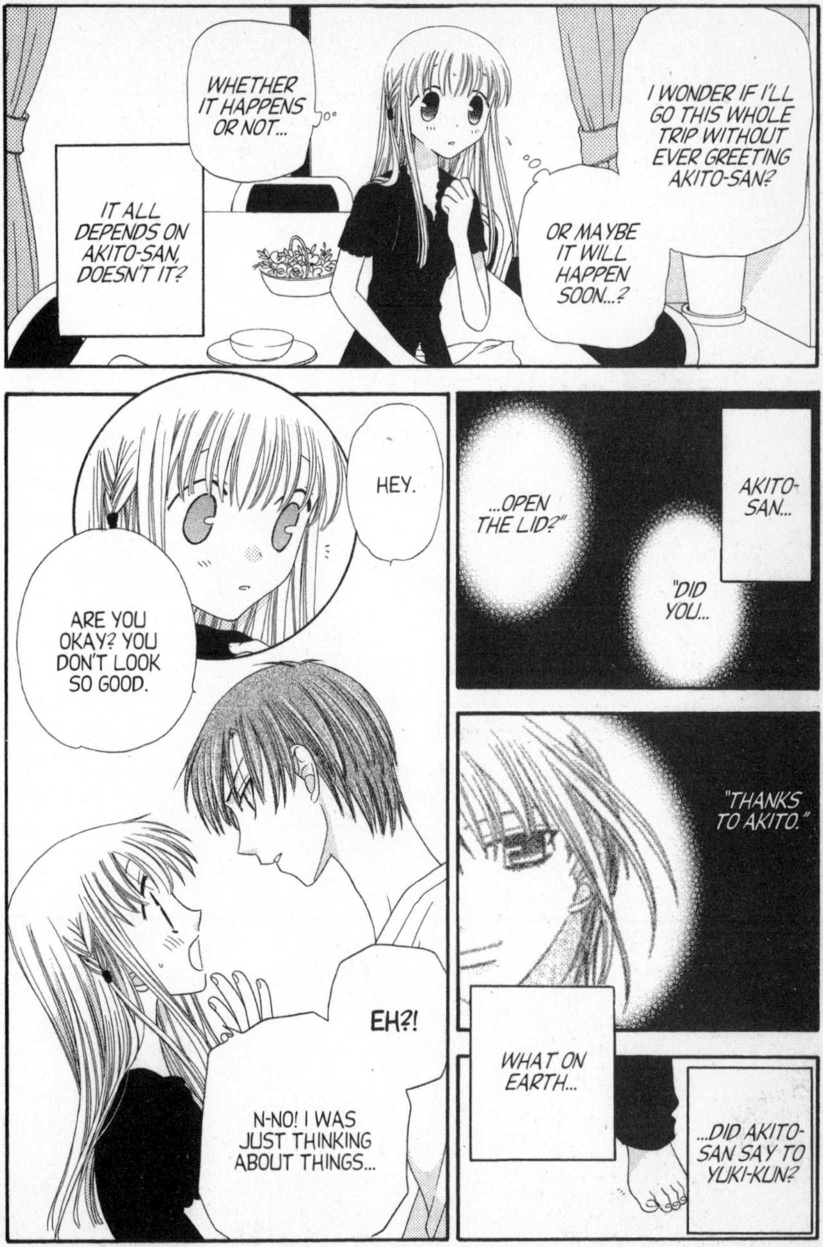
I WONDER IF I'LL GO THIS WHOLE TRIP WITHOUT EVER GREETING AKITO-SAN?
OR MAYBE IT WILL HAPPEN SOON...?
WHETHER IT HAPPENS OR NOT...
IT ALL DEPENDS ON AKITO-SAN, DOESN'T IT?
AKITO-SAN...
"DID YOU...
...OPEN THE LID?"
"THANKS TO AKITO."
WHAT ON EARTH...
...DID AKITO-SAN SAY TO YUKI-KUN?
HEY.
ARE YOU OKAY? YOU DON'T LOOK SO GOOD.
EH?!
N-NO! I WAS JUST THINKING ABOUT THINGS...

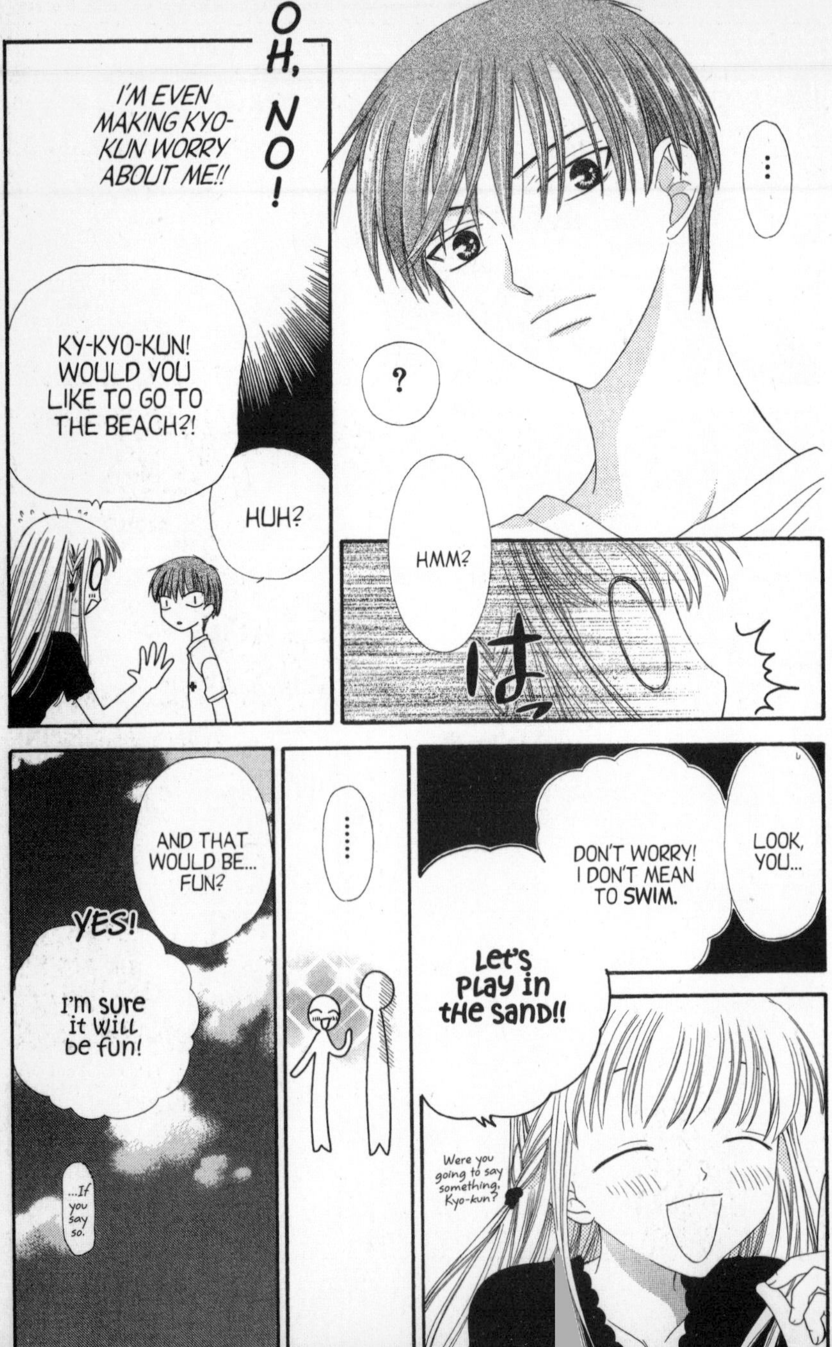
...
?
HMM?
はっ
OH, NO!
I'M EVEN MAKING KYO-KUN WORRY ABOUT ME!!
KY-KYO-KUN! WOULD YOU LIKE TO GO TO THE BEACH?!
HUH?
LOOK, YOU...
DON'T WORRY! I DON'T MEAN TO SWIM.
Let's play in the sand!!
Were you going to say something, Kyo-kun?
......
AND THAT WOULD BE... FUN?
YES!
I'm sure it will be fun!
...If you say so.

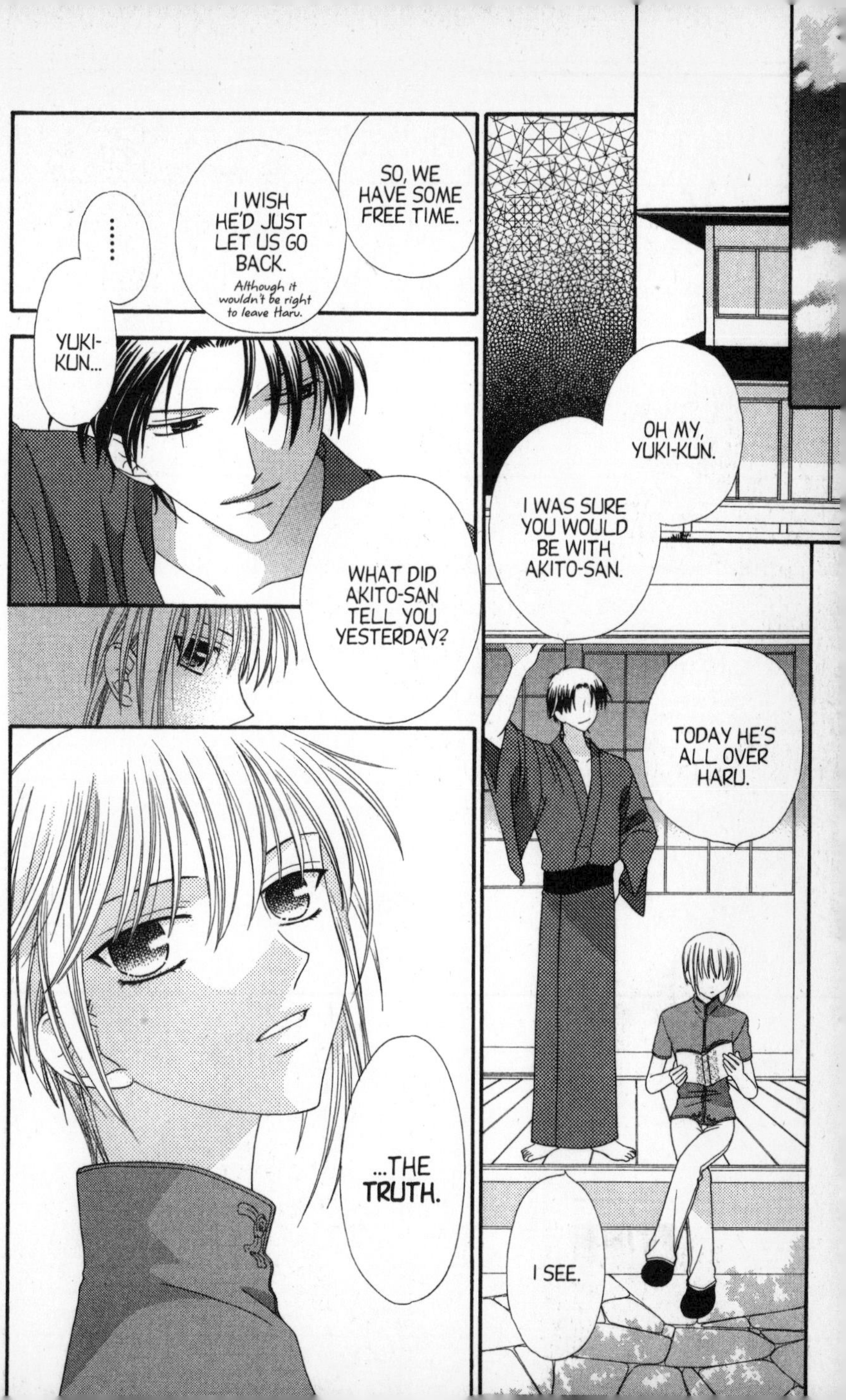
OH MY, YUKI-KUN.
I WAS SURE YOU WOULD BE WITH AKITO-SAN.
TODAY HE'S ALL OVER HARU.
I SEE.
SO, WE HAVE SOME FREE TIME.
I WISH HE'D JUST LET US GO BACK.
Although it wouldn't be right to leave Haru.
......
YUKI-KUN...
WHAT DID AKITO-SAN TELL YOU YESTERDAY?
...THE TRUTH.

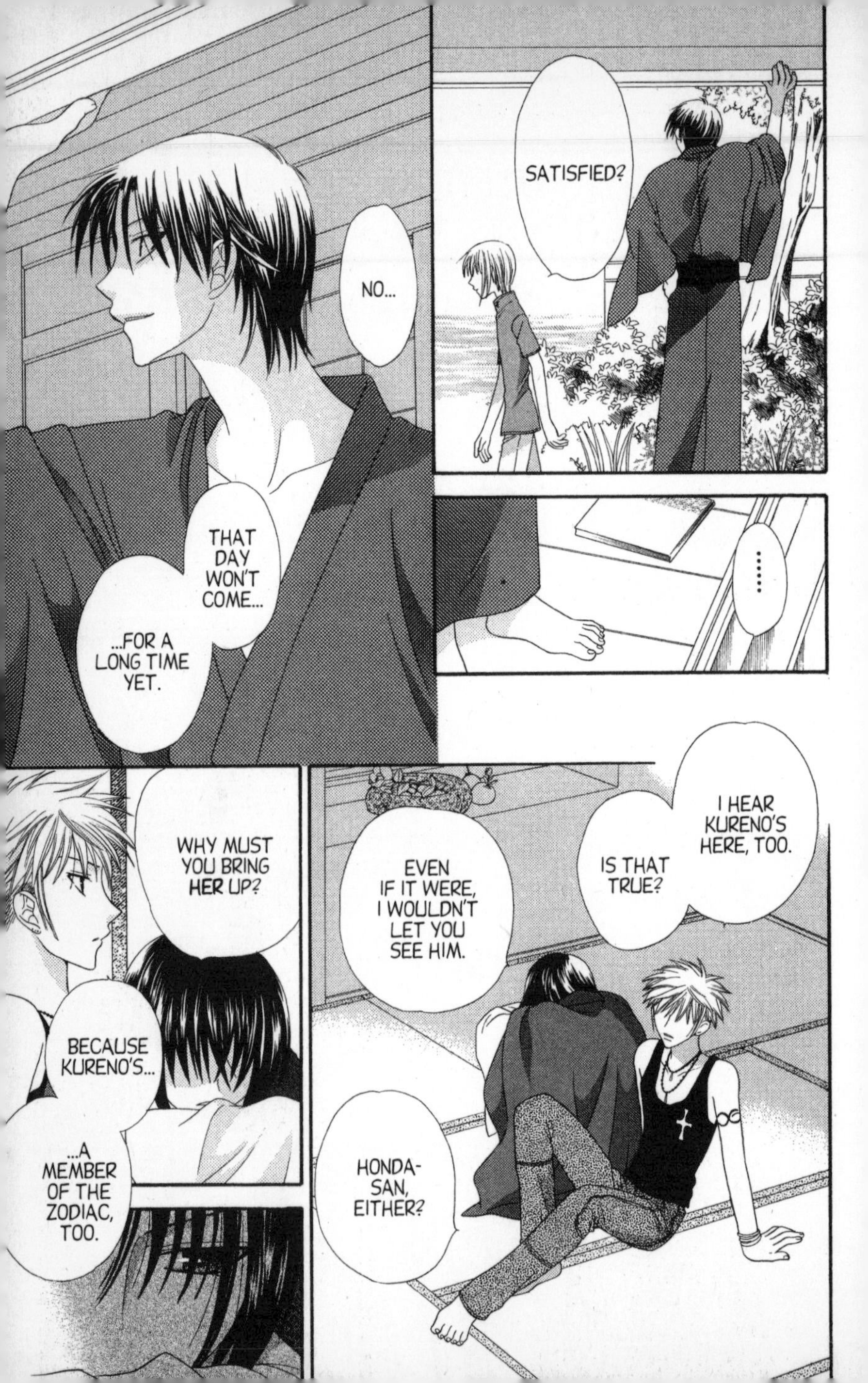
SATISFIED?
......
NO...
THAT DAY WON'T COME...
...FOR A LONG TIME YET.
I HEAR KURENO'S HERE, TOO.
IS THAT TRUE?
EVEN IF IT WERE, I WOULDN'T LET YOU SEE HIM.
HONDA-SAN, EITHER?
WHY MUST YOU BRING **HER** UP?
BECAUSE KURENO'S...
...A MEMBER OF THE ZODIAC, TOO.

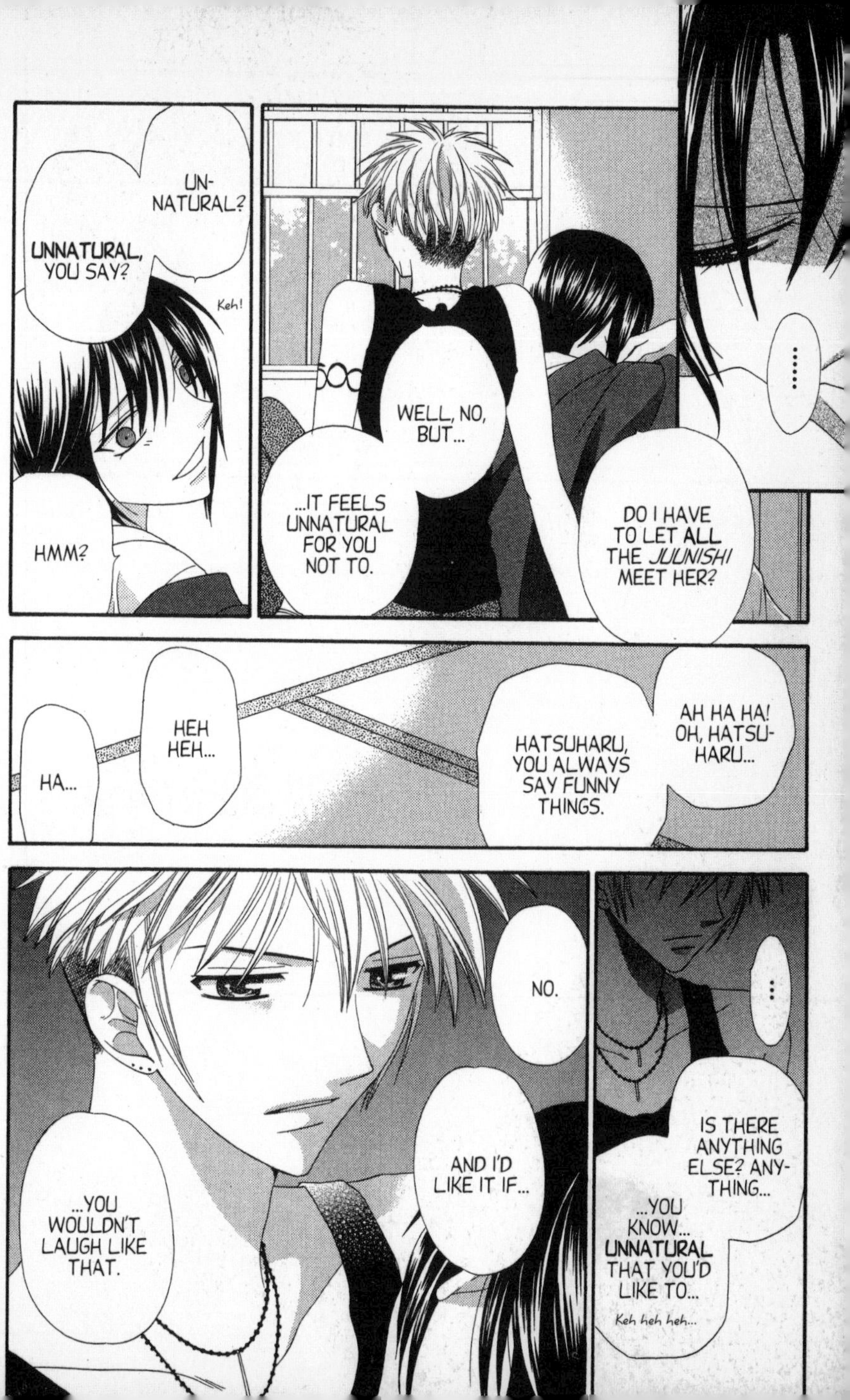
......
DO I HAVE TO LET ALL THE JUUNISHI MEET HER?
WELL, NO, BUT...
...IT FEELS UNNATURAL FOR YOU NOT TO.
UN-NATURAL?
UNNATURAL, YOU SAY?
Keh!
HMM?
AH HA HA! OH, HATSU-HARU...
HATSUHARU, YOU ALWAYS SAY FUNNY THINGS.
HEH HEH...
HA...
...
IS THERE ANYTHING ELSE? ANY-THING...
...YOU KNOW... UNNATURAL THAT YOU'D LIKE TO...
Keh heh heh...
NO.
AND I'D LIKE IT IF...
...YOU WOULDN'T LAUGH LIKE THAT.

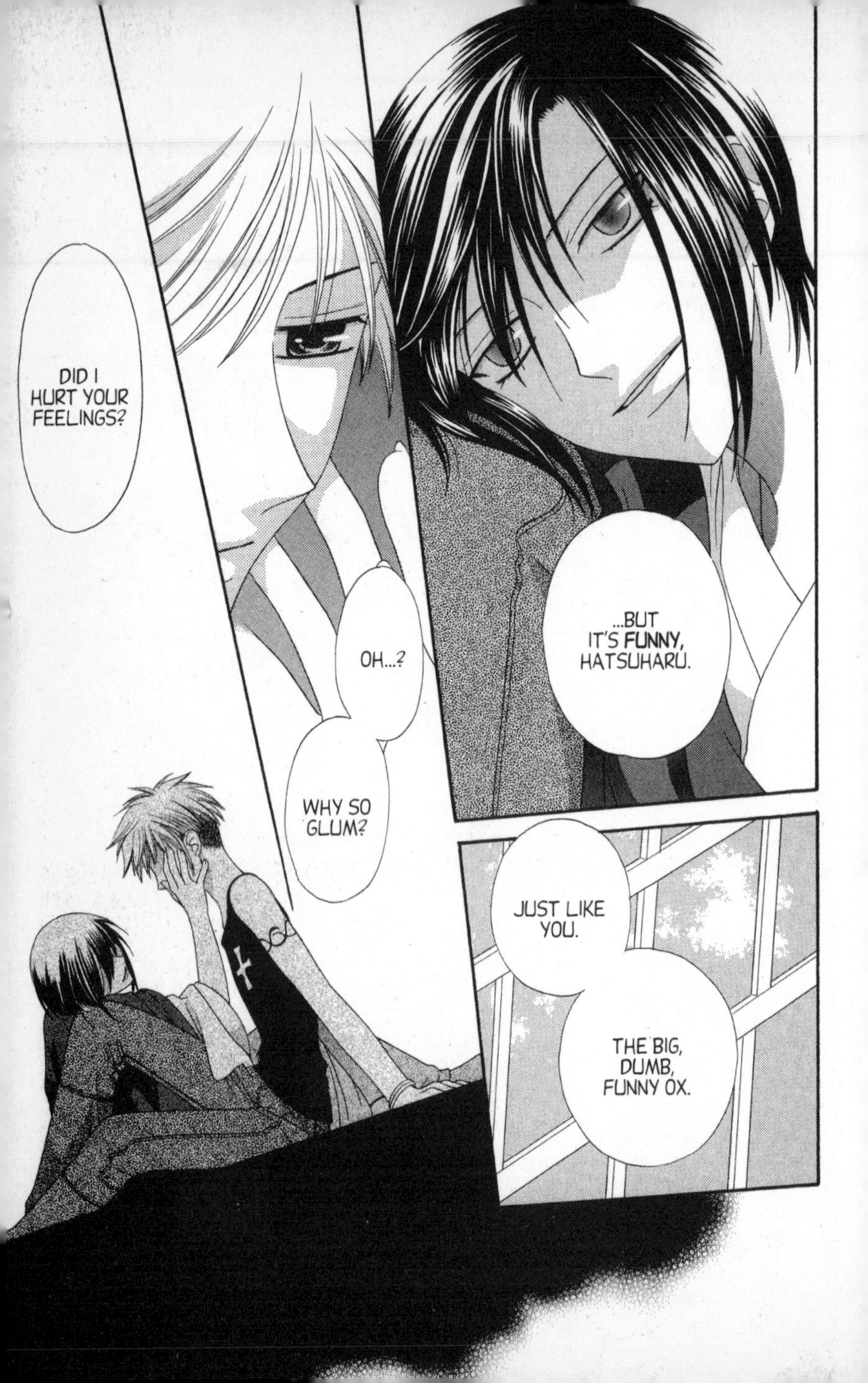
...BUT IT'S FUNNY, HATSUHARU.
JUST LIKE YOU.
THE BIG, DUMB, FUNNY OX.
OH...?
WHY SO GLUM?
DID I HURT YOUR FEELINGS?

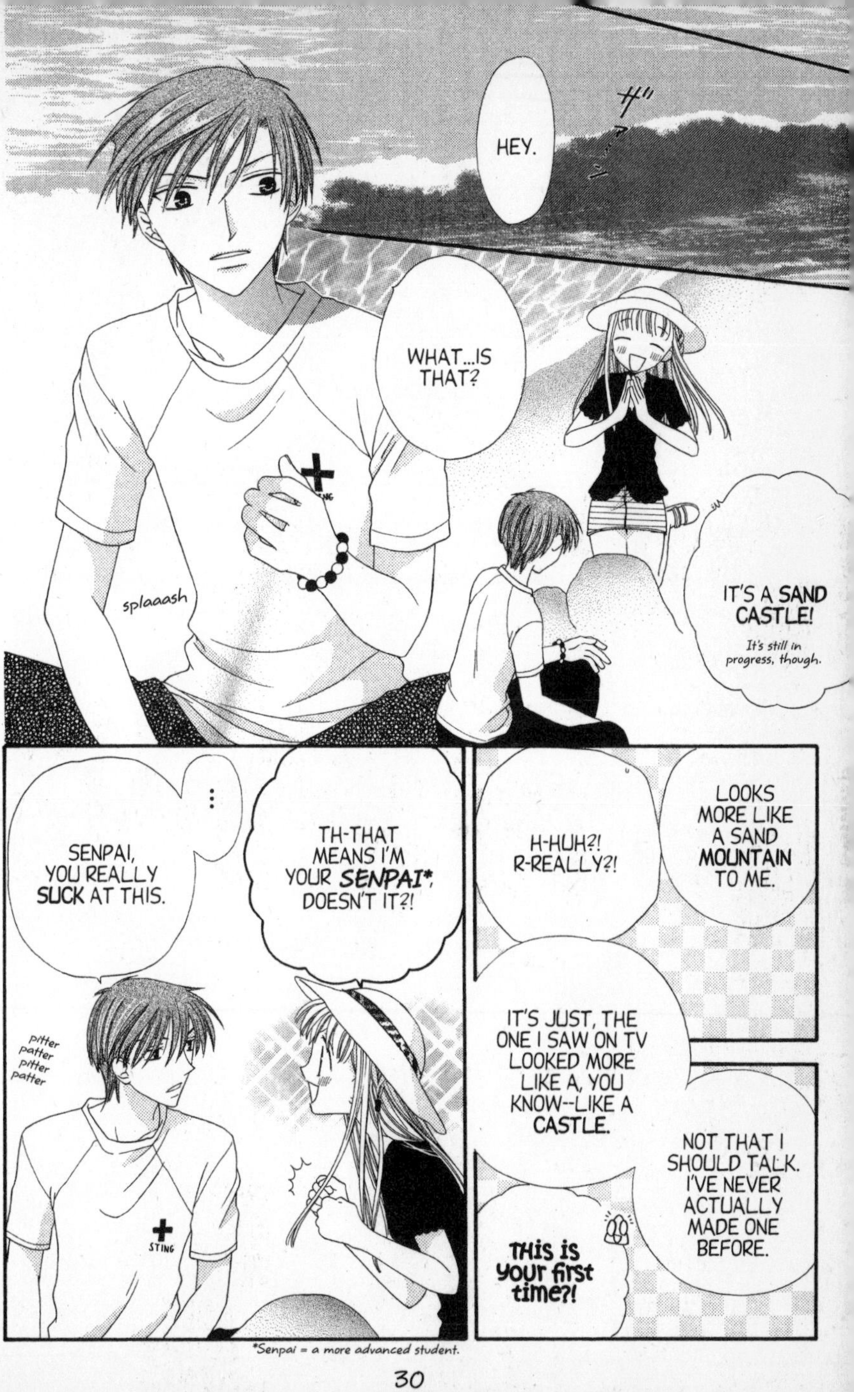

HEY.
splaaash
WHAT...IS THAT?
IT'S A SAND CASTLE!
It's still in progress, though.
LOOKS MORE LIKE A SAND MOUNTAIN TO ME.
H-HUH?! R-REALLY?!
IT'S JUST, THE ONE I SAW ON TV LOOKED MORE LIKE A, YOU KNOW--LIKE A CASTLE.
NOT THAT I SHOULD TALK. I'VE NEVER ACTUALLY MADE ONE BEFORE.
THIS is your first time?!
TH-THAT MEANS I'M YOUR SENPAI*, DOESN'T IT?!
...
SENPAI, YOU REALLY SUCK AT THIS.
pitter patter pitter patter

*Senpai = a more advanced student.

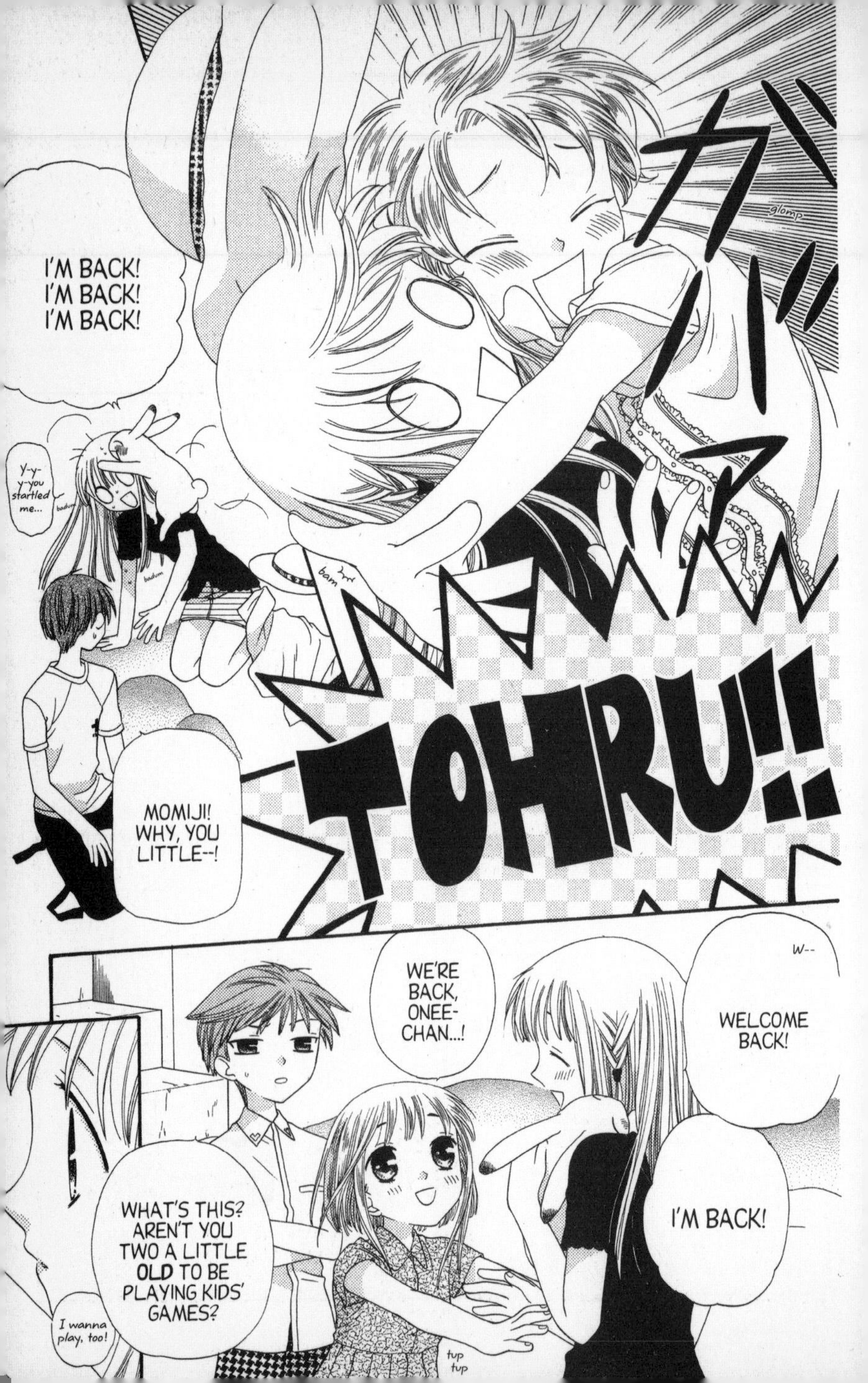
ガバッ
glomp
TOHRU!!
bam
I'M BACK! I'M BACK! I'M BACK!
Y-y-y-you startled me...
badum
badum
MOMIJI! WHY, YOU LITTLE--!
W--
WELCOME BACK!
I'M BACK!
WE'RE BACK, ONEE-CHAN...!
WHAT'S THIS? AREN'T YOU TWO A LITTLE **OLD** TO BE PLAYING KIDS' GAMES?
I wanna play, too!
tup tup

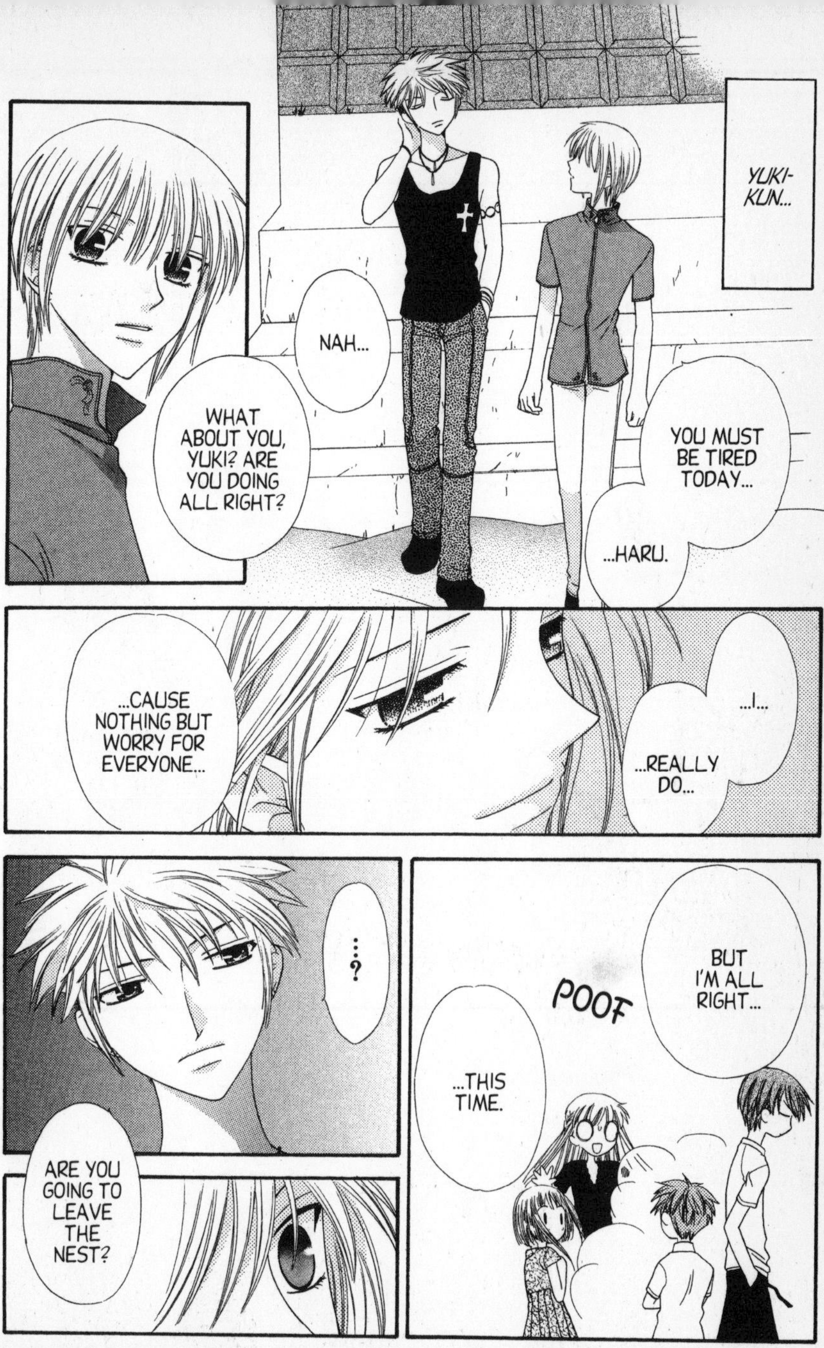
YUKI-KUN...
YOU MUST BE TIRED TODAY...
...HARU.
NAH...
WHAT ABOUT YOU, YUKI? ARE YOU DOING ALL RIGHT?
...I...
...REALLY DO...
...CAUSE NOTHING BUT WORRY FOR EVERYONE...
BUT I'M ALL RIGHT...
POOF
...THIS TIME.
...?
ARE YOU GOING TO LEAVE THE NEST?

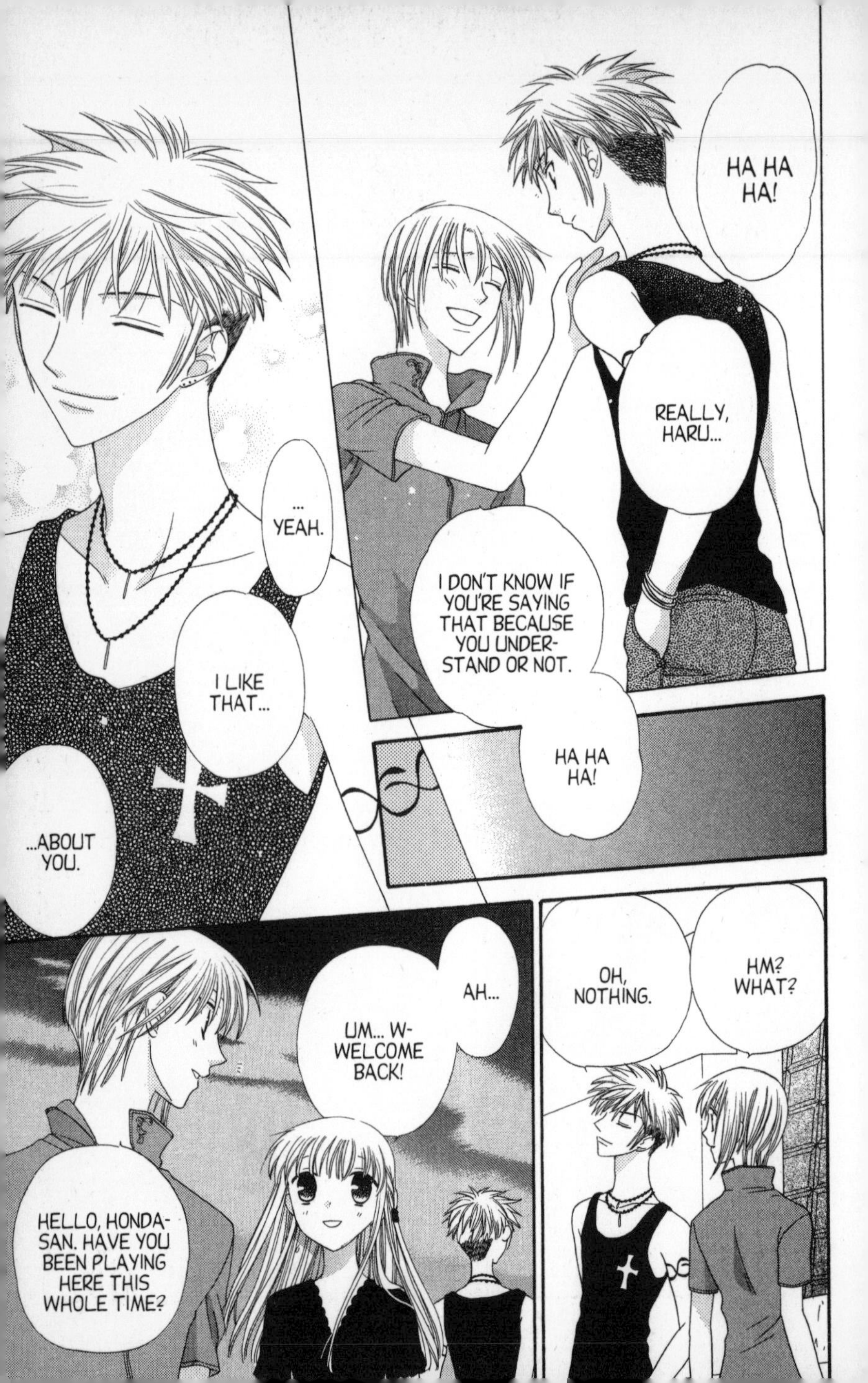
HA HA HA!
REALLY, HARU...
I DON'T KNOW IF YOU'RE SAYING THAT BECAUSE YOU UNDER-STAND OR NOT.
HA HA HA!
... YEAH.
I LIKE THAT...
...ABOUT YOU.
HM? WHAT?
OH, NOTHING.
AH...
UM... W-WELCOME BACK!
HELLO, HONDA-SAN. HAVE YOU BEEN PLAYING HERE THIS WHOLE TIME?

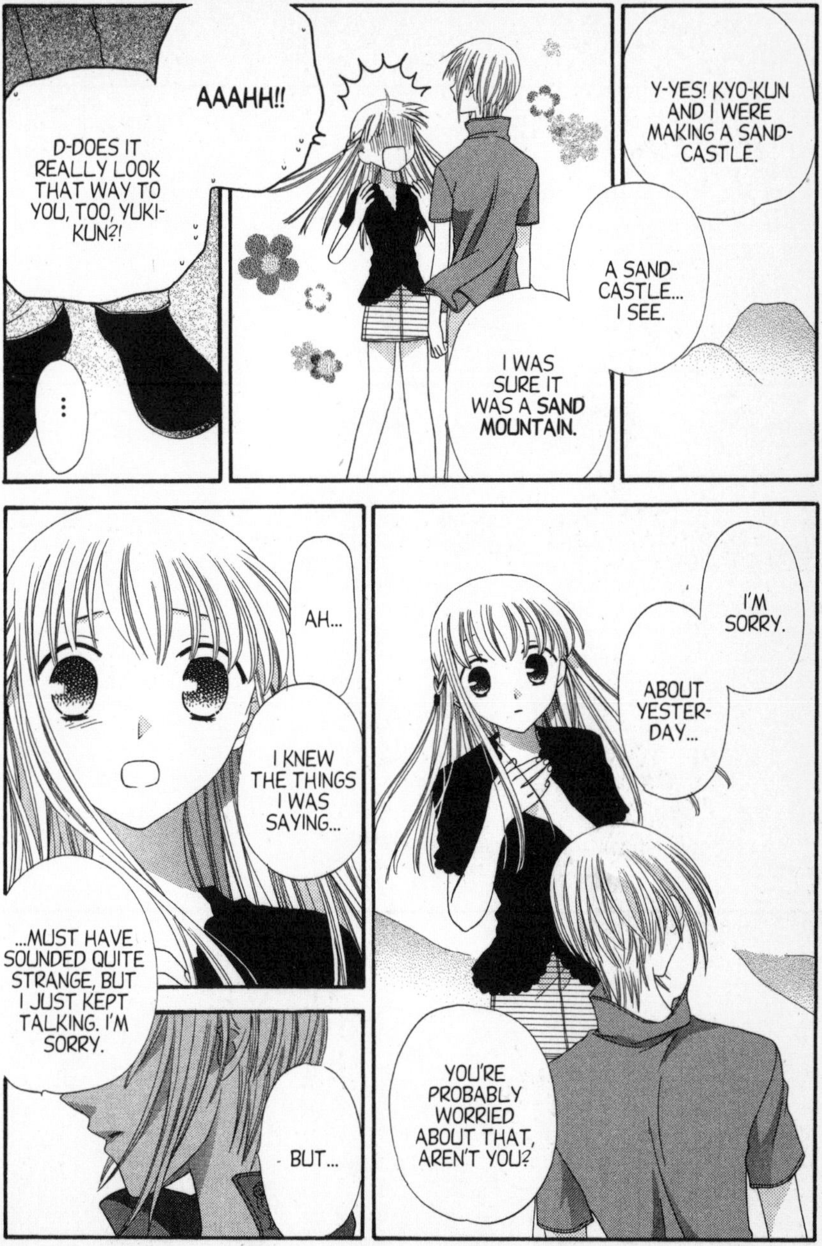
Y-YES! KYO-KUN AND I WERE MAKING A SAND-CASTLE.
A SAND-CASTLE... I SEE.
I WAS SURE IT WAS A **SAND MOUNTAIN.**
AAAHH!!
D-DOES IT REALLY LOOK THAT WAY TO YOU, TOO, YUKI-KUN?!
...
I'M SORRY.
ABOUT YESTERDAY...
YOU'RE PROBABLY WORRIED ABOUT THAT, AREN'T YOU?
AH...
I KNEW THE THINGS I WAS SAYING...
...MUST HAVE SOUNDED QUITE STRANGE, BUT I JUST KEPT TALKING. I'M SORRY.
BUT...

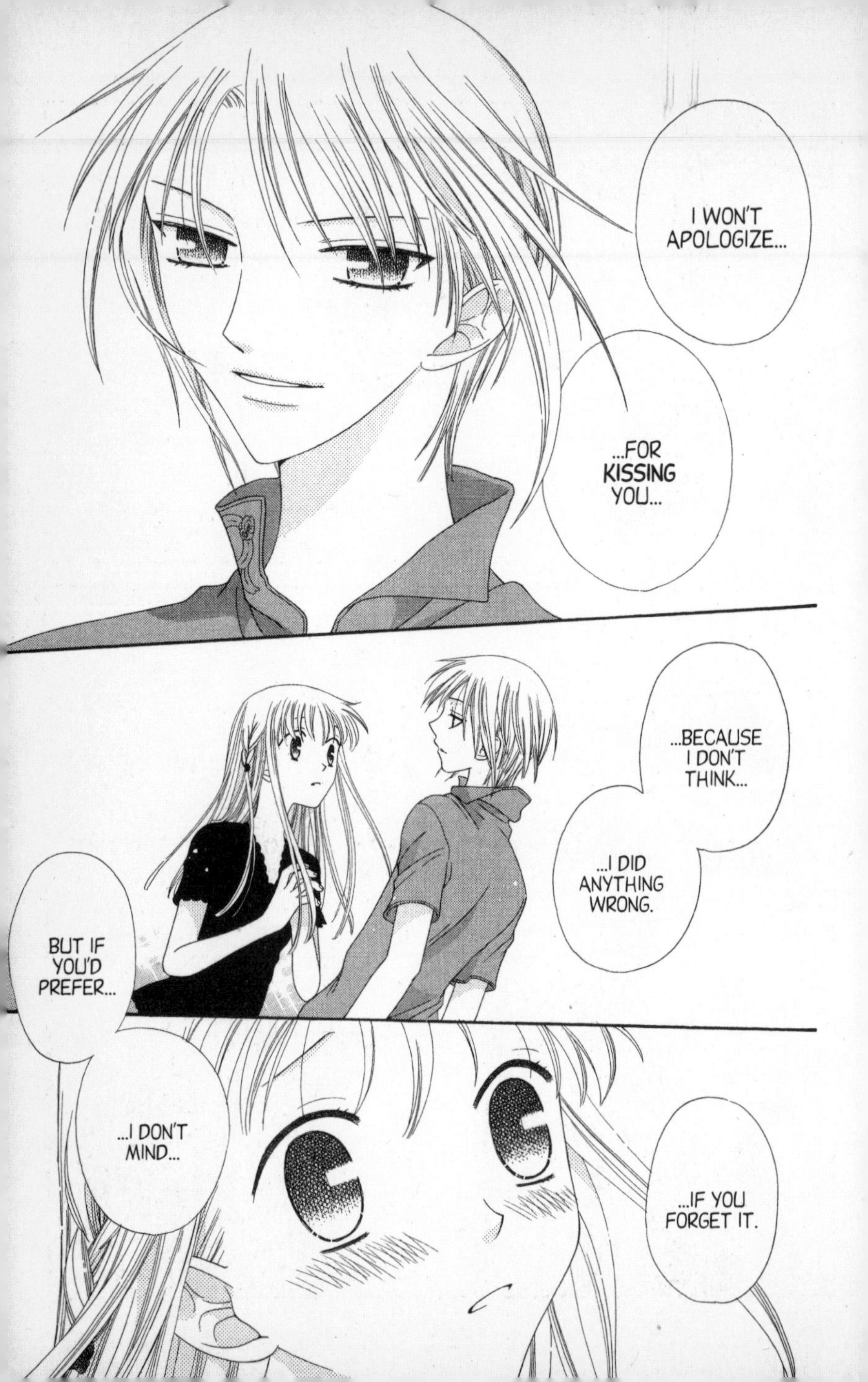

I WON'T APOLOGIZE...
...FOR KISSING YOU...
...BECAUSE I DON'T THINK...
...I DID ANYTHING WRONG.
BUT IF YOU'D PREFER...
...I DON'T MIND...
...IF YOU FORGET IT.

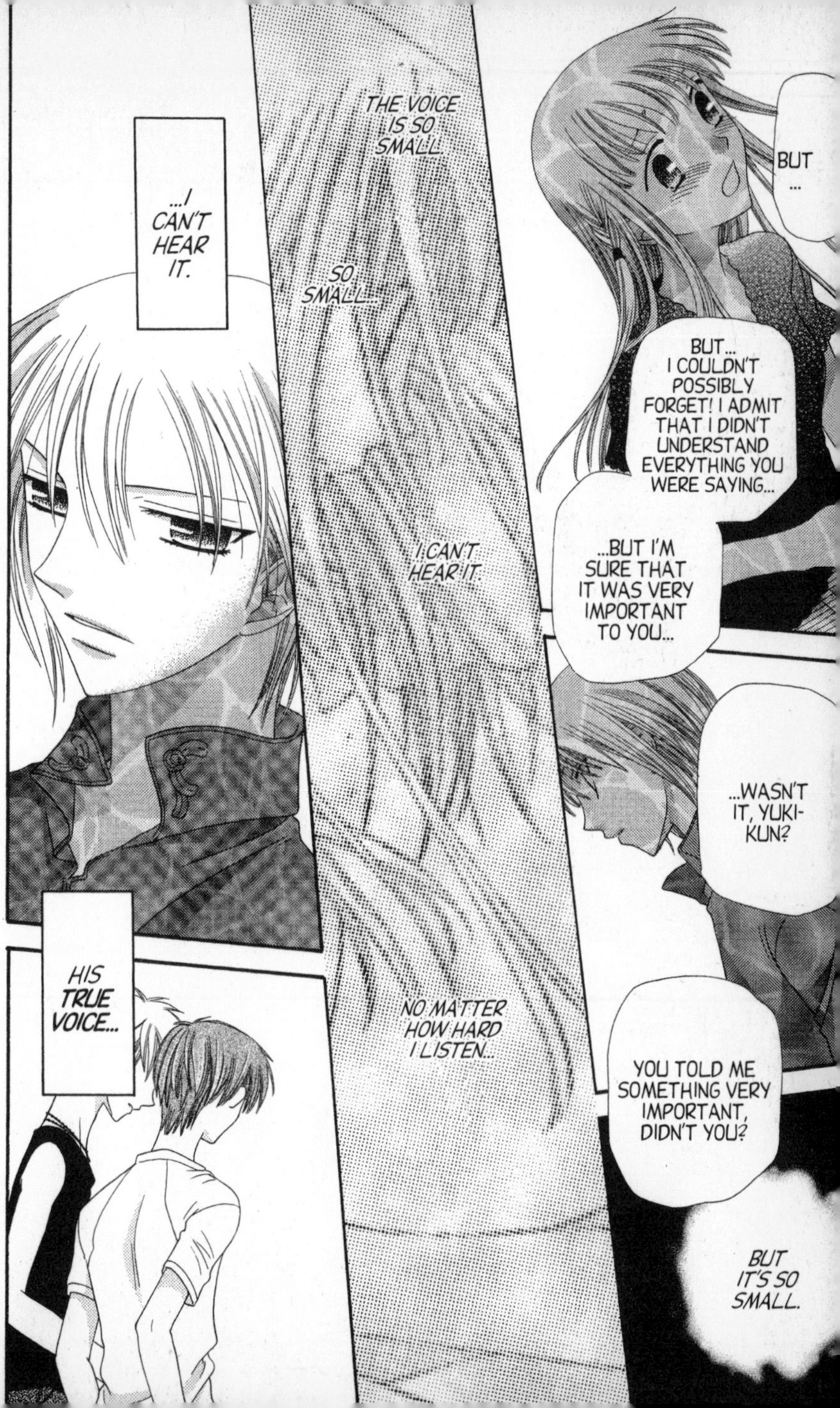
BUT ...
BUT... I COULDN'T POSSIBLY FORGET! I ADMIT THAT I DIDN'T UNDERSTAND EVERYTHING YOU WERE SAYING...
...BUT I'M SURE THAT IT WAS VERY IMPORTANT TO YOU...
...WASN'T IT, YUKI-KUN?
YOU TOLD ME SOMETHING VERY IMPORTANT, DIDN'T YOU?
BUT IT'S SO SMALL.
THE VOICE IS SO SMALL.
SO SMALL...
I CAN'T HEAR IT.
NO MATTER HOW HARD I LISTEN..
...I CAN'T HEAR IT.
HIS TRUE VOICE...

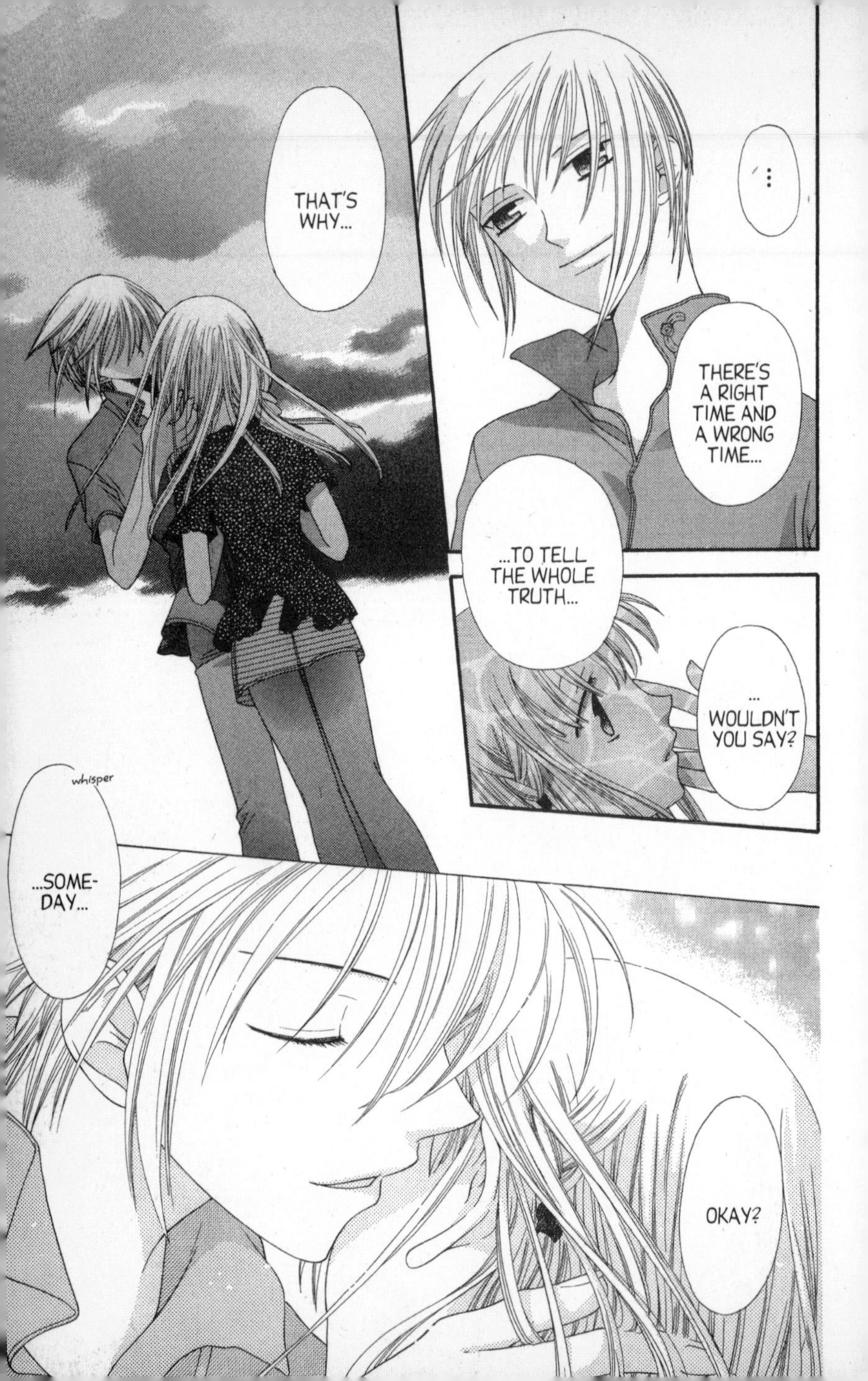
...
THERE'S A RIGHT TIME AND A WRONG TIME...
...TO TELL THE WHOLE TRUTH...
... WOULDN'T YOU SAY?
THAT'S WHY...
whisper
...SOME-DAY...
OKAY?

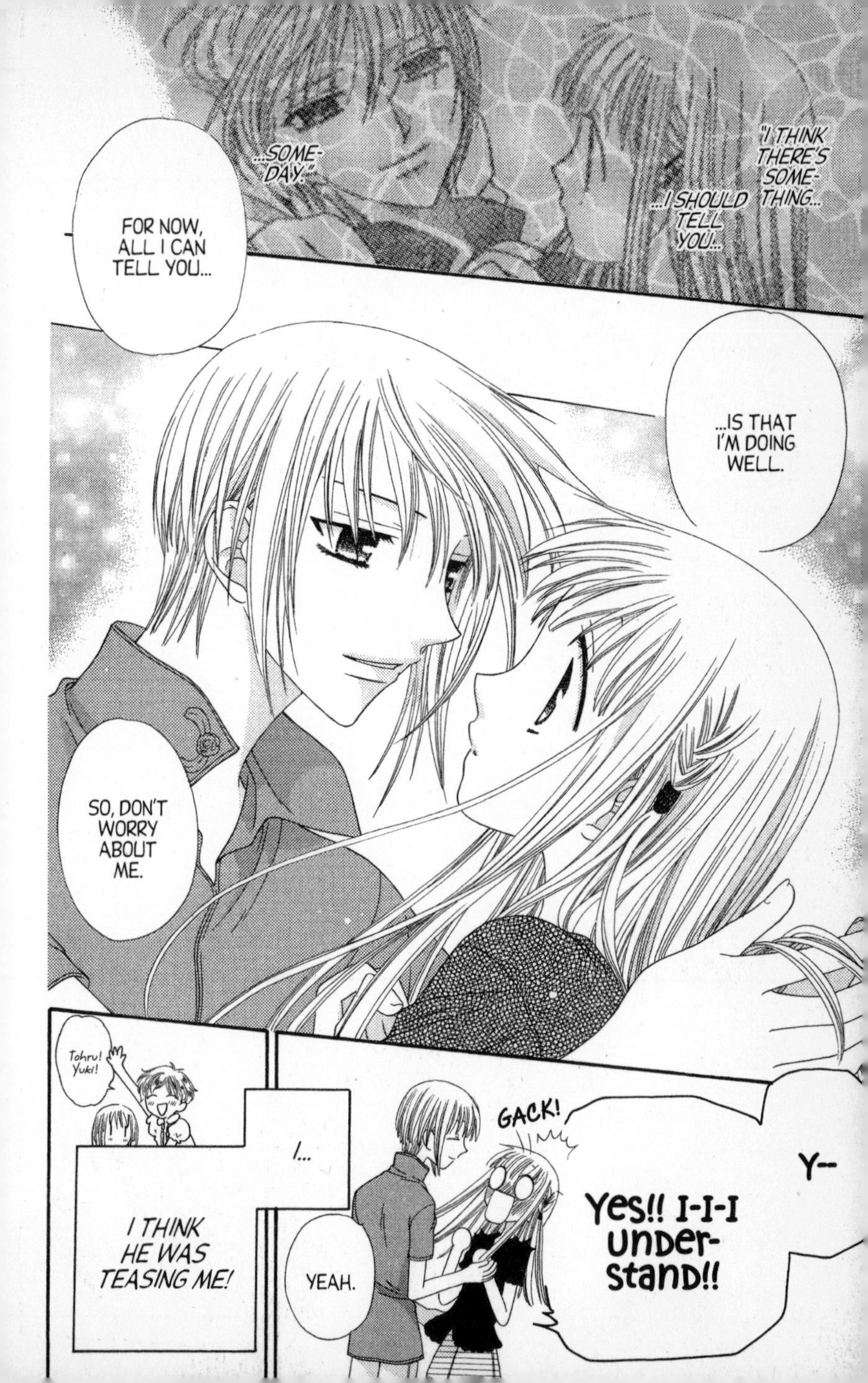

"I THINK THERE'S SOME-THING...
...I SHOULD TELL YOU...
...SOME-DAY."
FOR NOW, ALL I CAN TELL YOU...
...IS THAT I'M DOING WELL.
SO, DON'T WORRY ABOUT ME.
Y--
GACK!
Yes!! I-I-I under-stand!!
YEAH.
Tohru! Yuki!
I...
I THINK HE WAS TEASING ME!

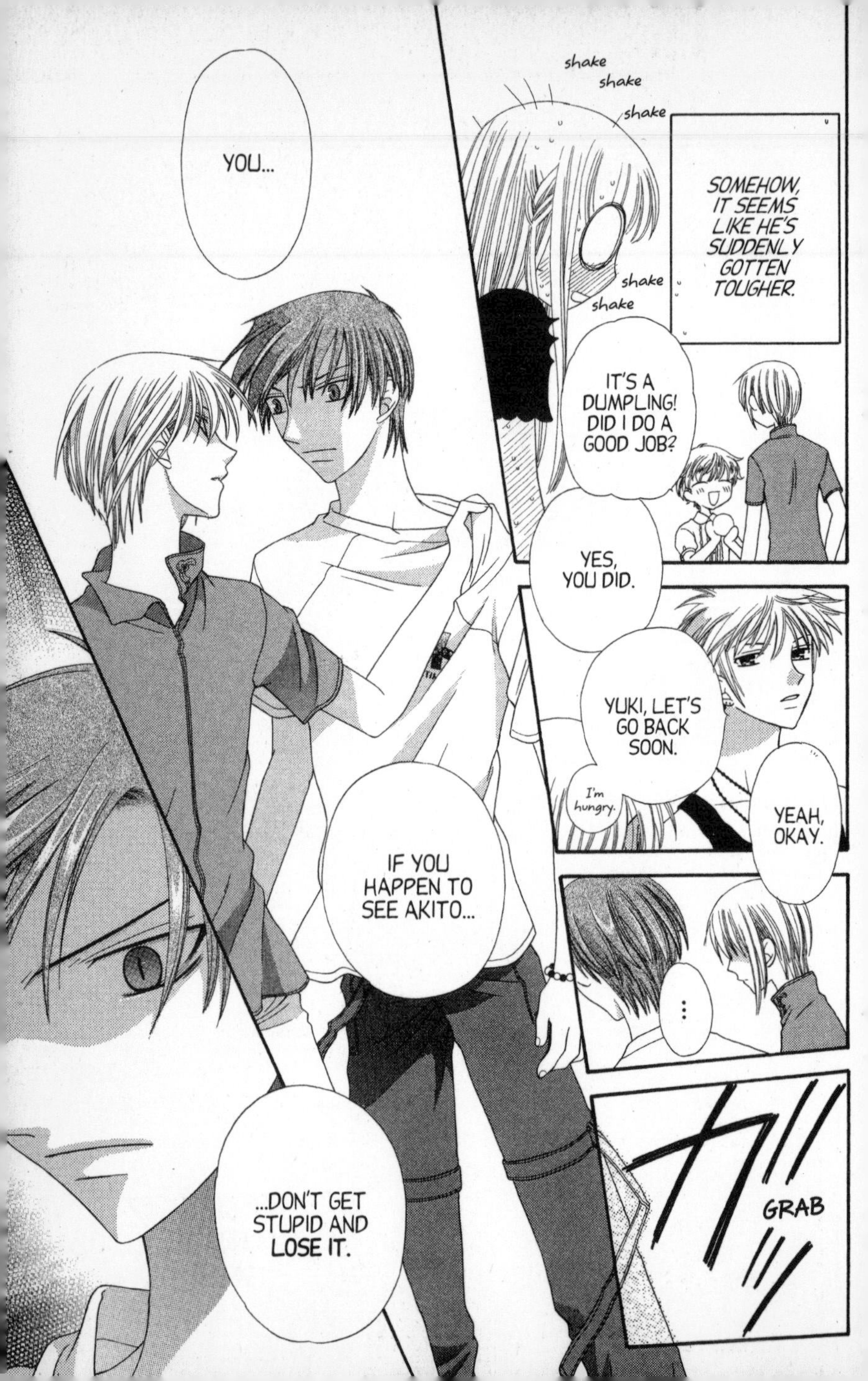
shake
shake
shake
SOMEHOW, IT SEEMS LIKE HE'S SUDDENLY GOTTEN TOUGHER.
shake
shake
IT'S A DUMPLING! DID I DO A GOOD JOB?
YES, YOU DID.
YUKI, LET'S GO BACK SOON.
I'm hungry.
YEAH, OKAY.
...
GRAB
YOU...
IF YOU HAPPEN TO SEE AKITO...
...DON'T GET STUPID AND LOSE IT.

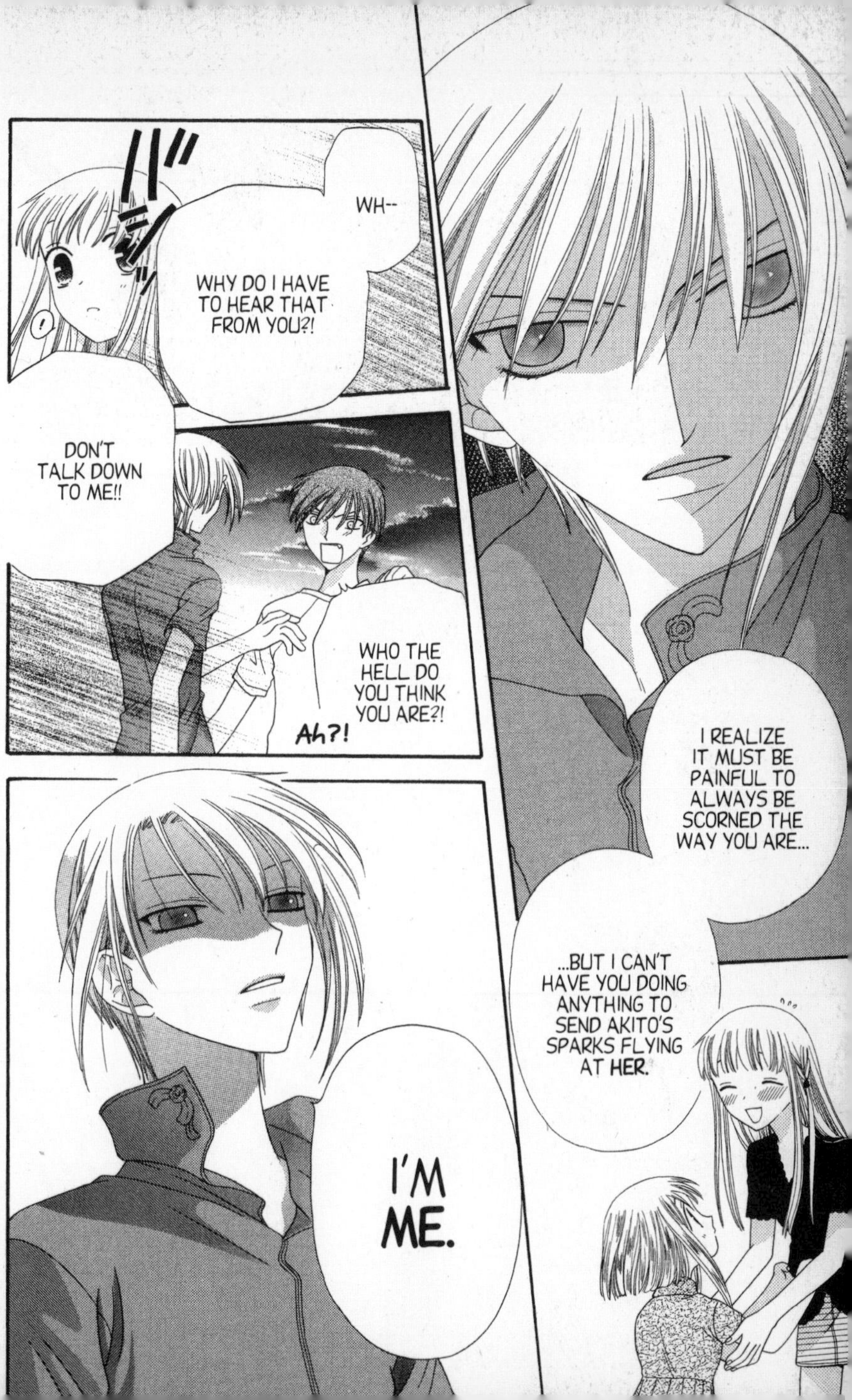
I REALIZE IT MUST BE PAINFUL TO ALWAYS BE SCORNED THE WAY YOU ARE...
...BUT I CAN'T HAVE YOU DOING ANYTHING TO SEND AKITO'S SPARKS FLYING AT **HER**.
WH--
WHY DO I HAVE TO HEAR THAT FROM YOU?!
DON'T TALK DOWN TO ME!!
WHO THE HELL DO YOU THINK YOU ARE?!
Ah?!
I'M **ME.**

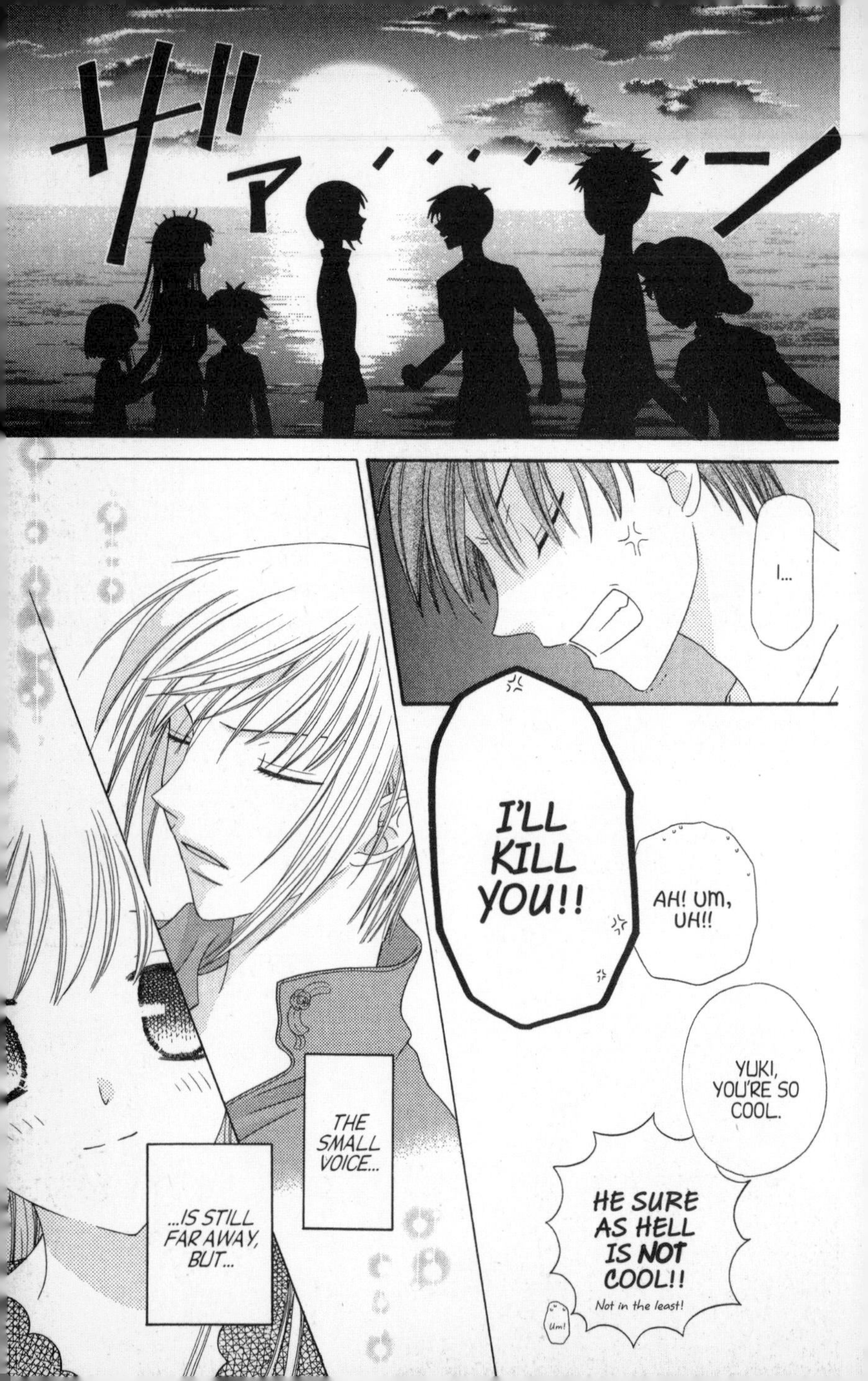
ザァ
I...
I'LL KILL YOU!!
AH! UM, UH!!
YUKI, YOU'RE SO COOL.
HE SURE AS HELL IS **NOT** COOL!!
Not in the least!
Um!
THE SMALL VOICE...
...IS STILL FAR AWAY, BUT...

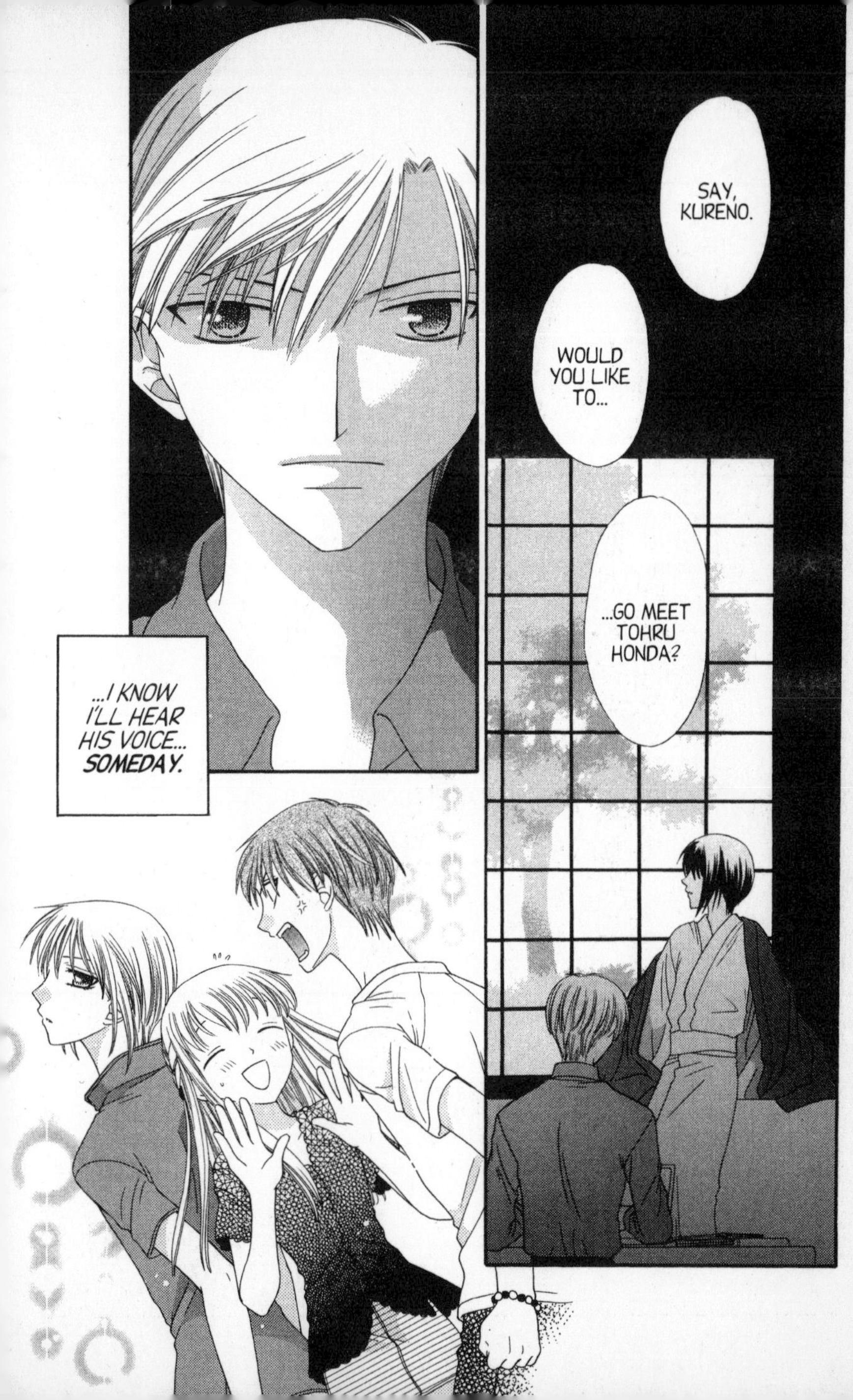
SAY, KURENO.
WOULD YOU LIKE TO...
...GO MEET TOHRU HONDA?
...I KNOW I'LL HEAR HIS VOICE... SOMEDAY.

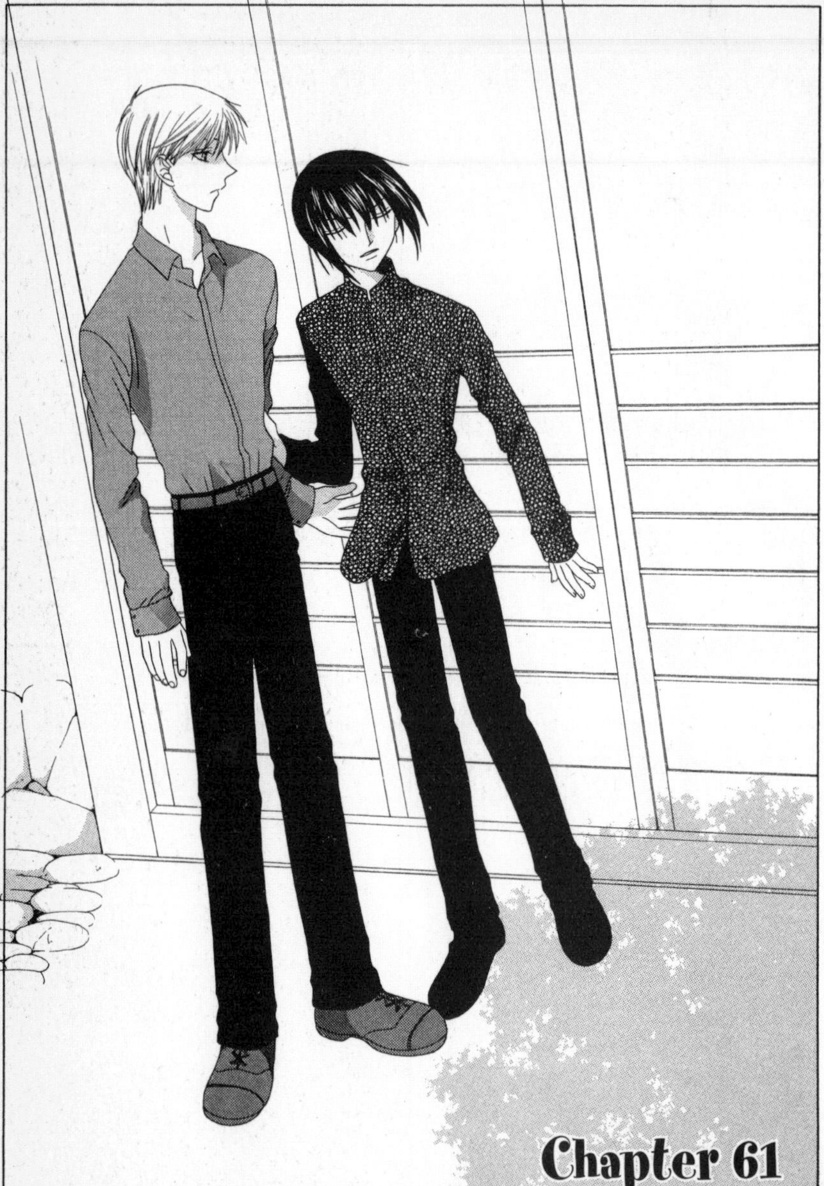
Chapter 61

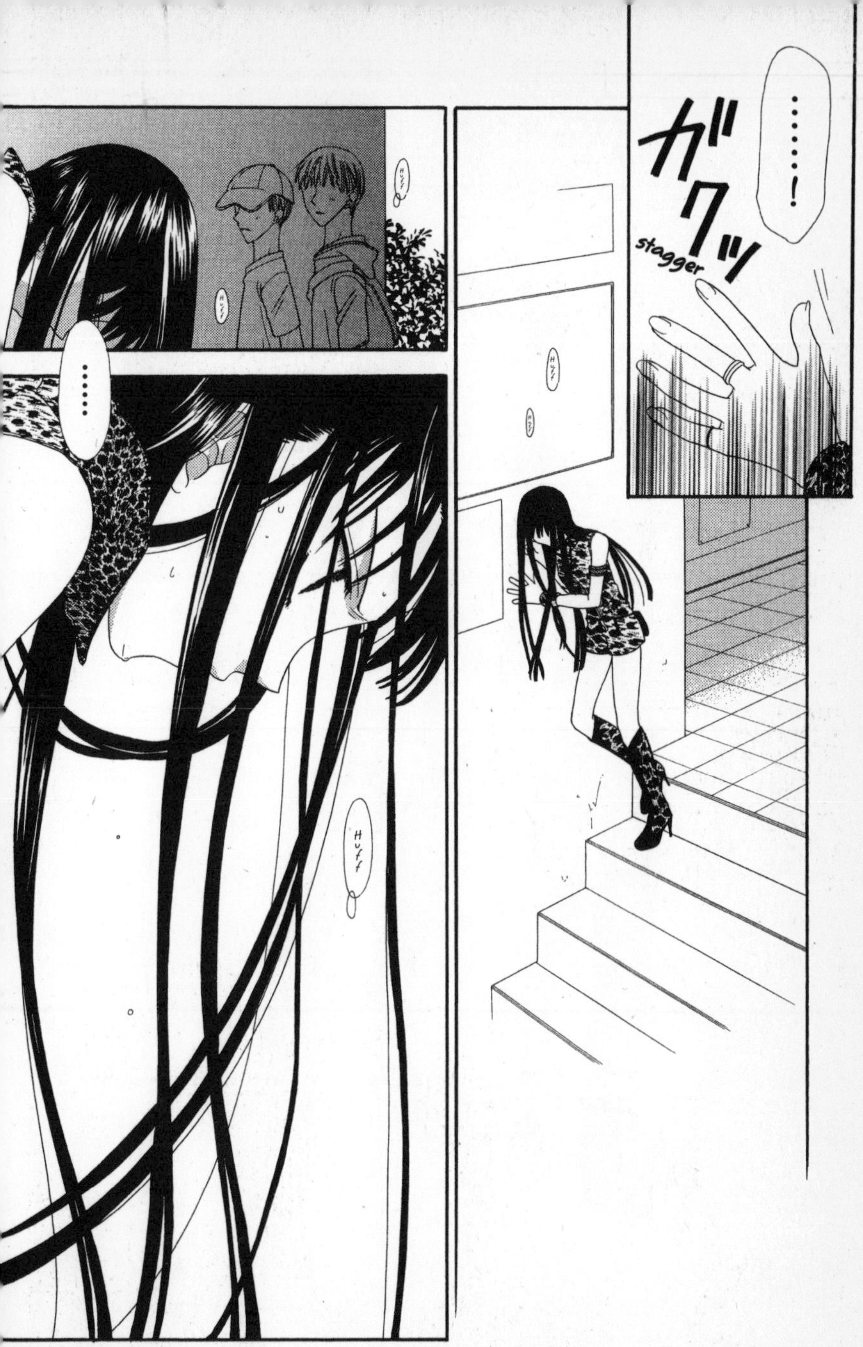
......!
ガクッ
stagger
Huff
Huff
Huff
Huff
......
Huff

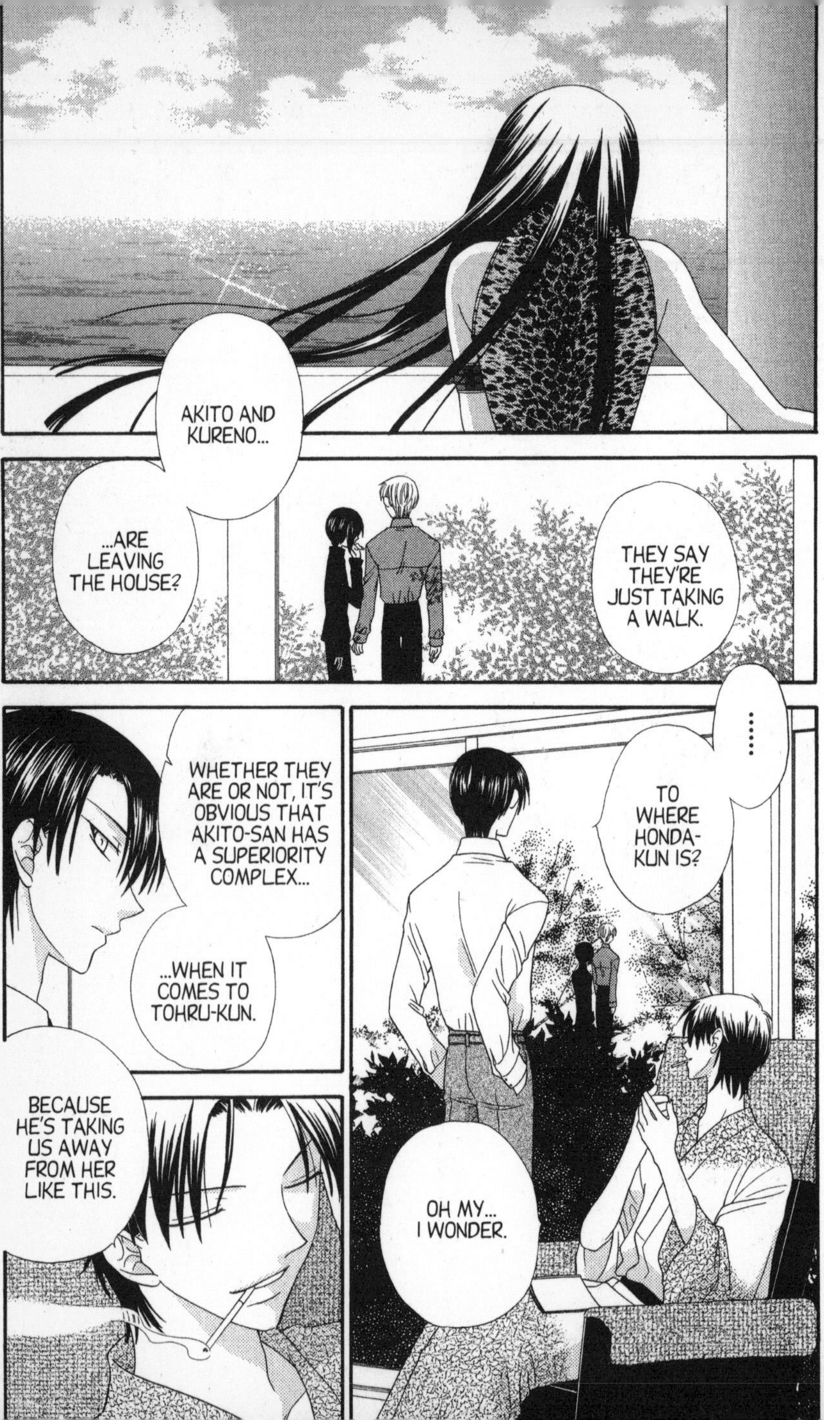
AKITO AND KURENO...
...ARE LEAVING THE HOUSE?
THEY SAY THEY'RE JUST TAKING A WALK.
......
TO WHERE HONDA-KUN IS?
OH MY... I WONDER.
WHETHER THEY ARE OR NOT, IT'S OBVIOUS THAT AKITO-SAN HAS A SUPERIORITY COMPLEX...
...WHEN IT COMES TO TOHRU-KUN.
BECAUSE HE'S TAKING US AWAY FROM HER LIKE THIS.

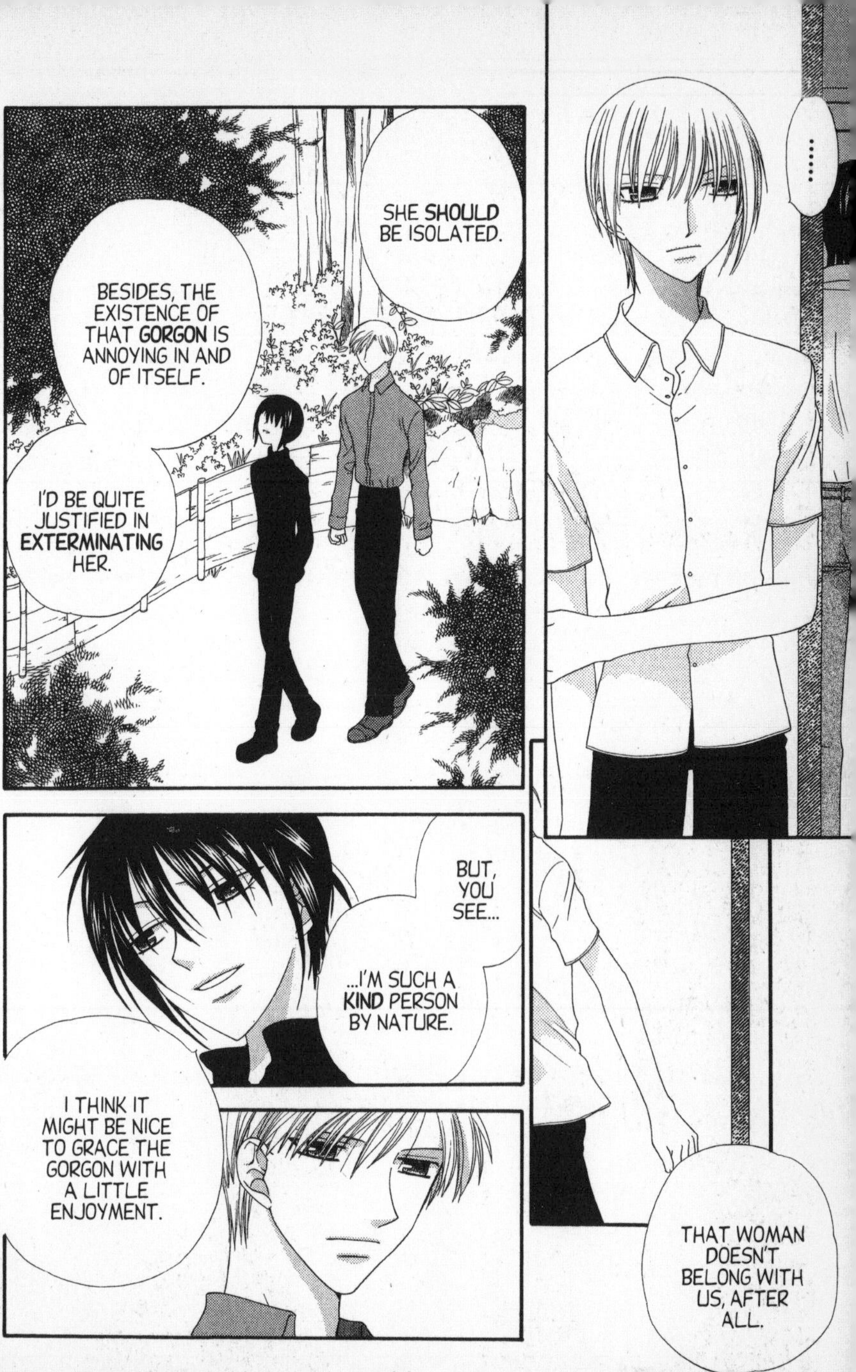
......
SHE SHOULD BE ISOLATED.
BESIDES, THE EXISTENCE OF THAT GORGON IS ANNOYING IN AND OF ITSELF.
I'D BE QUITE JUSTIFIED IN EXTERMINATING HER.
BUT, YOU SEE...
...I'M SUCH A KIND PERSON BY NATURE.
I THINK IT MIGHT BE NICE TO GRACE THE GORGON WITH A LITTLE ENJOYMENT.
THAT WOMAN DOESN'T BELONG WITH US, AFTER ALL.

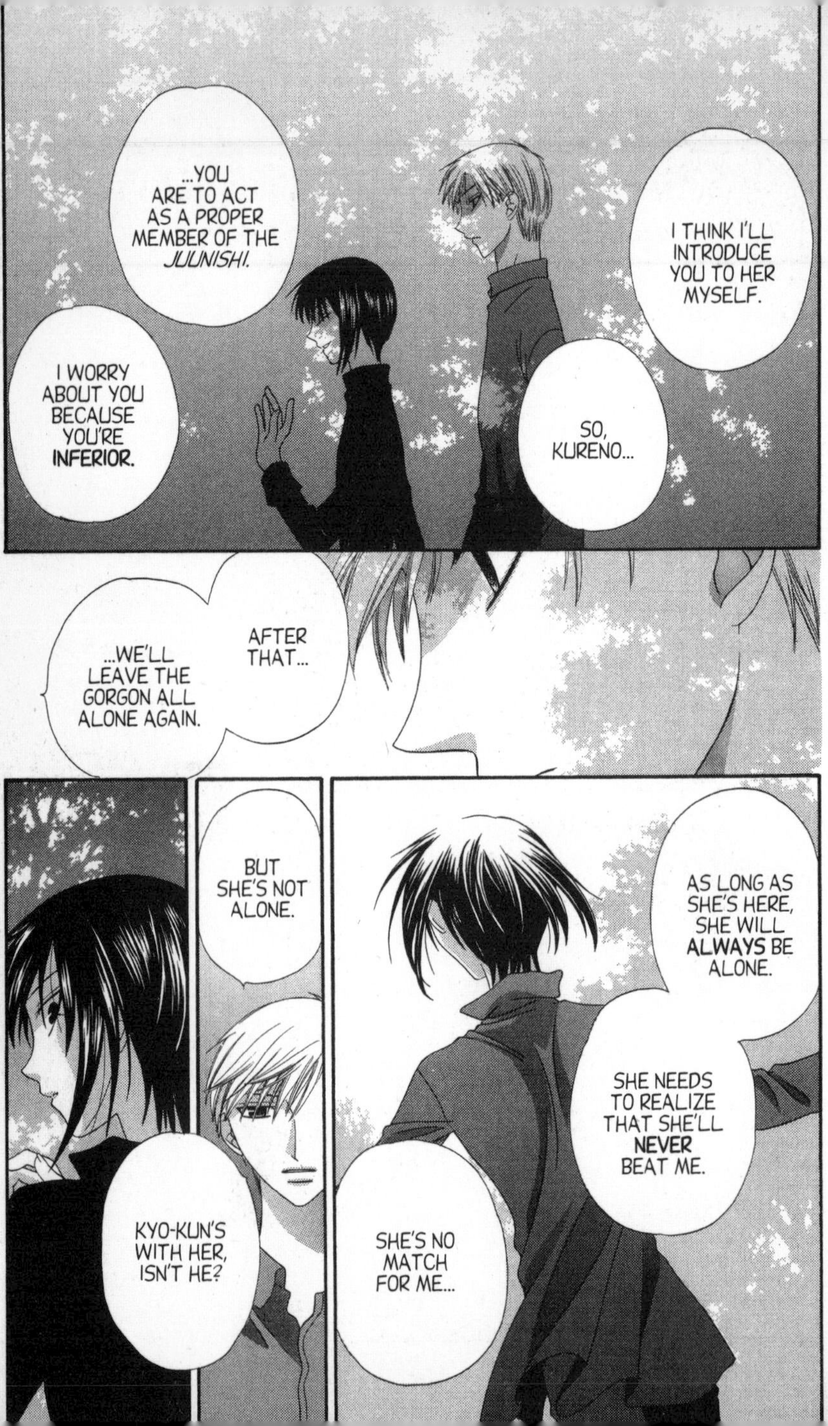
I THINK I'LL INTRODUCE YOU TO HER MYSELF.
SO, KURENO...
...YOU ARE TO ACT AS A PROPER MEMBER OF THE *JUUNISHI.*
I WORRY ABOUT YOU BECAUSE YOU'RE **INFERIOR.**
AFTER THAT...
...WE'LL LEAVE THE GORGON ALL ALONE AGAIN.
AS LONG AS SHE'S HERE, SHE WILL **ALWAYS** BE ALONE.
SHE NEEDS TO REALIZE THAT SHE'LL **NEVER** BEAT ME.
SHE'S NO MATCH FOR ME...
BUT SHE'S NOT ALONE.
KYO-KUN'S WITH HER, ISN'T HE?

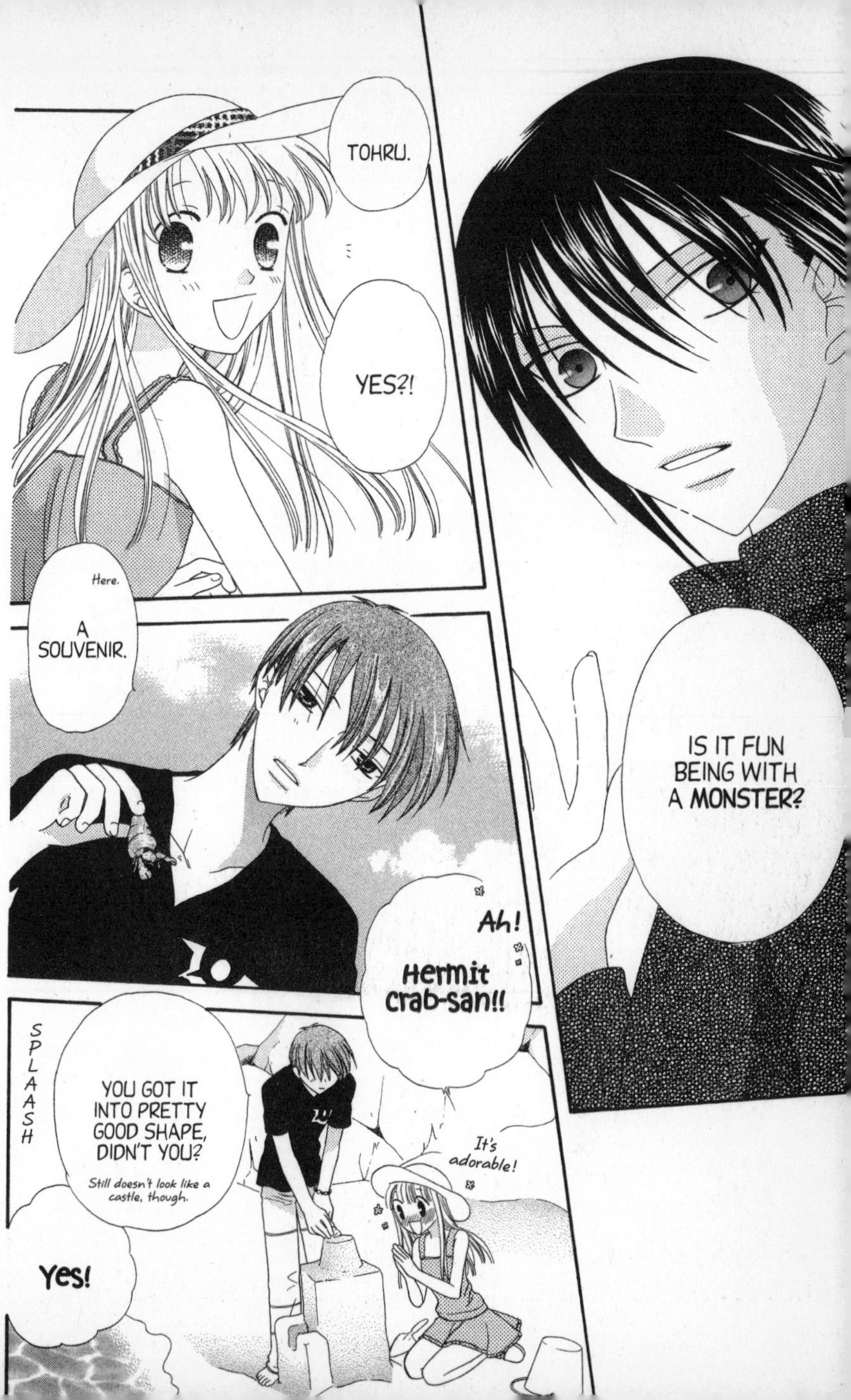
IS IT FUN BEING WITH A MONSTER?
TOHRU.
YES?!
Here.
A SOUVENIR.
Ah!
Hermit crab-san!!
It's adorable!
YOU GOT IT INTO PRETTY GOOD SHAPE, DIDN'T YOU?
Still doesn't look like a castle, though.
Yes!
SPLAASH

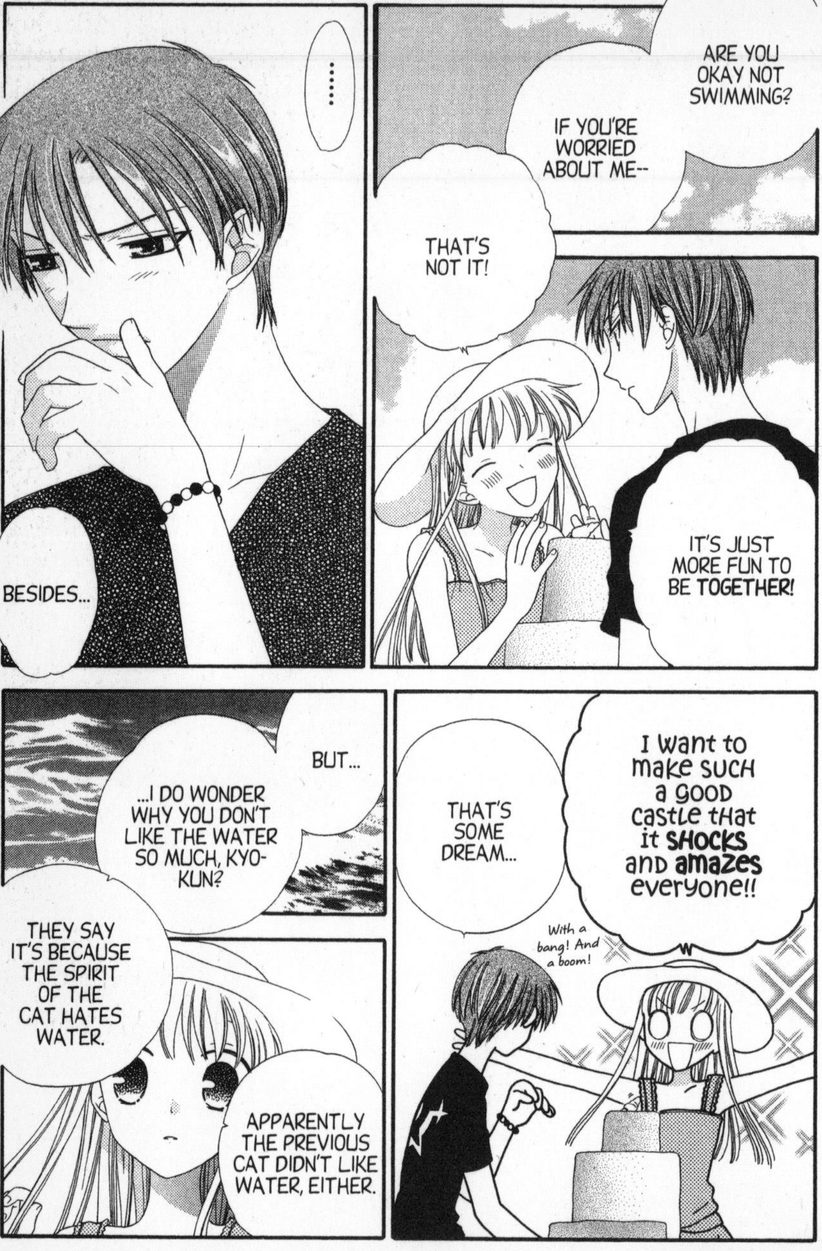
ARE YOU OKAY NOT SWIMMING?
IF YOU'RE WORRIED ABOUT ME--
THAT'S NOT IT!
IT'S JUST MORE FUN TO BE TOGETHER!
......
BESIDES...
I want to make such a good castle that it SHOCKS and amazes everyone!!
With a bang! And a boom!
THAT'S SOME DREAM...
BUT...
...I DO WONDER WHY YOU DON'T LIKE THE WATER SO MUCH, KYO-KUN?
THEY SAY IT'S BECAUSE THE SPIRIT OF THE CAT HATES WATER.
APPARENTLY THE PREVIOUS CAT DIDN'T LIKE WATER, EITHER.

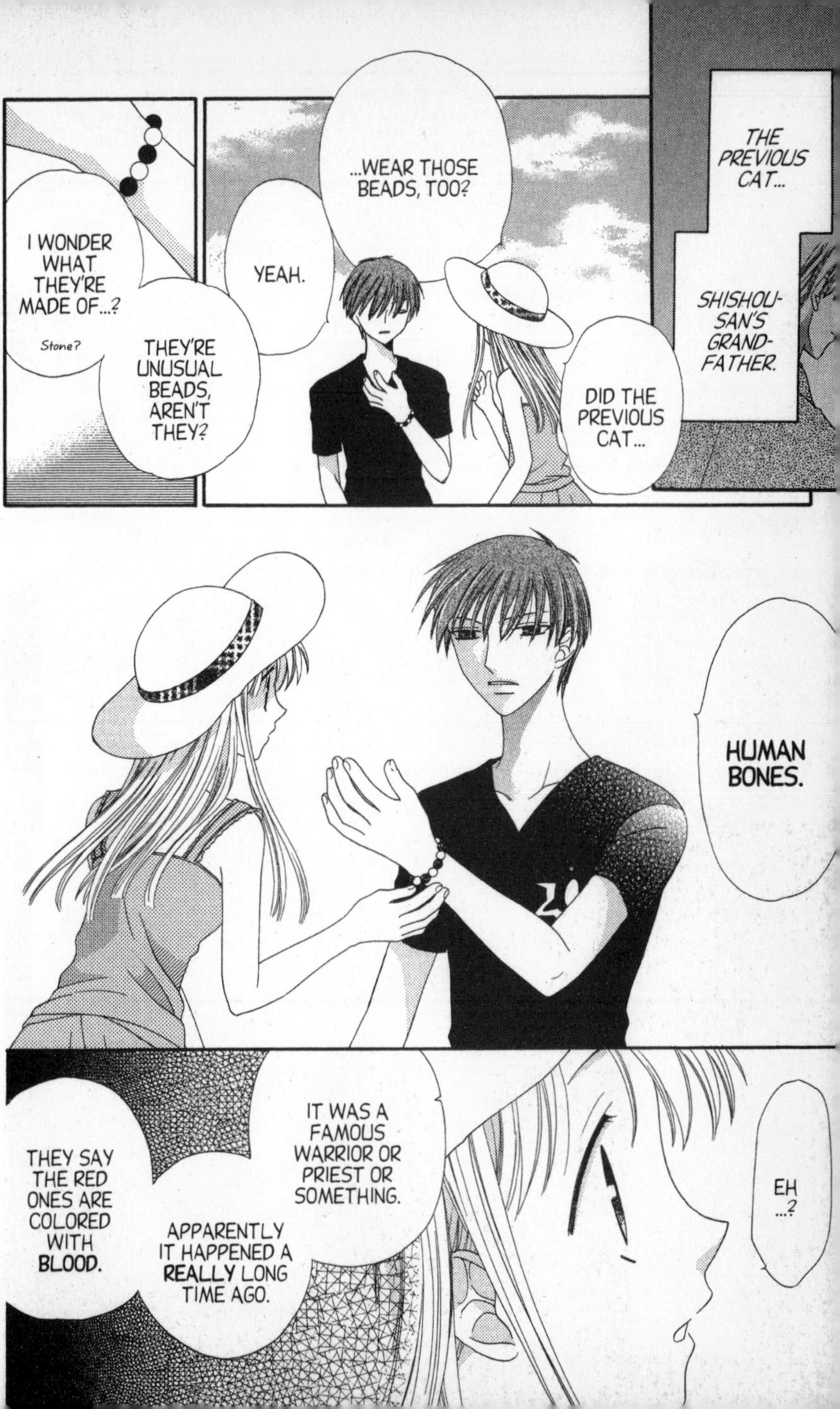
THE PREVIOUS CAT...
SHISHOU-SAN'S GRAND-FATHER.
DID THE PREVIOUS CAT...
...WEAR THOSE BEADS, TOO?
YEAH.
THEY'RE UNUSUAL BEADS, AREN'T THEY?
I WONDER WHAT THEY'RE MADE OF...?
Stone?
HUMAN BONES.
EH ...?
IT WAS A FAMOUS WARRIOR OR PRIEST OR SOMETHING.
APPARENTLY IT HAPPENED A REALLY LONG TIME AGO.
THEY SAY THE RED ONES ARE COLORED WITH BLOOD.

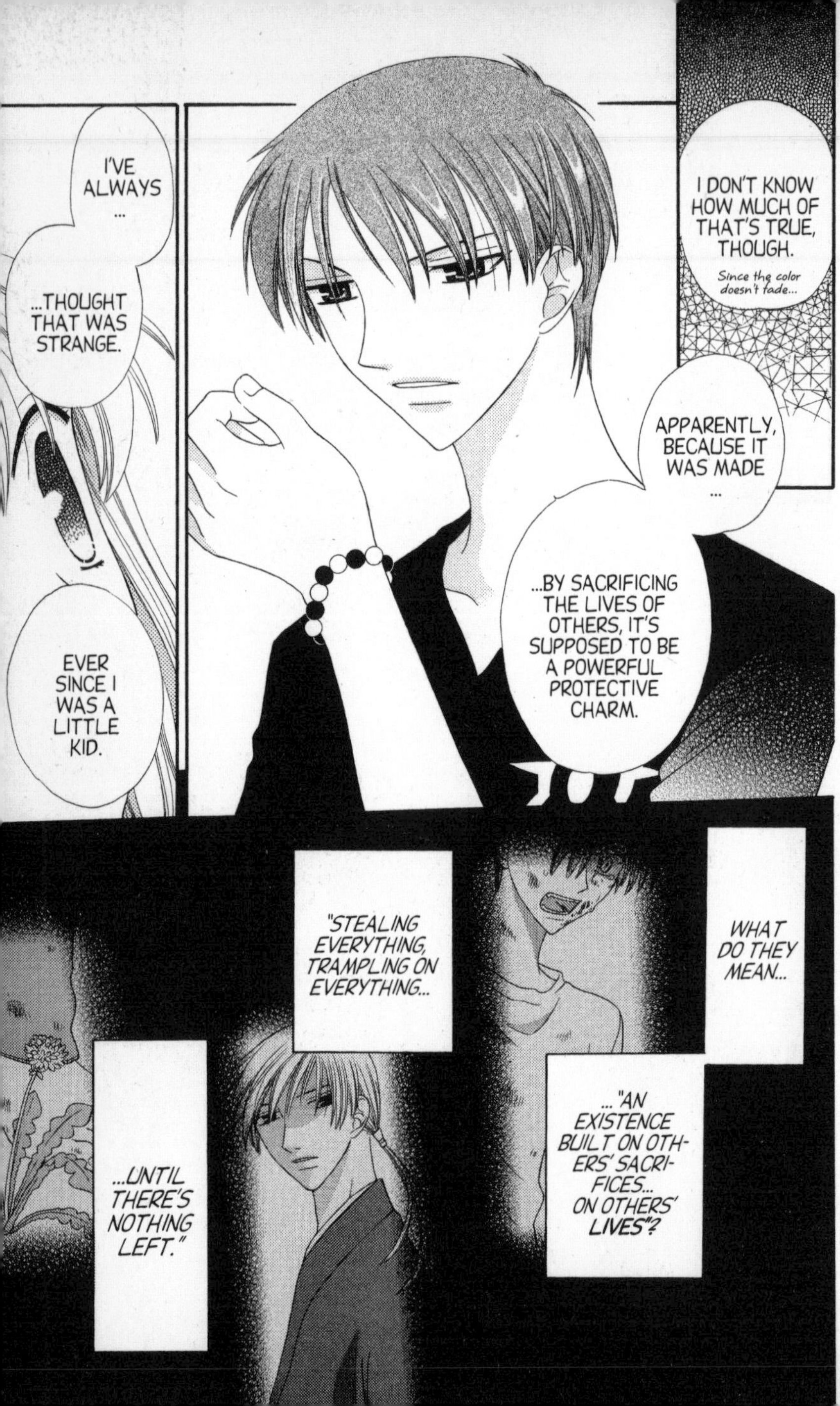
I DON'T KNOW HOW MUCH OF THAT'S TRUE, THOUGH.
Since the color doesn't fade...
APPARENTLY, BECAUSE IT WAS MADE ...
...BY SACRIFICING THE LIVES OF OTHERS, IT'S SUPPOSED TO BE A POWERFUL PROTECTIVE CHARM.
I'VE ALWAYS ...
...THOUGHT THAT WAS STRANGE.
EVER SINCE I WAS A LITTLE KID.
WHAT DO THEY MEAN...
..."AN EXISTENCE BUILT ON OTHERS' SACRIFICES... ON OTHERS' LIVES"?
"STEALING EVERYTHING, TRAMPLING ON EVERYTHING...
...UNTIL THERE'S NOTHING LEFT."

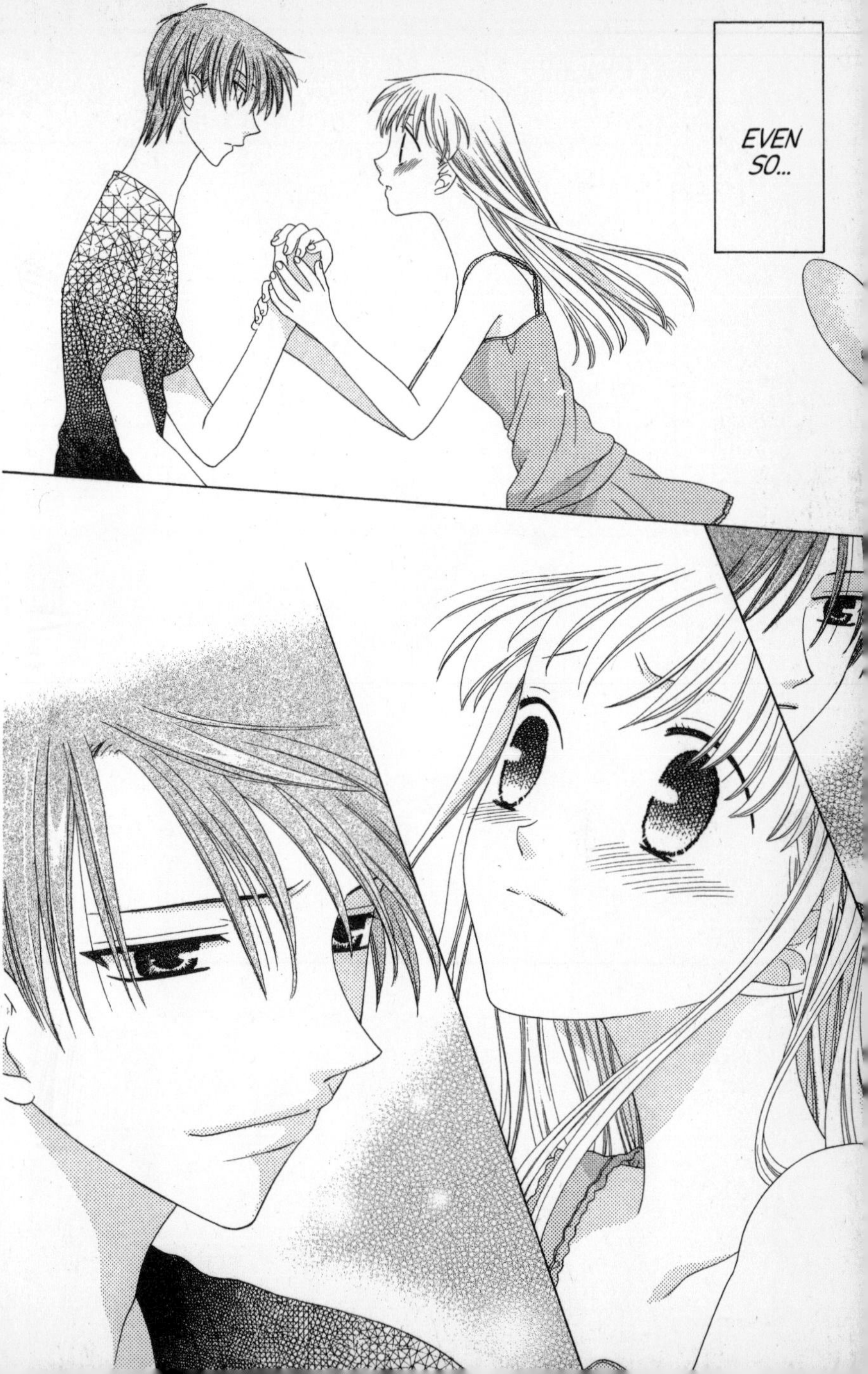
EVEN SO...

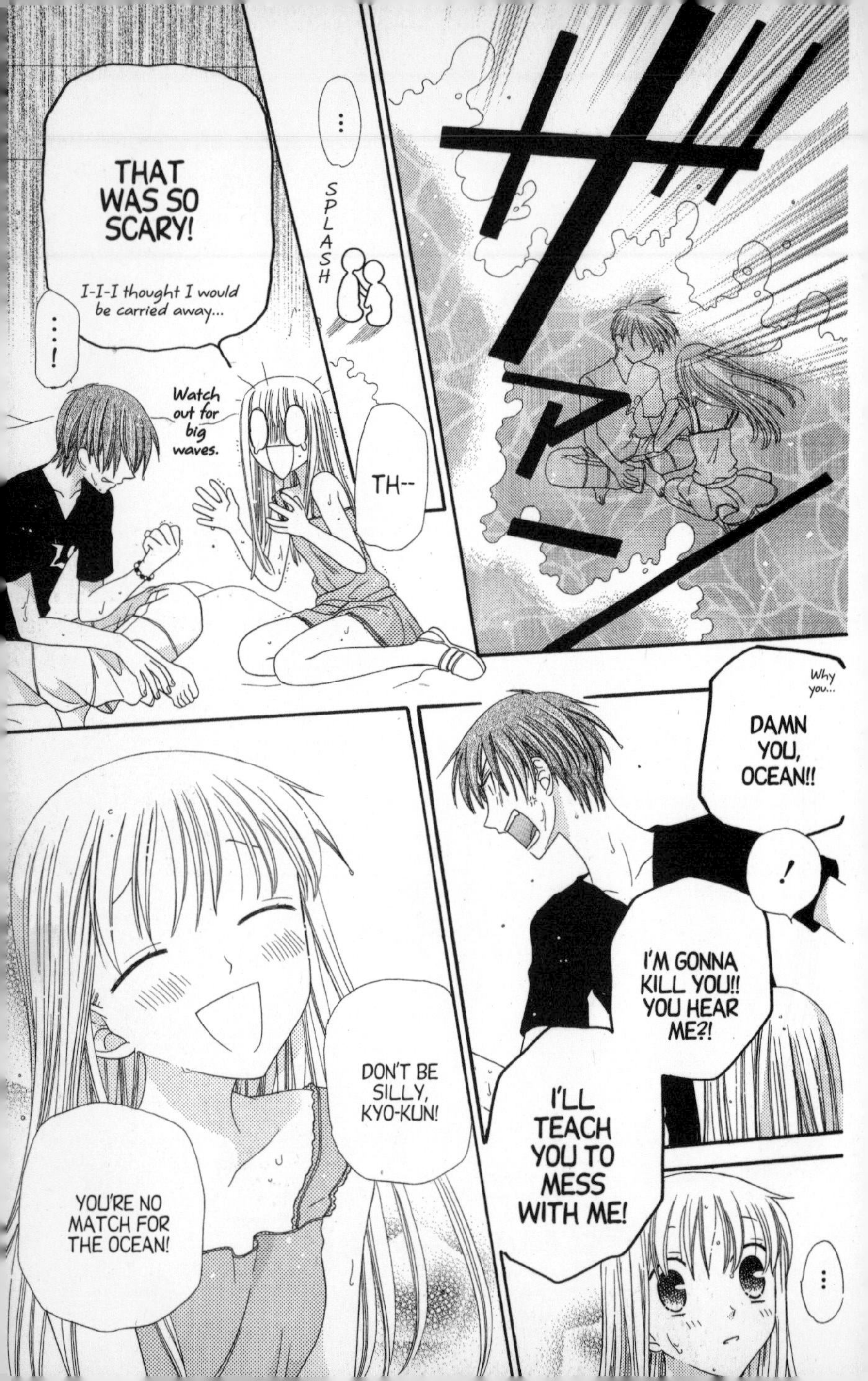
…
SPLASH
THAT WAS SO SCARY!
I-I-I thought I would be carried away...
…!
TH--
Watch out for big waves.
Why you...
DAMN YOU, OCEAN!!
!
I'M GONNA KILL YOU!! YOU HEAR ME?!
I'LL TEACH YOU TO MESS WITH ME!
…
DON'T BE SILLY, KYO-KUN!
YOU'RE NO MATCH FOR THE OCEAN!

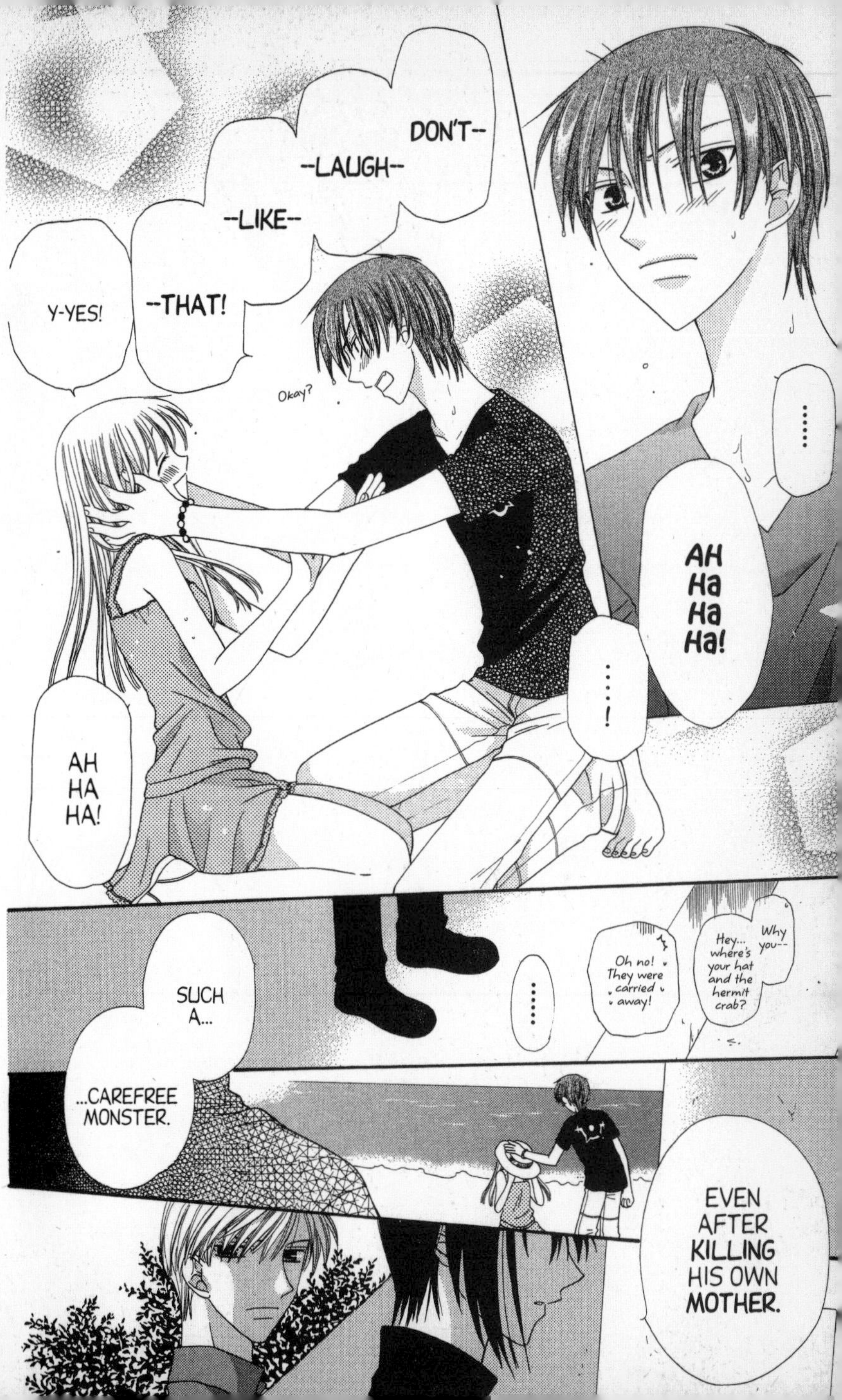
......
AH Ha Ha Ha!
DON'T--
--LAUGH--
--LIKE--
--THAT!
Y-YES!
Okay?
....!
AH HA HA!
Why you--
Hey... where's your hat and the hermit crab?
Oh no! They were carried away!
......
SUCH A...
...CAREFREE MONSTER.
EVEN AFTER KILLING HIS OWN MOTHER.

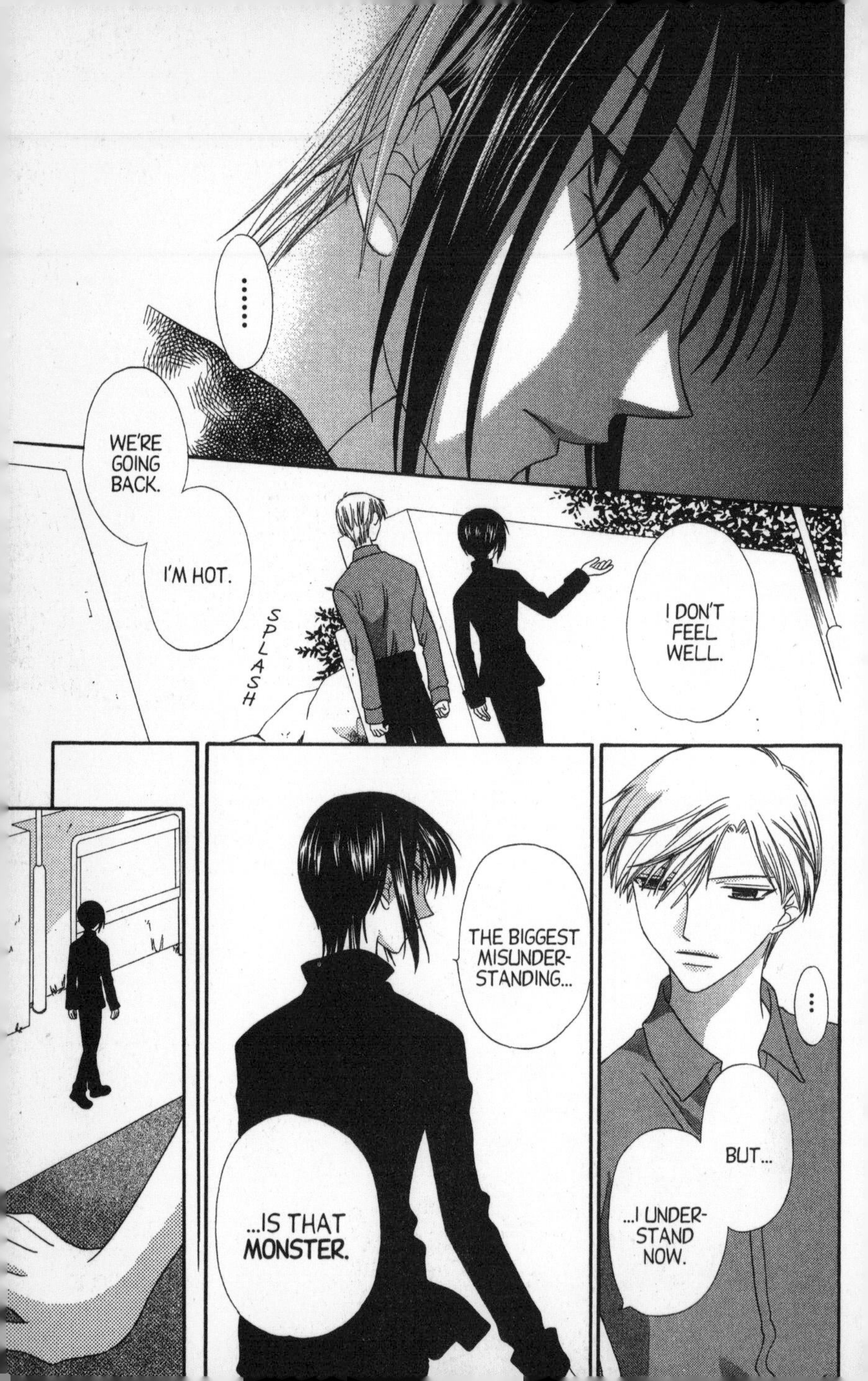
......
I DON'T FEEL WELL.
WE'RE GOING BACK.
I'M HOT.
SPLASH
...
BUT...
...I UNDER-STAND NOW.
THE BIGGEST MISUNDER-STANDING...
...IS THAT MONSTER.

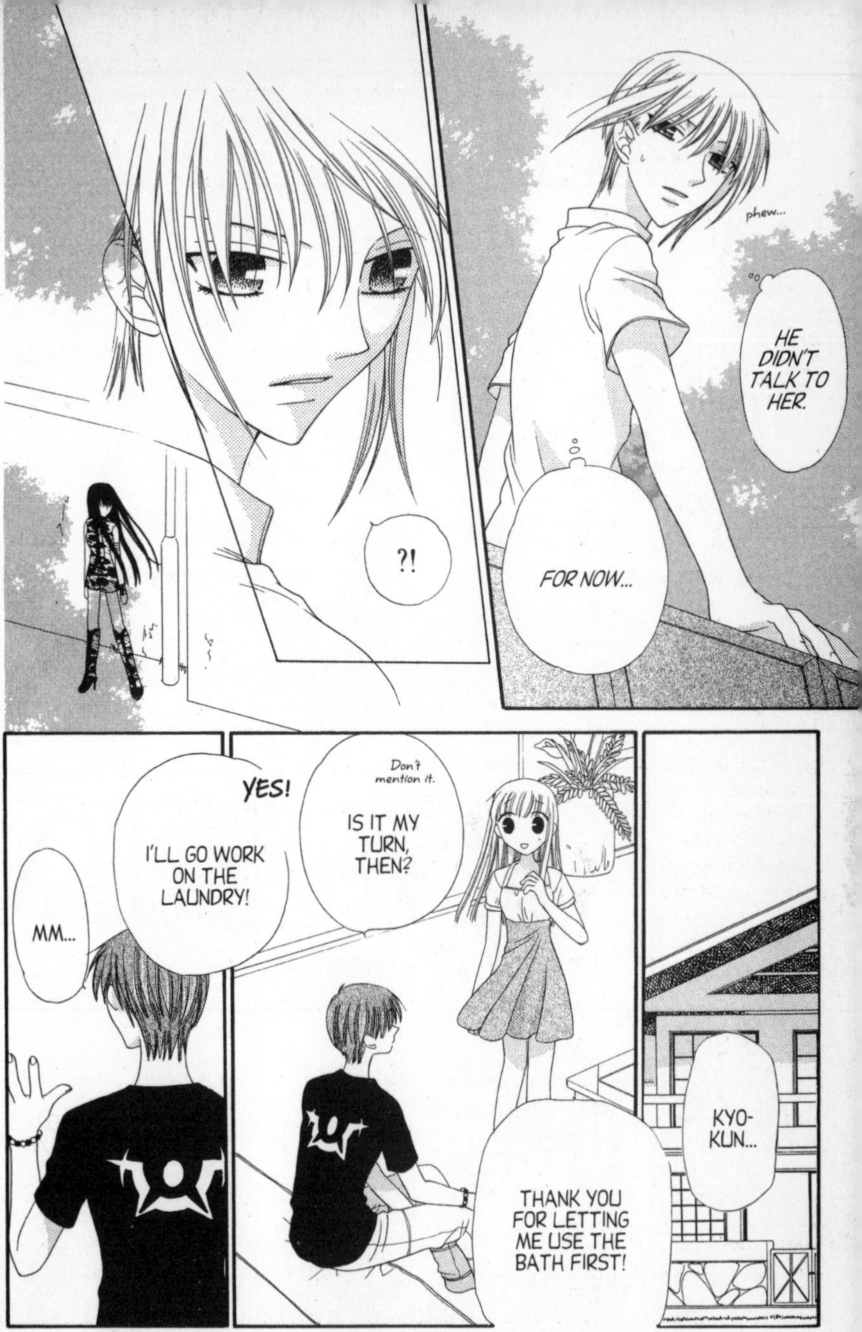
phew...
HE DIDN'T TALK TO HER.
FOR NOW...
?!
KYO-KUN...
THANK YOU FOR LETTING ME USE THE BATH FIRST!
Don't mention it.
IS IT MY TURN, THEN?
YES!
I'LL GO WORK ON THE LAUNDRY!
MM...

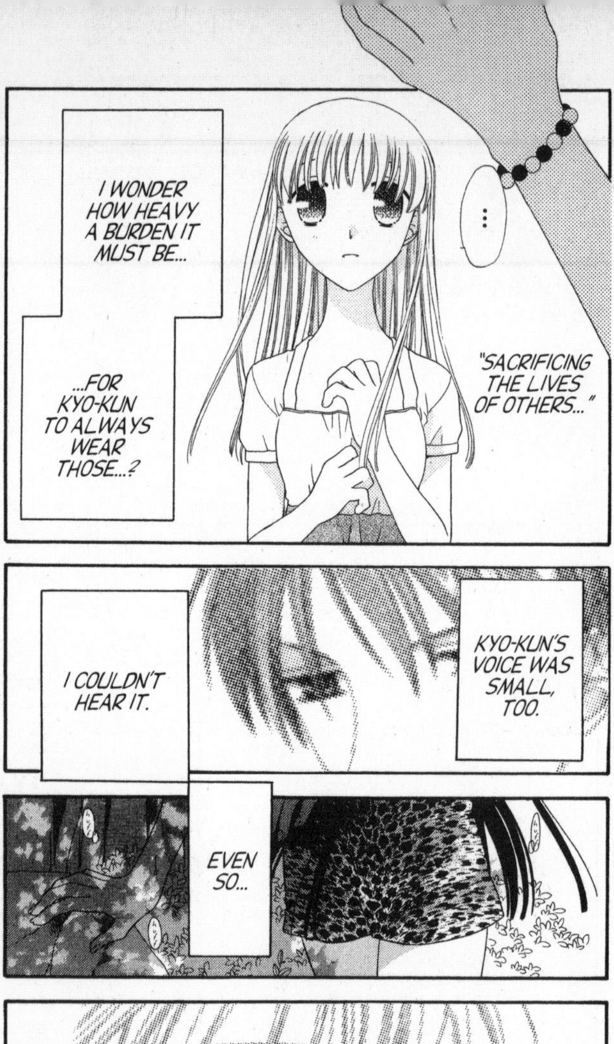
…
"SACRIFICING THE LIVES OF OTHERS…"
I WONDER HOW HEAVY A BURDEN IT MUST BE…
…FOR KYO-KUN TO ALWAYS WEAR THOSE…?
KYO-KUN'S VOICE WAS SMALL, TOO.
I COULDN'T HEAR IT.
EVEN SO…
"SOMEDAY… OKAY?"
…I WONDER IF I SHOULD DO EVERYTHING IN MY POWER TO TRY TO HEAR.

Okami-san

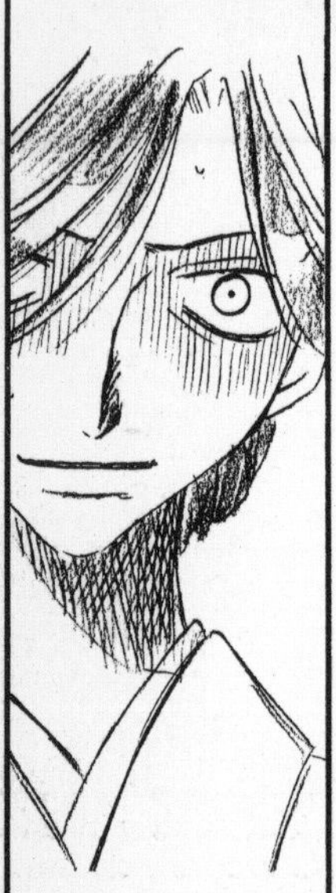

If Okami-san ever came at me with all that tension, I would either run away with all my might, or be scared stiff. At least when she speaks with Ritchan she can be quiet. She's not always thorough in fulfill-ing her duties as hostess--could it be calculated neglect? Is she as shameless as her son? Anyway, because she shouts a lot, I have a hard time fitting all her lines inside her balloons.

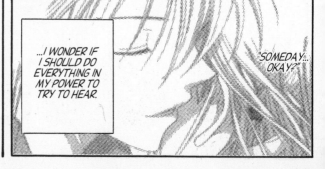

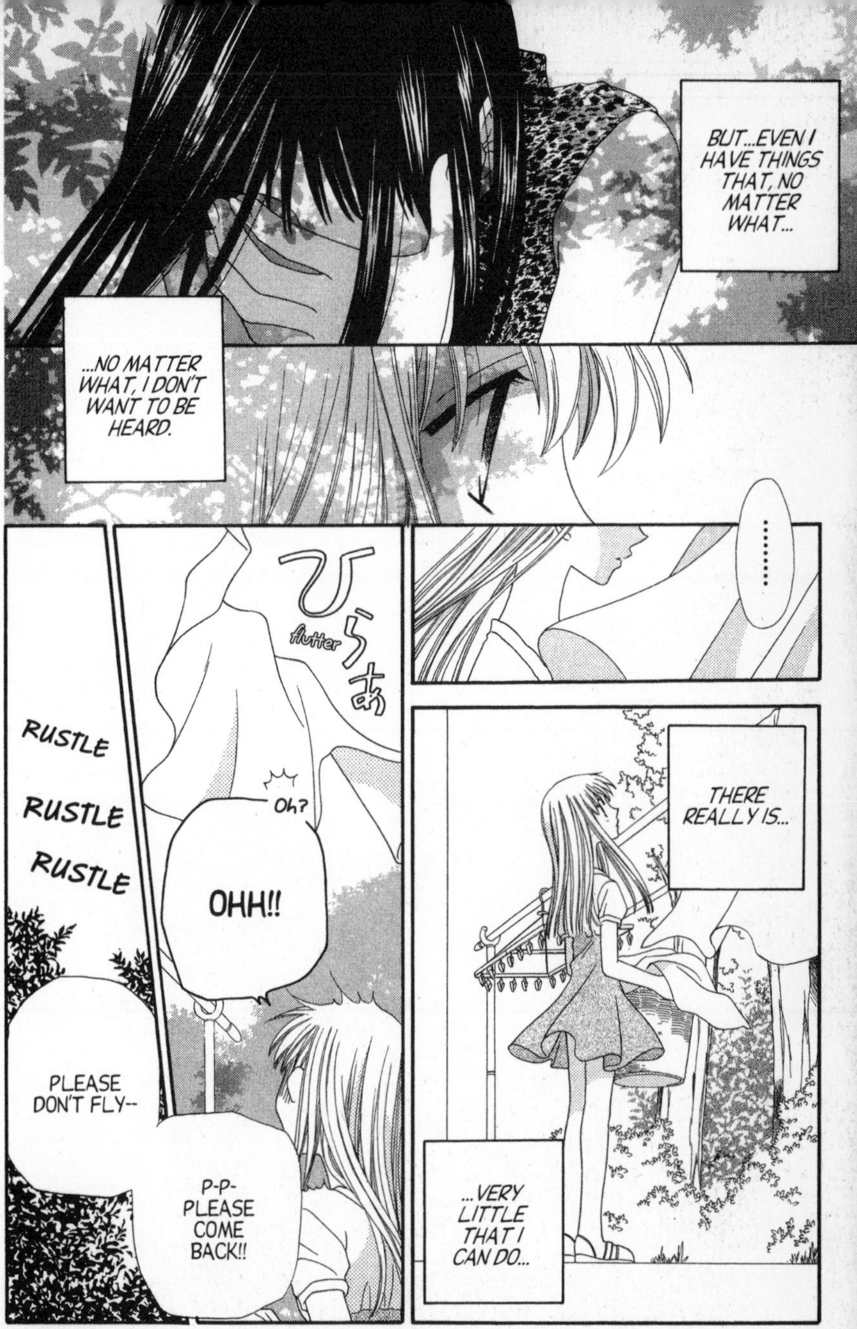
BUT...EVEN I HAVE THINGS THAT, NO MATTER WHAT...
...NO MATTER WHAT, I DON'T WANT TO BE HEARD.
......
THERE REALLY IS...
...VERY LITTLE THAT I CAN DO...
ひらあ
flutter
Oh?
OHH!!
RUSTLE
RUSTLE
RUSTLE
PLEASE DON'T FLY--
P-P-PLEASE COME BACK!!

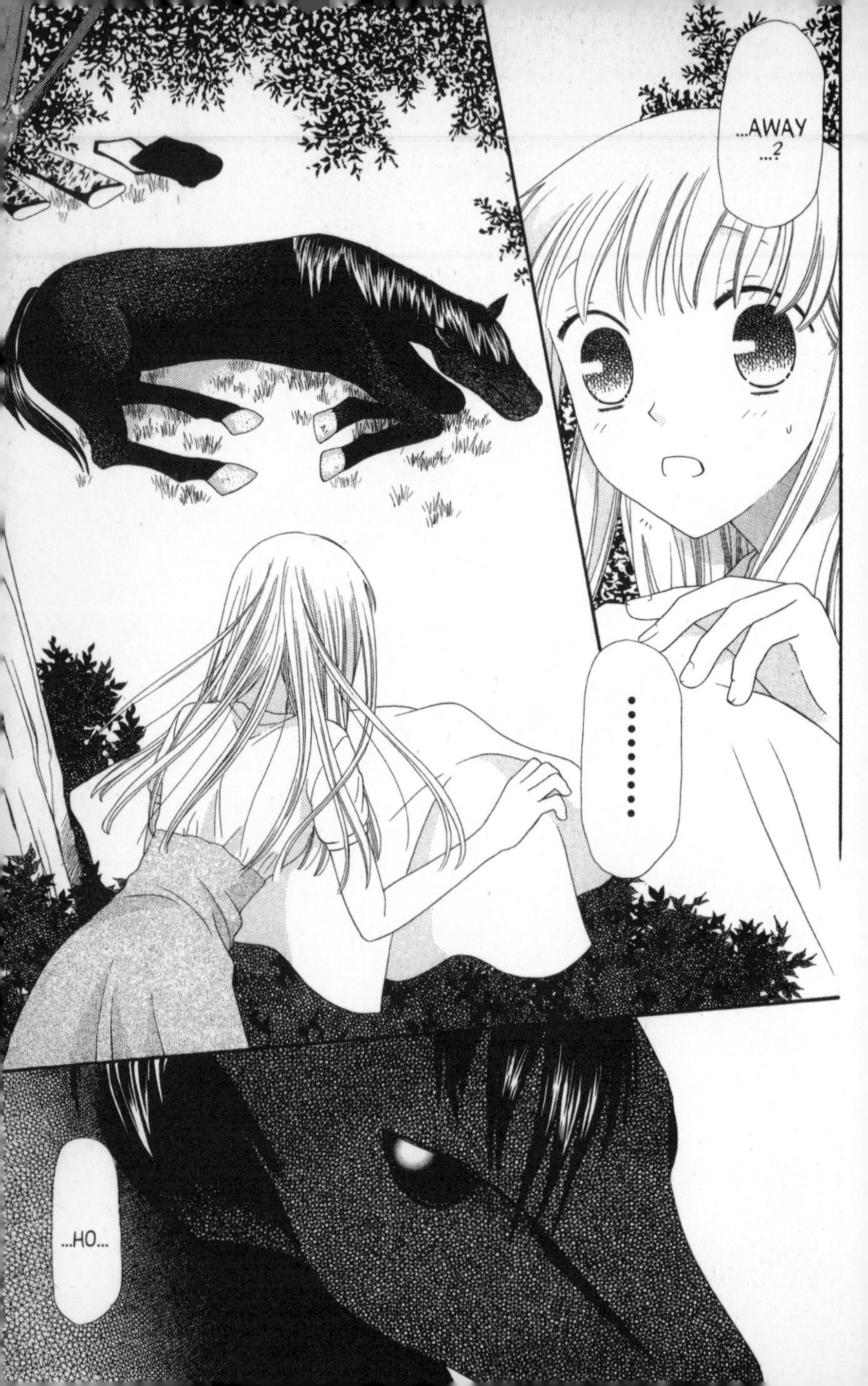
...AWAY...?
....
...HO...

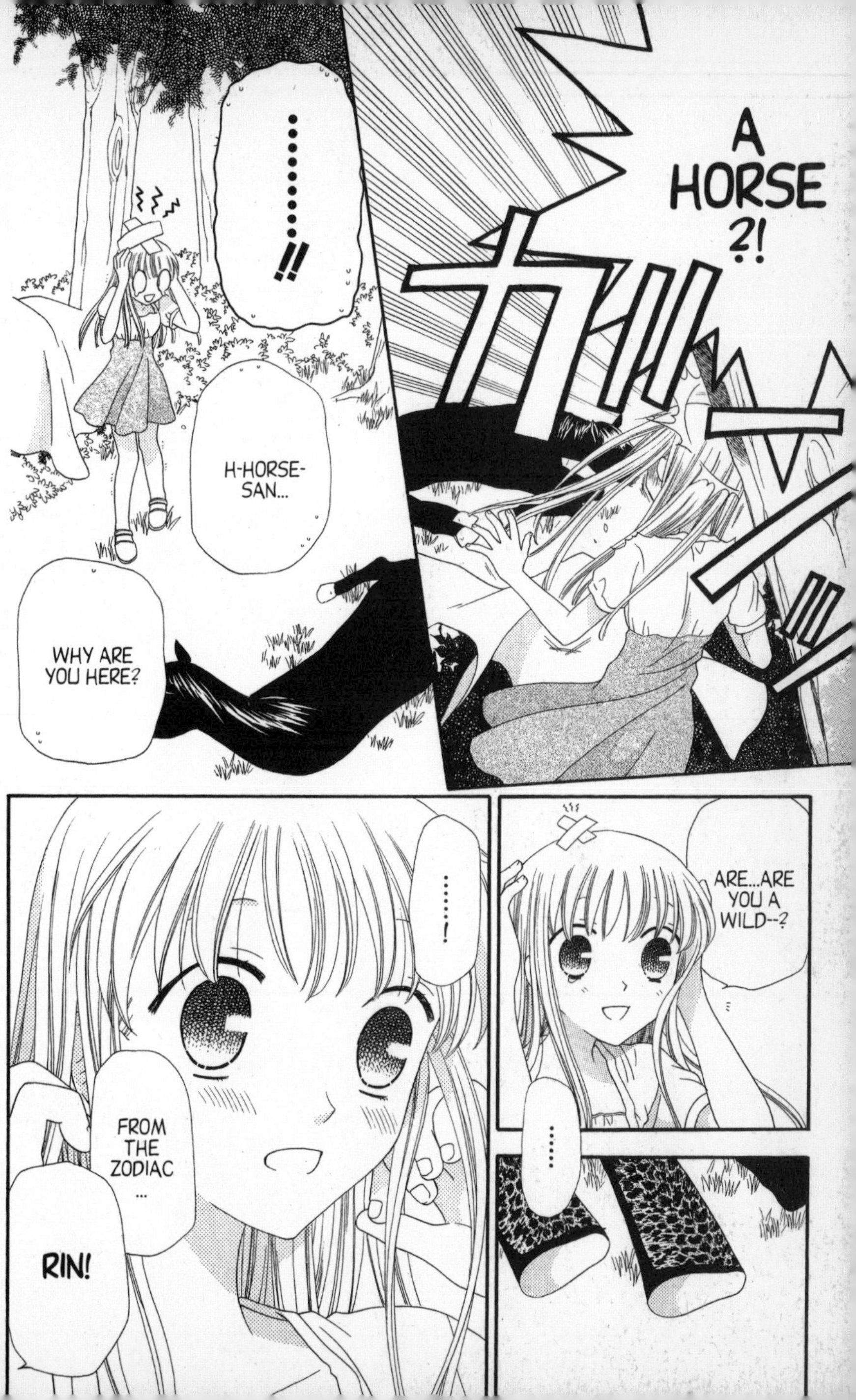
A HORSE ?!
カッ
......!!
H-HORSE-SAN...
WHY ARE YOU HERE?
ARE...ARE YOU A WILD--?
......
......!
FROM THE ZODIAC ...
RIN!

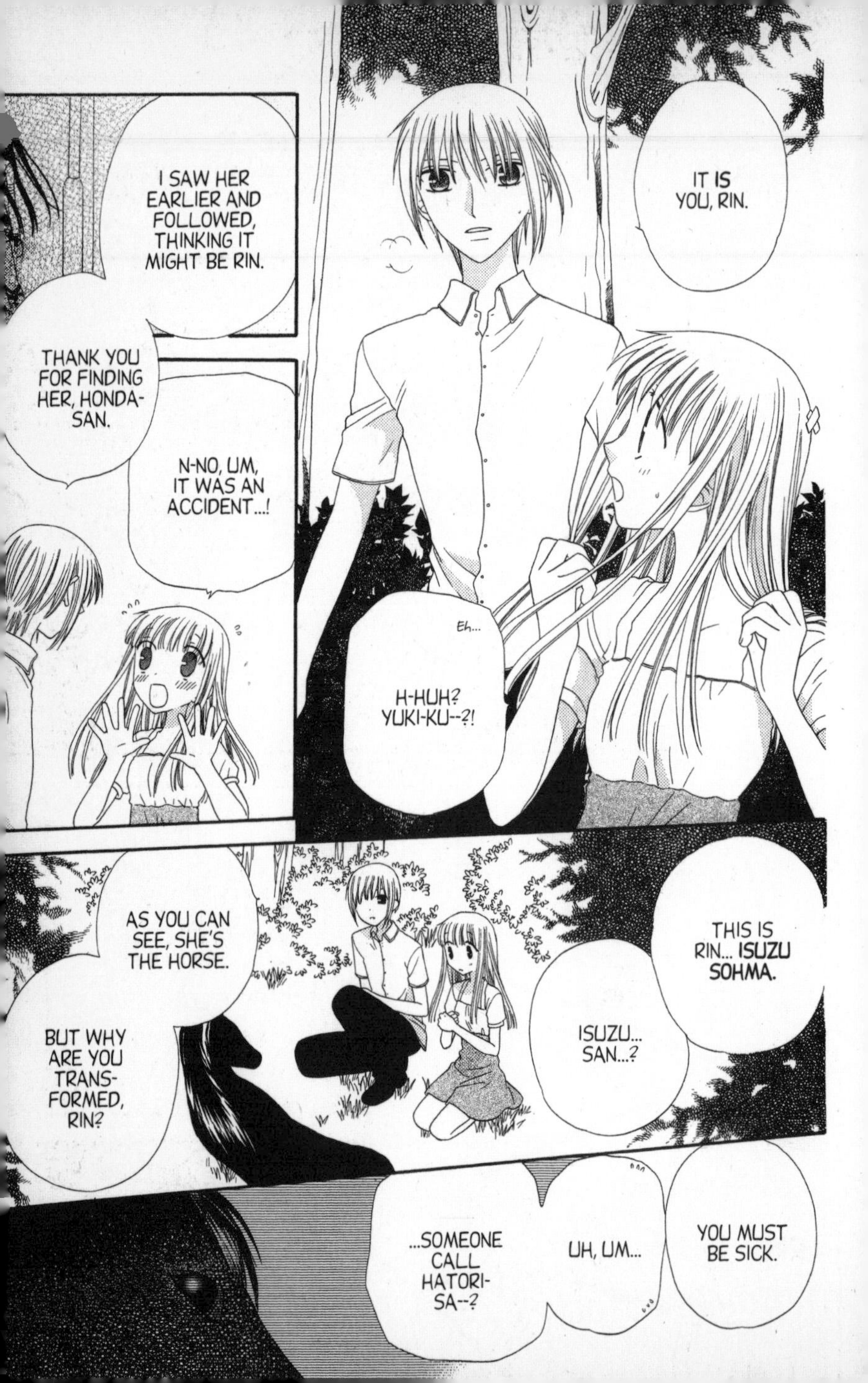
IT IS YOU, RIN.
Eh...
H-HUH? YUKI-KU--?!
I SAW HER EARLIER AND FOLLOWED, THINKING IT MIGHT BE RIN.
THANK YOU FOR FINDING HER, HONDA-SAN.
N-NO, UM, IT WAS AN ACCIDENT...!
THIS IS RIN... **ISUZU SOHMA.**
ISUZU... SAN...?
AS YOU CAN SEE, SHE'S THE HORSE.
BUT WHY ARE YOU TRANSFORMED, RIN?
YOU MUST BE SICK.
UH, UM...
...SOMEONE CALL HATORI-SA--?

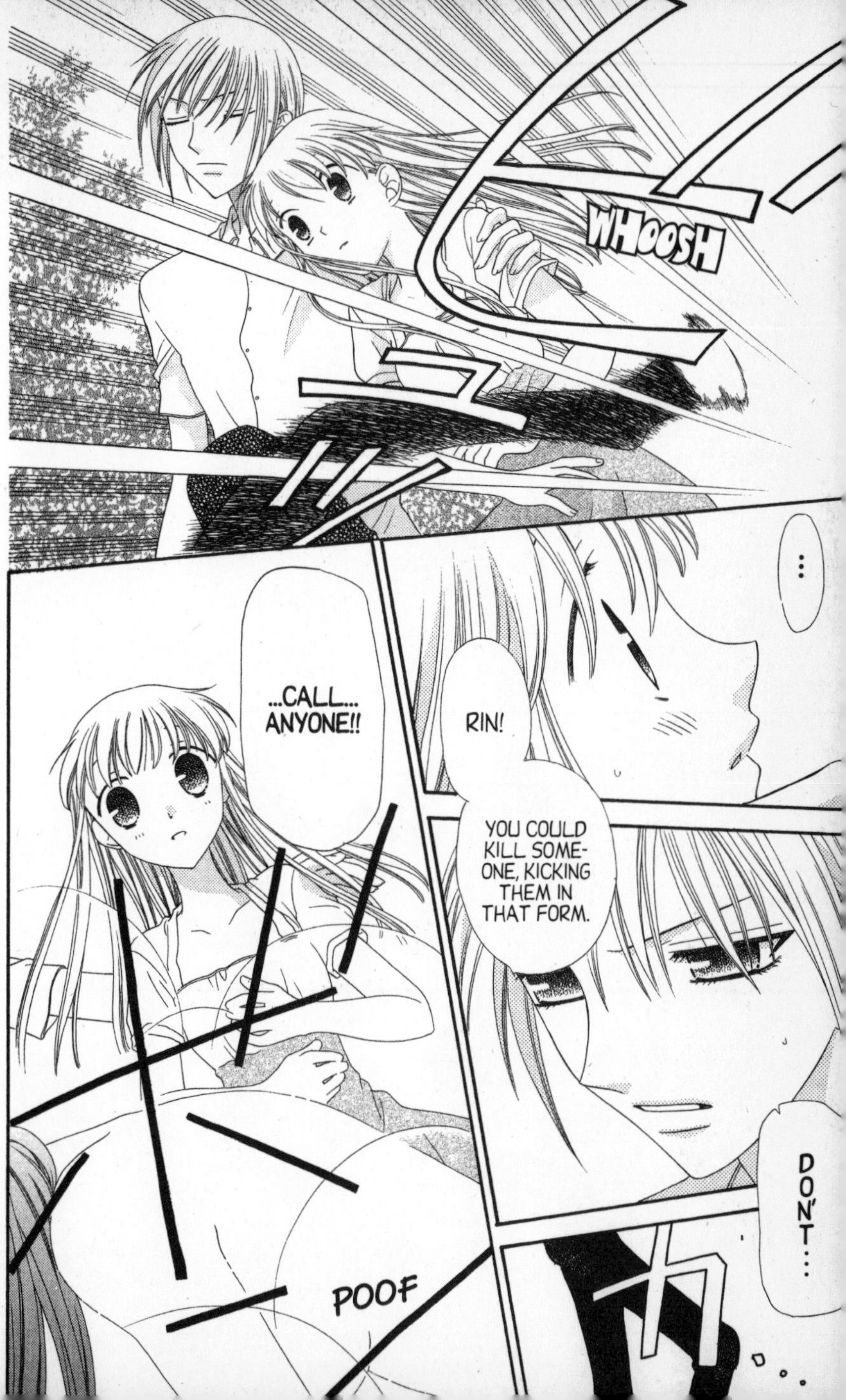
WHOOSH
...
RIN!
YOU COULD KILL SOME-ONE, KICKING THEM IN THAT FORM.
DON'T...
...CALL... ANYONE!!
POOF

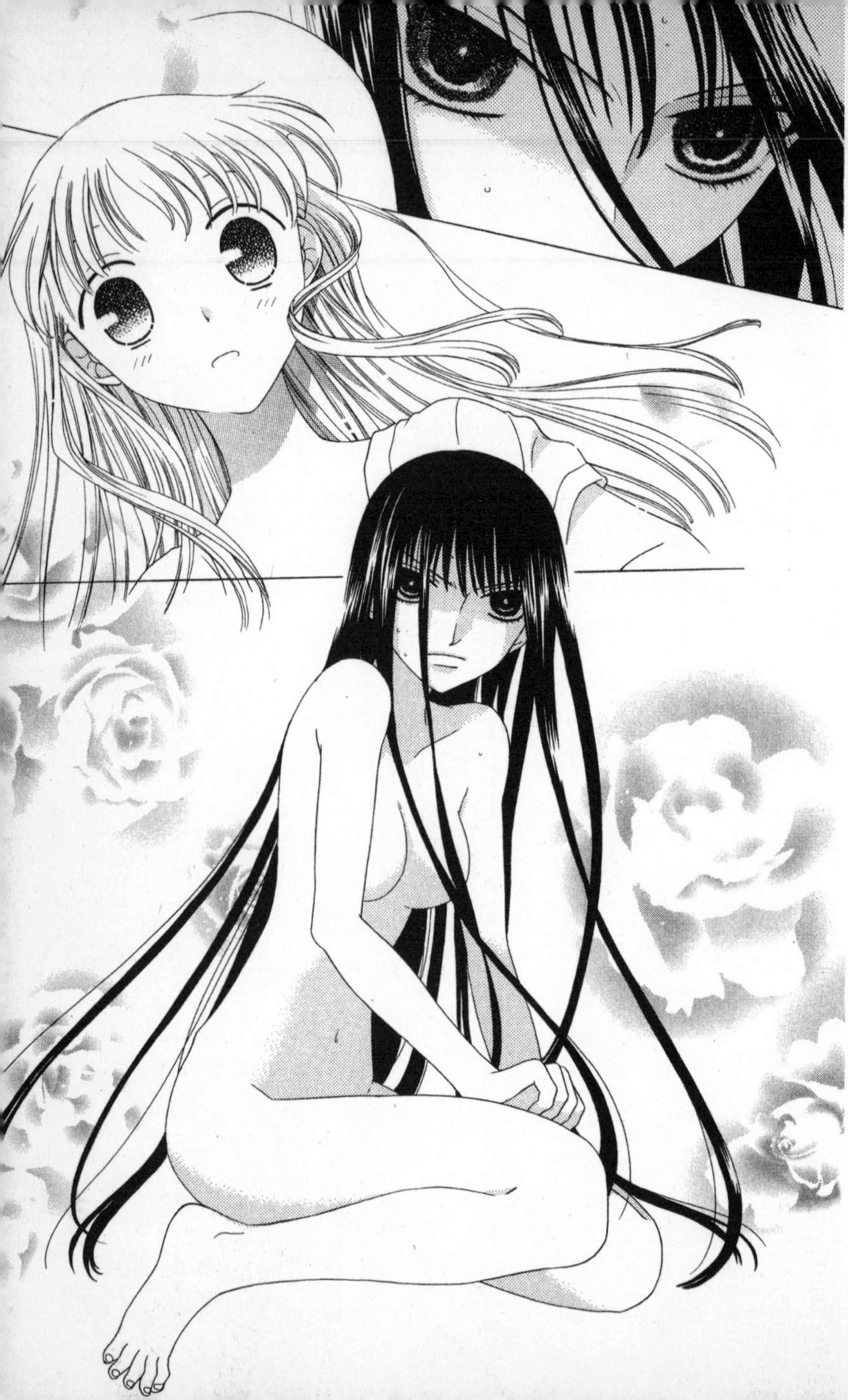

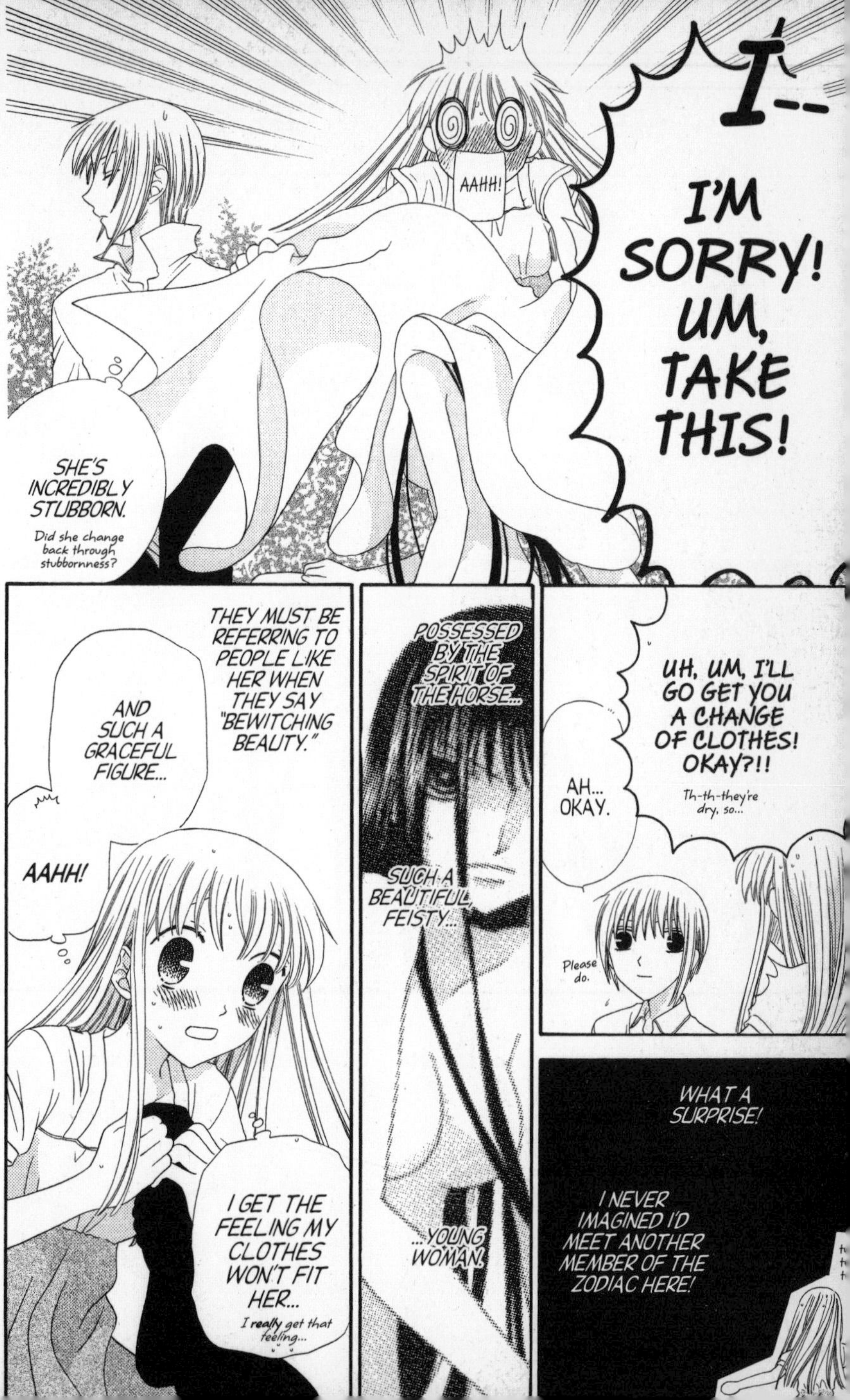
I--
I'M SORRY! UM, TAKE THIS!
AAHH!
SHE'S INCREDIBLY STUBBORN.
Did she change back through stubbornness?
UH, UM, I'LL GO GET YOU A CHANGE OF CLOTHES! OKAY?!!
Th-th-they're dry, so...
AH... OKAY.
Please do.
WHAT A SURPRISE!
I NEVER IMAGINED I'D MEET ANOTHER MEMBER OF THE ZODIAC HERE!
POSSESSED BY THE SPIRIT OF THE HORSE...
SUCH A BEAUTIFUL, FEISTY...
...YOUNG WOMAN!
THEY MUST BE REFERRING TO PEOPLE LIKE HER WHEN THEY SAY "BEWITCHING BEAUTY."
AND SUCH A GRACEFUL FIGURE...
AAHH!
I GET THE FEELING MY CLOTHES WON'T FIT HER...
I **really** get that feeling...

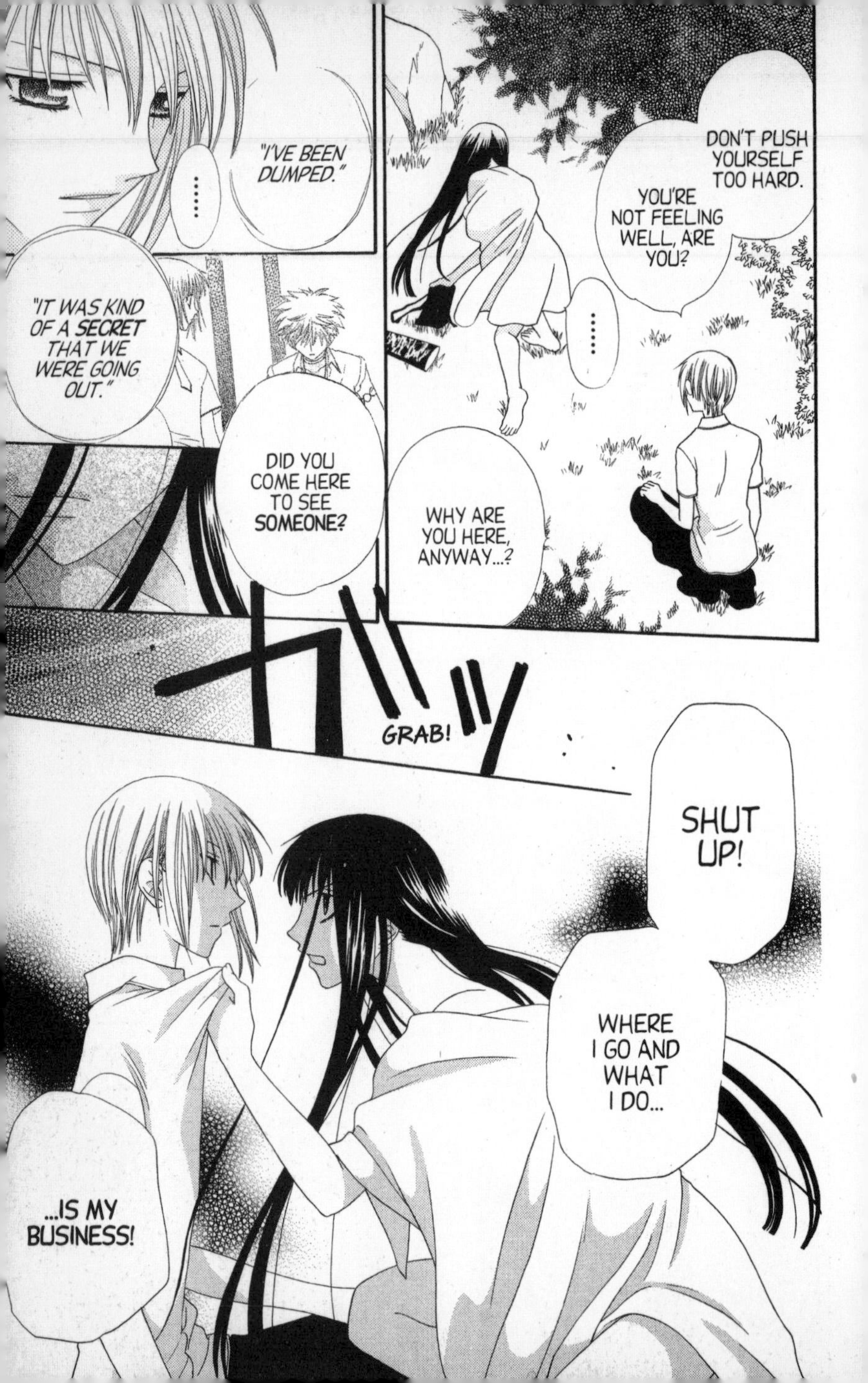
DON'T PUSH YOURSELF TOO HARD.
YOU'RE NOT FEELING WELL, ARE YOU?
……
WHY ARE YOU HERE, ANYWAY...?
"I'VE BEEN DUMPED."
……
"IT WAS KIND OF A SECRET THAT WE WERE GOING OUT."
DID YOU COME HERE TO SEE SOMEONE?
GRAB!
SHUT UP!
WHERE I GO AND WHAT I DO...
...IS MY BUSINESS!

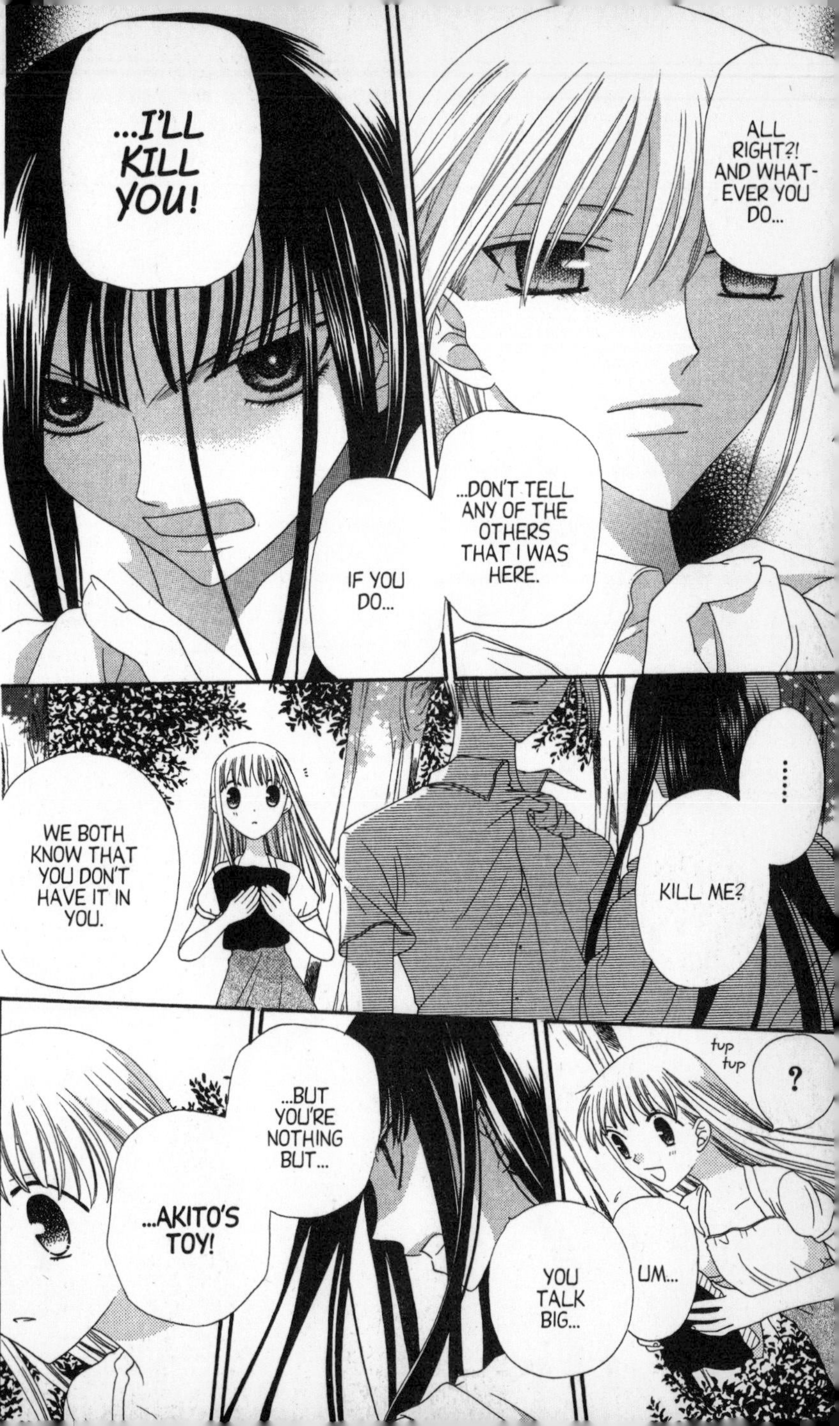
ALL RIGHT?! AND WHAT-EVER YOU DO...
...DON'T TELL ANY OF THE OTHERS THAT I WAS HERE.
IF YOU DO...
...I'LL KILL YOU!
......
KILL ME?
WE BOTH KNOW THAT YOU DON'T HAVE IT IN YOU.
tup tup
?
UM...
YOU TALK BIG...
...BUT YOU'RE NOTHING BUT...
...AKITO'S TOY!

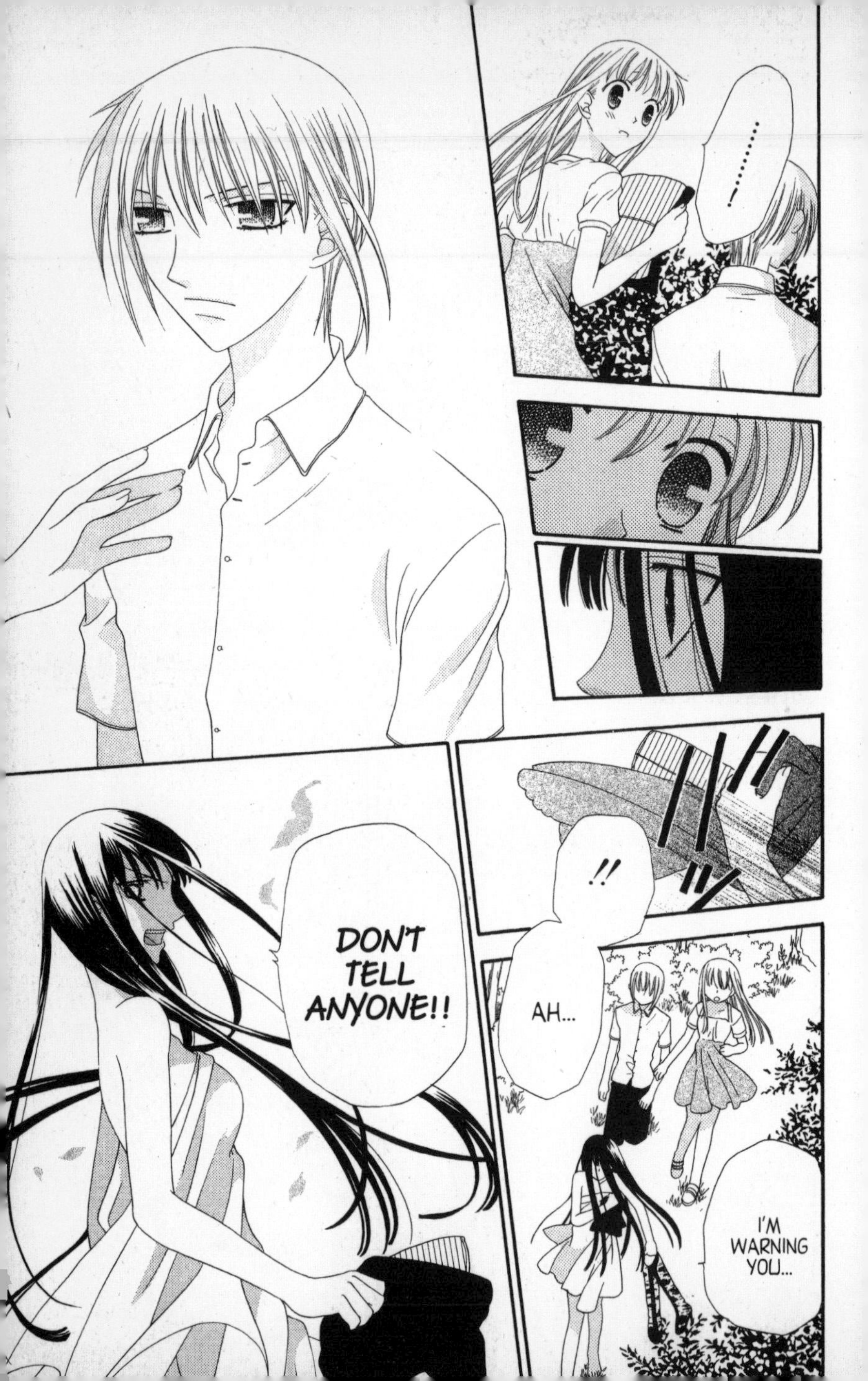
……!
!!
AH...
I'M WARNING YOU...
DON'T TELL ANYONE!!

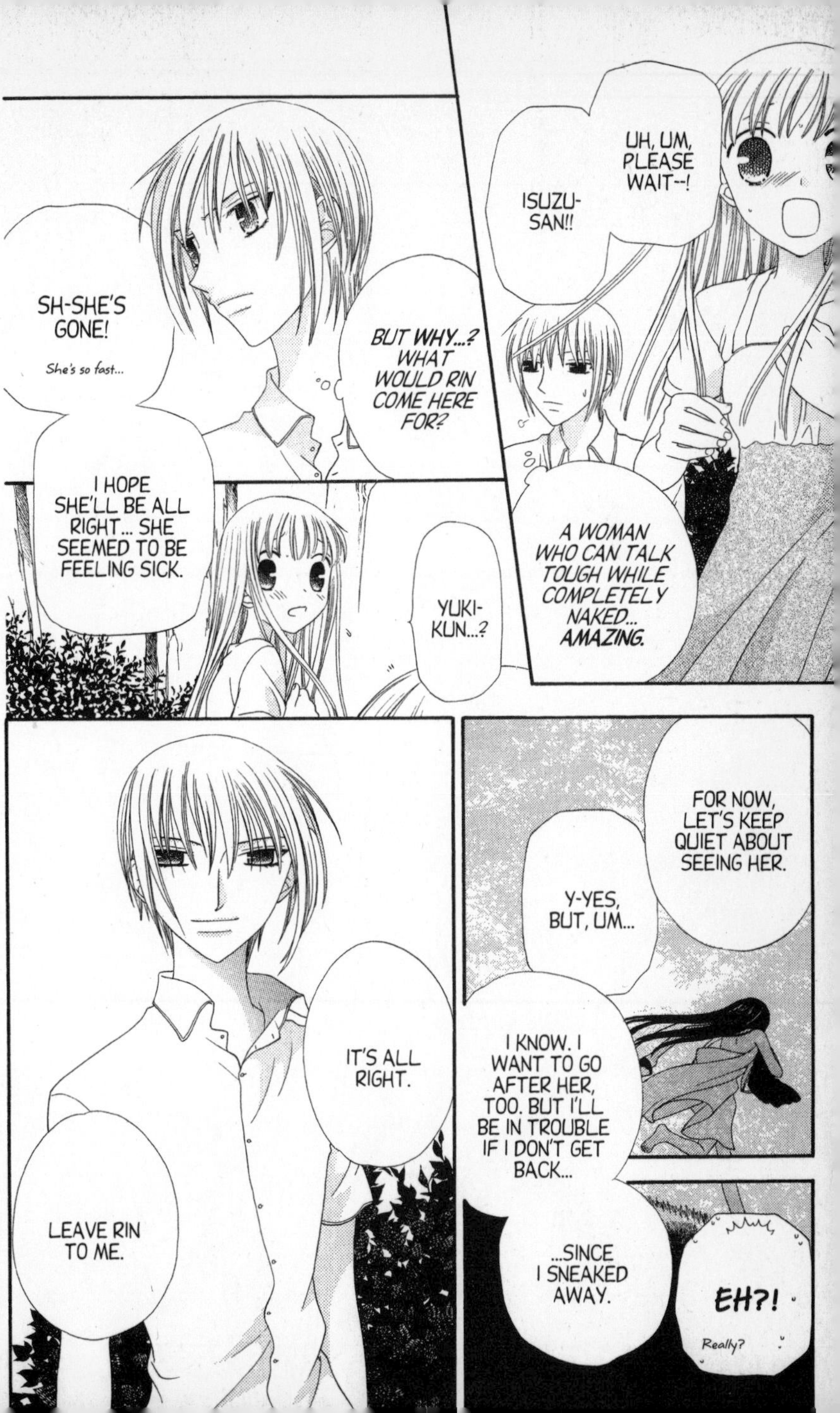
UH, UM, PLEASE WAIT--!
ISUZU-SAN!!
A WOMAN WHO CAN TALK TOUGH WHILE COMPLETELY NAKED... AMAZING.
SH-SHE'S GONE!
She's so fast...
BUT WHY...? WHAT WOULD RIN COME HERE FOR?
I HOPE SHE'LL BE ALL RIGHT... SHE SEEMED TO BE FEELING SICK.
YUKI-KUN...?
FOR NOW, LET'S KEEP QUIET ABOUT SEEING HER.
Y-YES, BUT, UM...
I KNOW. I WANT TO GO AFTER HER, TOO. BUT I'LL BE IN TROUBLE IF I DON'T GET BACK...
...SINCE I SNEAKED AWAY.
EH?!
Really?
IT'S ALL RIGHT.
LEAVE RIN TO ME.

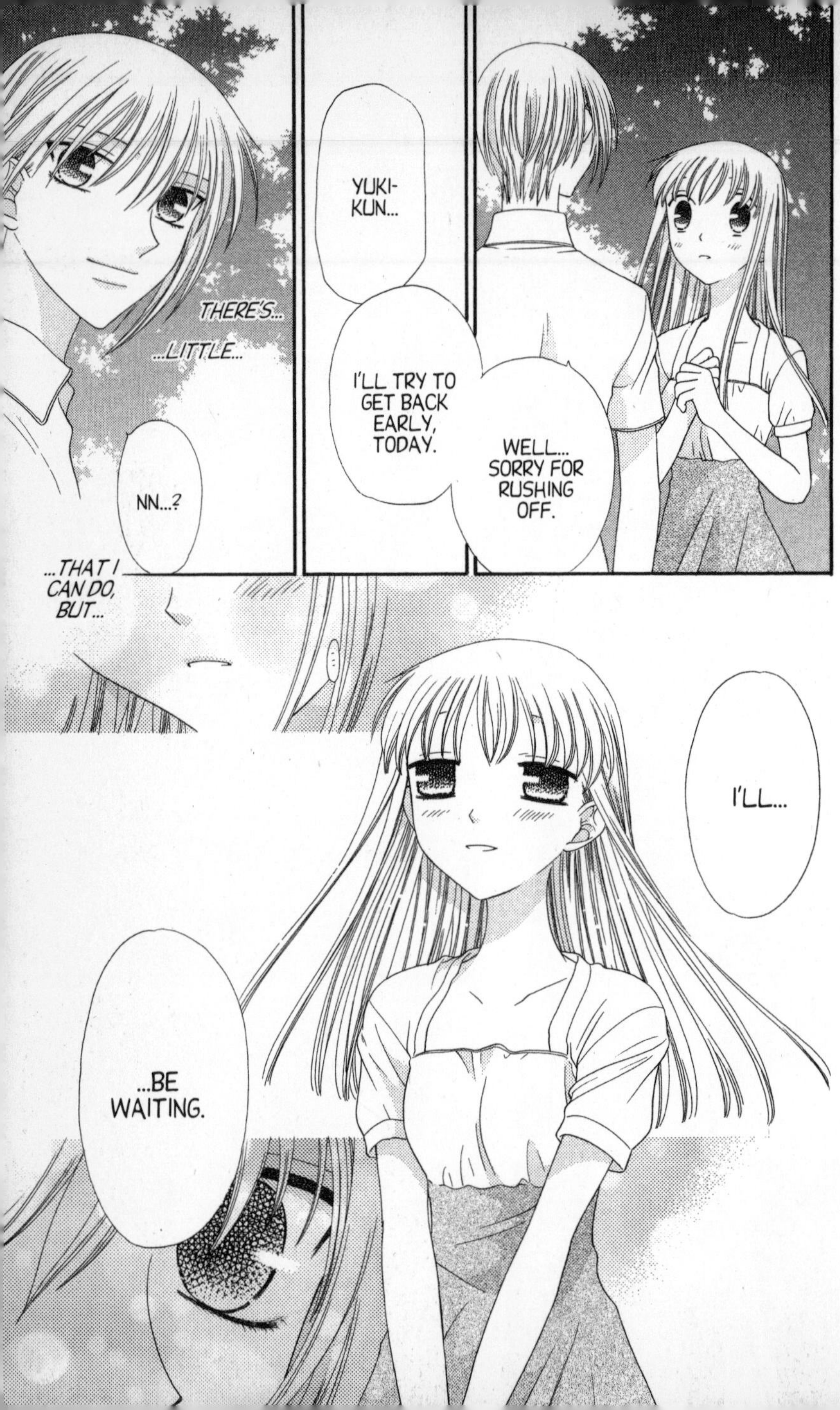

WELL... SORRY FOR RUSHING OFF.
YUKI-KUN...
I'LL TRY TO GET BACK EARLY, TODAY.
THERE'S...
...LITTLE...
NN...?
...THAT I CAN DO, BUT...
I'LL...
...BE WAITING.

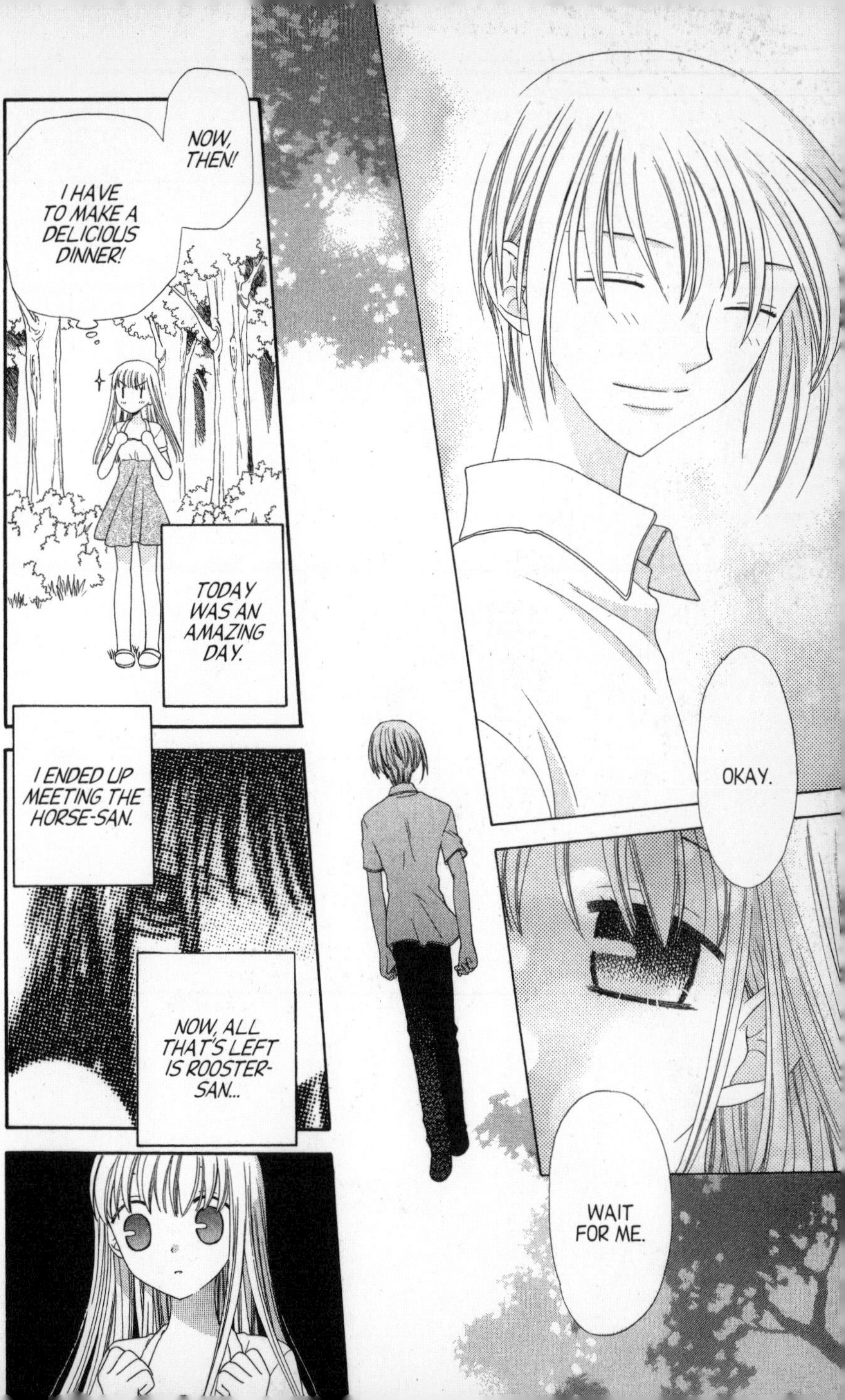
OKAY.
WAIT FOR ME.
NOW, THEN! I HAVE TO MAKE A DELICIOUS DINNER!
TODAY WAS AN AMAZING DAY.
I ENDED UP MEETING THE HORSE-SAN.
NOW, ALL THAT'S LEFT IS ROOSTER-SAN...

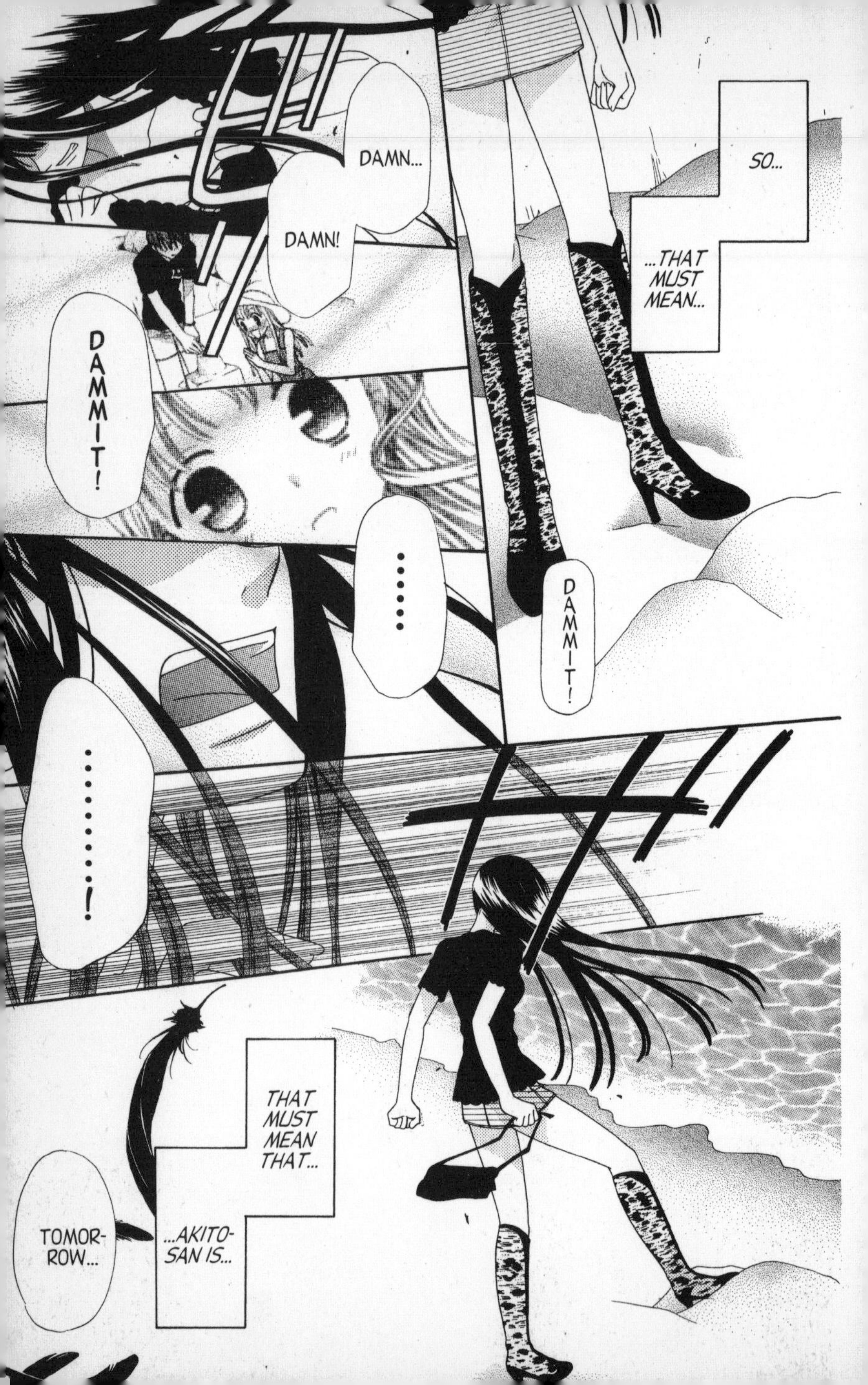
SO...
...THAT MUST MEAN...
DAMMIT!
DAMN...
DAMN!
DAMMIT!
.....
.......!
THAT MUST MEAN THAT...
...AKITO-SAN IS...
TOMOR-ROW...

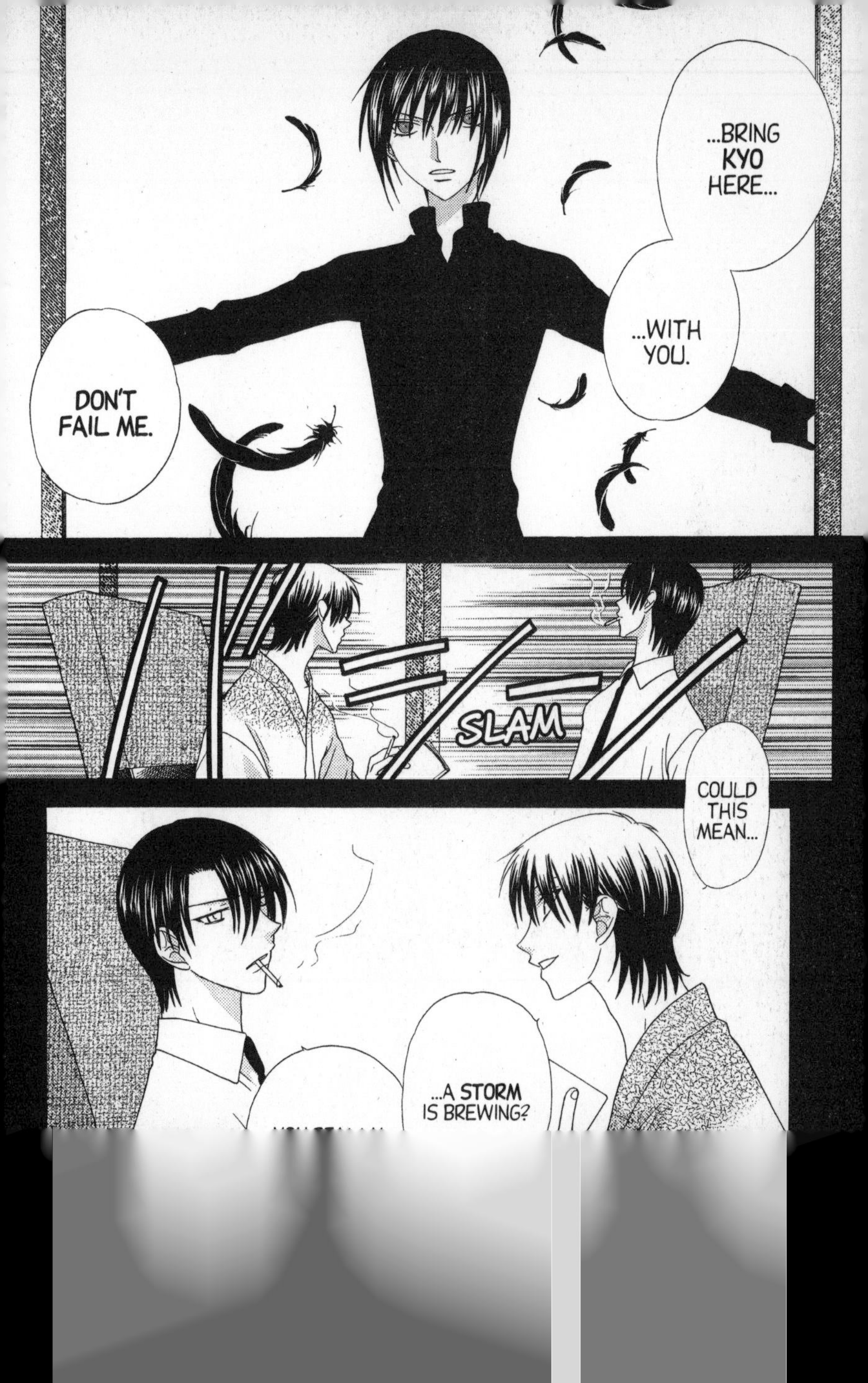
...BRING KYO HERE...
...WITH YOU.
DON'T FAIL ME.
SLAM
COULD THIS MEAN...
...A STORM IS BREWING?

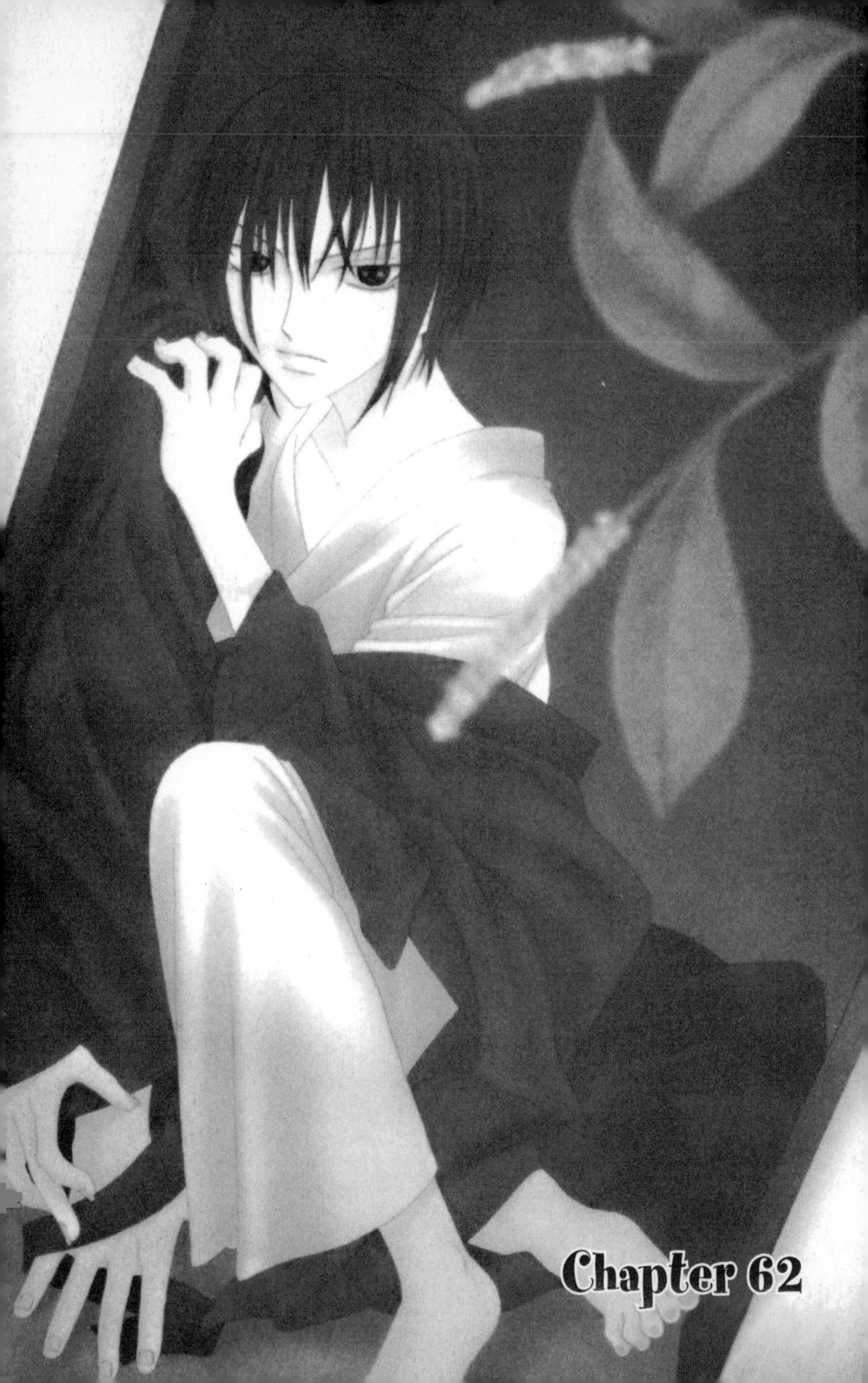
Chapter 62

Filler Sketch

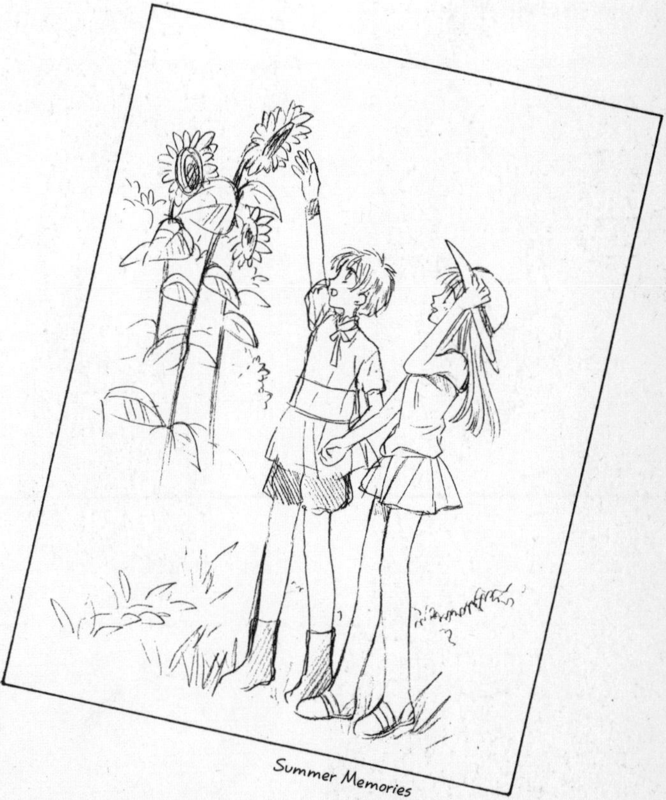

Summer Memories

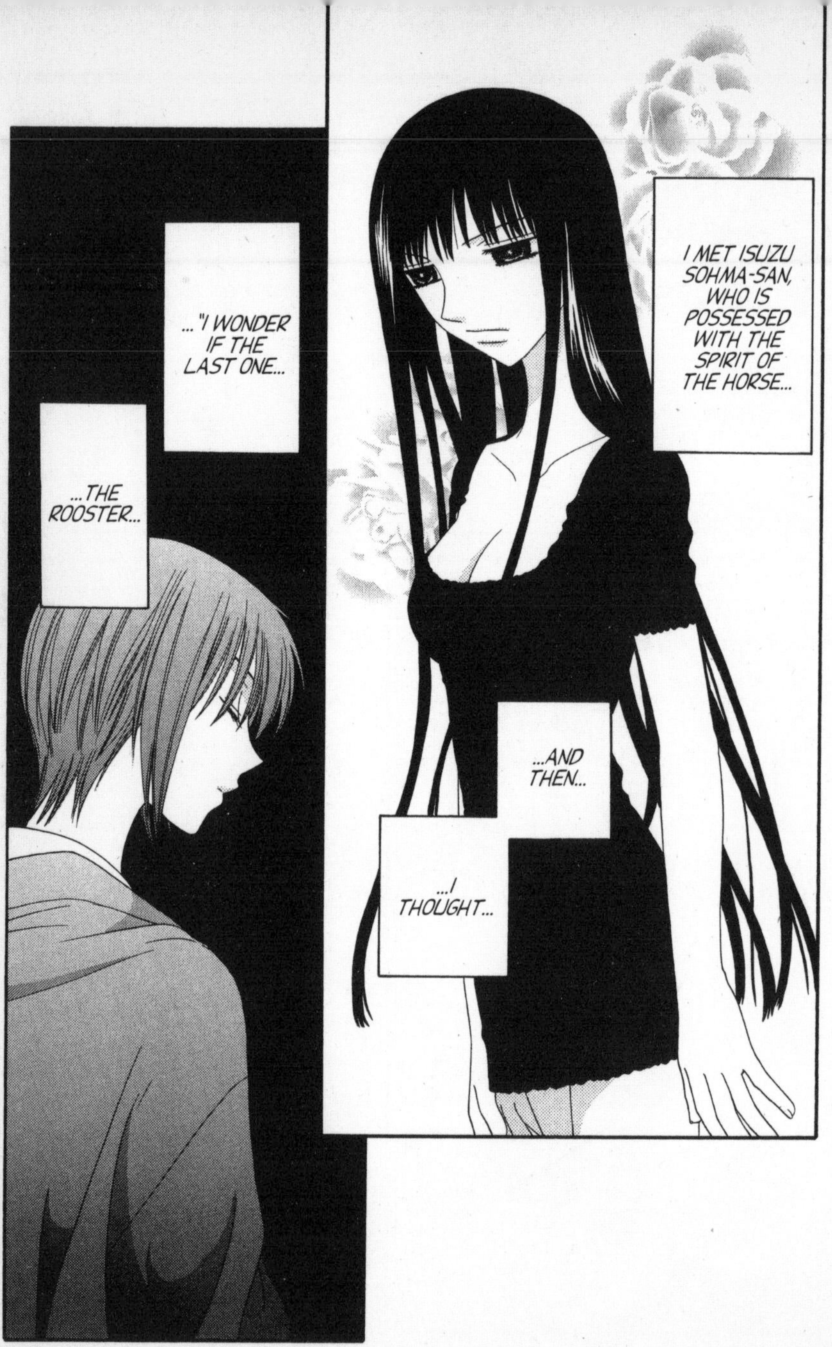
I MET ISUZU SOHMA-SAN, WHO IS POSSESSED WITH THE SPIRIT OF THE HORSE...
...AND THEN...
...I THOUGHT...
..."I WONDER IF THE LAST ONE...
...THE ROOSTER...

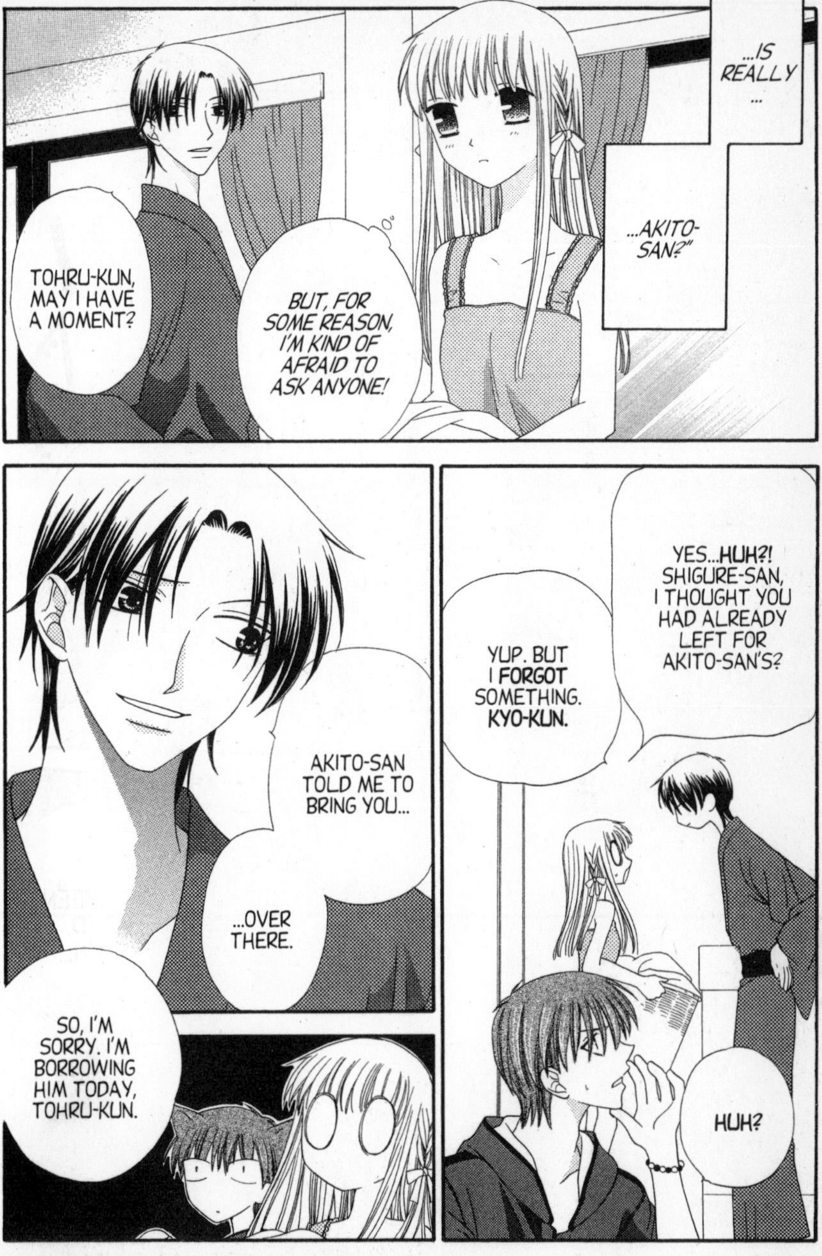
...IS REALLY ...
...AKITO-SAN?"
BUT, FOR SOME REASON, I'M KIND OF AFRAID TO ASK ANYONE!
TOHRU-KUN, MAY I HAVE A MOMENT?
YES...**HUH?!** SHIGURE-SAN, I THOUGHT YOU HAD ALREADY LEFT FOR AKITO-SAN'S?
YUP. BUT I **FORGOT** SOMETHING. **KYO-KUN.**
HUH?
AKITO-SAN TOLD ME TO BRING YOU...
...OVER THERE.
SO, I'M SORRY. I'M BORROWING HIM TODAY, TOHRU-KUN.

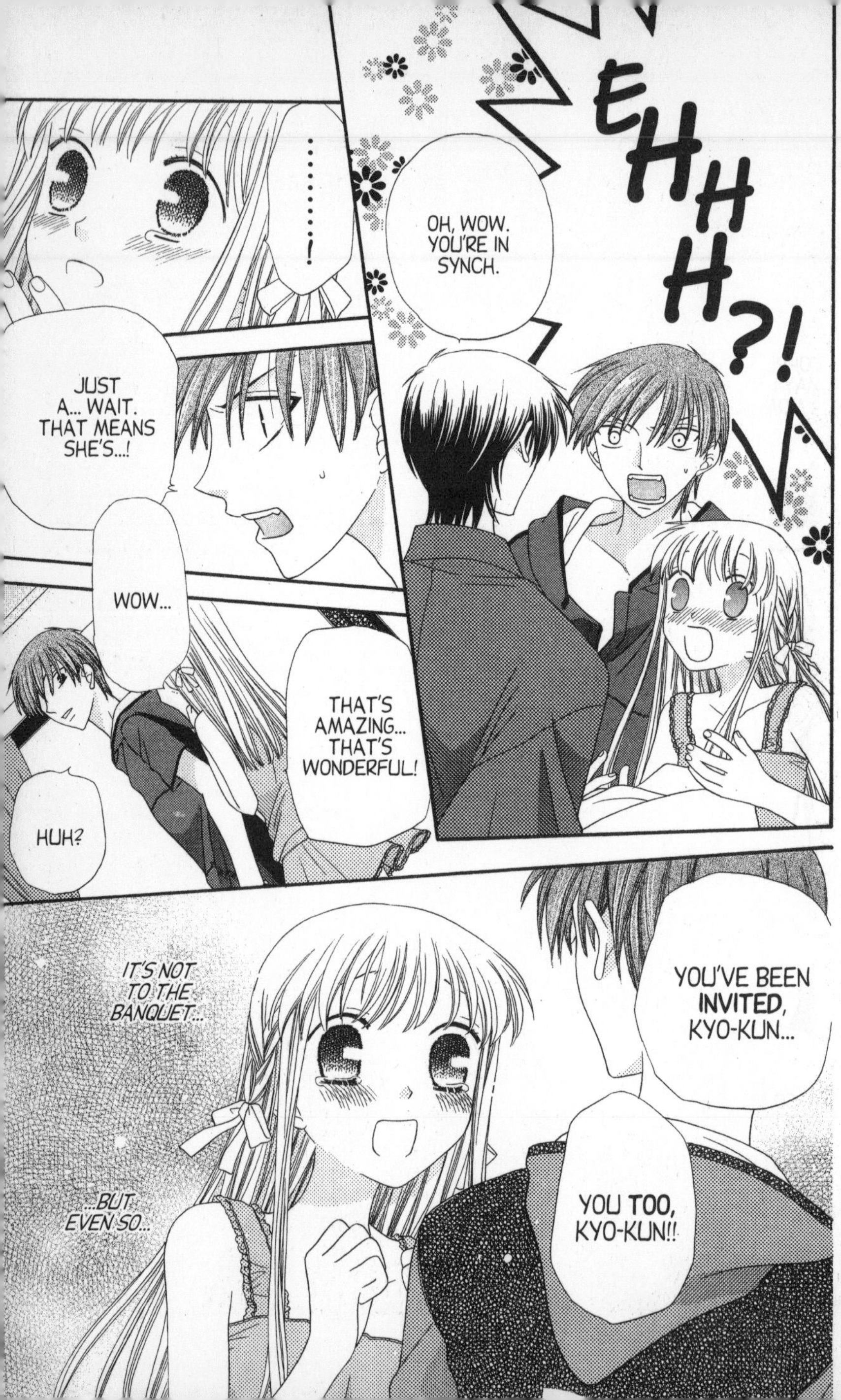

EHHHH?!
OH, WOW. YOU'RE IN SYNCH.
....!
JUST A... WAIT. THAT MEANS SHE'S...!
WOW...
THAT'S AMAZING... THAT'S WONDERFUL!
HUH?
YOU'VE BEEN **INVITED**, KYO-KUN...
YOU **TOO**, KYO-KUN!!
IT'S NOT TO THE BANQUET...
...BUT EVEN SO...

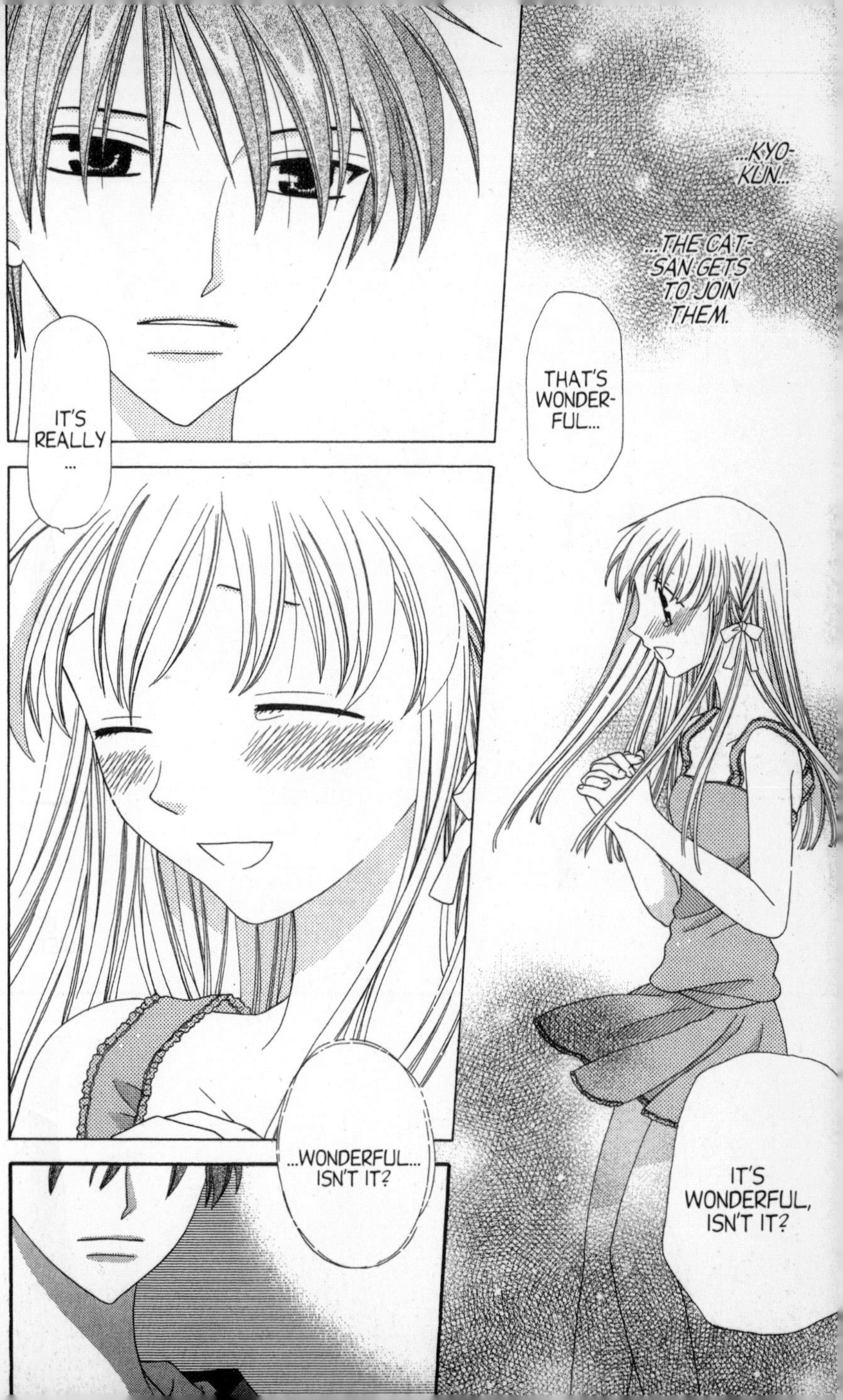
...KYO-KUN...
...THE CAT-SAN GETS TO JOIN THEM.
THAT'S WONDERFUL...
IT'S WONDERFUL, ISN'T IT?
IT'S REALLY ...
...WONDERFUL... ISN'T IT?

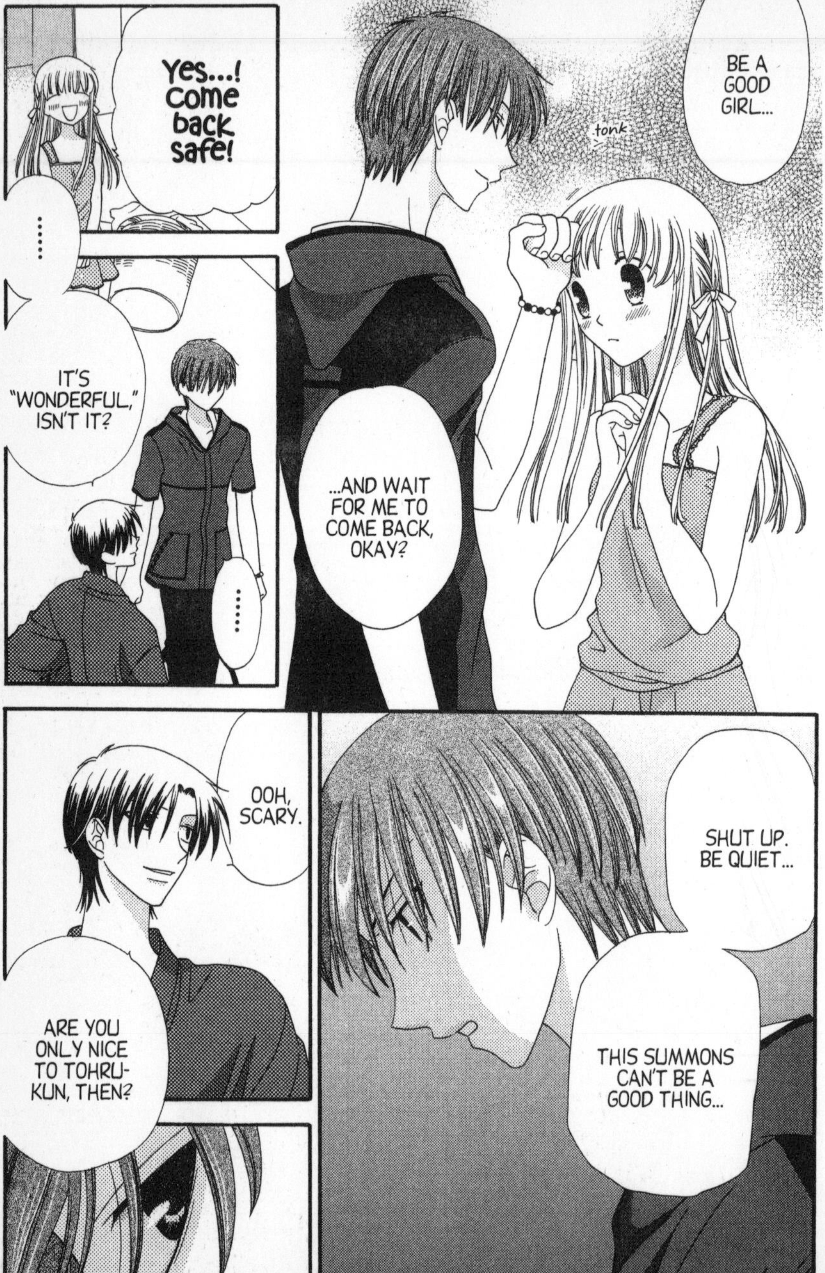
BE A GOOD GIRL...
tonk
...AND WAIT FOR ME TO COME BACK, OKAY?
Yes...! Come back safe!
......
IT'S "WONDERFUL," ISN'T IT?
......
SHUT UP. BE QUIET...
THIS SUMMONS CAN'T BE A GOOD THING...
OOH, SCARY.
ARE YOU ONLY NICE TO TOHRU-KUN, THEN?

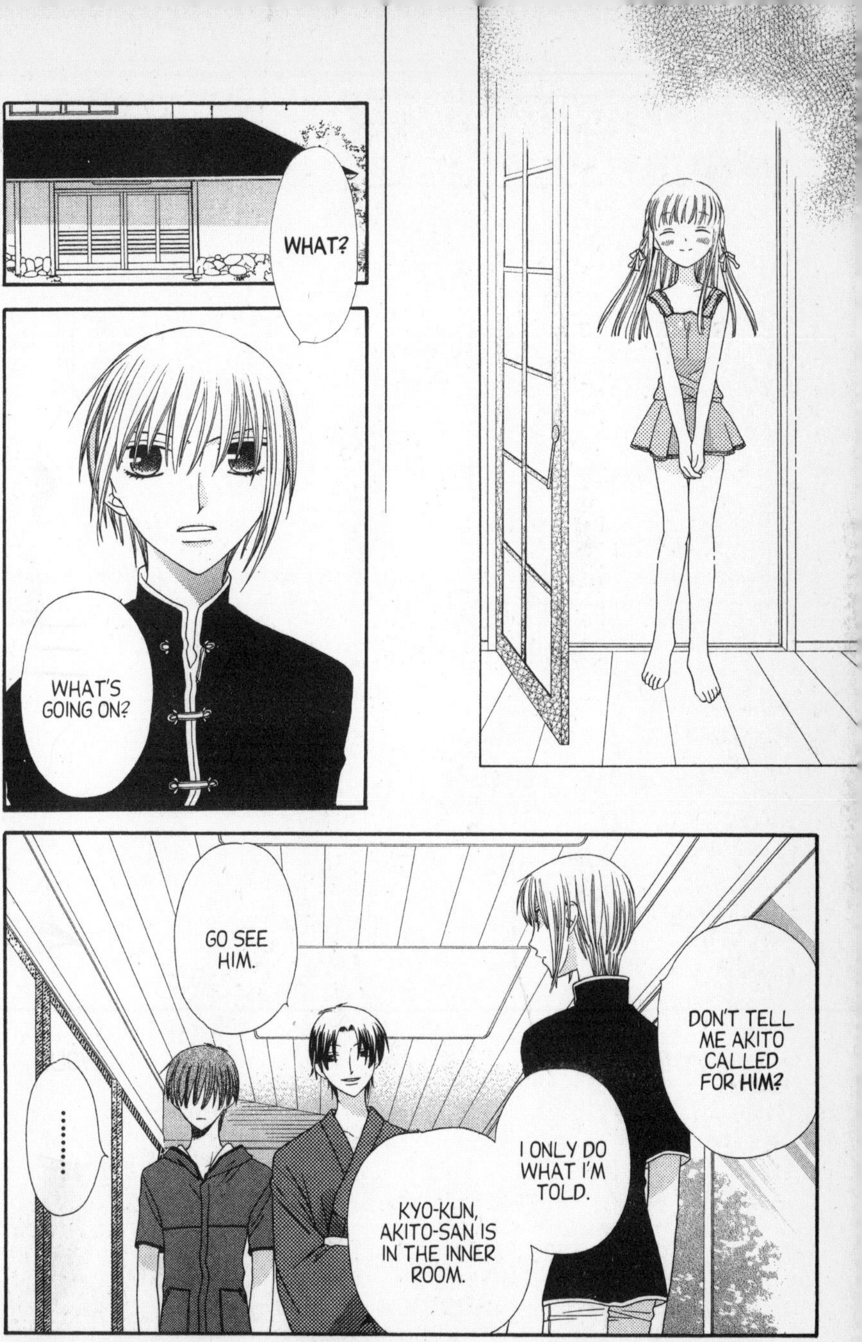
WHAT?
WHAT'S GOING ON?
DON'T TELL ME AKITO CALLED FOR HIM?
I ONLY DO WHAT I'M TOLD.
KYO-KUN, AKITO-SAN IS IN THE INNER ROOM.
GO SEE HIM.
......

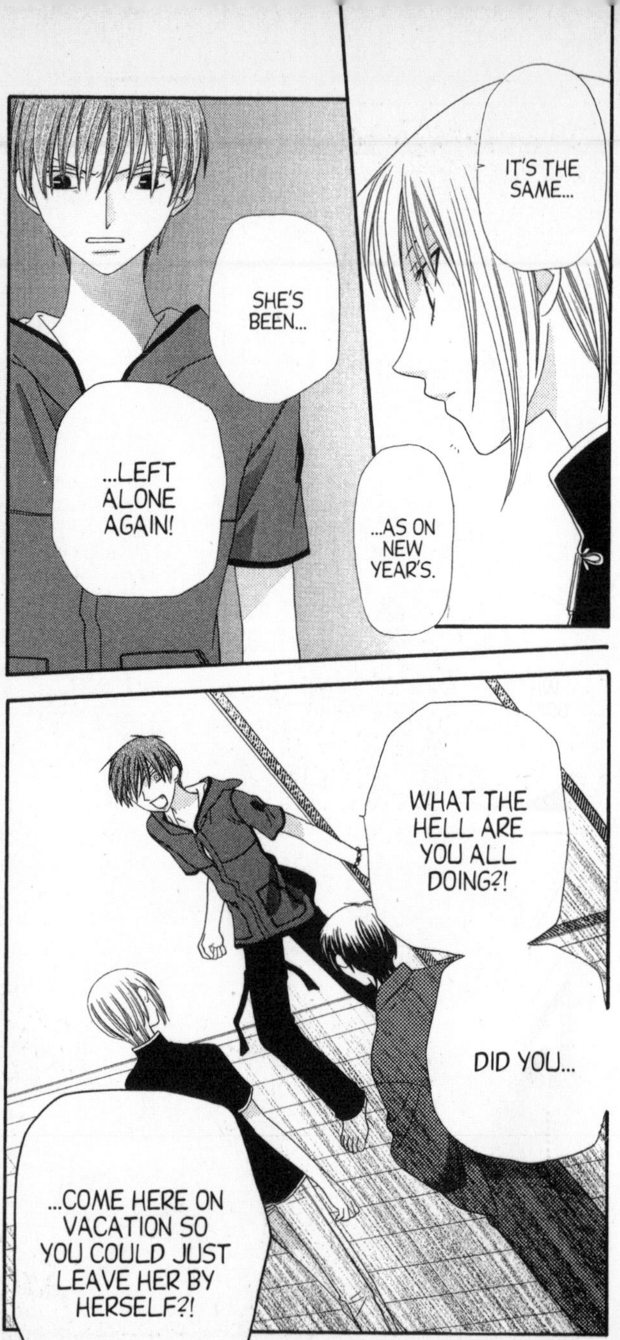
IT'S THE SAME...
...AS ON NEW YEAR'S.
SHE'S BEEN...
...LEFT ALONE AGAIN!
WHAT THE HELL ARE YOU ALL DOING?!
DID YOU...
...COME HERE ON VACATION SO YOU COULD JUST LEAVE HER BY HERSELF?!

Kana

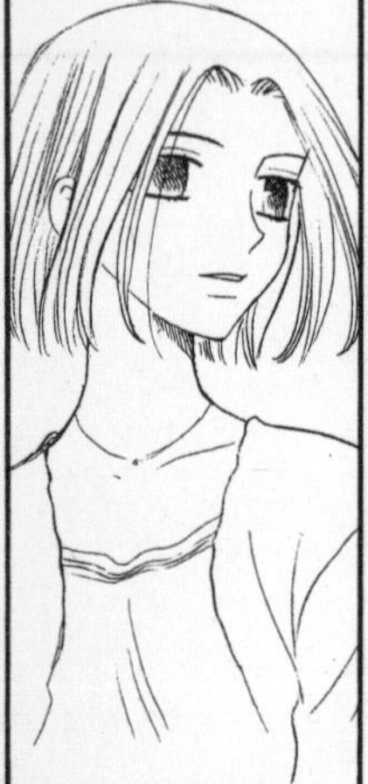

Actually, I've been asked the "When snow melts..." question. A loooong time ago. At the time, I thought I would be moved to tears if I heard them answer "It becomes spring." Because I, of course, would have answered, "It becomes water."

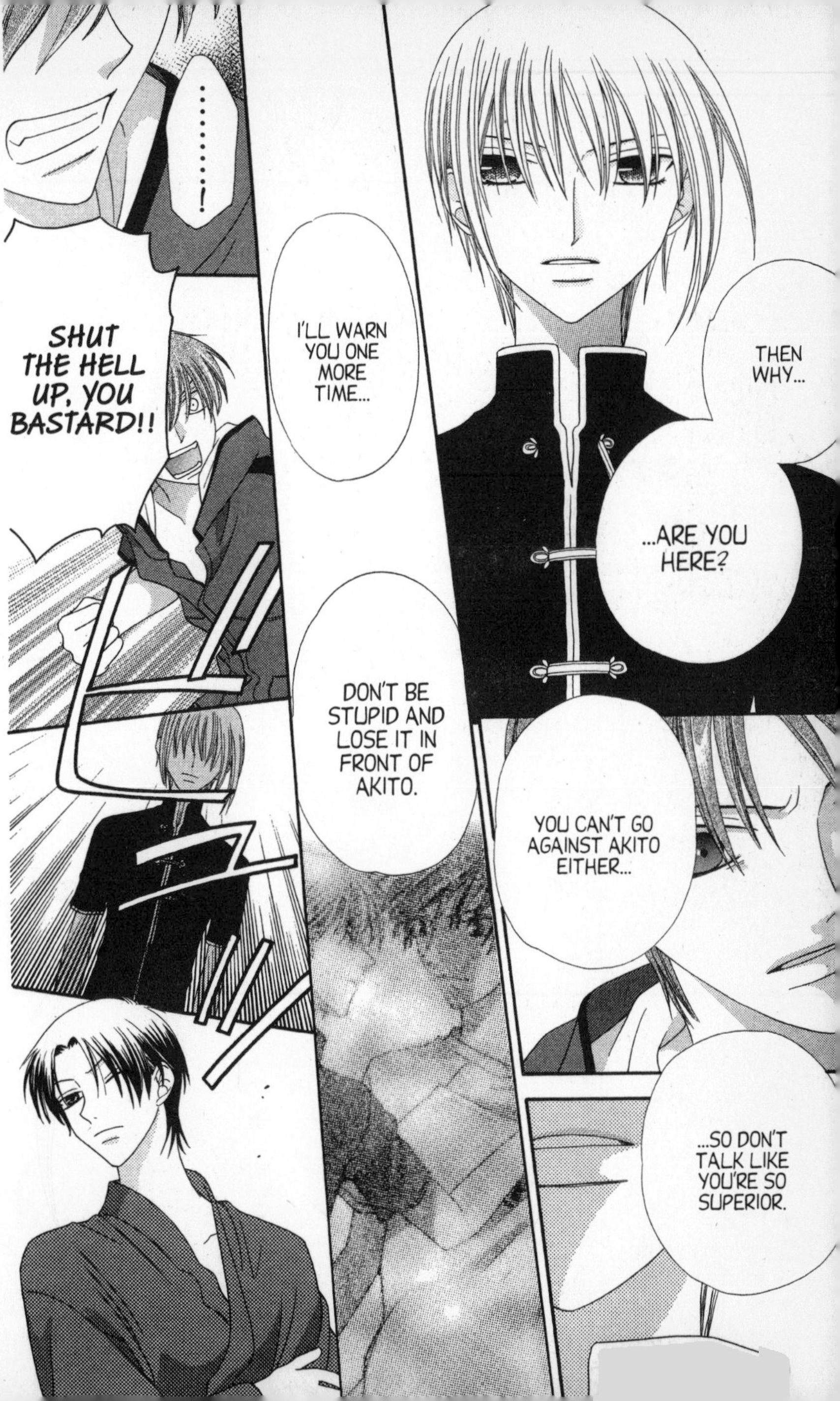
THEN WHY...
...ARE YOU HERE?
YOU CAN'T GO AGAINST AKITO EITHER...
...SO DON'T TALK LIKE YOU'RE SO SUPERIOR.
I'LL WARN YOU ONE MORE TIME...
DON'T BE STUPID AND LOSE IT IN FRONT OF AKITO.
......!
SHUT THE HELL UP, YOU BASTARD!!

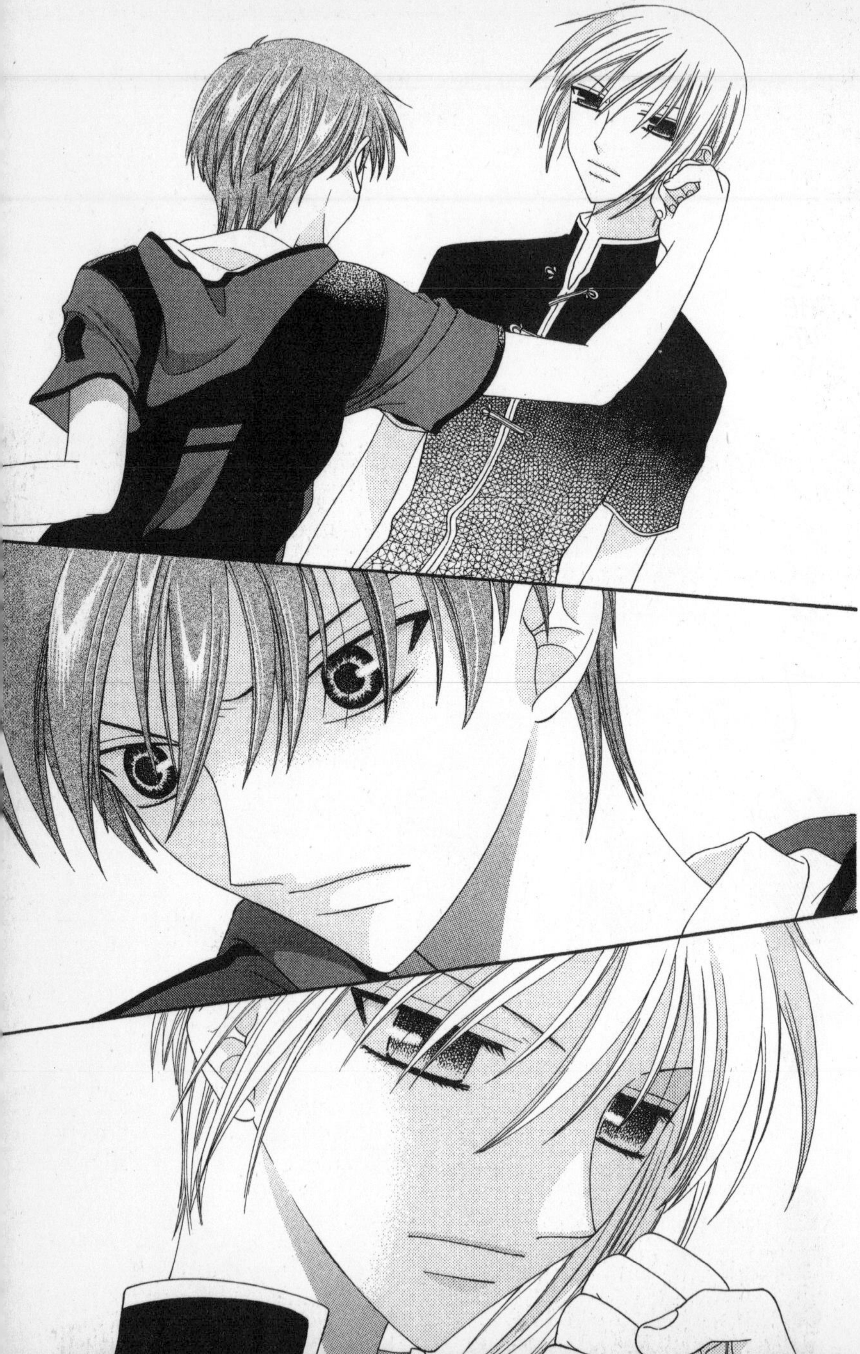

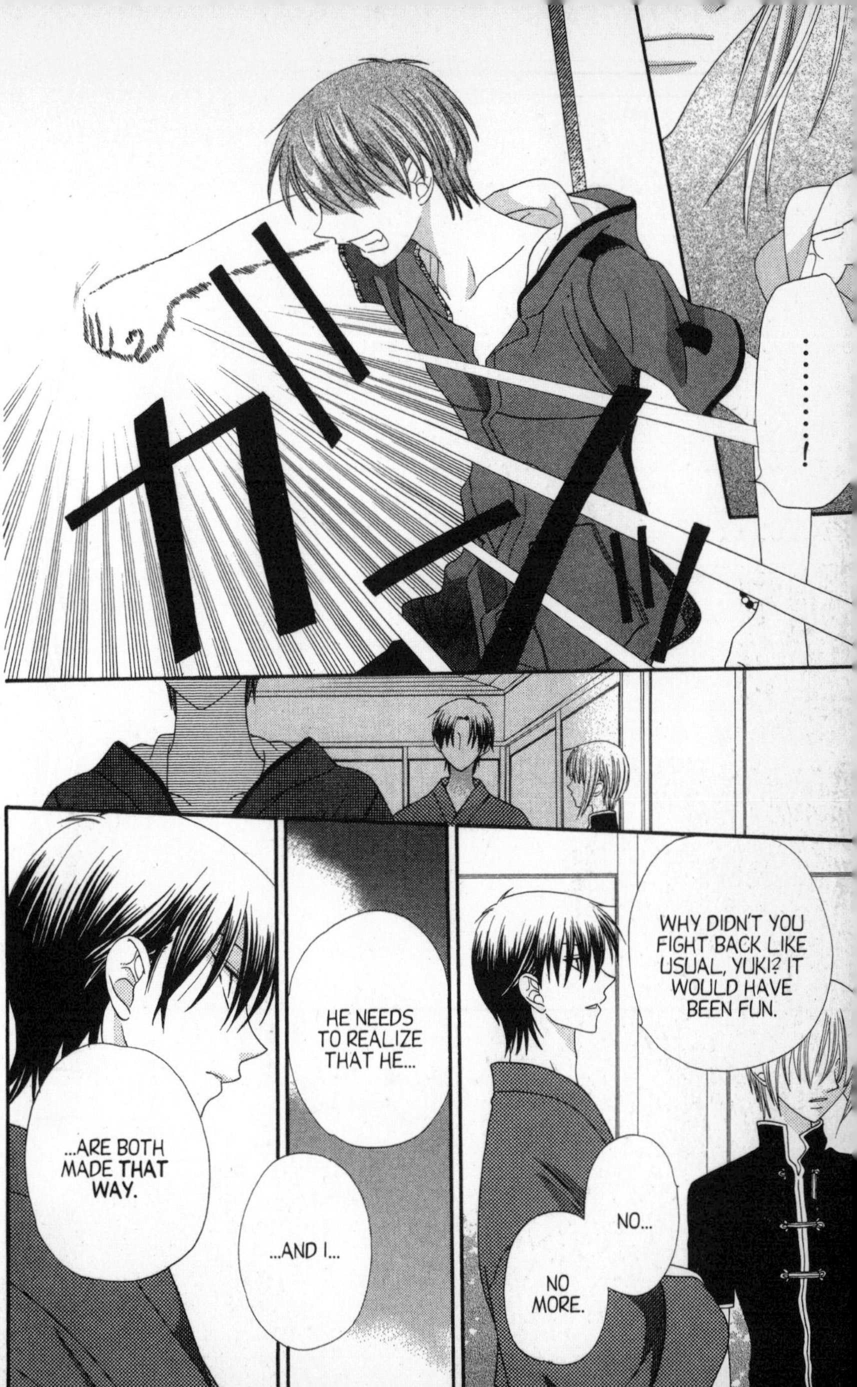
......!
ガンッ
WHY DIDN'T YOU FIGHT BACK LIKE USUAL, YUKI? IT WOULD HAVE BEEN FUN.
NO...
NO MORE.
HE NEEDS TO REALIZE THAT HE...
...AND I...
...ARE BOTH MADE THAT WAY.

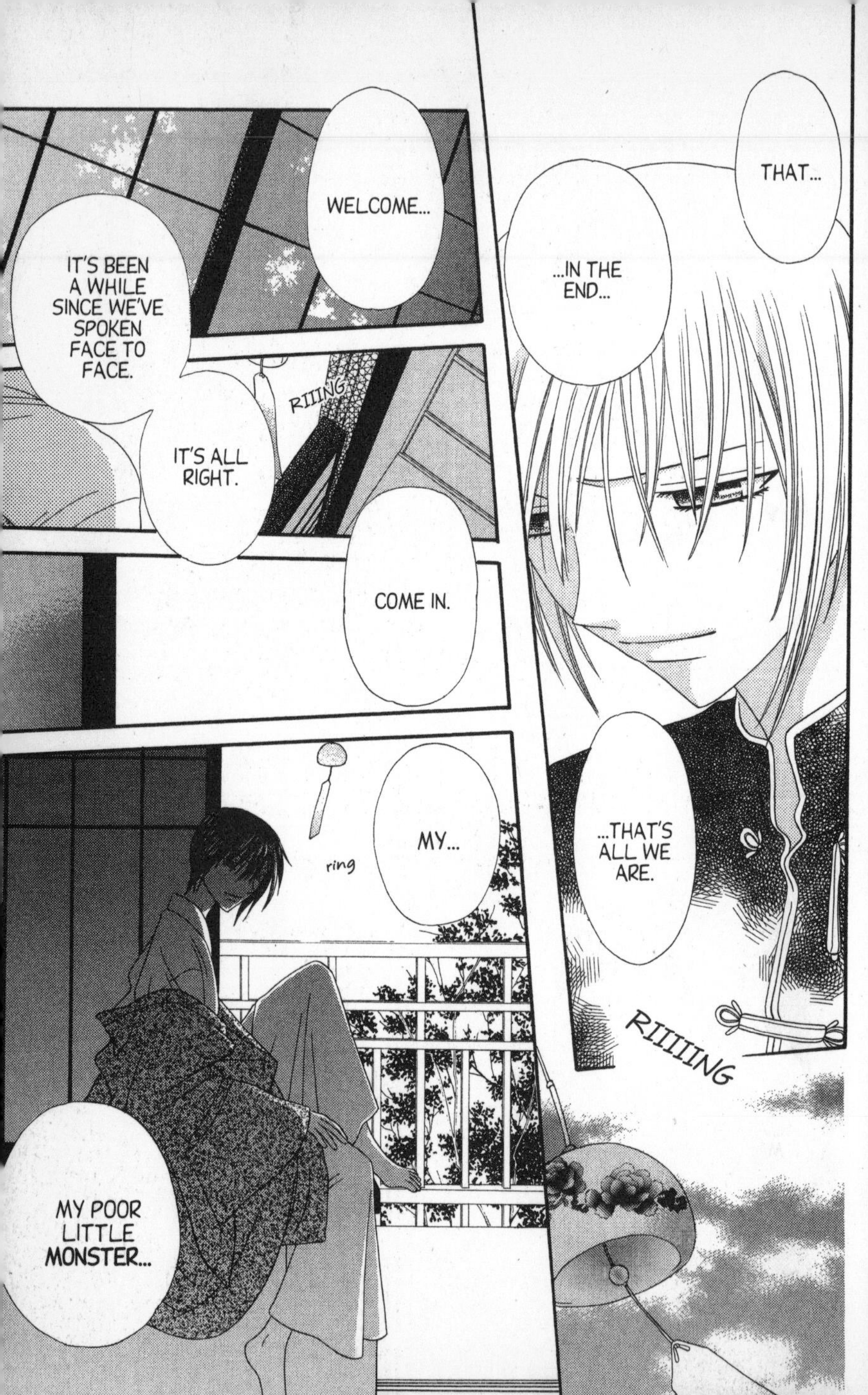
THAT...
...IN THE END...
...THAT'S ALL WE ARE.
RIIIIING
WELCOME...
IT'S BEEN A WHILE SINCE WE'VE SPOKEN FACE TO FACE.
RIIING
IT'S ALL RIGHT.
COME IN.
MY...
ring
MY POOR LITTLE MONSTER...

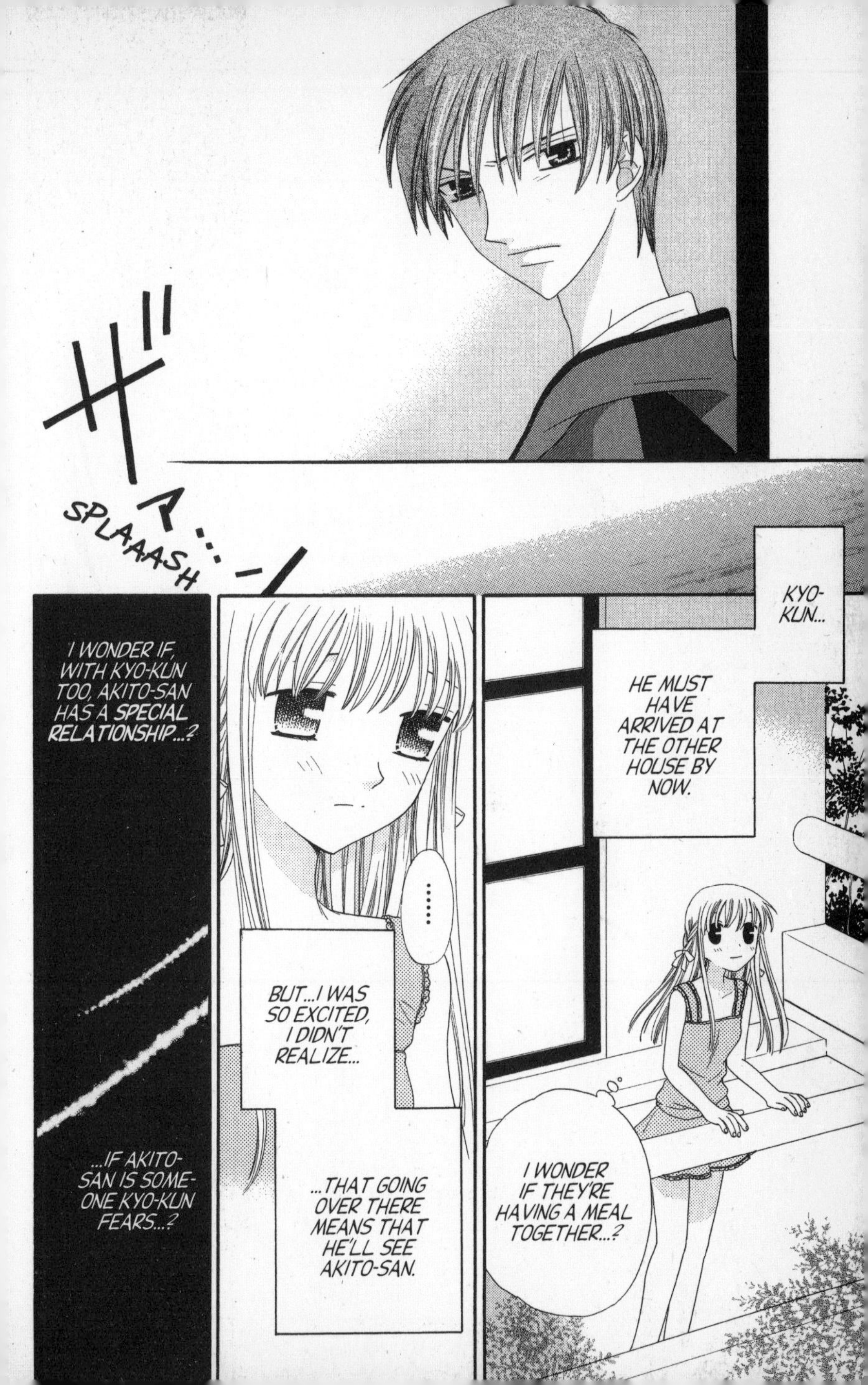
SPLAAASH
KYO-KUN...
HE MUST HAVE ARRIVED AT THE OTHER HOUSE BY NOW.
I WONDER IF THEY'RE HAVING A MEAL TOGETHER...?
......
BUT...I WAS SO EXCITED, I DIDN'T REALIZE...
...THAT GOING OVER THERE MEANS THAT HE'LL SEE AKITO-SAN.
I WONDER IF, WITH KYO-KUN TOO, AKITO-SAN HAS A SPECIAL RELATIONSHIP...?
...IF AKITO-SAN IS SOMEONE KYO-KUN FEARS...?

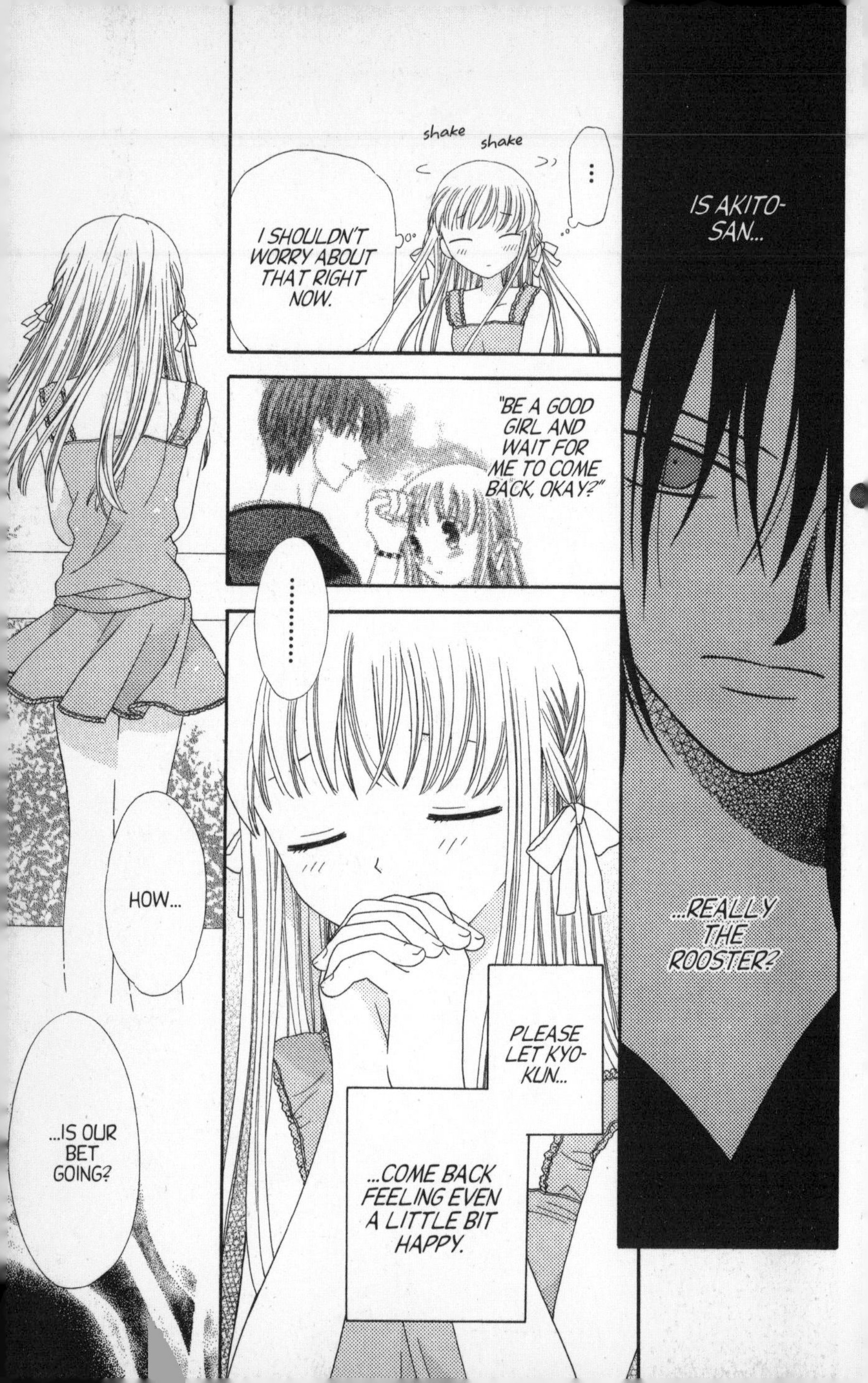
IS AKITO-SAN...
...REALLY THE ROOSTER?
...
shake shake
I SHOULDN'T WORRY ABOUT THAT RIGHT NOW.
"BE A GOOD GIRL AND WAIT FOR ME TO COME BACK, OKAY?"
....
PLEASE LET KYO-KUN...
...COME BACK FEELING EVEN A LITTLE BIT HAPPY.
HOW...
...IS OUR BET GOING?

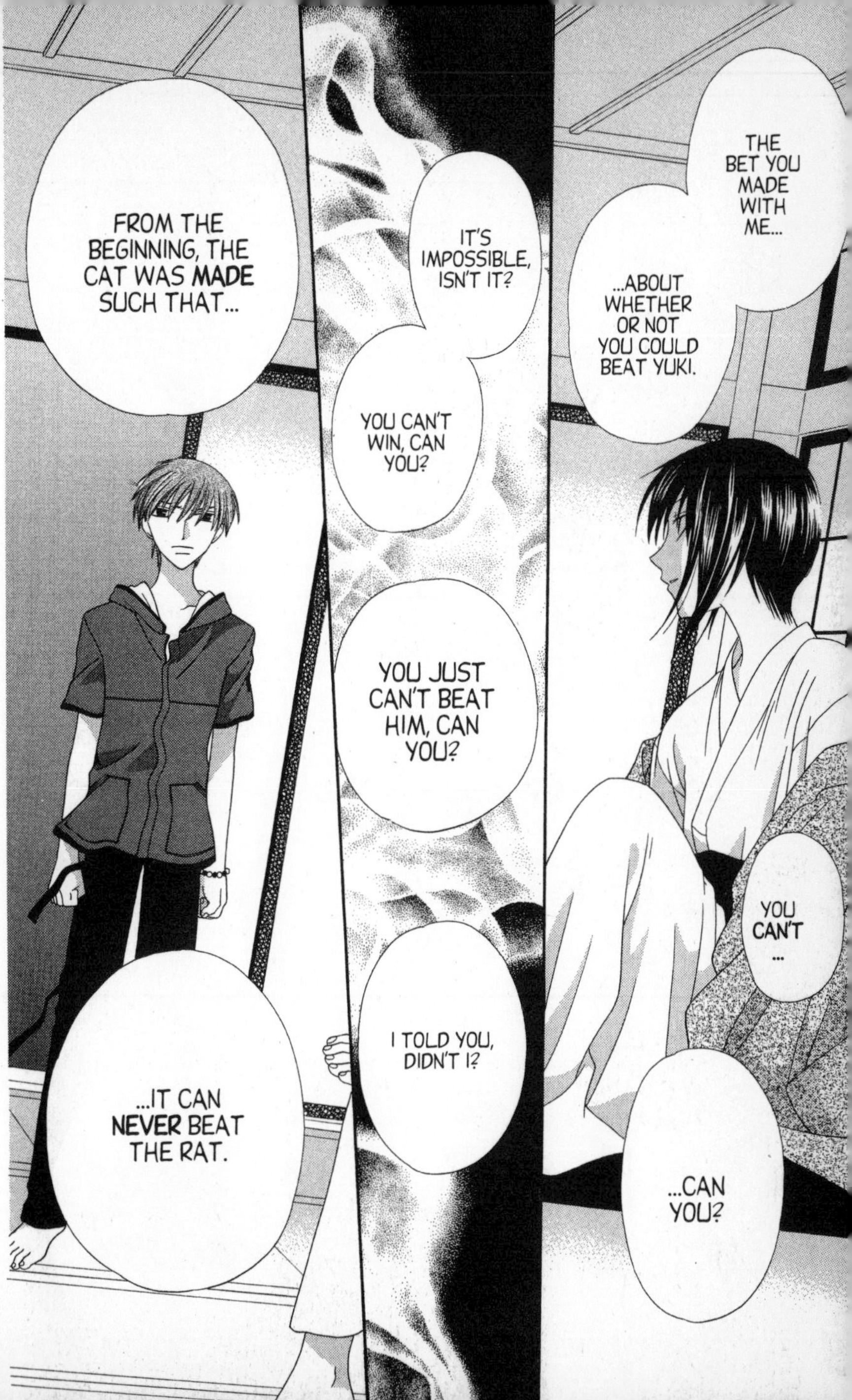
THE BET YOU MADE WITH ME...
...ABOUT WHETHER OR NOT YOU COULD BEAT YUKI.
YOU CAN'T ...
...CAN YOU?
IT'S IMPOSSIBLE, ISN'T IT?
YOU CAN'T WIN, CAN YOU?
YOU JUST CAN'T BEAT HIM, CAN YOU?
I TOLD YOU, DIDN'T I?
FROM THE BEGINNING, THE CAT WAS MADE SUCH THAT...
...IT CAN NEVER BEAT THE RAT.

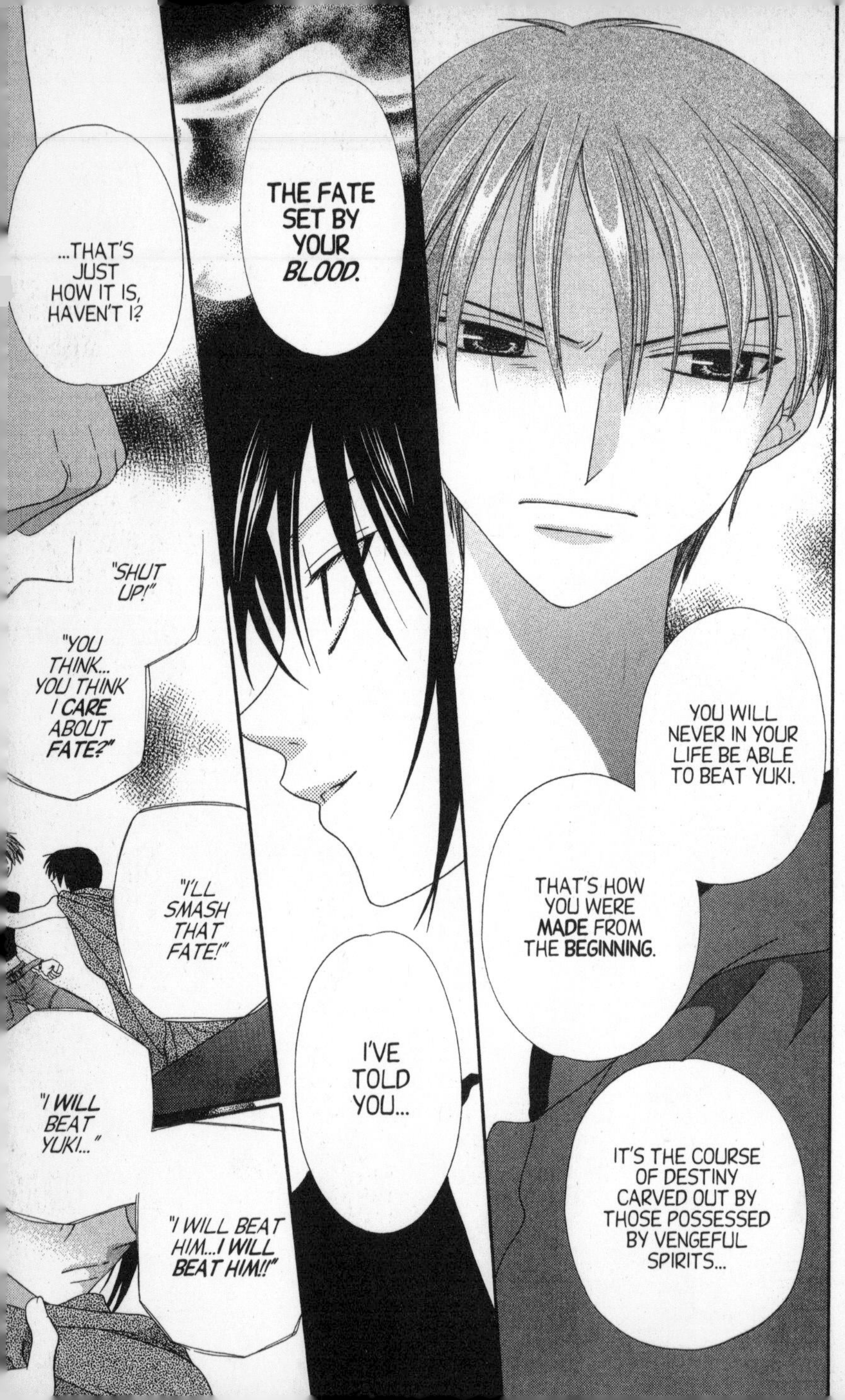
YOU WILL NEVER IN YOUR LIFE BE ABLE TO BEAT YUKI.
THAT'S HOW YOU WERE MADE FROM THE BEGINNING.
IT'S THE COURSE OF DESTINY CARVED OUT BY THOSE POSSESSED BY VENGEFUL SPIRITS...
THE FATE SET BY YOUR BLOOD.
I'VE TOLD YOU...
...THAT'S JUST HOW IT IS, HAVEN'T I?
"SHUT UP!"
"YOU THINK... YOU THINK I CARE ABOUT FATE?"
"I'LL SMASH THAT FATE!"
"I WILL BEAT YUKI..."
"I WILL BEAT HIM...I WILL BEAT HIM!!"

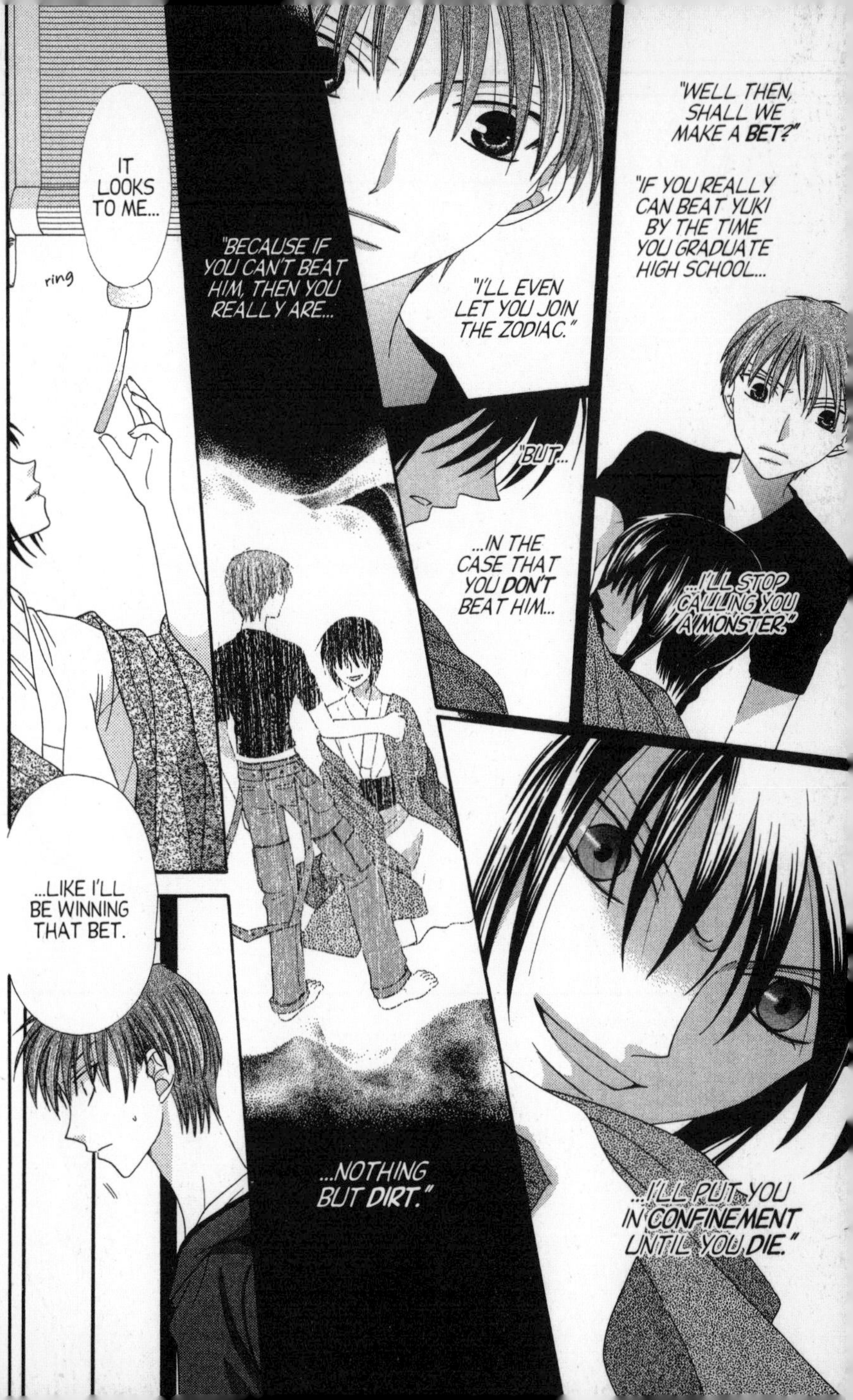
"WELL THEN, SHALL WE MAKE A BET?"
"IF YOU REALLY CAN BEAT YUKI BY THE TIME YOU GRADUATE HIGH SCHOOL...
...I'LL STOP CALLING YOU A MONSTER."
"I'LL EVEN LET YOU JOIN THE ZODIAC."
"BUT...
...IN THE CASE THAT YOU DON'T BEAT HIM...
...I'LL PUT YOU IN CONFINEMENT UNTIL YOU DIE."
"BECAUSE IF YOU CAN'T BEAT HIM, THEN YOU REALLY ARE...
...NOTHING BUT DIRT."
IT LOOKS TO ME...
ring
...LIKE I'LL BE WINNING THAT BET.

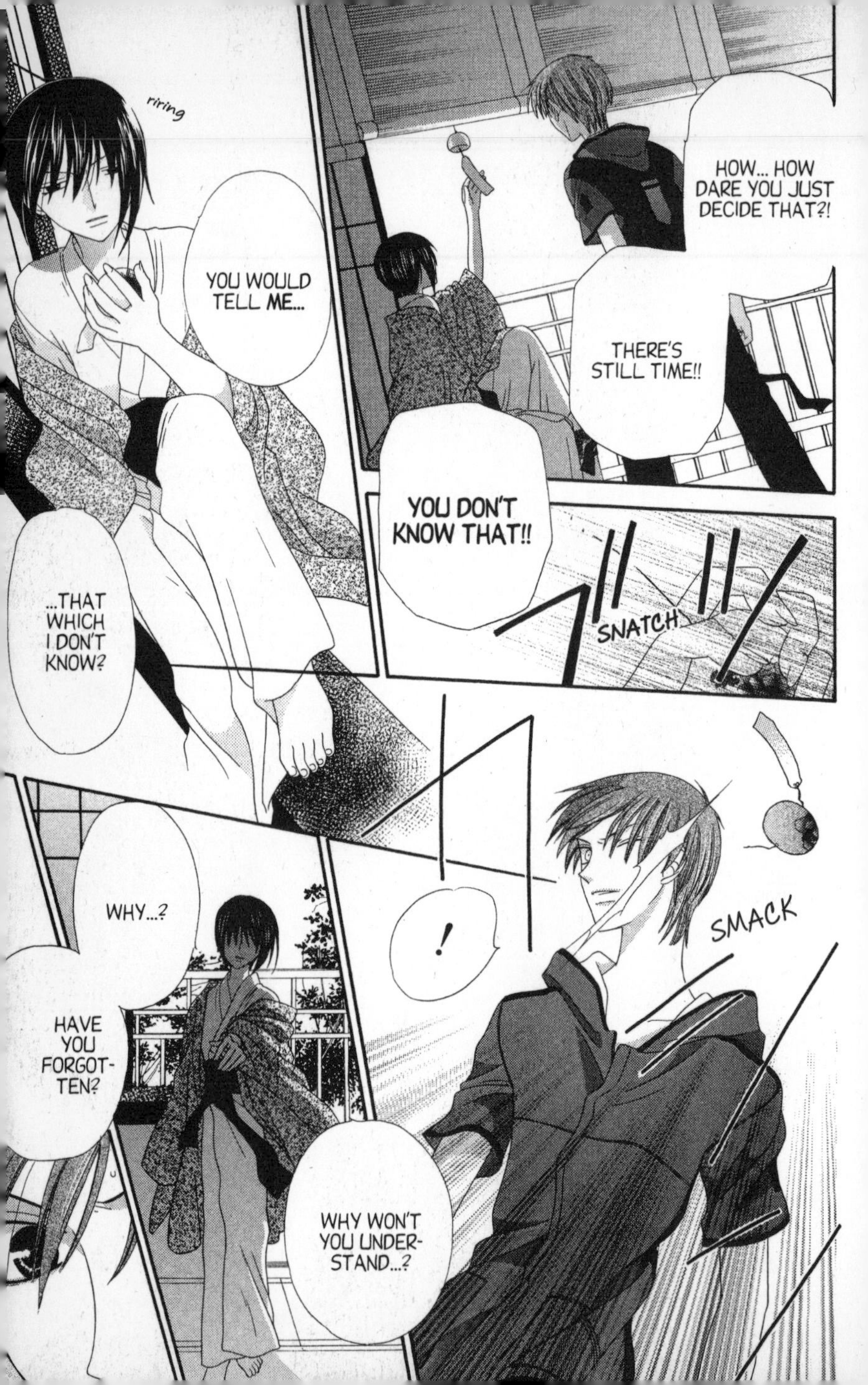
HOW... HOW DARE YOU JUST DECIDE THAT?!
THERE'S STILL TIME!!
YOU DON'T KNOW THAT!!
SNATCH
riring
YOU WOULD TELL ME...
...THAT WHICH I DON'T KNOW?
SMACK
!
WHY WON'T YOU UNDERSTAND...?
WHY...?
HAVE YOU FORGOT-TEN?

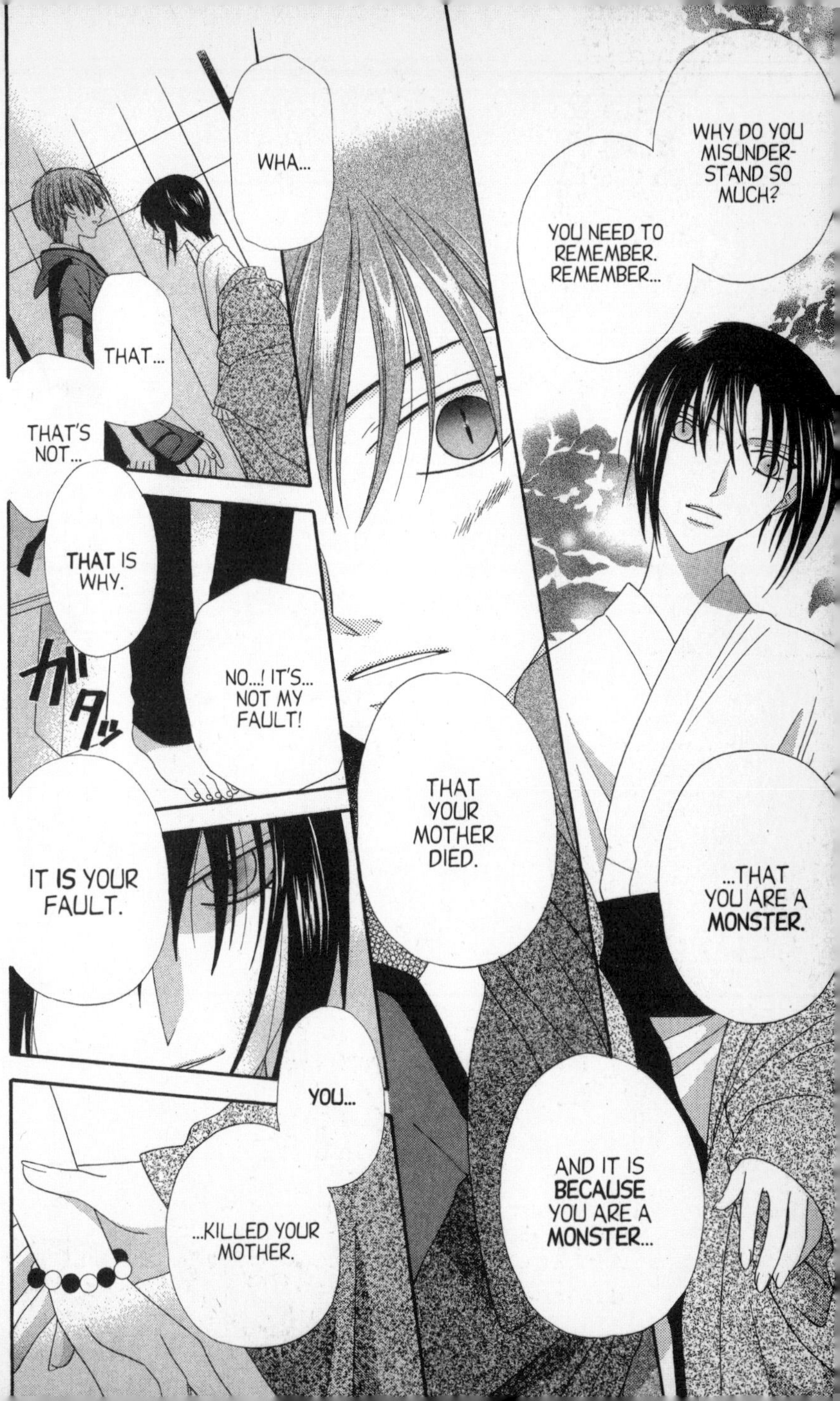
WHY DO YOU MISUNDERSTAND SO MUCH?
YOU NEED TO REMEMBER. REMEMBER...
WHA...
THAT...
THAT'S NOT...
THAT IS WHY.
NO...! IT'S... NOT MY FAULT!
ガタッ
IT IS YOUR FAULT.
THAT YOUR MOTHER DIED.
...THAT YOU ARE A MONSTER.
AND IT IS BECAUSE YOU ARE A MONSTER...
YOU...
...KILLED YOUR MOTHER.

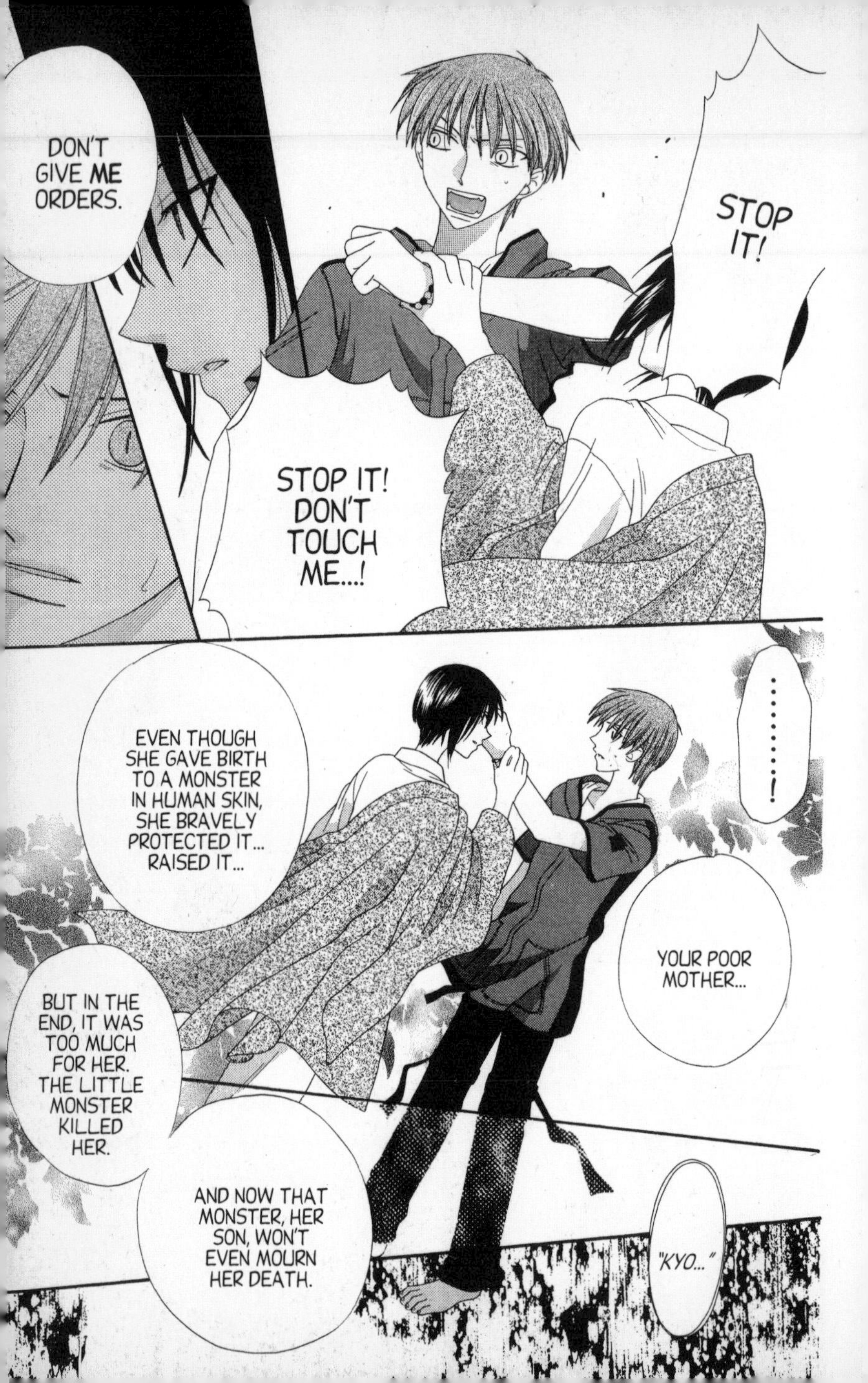
STOP IT!
STOP IT! DON'T TOUCH ME...!
DON'T GIVE ME ORDERS.
......!
EVEN THOUGH SHE GAVE BIRTH TO A MONSTER IN HUMAN SKIN, SHE BRAVELY PROTECTED IT... RAISED IT...
YOUR POOR MOTHER...
BUT IN THE END, IT WAS TOO MUCH FOR HER. THE LITTLE MONSTER KILLED HER.
AND NOW THAT MONSTER, HER SON, WON'T EVEN MOURN HER DEATH.
"KYO..."

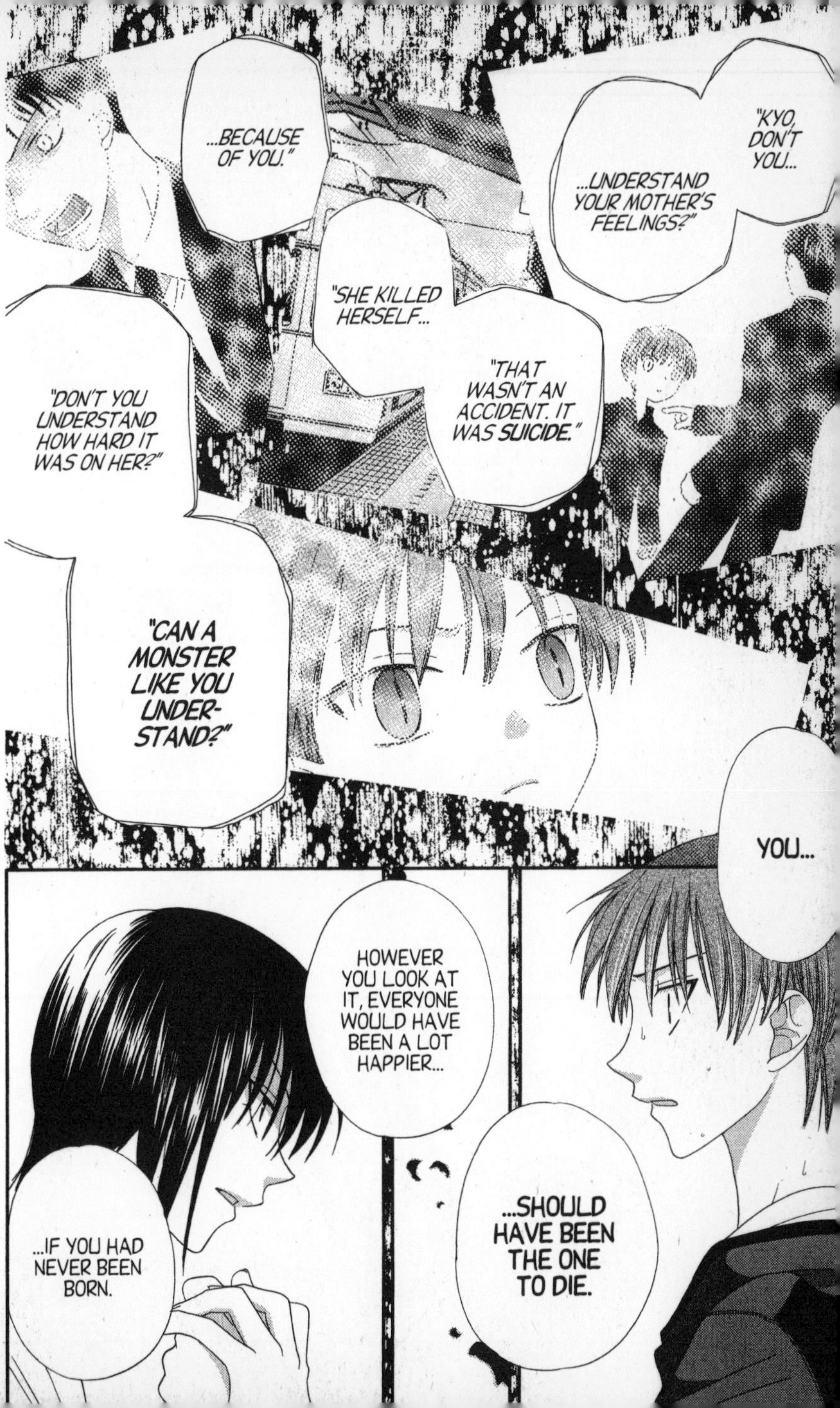
"KYO, DON'T YOU...
...UNDERSTAND YOUR MOTHER'S FEELINGS?"
"SHE KILLED HERSELF...
...BECAUSE OF YOU."
"THAT WASN'T AN ACCIDENT. IT WAS SUICIDE."
"DON'T YOU UNDERSTAND HOW HARD IT WAS ON HER?"
"CAN A MONSTER LIKE YOU UNDER-STAND?"
YOU...
...SHOULD HAVE BEEN THE ONE TO DIE.
HOWEVER YOU LOOK AT IT, EVERYONE WOULD HAVE BEEN A LOT HAPPIER...
...IF YOU HAD NEVER BEEN BORN.

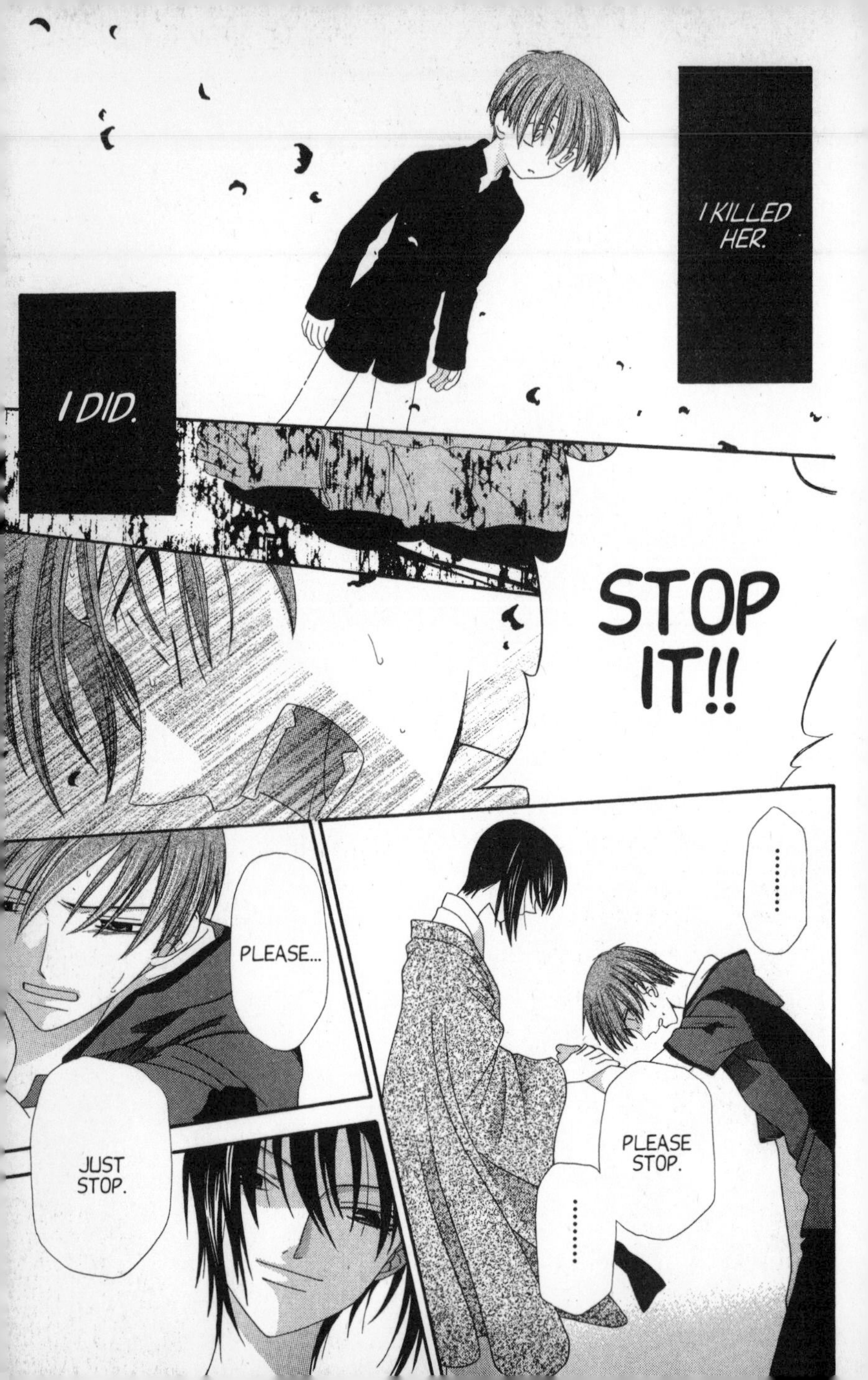
I KILLED HER.
I DID.
STOP IT!!
......
PLEASE STOP.
......
PLEASE...
JUST STOP.

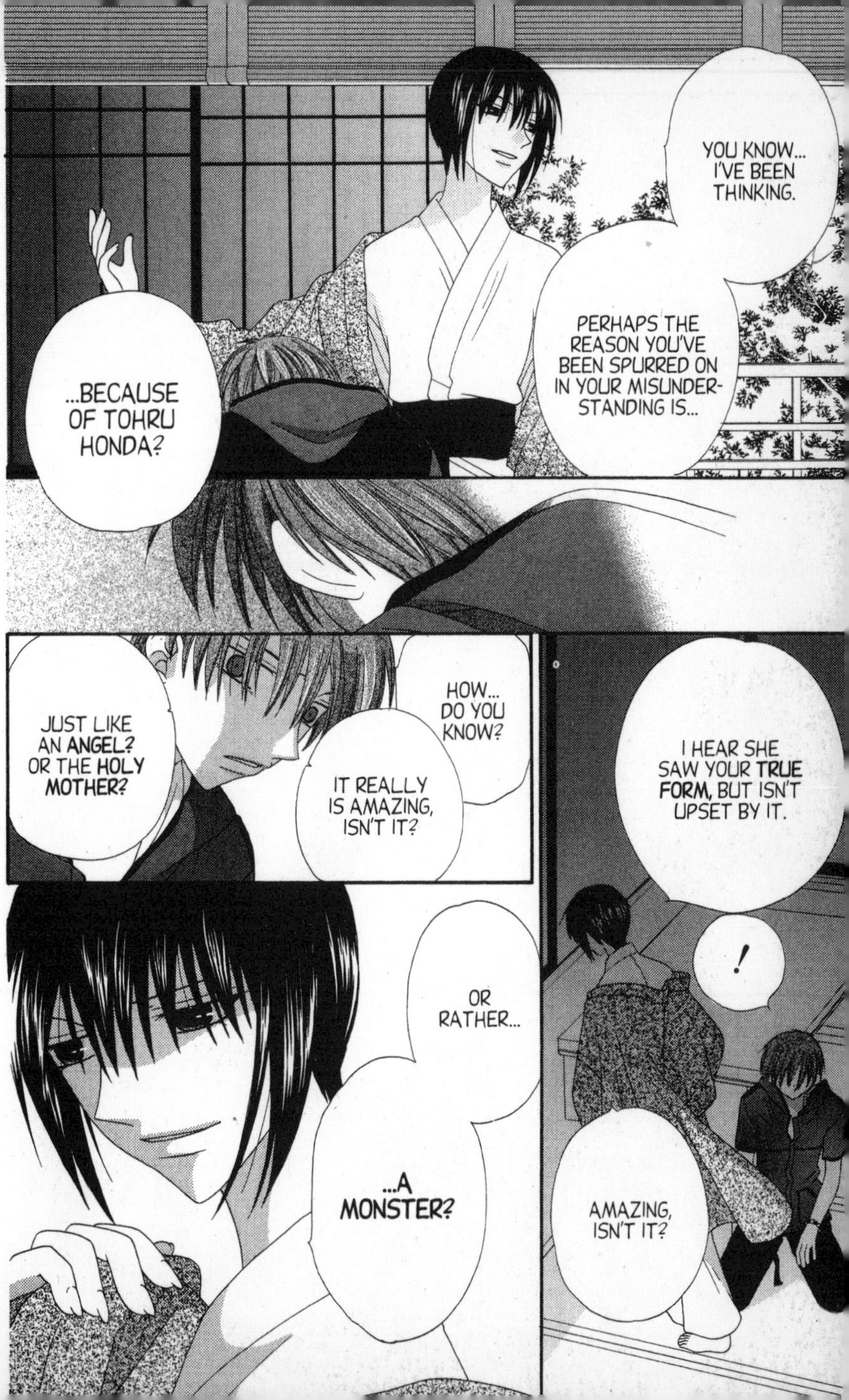
YOU KNOW... I'VE BEEN THINKING.
PERHAPS THE REASON YOU'VE BEEN SPURRED ON IN YOUR MISUNDER-STANDING IS...
...BECAUSE OF TOHRU HONDA?
I HEAR SHE SAW YOUR **TRUE FORM,** BUT ISN'T UPSET BY IT.
!
AMAZING, ISN'T IT?
HOW... DO YOU KNOW?
IT REALLY IS AMAZING, ISN'T IT?
JUST LIKE AN **ANGEL?** OR THE **HOLY MOTHER?**
OR RATHER...
...A **MONSTER?**

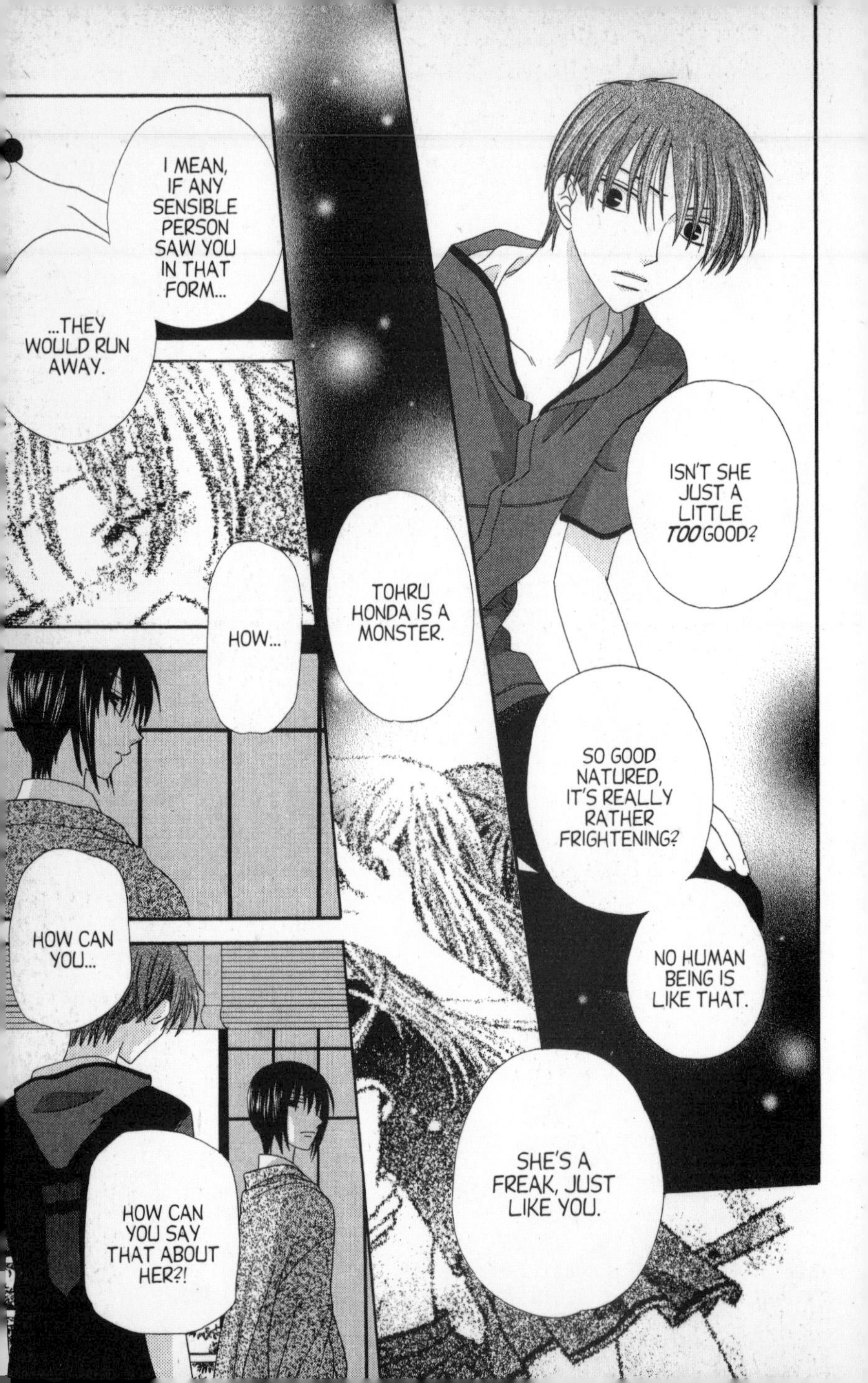
ISN'T SHE JUST A LITTLE TOO GOOD?
SO GOOD NATURED, IT'S REALLY RATHER FRIGHTENING?
NO HUMAN BEING IS LIKE THAT.
SHE'S A FREAK, JUST LIKE YOU.
TOHRU HONDA IS A MONSTER.
HOW...
I MEAN, IF ANY SENSIBLE PERSON SAW YOU IN THAT FORM...
...THEY WOULD RUN AWAY.
HOW CAN YOU...
HOW CAN YOU SAY THAT ABOUT HER?!

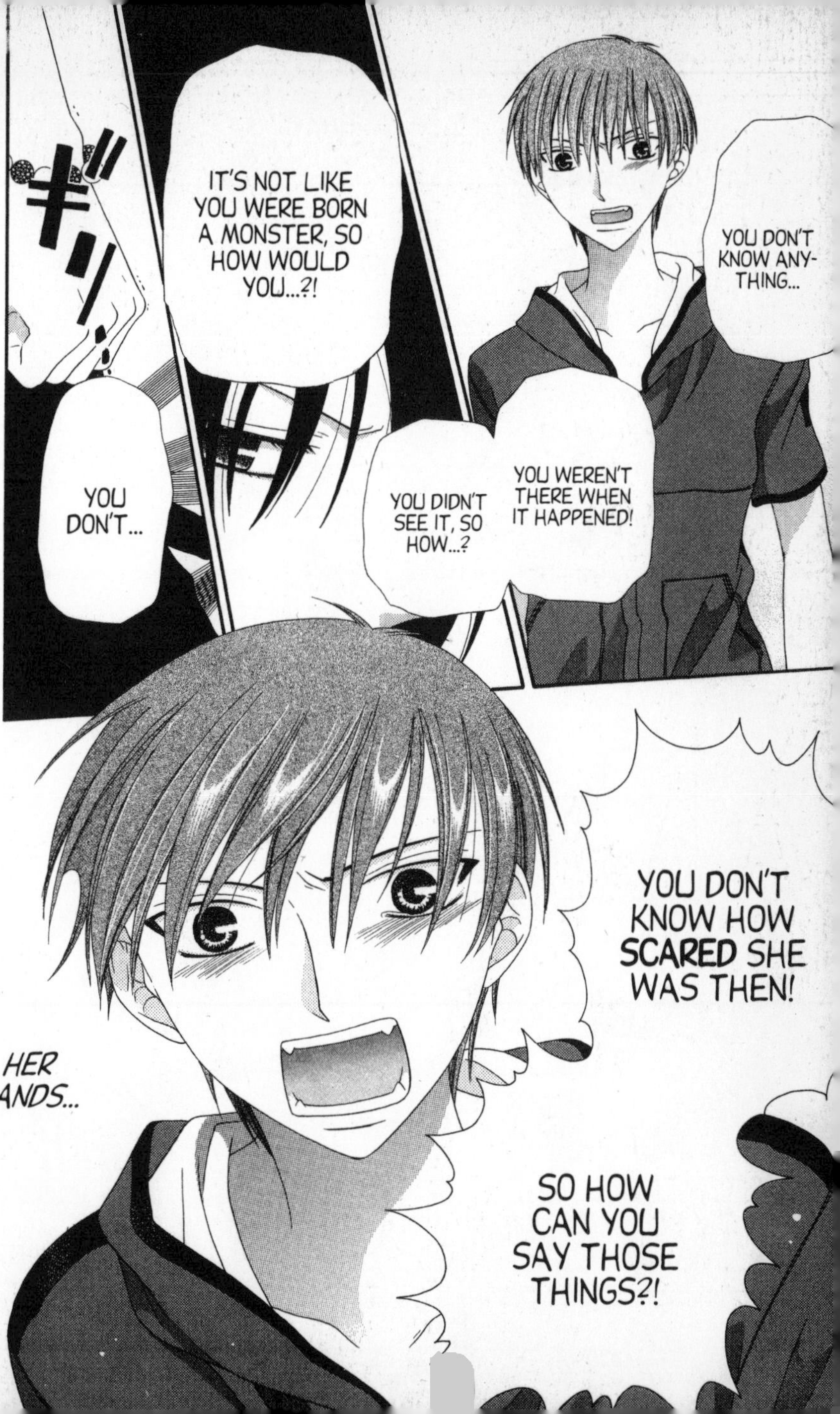

YOU DON'T KNOW ANYTHING...
YOU WEREN'T THERE WHEN IT HAPPENED!
YOU DIDN'T SEE IT, SO HOW...?
IT'S NOT LIKE YOU WERE BORN A MONSTER, SO HOW WOULD YOU...?!
ギリ
YOU DON'T...
YOU DON'T KNOW HOW **SCARED** SHE WAS THEN!
SO HOW CAN YOU SAY THOSE THINGS?!
HER HANDS...

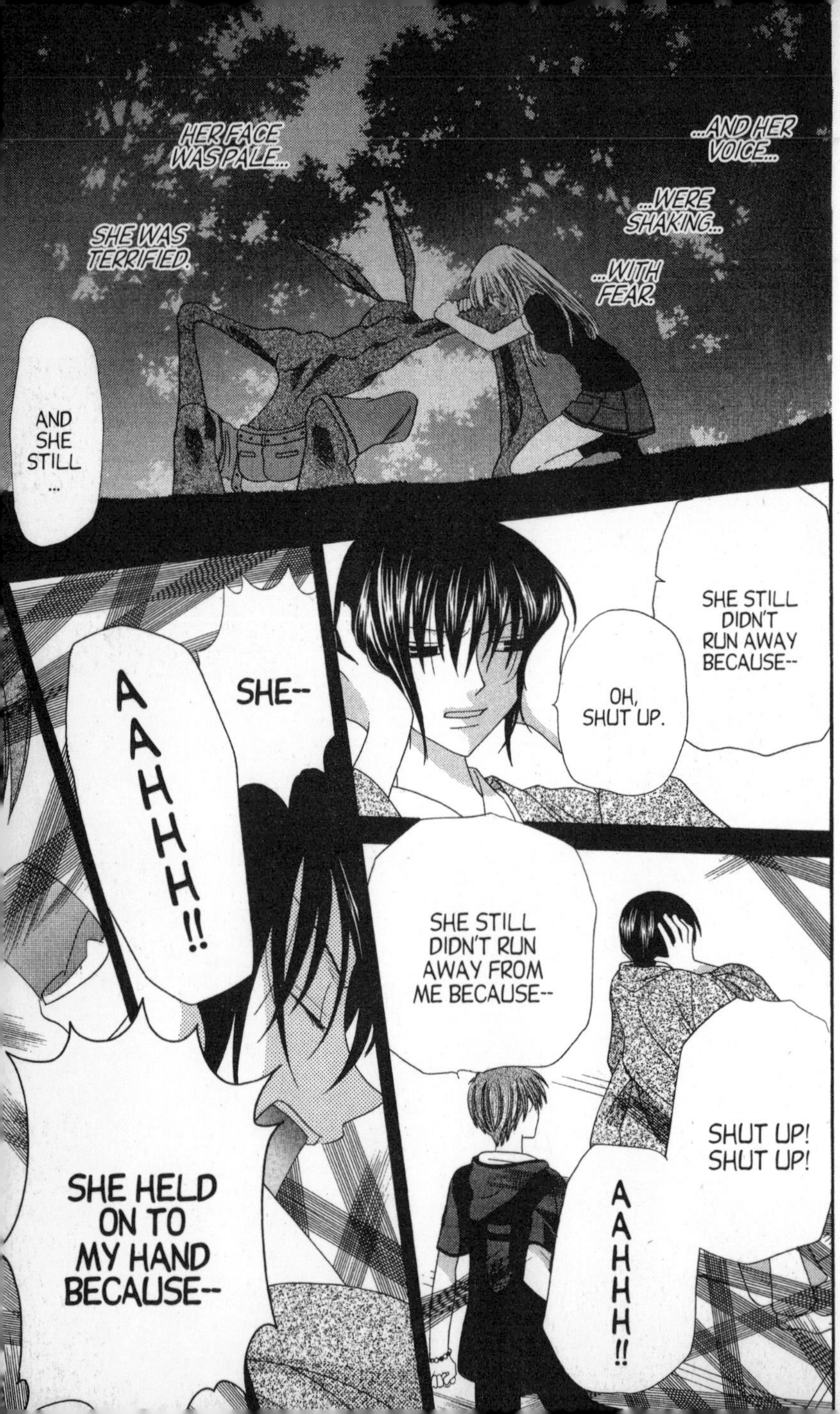
HER FACE WAS PALE...
...AND HER VOICE...
...WERE SHAKING...
...WITH FEAR.
SHE WAS TERRIFIED.
AND SHE STILL ...
SHE STILL DIDN'T RUN AWAY BECAUSE--
OH, SHUT UP.
SHE--
AAHHHH!!
SHE STILL DIDN'T RUN AWAY FROM ME BECAUSE--
SHUT UP! SHUT UP!
AAHHHH!!
SHE HELD ON TO MY HAND BECAUSE--

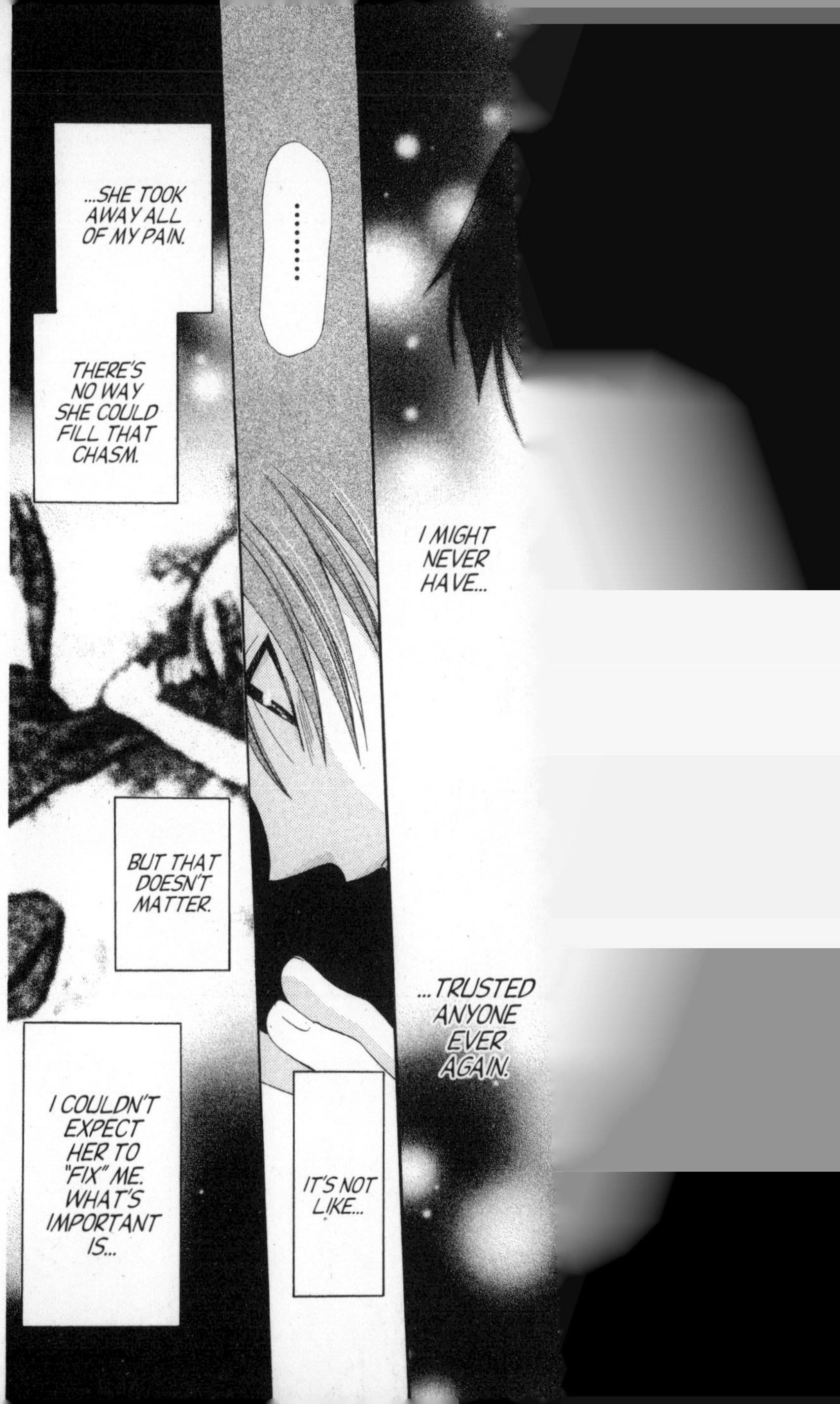
I MIGHT NEVER HAVE...
...TRUSTED ANYONE EVER AGAIN.
....
IT'S NOT LIKE...
...SHE TOOK AWAY ALL OF MY PAIN.
THERE'S NO WAY SHE COULD FILL THAT CHASM.
BUT THAT DOESN'T MATTER.
I COULDN'T EXPECT HER TO "FIX" ME. WHAT'S IMPORTANT IS...

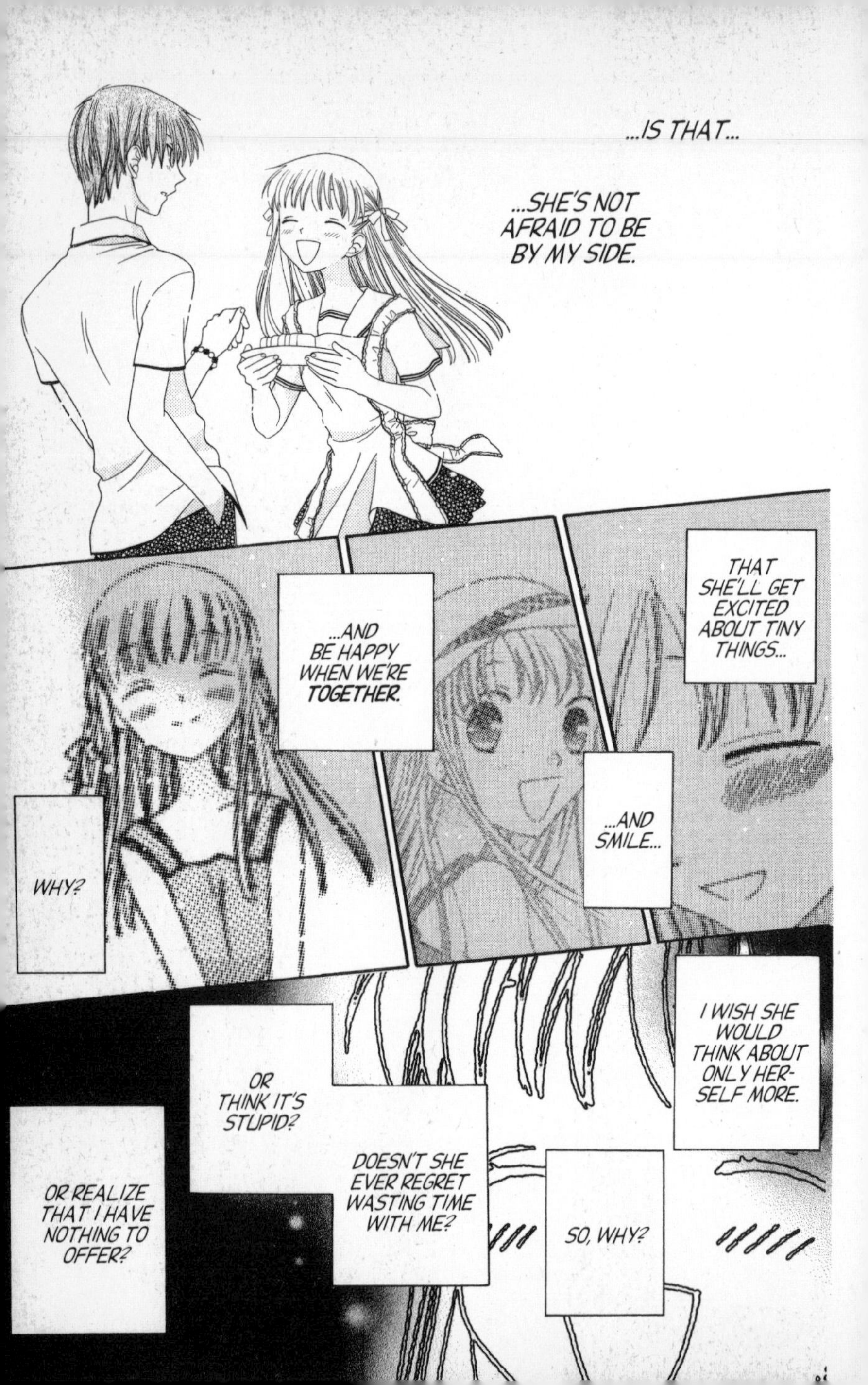
...IS THAT...
...SHE'S NOT AFRAID TO BE BY MY SIDE.
THAT SHE'LL GET EXCITED ABOUT TINY THINGS...
...AND SMILE...
...AND BE HAPPY WHEN WE'RE TOGETHER.
WHY?
I WISH SHE WOULD THINK ABOUT ONLY HER-SELF MORE.
SO, WHY?
DOESN'T SHE EVER REGRET WASTING TIME WITH ME?
OR THINK IT'S STUPID?
OR REALIZE THAT I HAVE NOTHING TO OFFER?

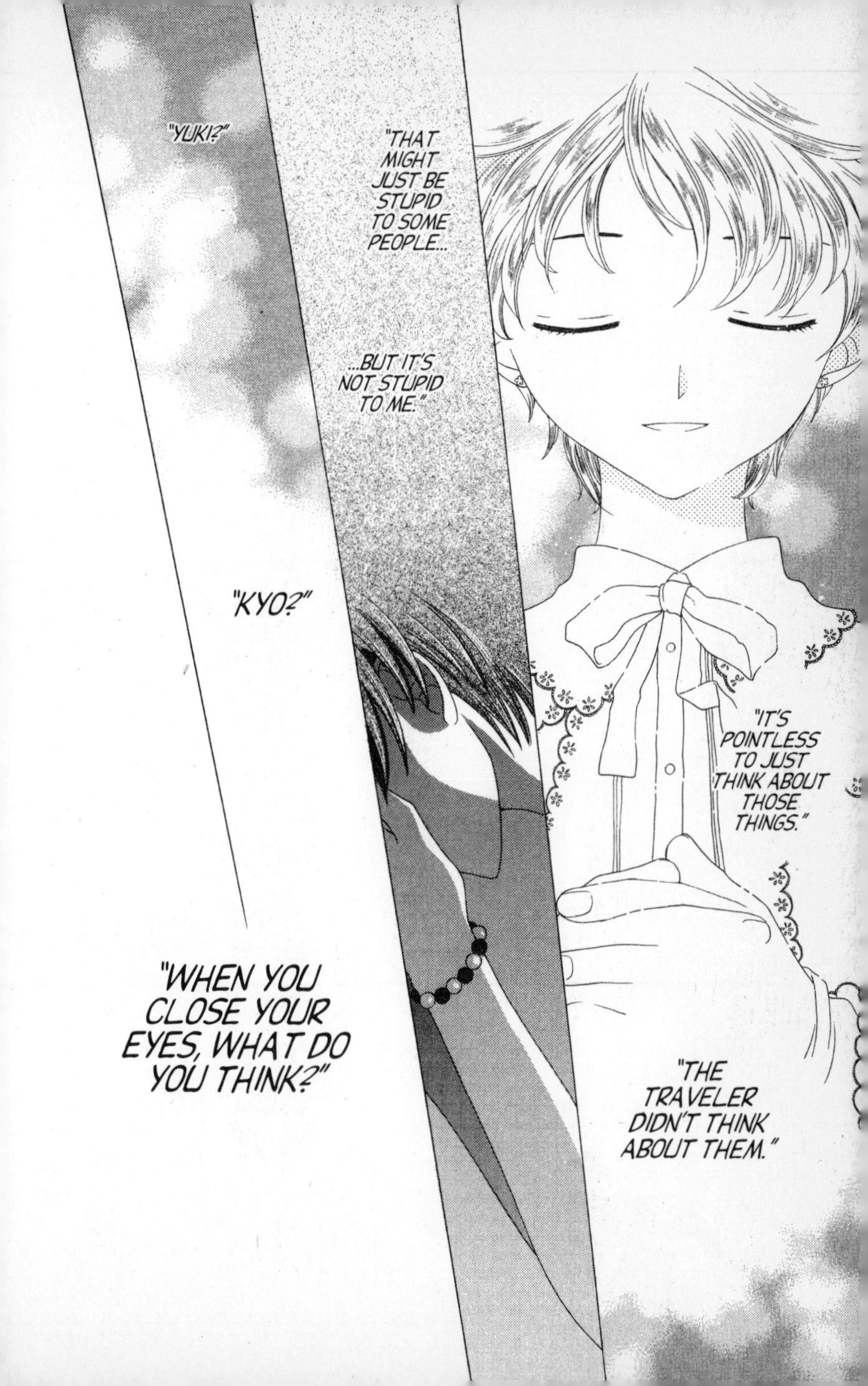
"IT'S POINTLESS TO JUST THINK ABOUT THOSE THINGS."
"THE TRAVELER DIDN'T THINK ABOUT THEM."
"THAT MIGHT JUST BE STUPID TO SOME PEOPLE...
...BUT IT'S NOT STUPID TO ME."
"YUKI?"
"KYO?"
"WHEN YOU CLOSE YOUR EYES, WHAT DO YOU THINK?"

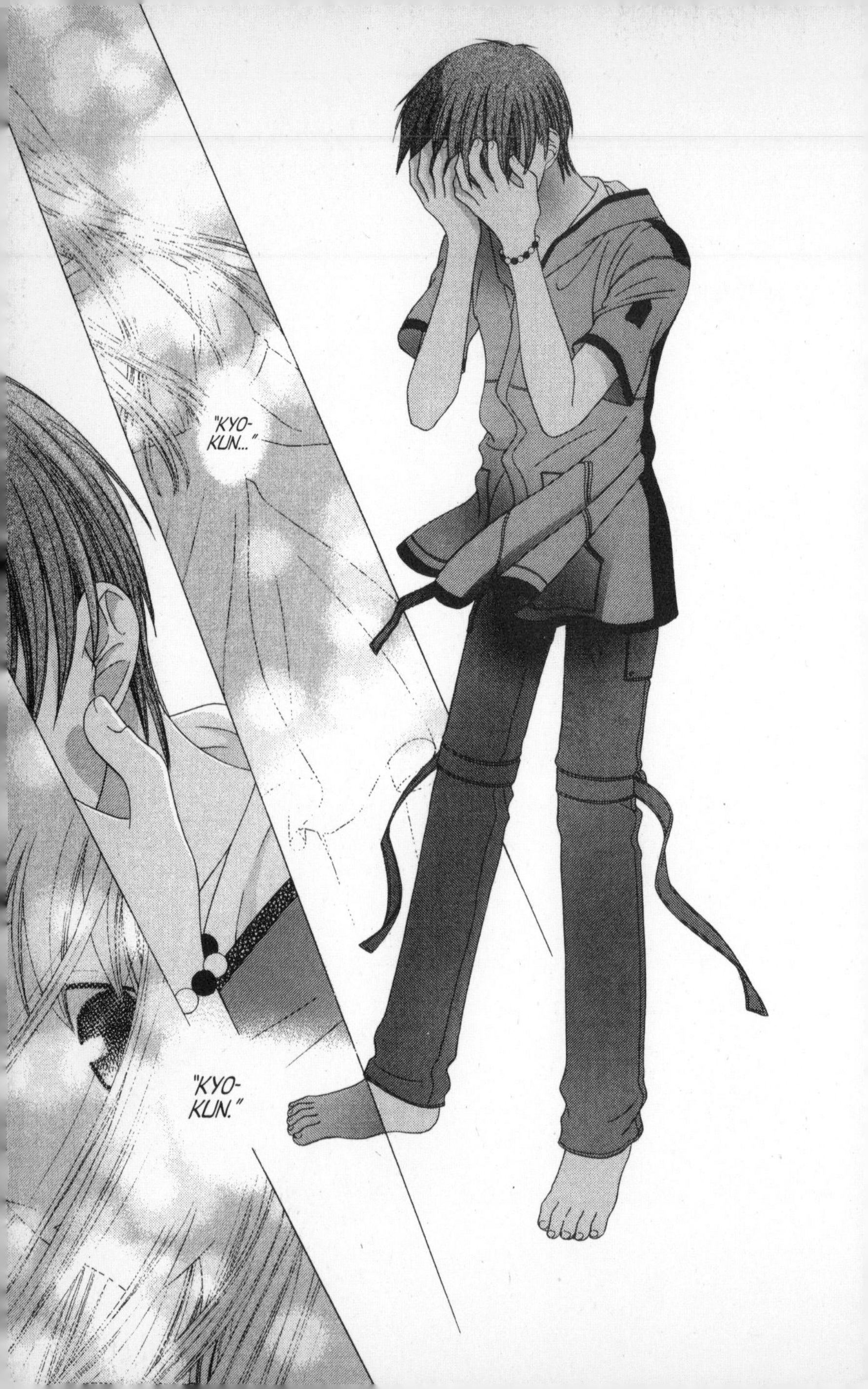
"KYO-KUN..."
"KYO-KUN."

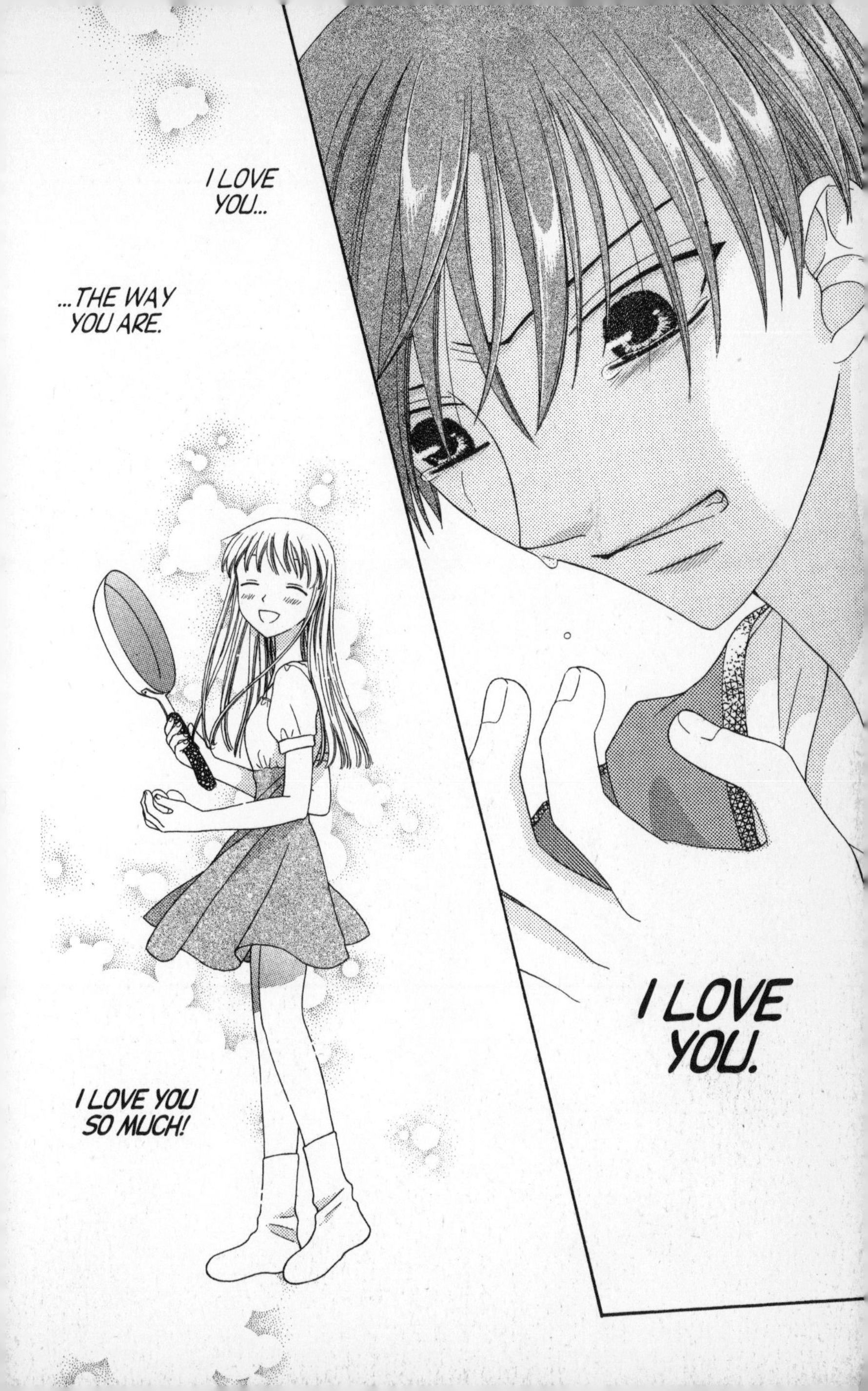
I LOVE YOU.
I LOVE YOU...
...THE WAY YOU ARE.
I LOVE YOU SO MUCH!

Chapter 63

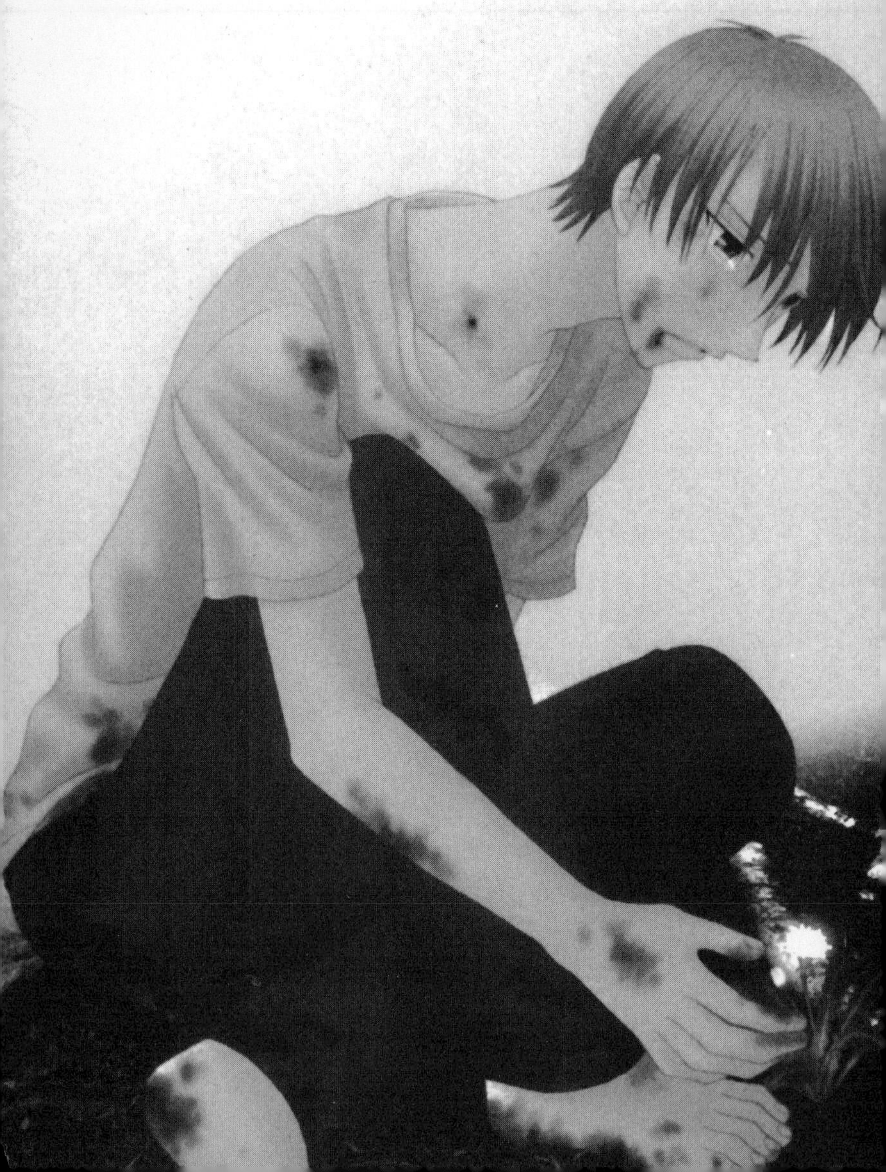

Filler
Sketch

Somehow, it seems like I've gotten into a rut of only drawing girls.
By the way, this is Kagura.

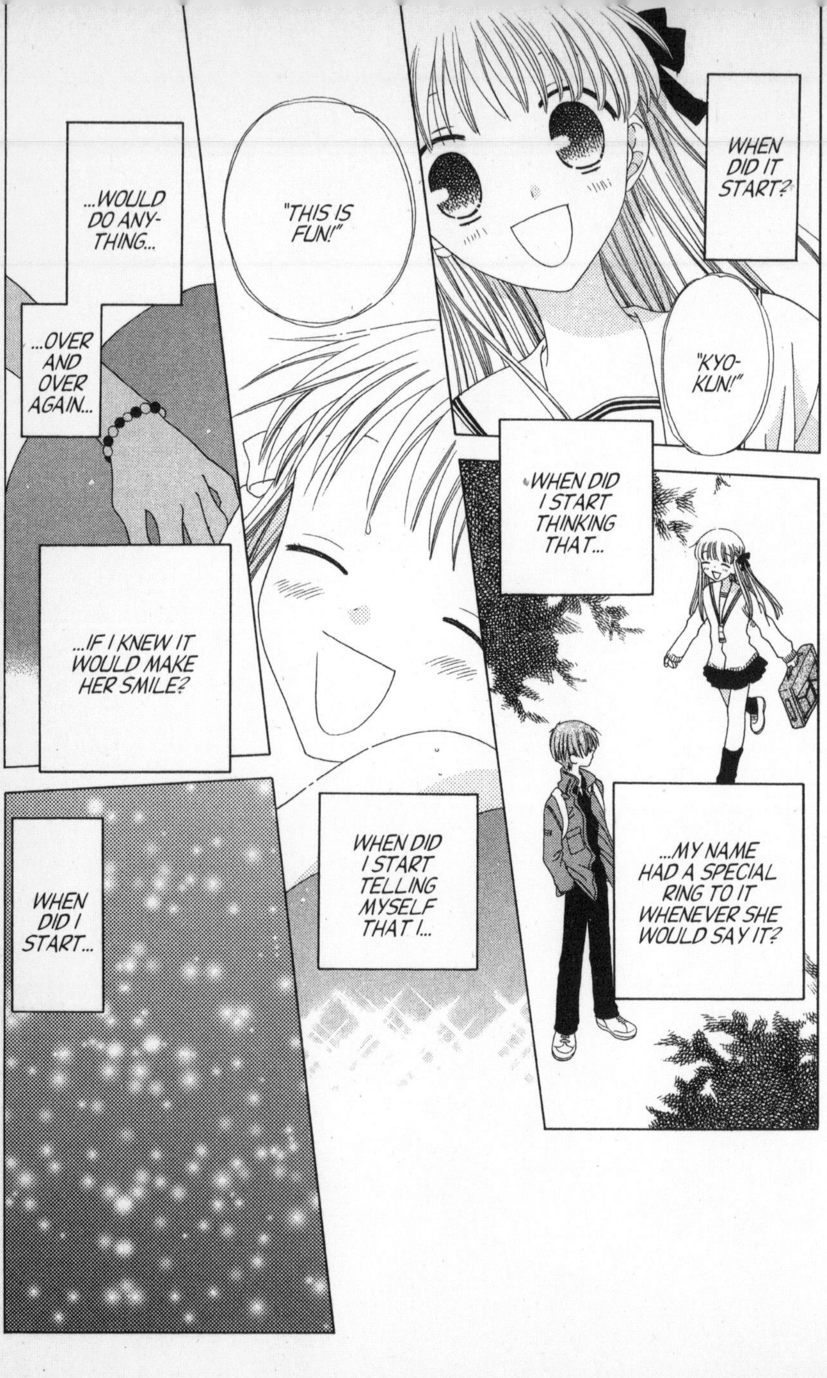
WHEN DID IT START?
"KYO-KUN!"
WHEN DID I START THINKING THAT...
...MY NAME HAD A SPECIAL RING TO IT WHENEVER SHE WOULD SAY IT?
"THIS IS FUN!"
WHEN DID I START TELLING MYSELF THAT I...
...WOULD DO ANY-THING...
...OVER AND OVER AGAIN...
...IF I KNEW IT WOULD MAKE HER SMILE?
WHEN DID I START...

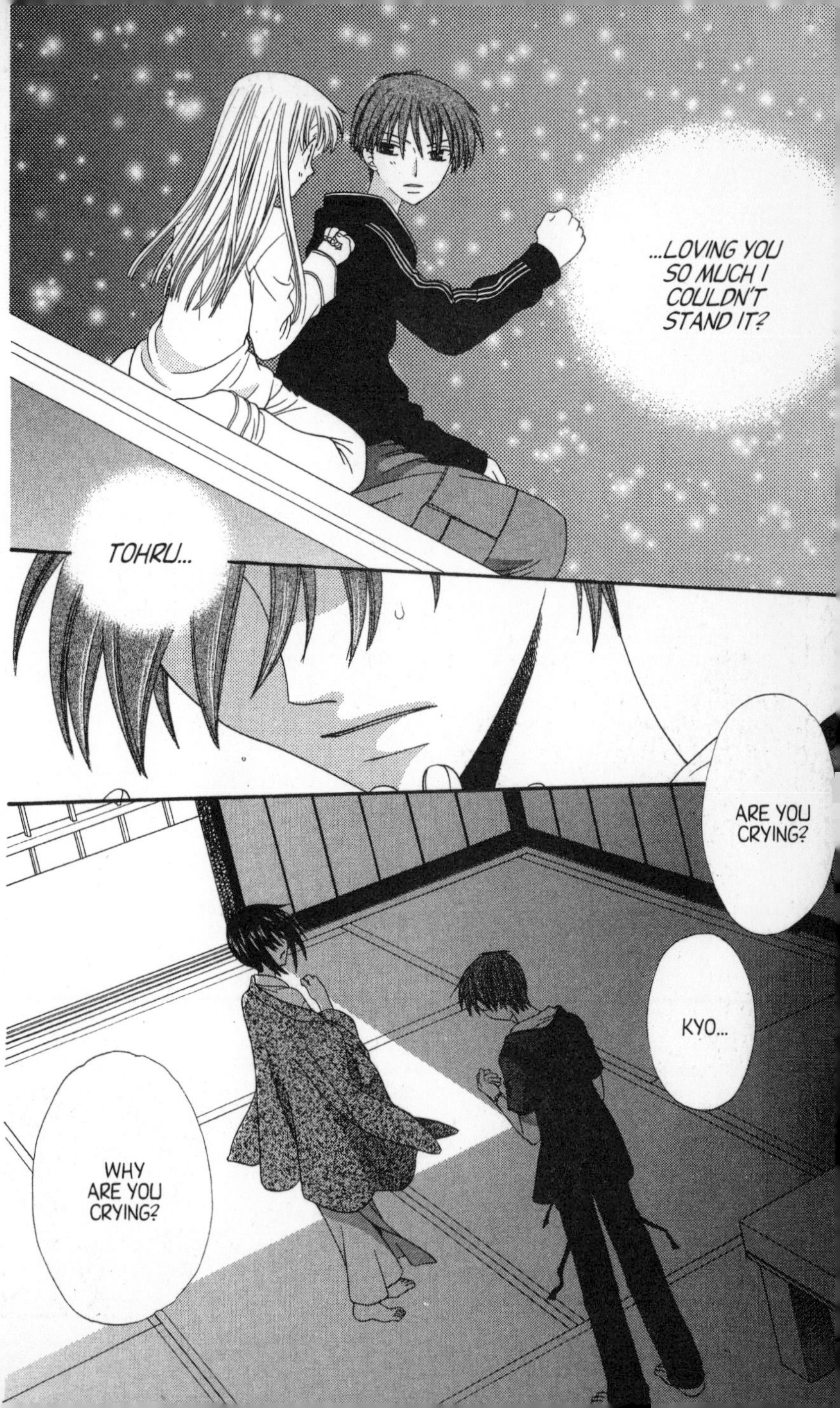
...LOVING YOU SO MUCH I COULDN'T STAND IT?
TOHRU...
ARE YOU CRYING?
KYO...
WHY ARE YOU CRYING?

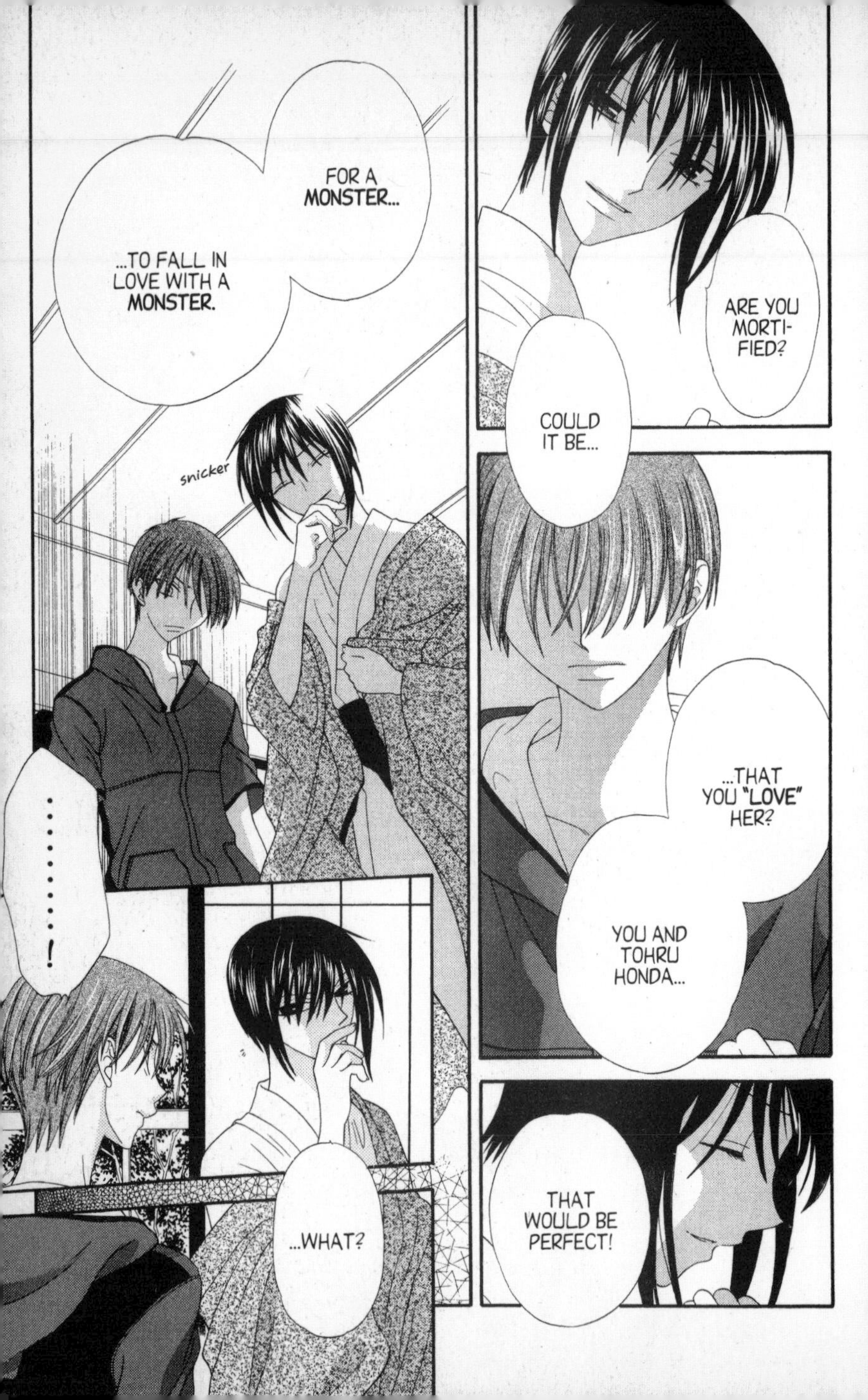
ARE YOU MORTI-FIED?
COULD IT BE...
...THAT YOU "LOVE" HER?
YOU AND TOHRU HONDA...
THAT WOULD BE PERFECT!
FOR A MONSTER...
...TO FALL IN LOVE WITH A MONSTER.
snicker
......!
...WHAT?

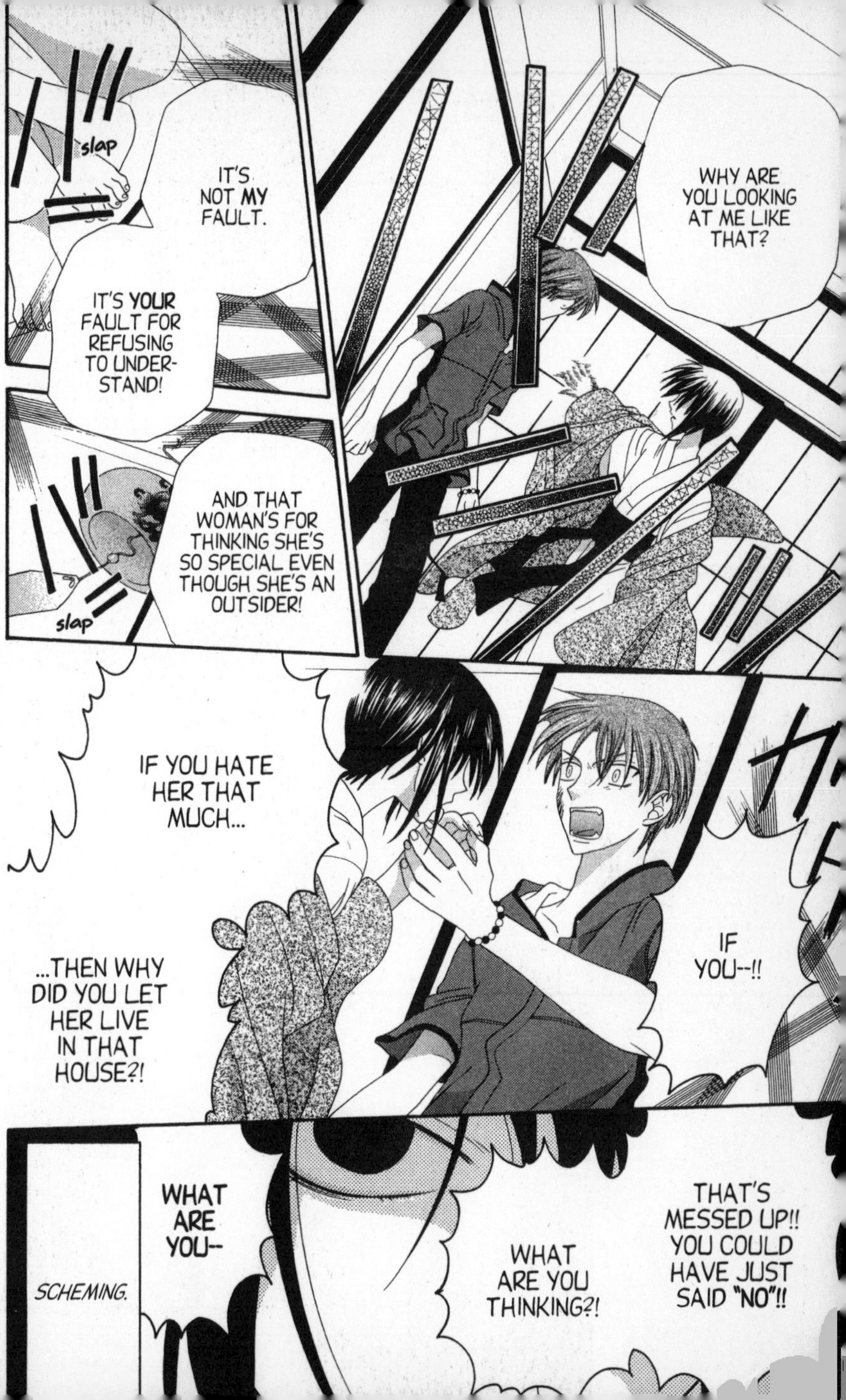
WHY ARE YOU LOOKING AT ME LIKE THAT?
slap
IT'S NOT MY FAULT.
IT'S **YOUR** FAULT FOR REFUSING TO UNDER-STAND!
AND THAT WOMAN'S FOR THINKING SHE'S SO SPECIAL EVEN THOUGH SHE'S AN OUTSIDER!
slap
IF YOU--!!
IF YOU HATE HER THAT MUCH...
...THEN WHY DID YOU LET HER LIVE IN THAT HOUSE?!
THAT'S MESSED UP!! YOU COULD HAVE JUST SAID "**NO**"!!
WHAT ARE YOU THINKING?!
WHAT ARE YOU--
SCHEMING.

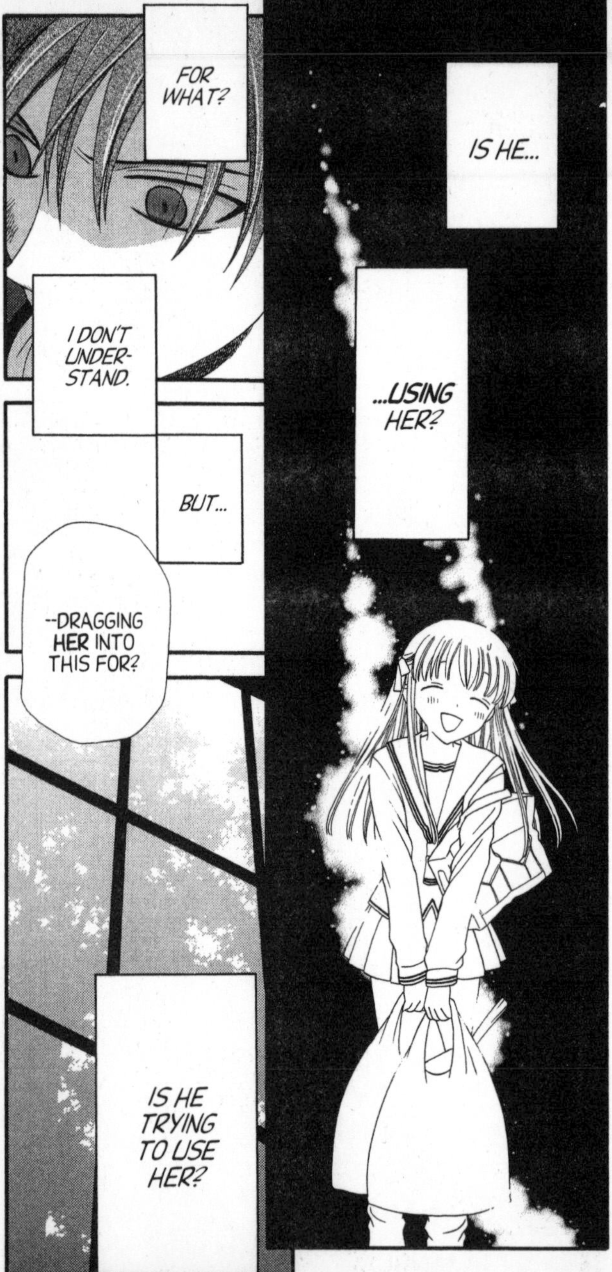
IS HE...
...USING HER?
FOR WHAT?
I DON'T UNDER-STAND.
BUT...
--DRAGGING HER INTO THIS FOR?
IS HE TRYING TO USE HER?

Mayu-chan-sensei

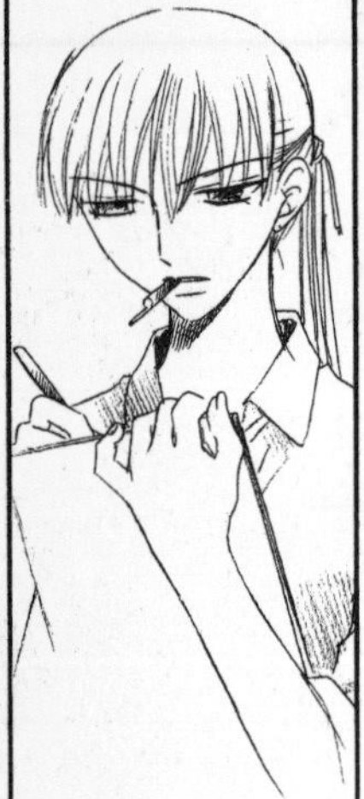

She might be the type who's kind of sad that she's a woman. That might be why Shigure likes her. Poor thing... At any rate, she's popular among the female students and has problems like getting love letters from them. Also, she's secretly insecure about how tall she is. But Hatori is tall, too, so they might look pretty good together as a tall couple.

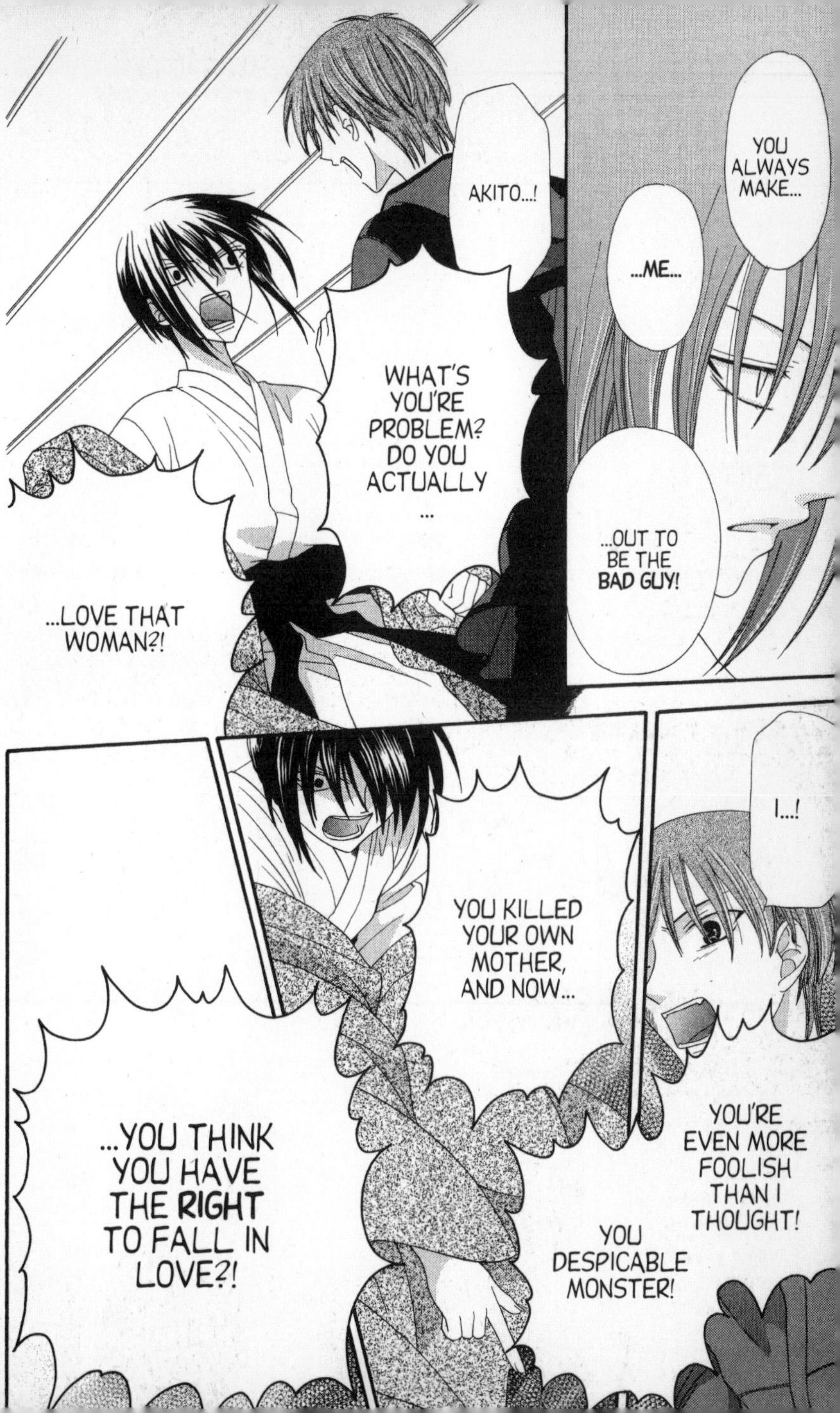
YOU ALWAYS MAKE...
...ME...
...OUT TO BE THE BAD GUY!
AKITO...!
WHAT'S YOU'RE PROBLEM? DO YOU ACTUALLY ...
...LOVE THAT WOMAN?!
I...!
YOU KILLED YOUR OWN MOTHER, AND NOW...
...YOU THINK YOU HAVE THE RIGHT TO FALL IN LOVE?!
YOU'RE EVEN MORE FOOLISH THAN I THOUGHT!
YOU DESPICABLE MONSTER!

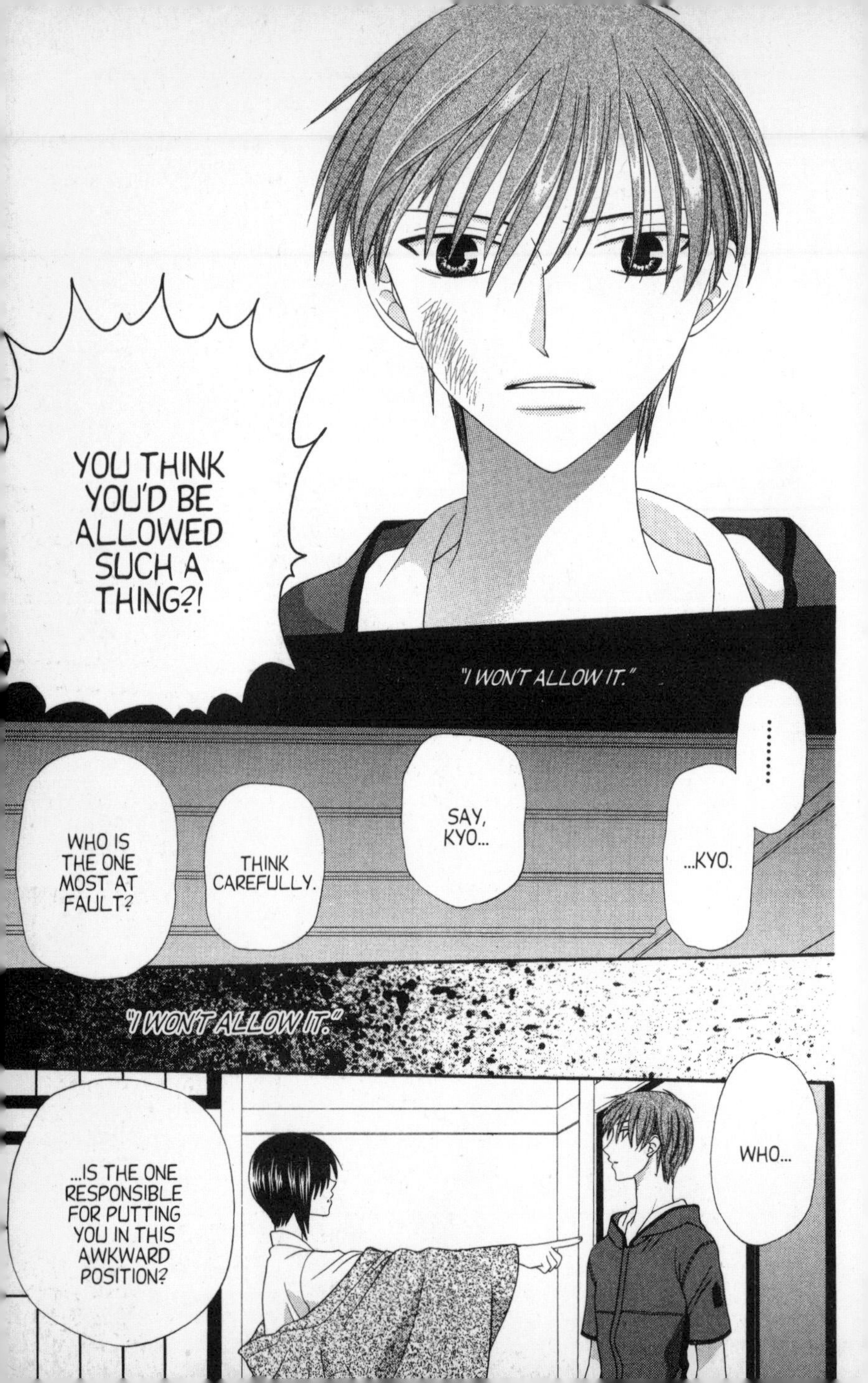
YOU THINK YOU'D BE ALLOWED SUCH A THING?!
"I WON'T ALLOW IT."
......
...KYO.
SAY, KYO...
THINK CAREFULLY.
WHO IS THE ONE MOST AT FAULT?
"I WON'T ALLOW IT."
WHO...
...IS THE ONE RESPONSIBLE FOR PUTTING YOU IN THIS AWKWARD POSITION?

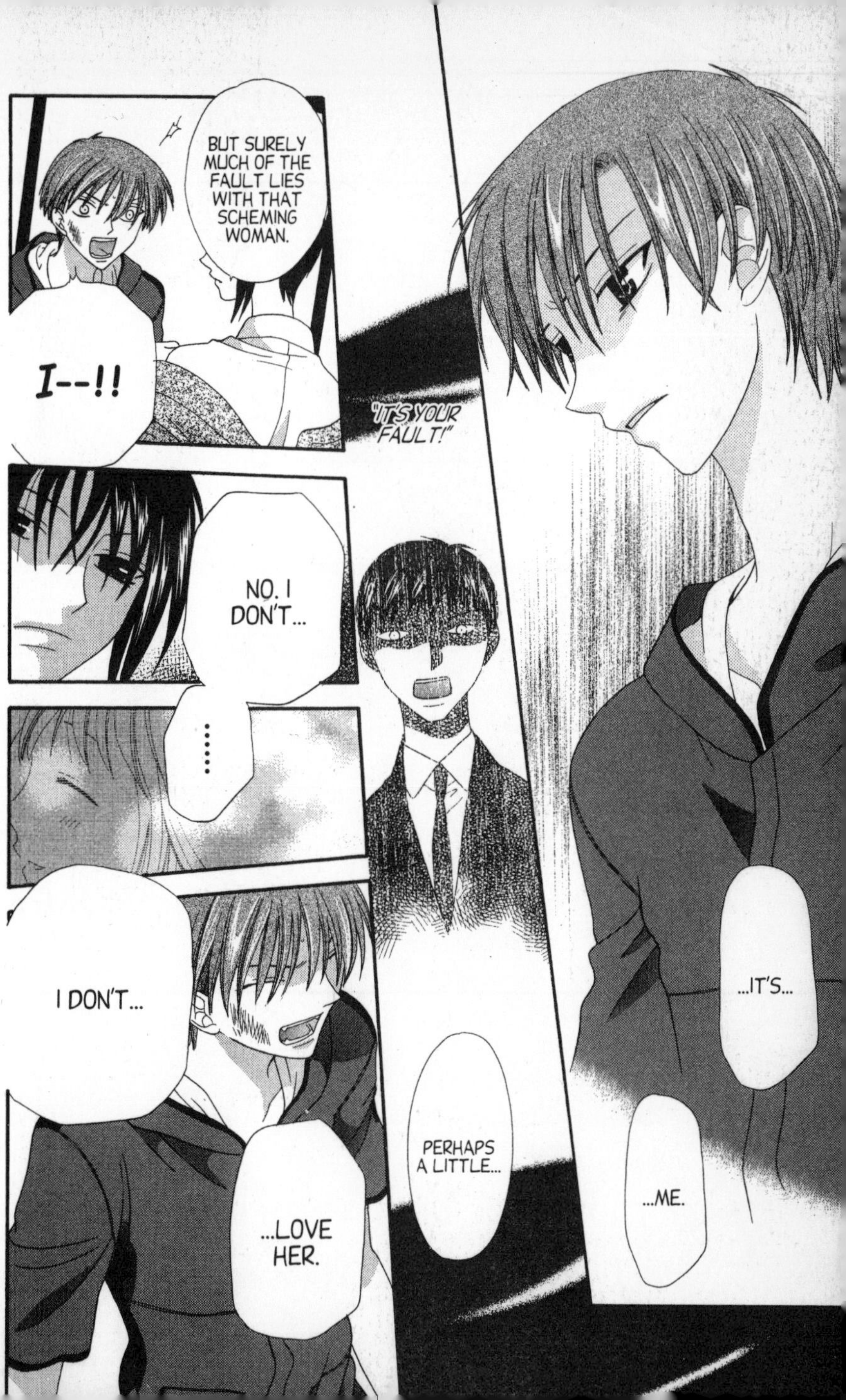
...IT'S...
...ME.
"IT'S YOUR FAULT!"
PERHAPS A LITTLE...
BUT SURELY MUCH OF THE FAULT LIES WITH THAT SCHEMING WOMAN.
I--!!
NO. I DON'T...
......
I DON'T...
...LOVE HER.

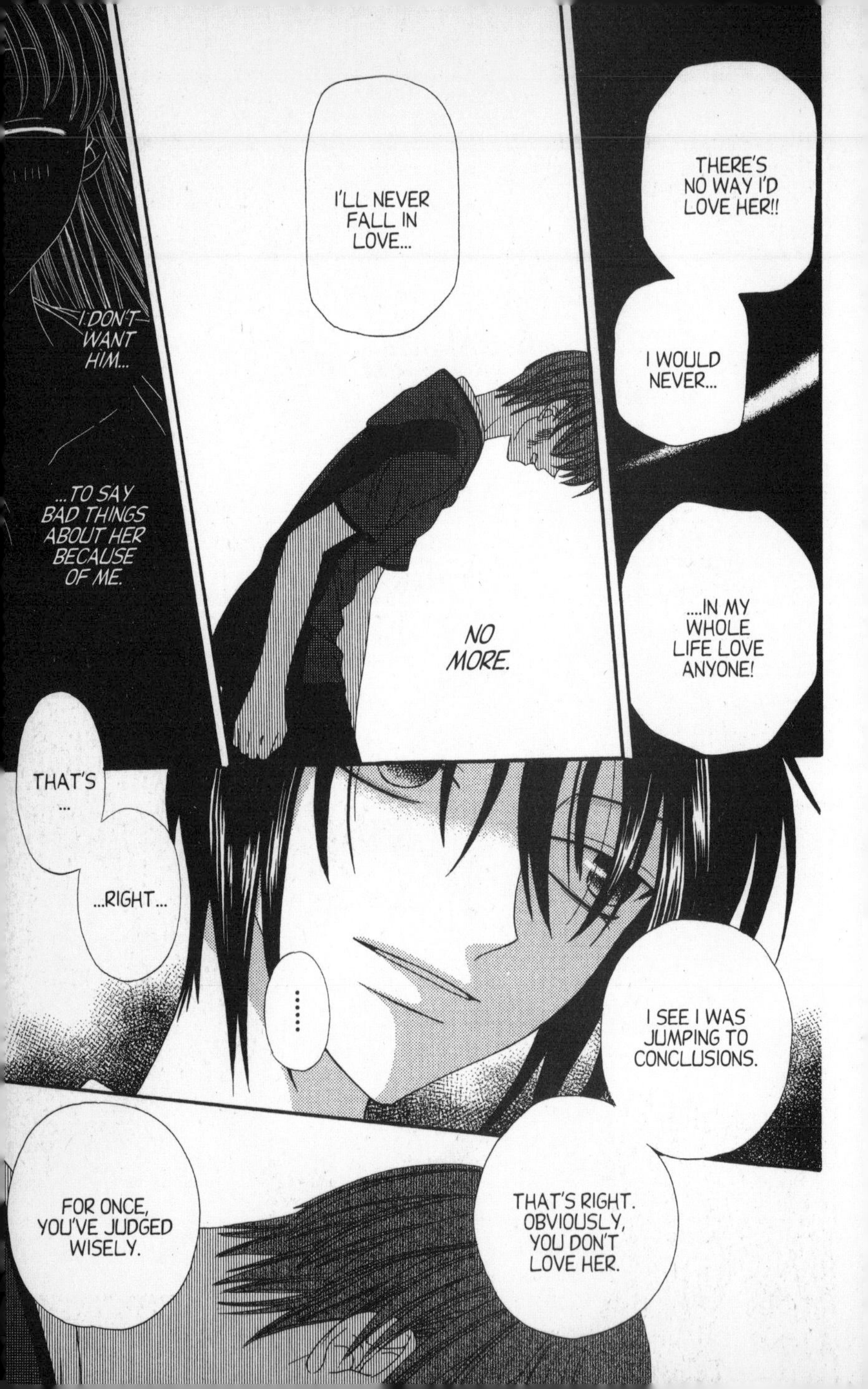

THERE'S NO WAY I'D LOVE HER!!
I WOULD NEVER...
....IN MY WHOLE LIFE LOVE ANYONE!
I'LL NEVER FALL IN LOVE...
NO MORE.
I DON'T WANT HIM...
...TO SAY BAD THINGS ABOUT HER BECAUSE OF ME.
I SEE I WAS JUMPING TO CONCLUSIONS.
......
THAT'S ...
...RIGHT...
THAT'S RIGHT. OBVIOUSLY, YOU DON'T LOVE HER.
FOR ONCE, YOU'VE JUDGED WISELY.

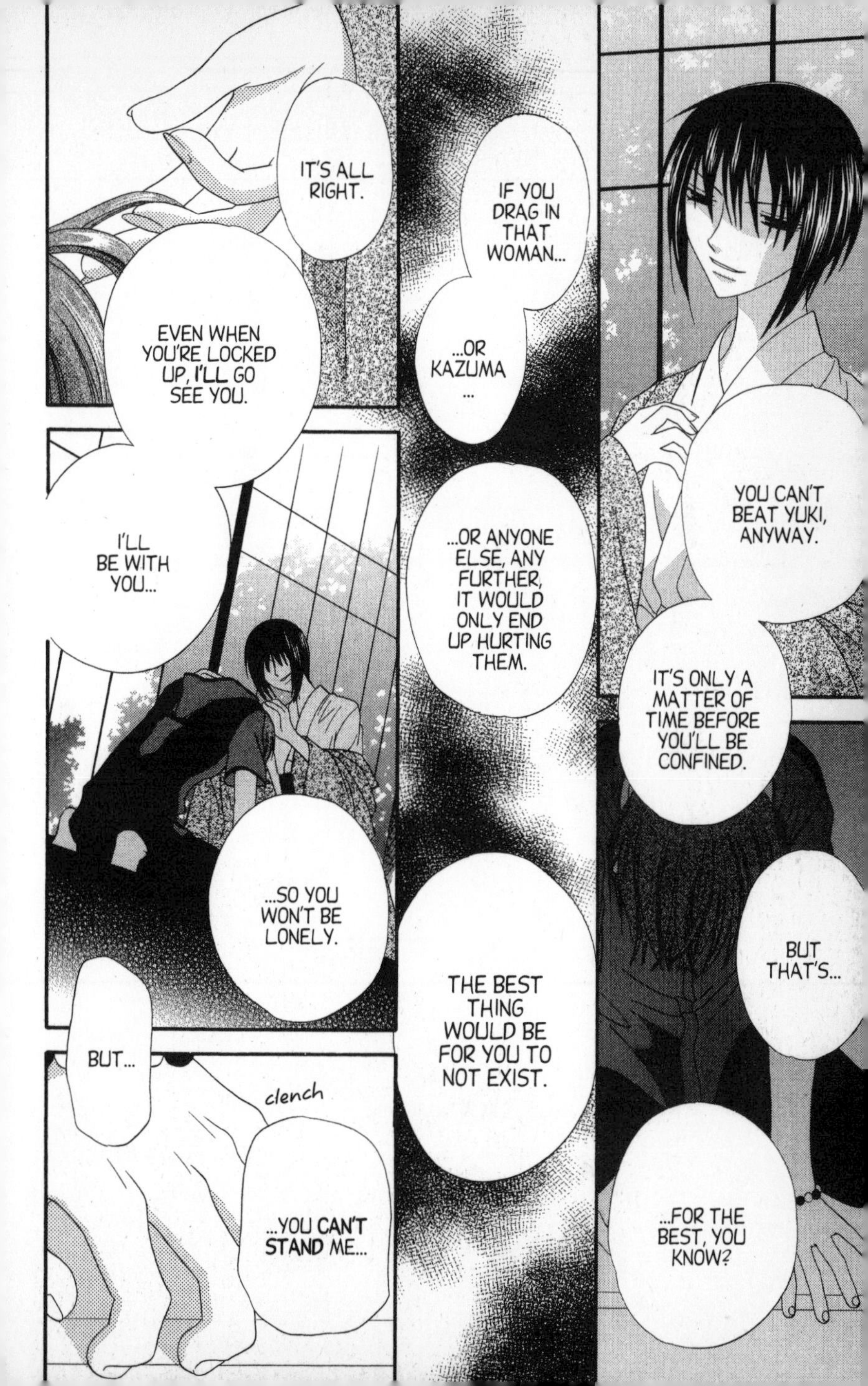
YOU CAN'T BEAT YUKI, ANYWAY.
IT'S ONLY A MATTER OF TIME BEFORE YOU'LL BE CONFINED.
BUT THAT'S...
...FOR THE BEST, YOU KNOW?
IF YOU DRAG IN THAT WOMAN...
...OR KAZUMA...
...OR ANYONE ELSE, ANY FURTHER, IT WOULD ONLY END UP HURTING THEM.
THE BEST THING WOULD BE FOR YOU TO NOT EXIST.
IT'S ALL RIGHT.
EVEN WHEN YOU'RE LOCKED UP, I'LL GO SEE YOU.
I'LL BE WITH YOU...
...SO YOU WON'T BE LONELY.
BUT...
clench
...YOU CAN'T STAND ME...

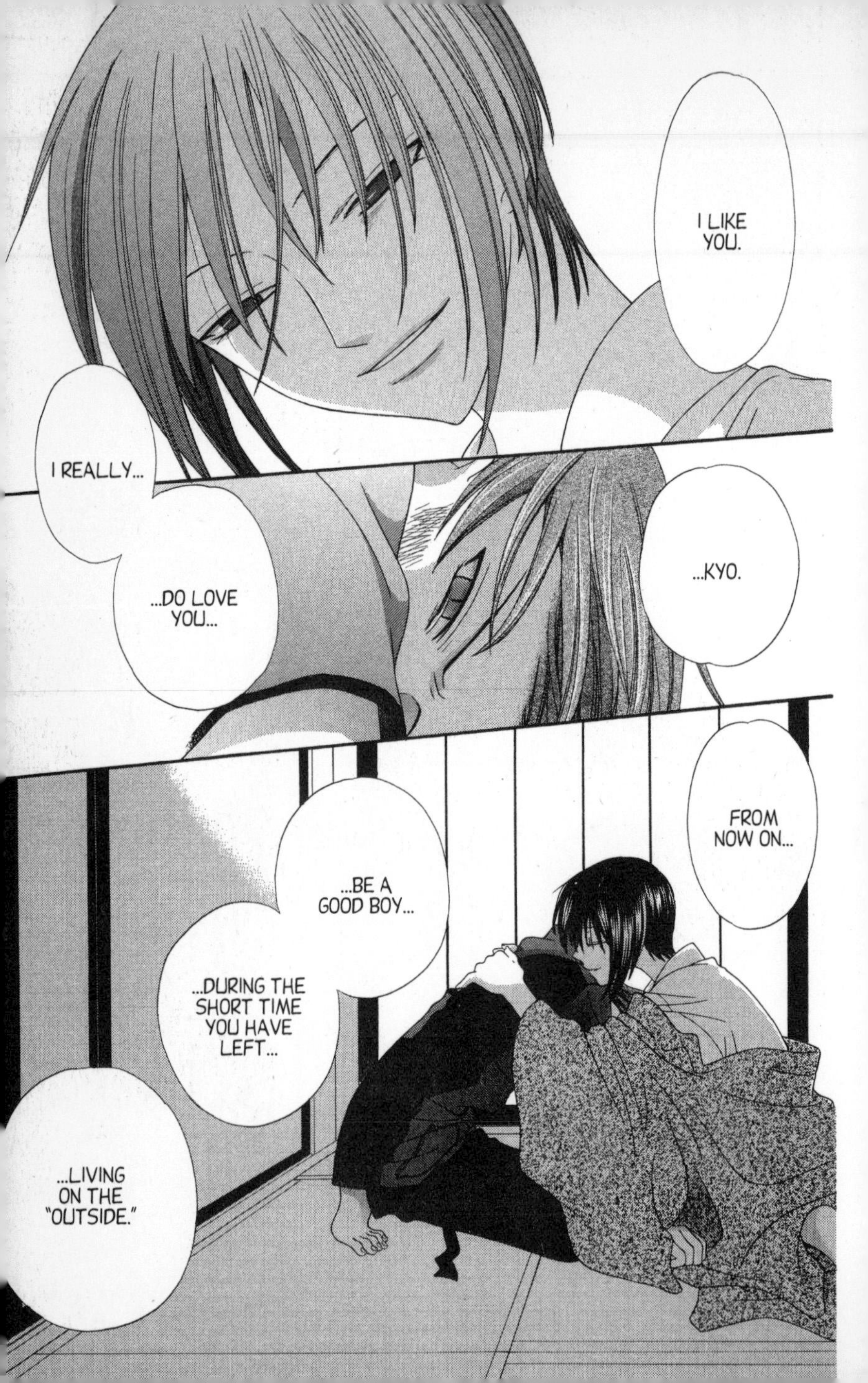
I LIKE YOU.
I REALLY...
...DO LOVE YOU...
...KYO.
FROM NOW ON...
...BE A GOOD BOY...
...DURING THE SHORT TIME YOU HAVE LEFT...
...LIVING ON THE "OUTSIDE."

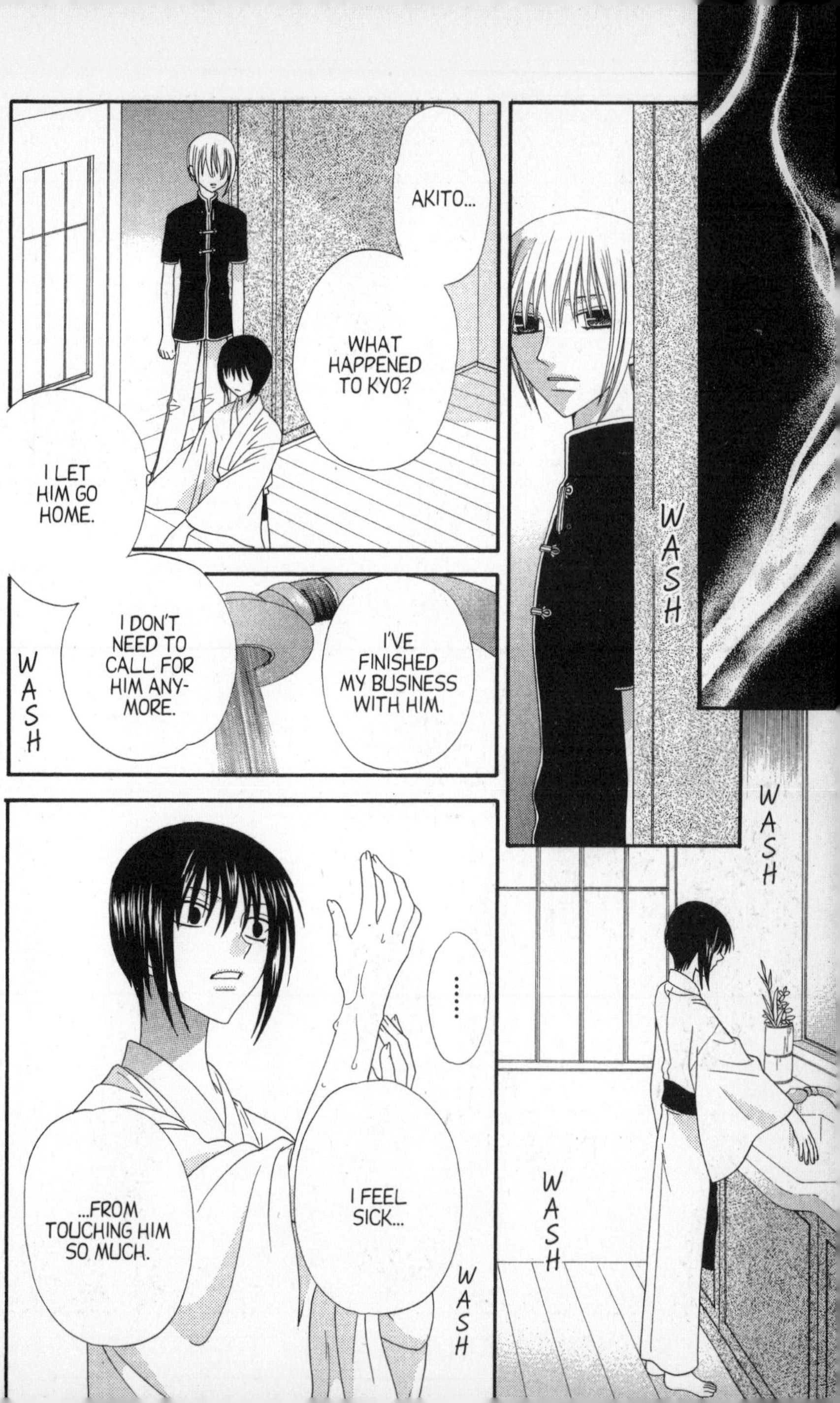
WASH
AKITO...
WHAT HAPPENED TO KYO?
I LET HIM GO HOME.
I'VE FINISHED MY BUSINESS WITH HIM.
I DON'T NEED TO CALL FOR HIM ANY-MORE.
WASH
WASH
WASH
......
I FEEL SICK...
...FROM TOUCHING HIM SO MUCH.
WASH

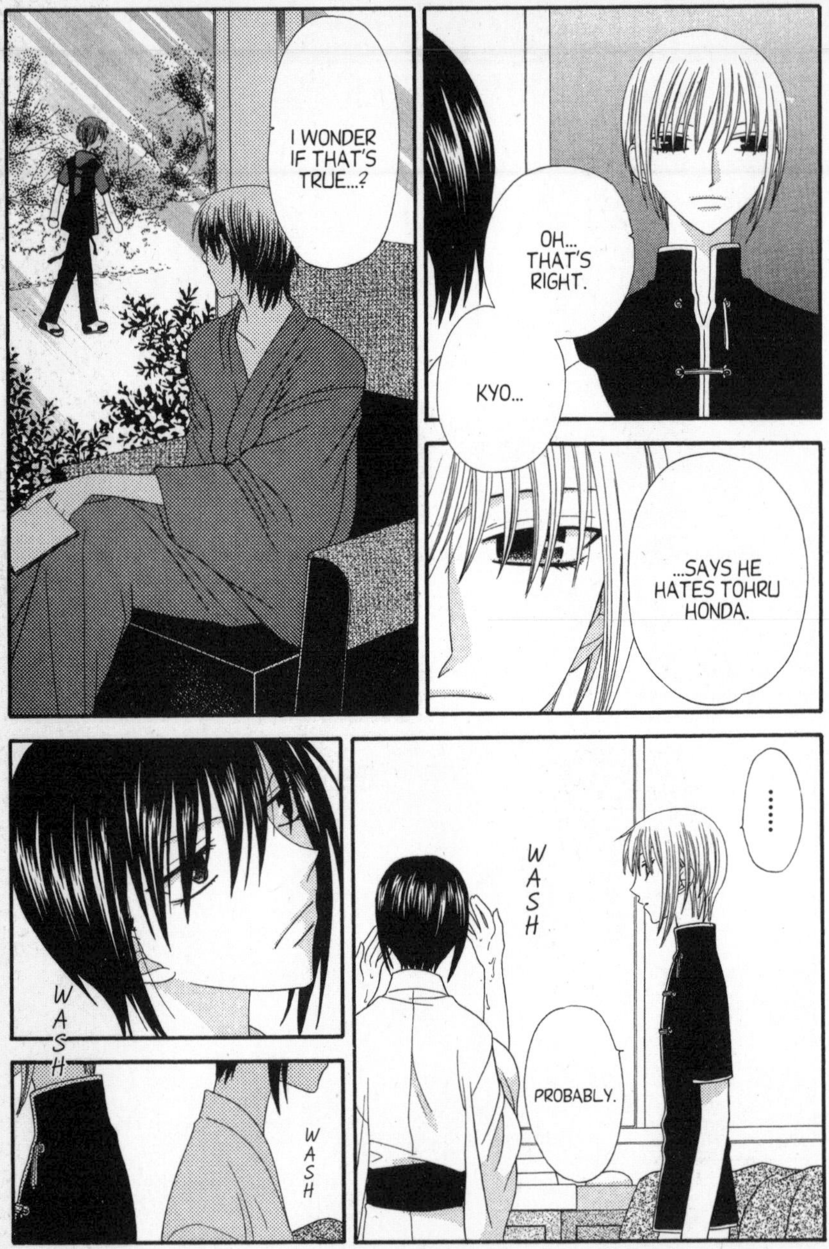
OH... THAT'S RIGHT.
KYO...
...SAYS HE HATES TOHRU HONDA.
I WONDER IF THAT'S TRUE...?
......
WASH
PROBABLY.
WASH
WASH

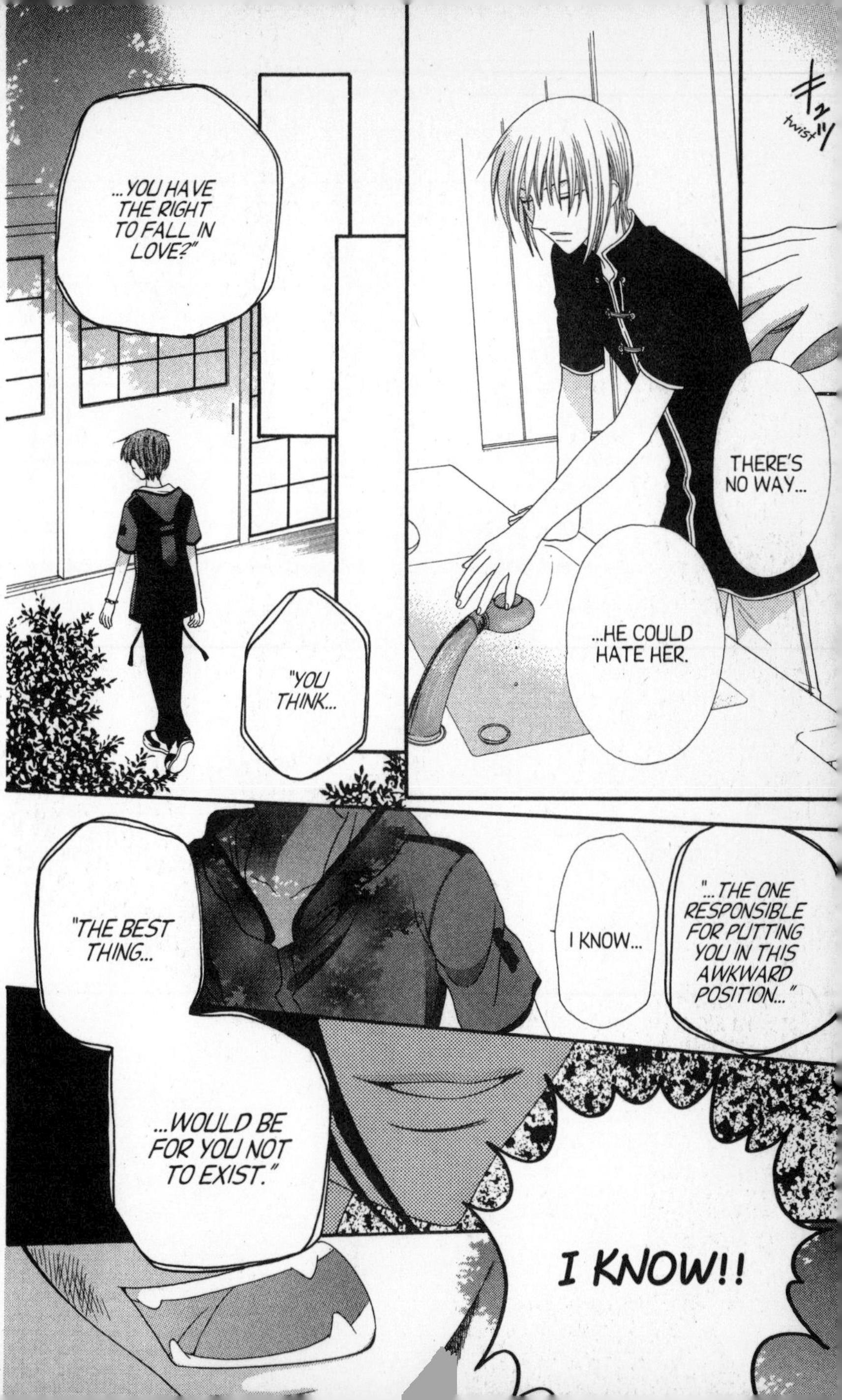
twist
THERE'S NO WAY...
...HE COULD HATE HER.
"YOU THINK...
...YOU HAVE THE RIGHT TO FALL IN LOVE?"
"...THE ONE RESPONSIBLE FOR PUTTING YOU IN THIS AWKWARD POSITION..."
I KNOW...
"THE BEST THING...
...WOULD BE FOR YOU NOT TO EXIST."
I KNOW!!

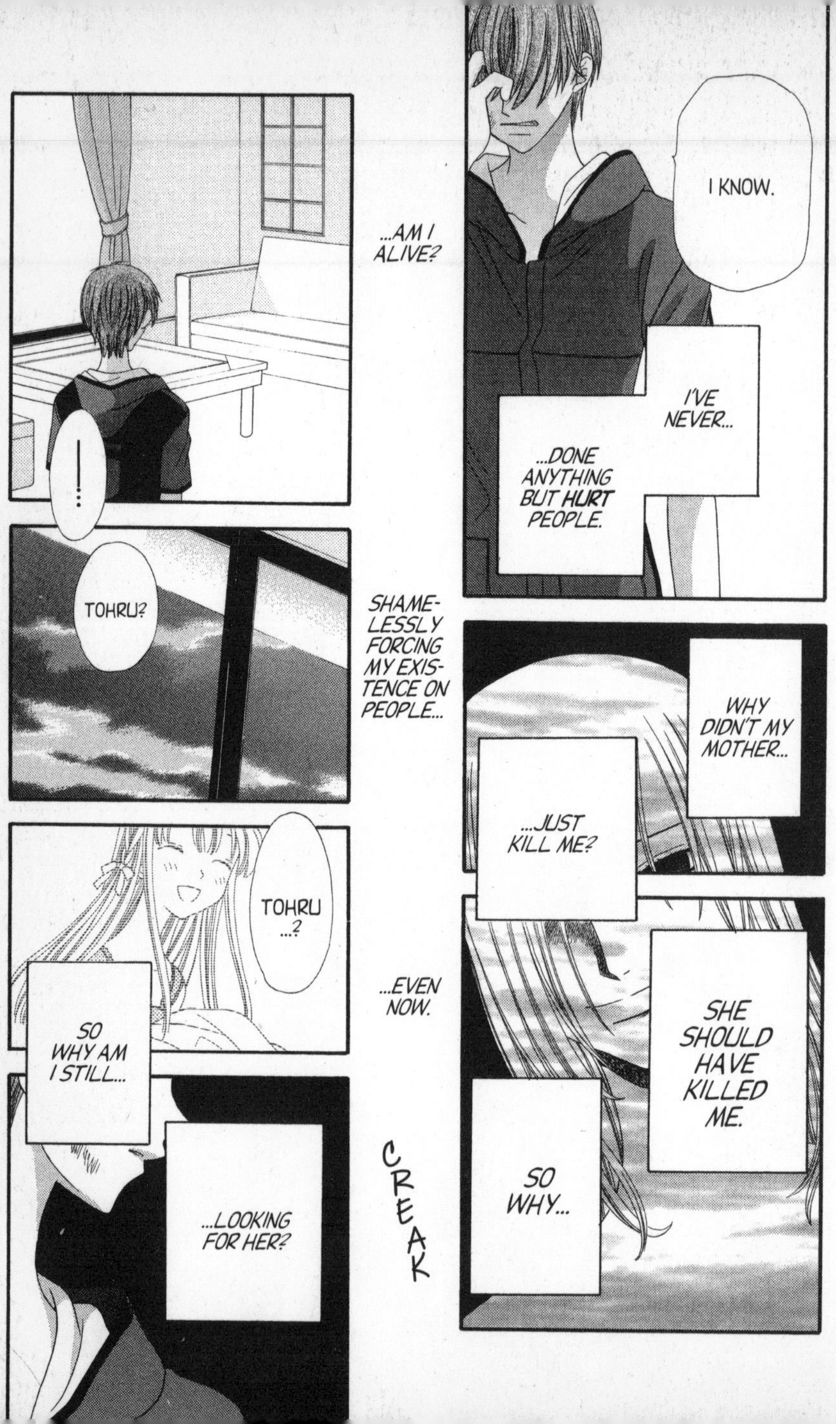
I KNOW.
I'VE NEVER...
...DONE ANYTHING BUT HURT PEOPLE.
WHY DIDN'T MY MOTHER...
...JUST KILL ME?
SHE SHOULD HAVE KILLED ME.
SO WHY...
...AM I ALIVE?
SHAMELESSLY FORCING MY EXISTENCE ON PEOPLE...
...EVEN NOW.
!...
TOHRU?
TOHRU ...?
SO WHY AM I STILL...
...LOOKING FOR HER?
CREAK

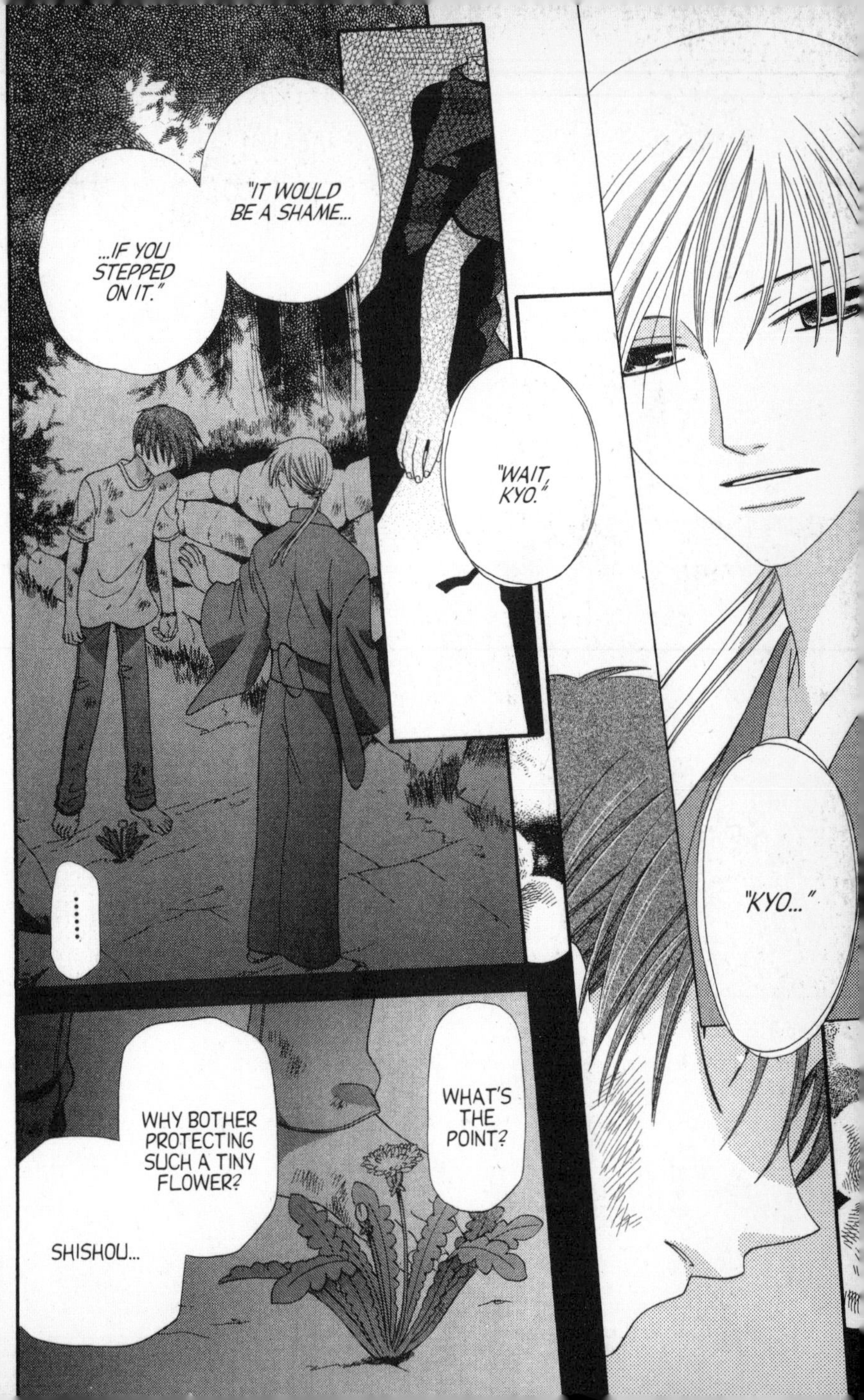
"KYO..."
"WAIT, KYO."
"IT WOULD BE A SHAME...
...IF YOU STEPPED ON IT."
......
WHAT'S THE POINT?
WHY BOTHER PROTECTING SUCH A TINY FLOWER?
SHISHOU...

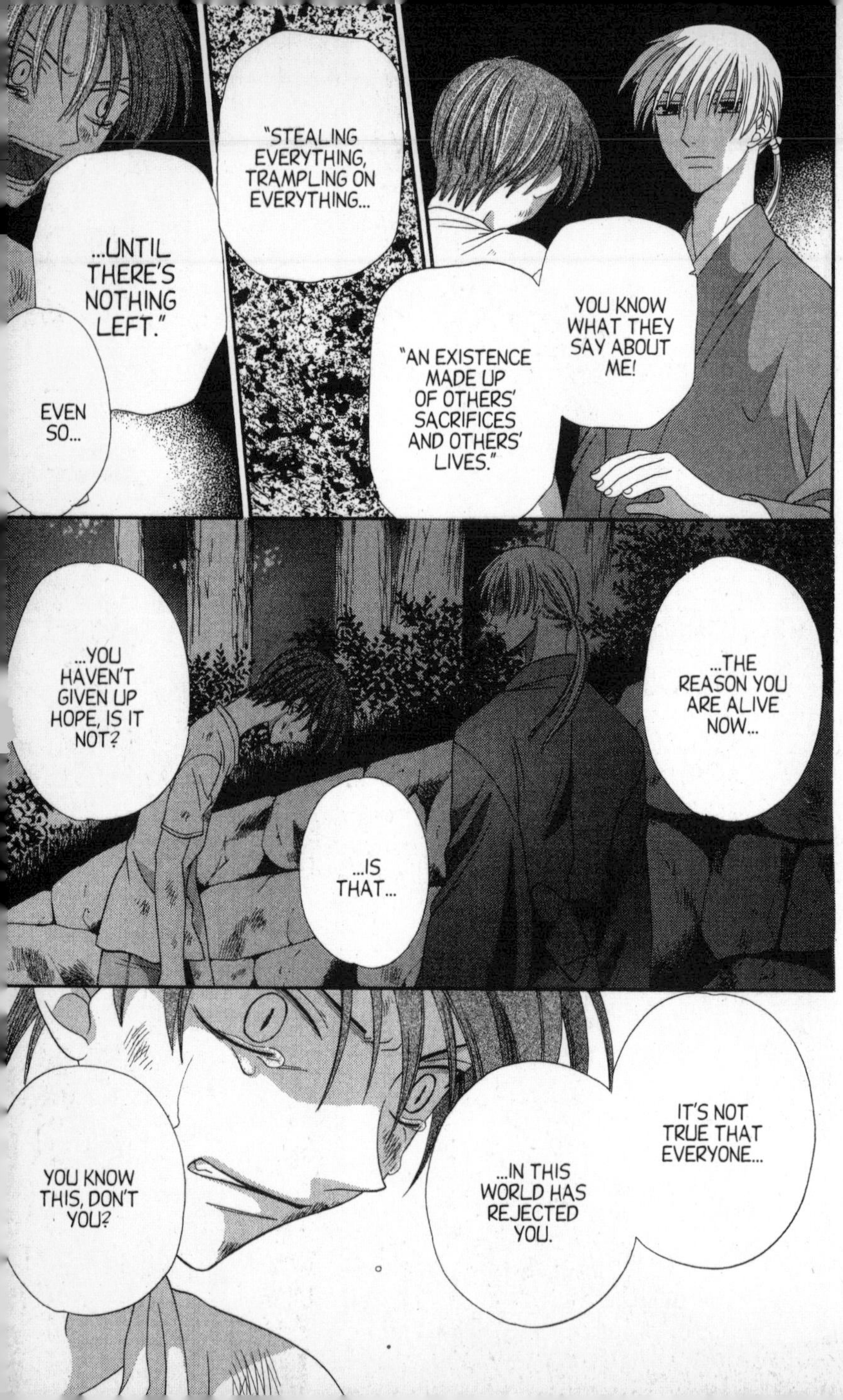
YOU KNOW WHAT THEY SAY ABOUT ME!
"AN EXISTENCE MADE UP OF OTHERS' SACRIFICES AND OTHERS' LIVES."
"STEALING EVERYTHING, TRAMPLING ON EVERYTHING...
...UNTIL THERE'S NOTHING LEFT."
EVEN SO...
...THE REASON YOU ARE ALIVE NOW...
...IS THAT...
...YOU HAVEN'T GIVEN UP HOPE, IS IT NOT?
IT'S NOT TRUE THAT EVERYONE...
...IN THIS WORLD HAS REJECTED YOU.
YOU KNOW THIS, DON'T YOU?

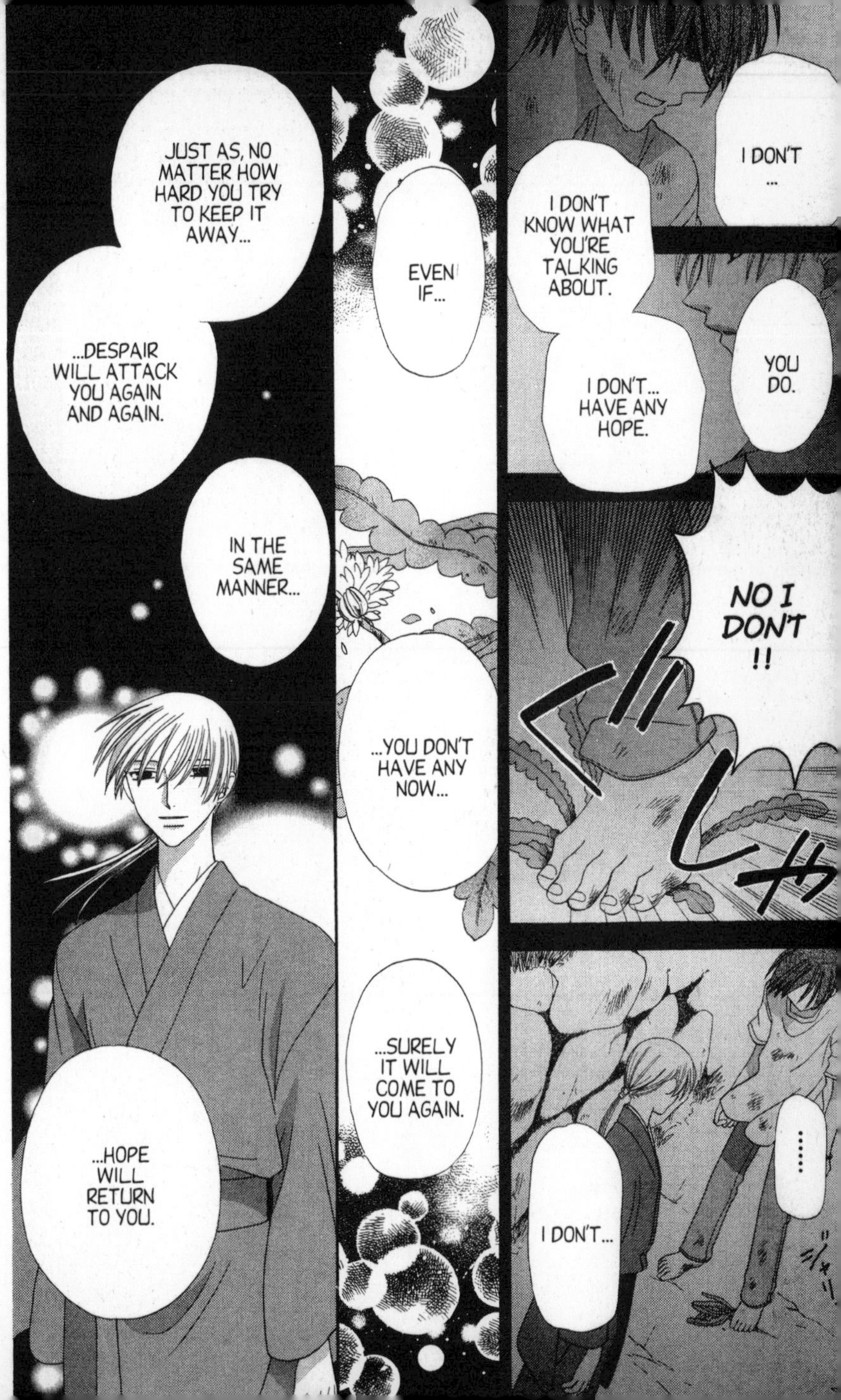
I DON'T ...
I DON'T KNOW WHAT YOU'RE TALKING ABOUT.
YOU DO.
I DON'T... HAVE ANY HOPE.
NO I DON'T !!
......
I DON'T...
EVEN IF...
...YOU DON'T HAVE ANY NOW...
...SURELY IT WILL COME TO YOU AGAIN.
JUST AS, NO MATTER HOW HARD YOU TRY TO KEEP IT AWAY...
...DESPAIR WILL ATTACK YOU AGAIN AND AGAIN.
IN THE SAME MANNER...
...HOPE WILL RETURN TO YOU.

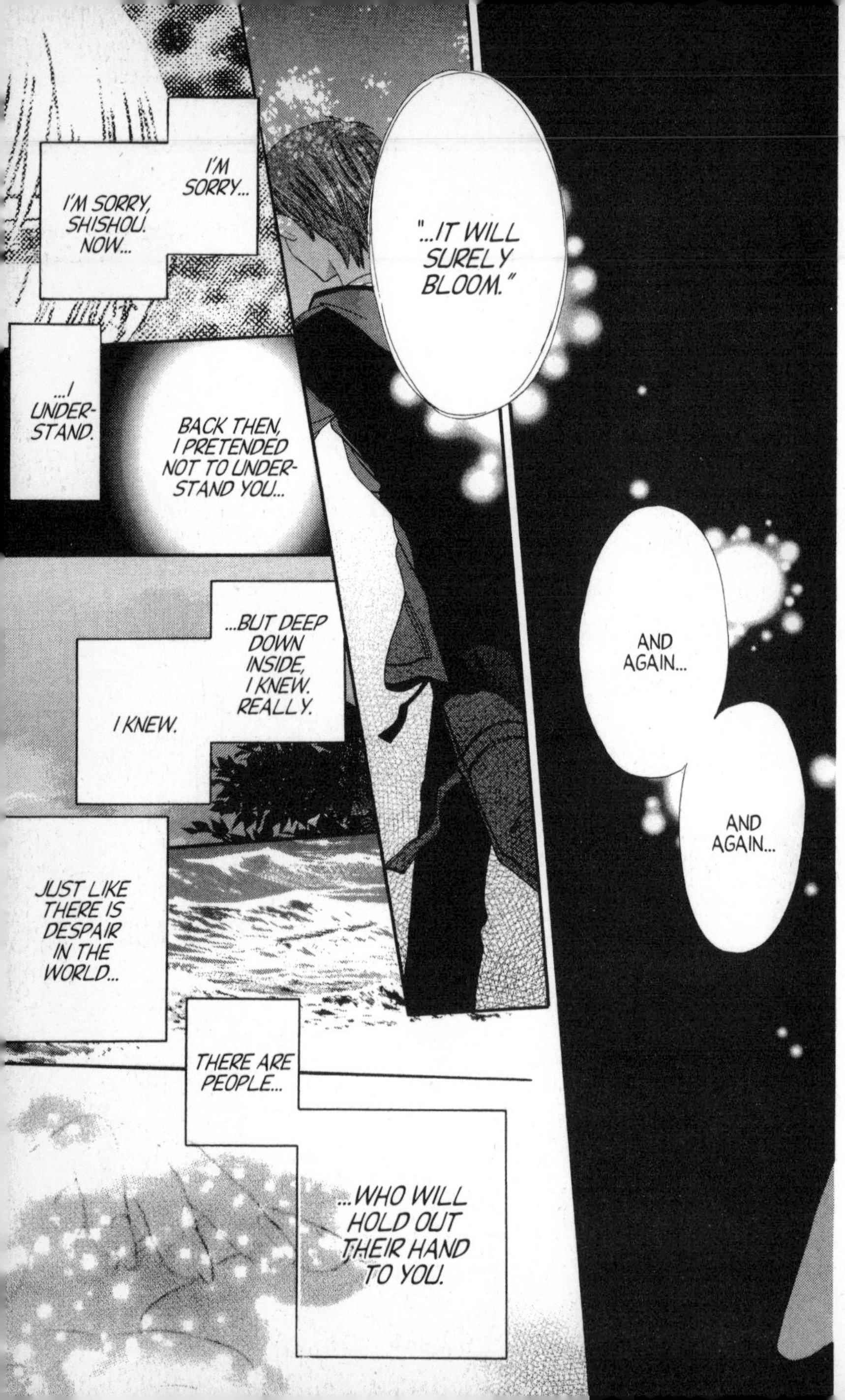
"...IT WILL SURELY BLOOM."
AND AGAIN...
AND AGAIN...
I'M SORRY...
I'M SORRY, SHISHOU. NOW...
BACK THEN, I PRETENDED NOT TO UNDER-STAND YOU...
...I UNDER-STAND.
...BUT DEEP DOWN INSIDE, I KNEW. REALLY.
I KNEW.
JUST LIKE THERE IS DESPAIR IN THE WORLD...
THERE ARE PEOPLE...
...WHO WILL HOLD OUT THEIR HAND TO YOU.

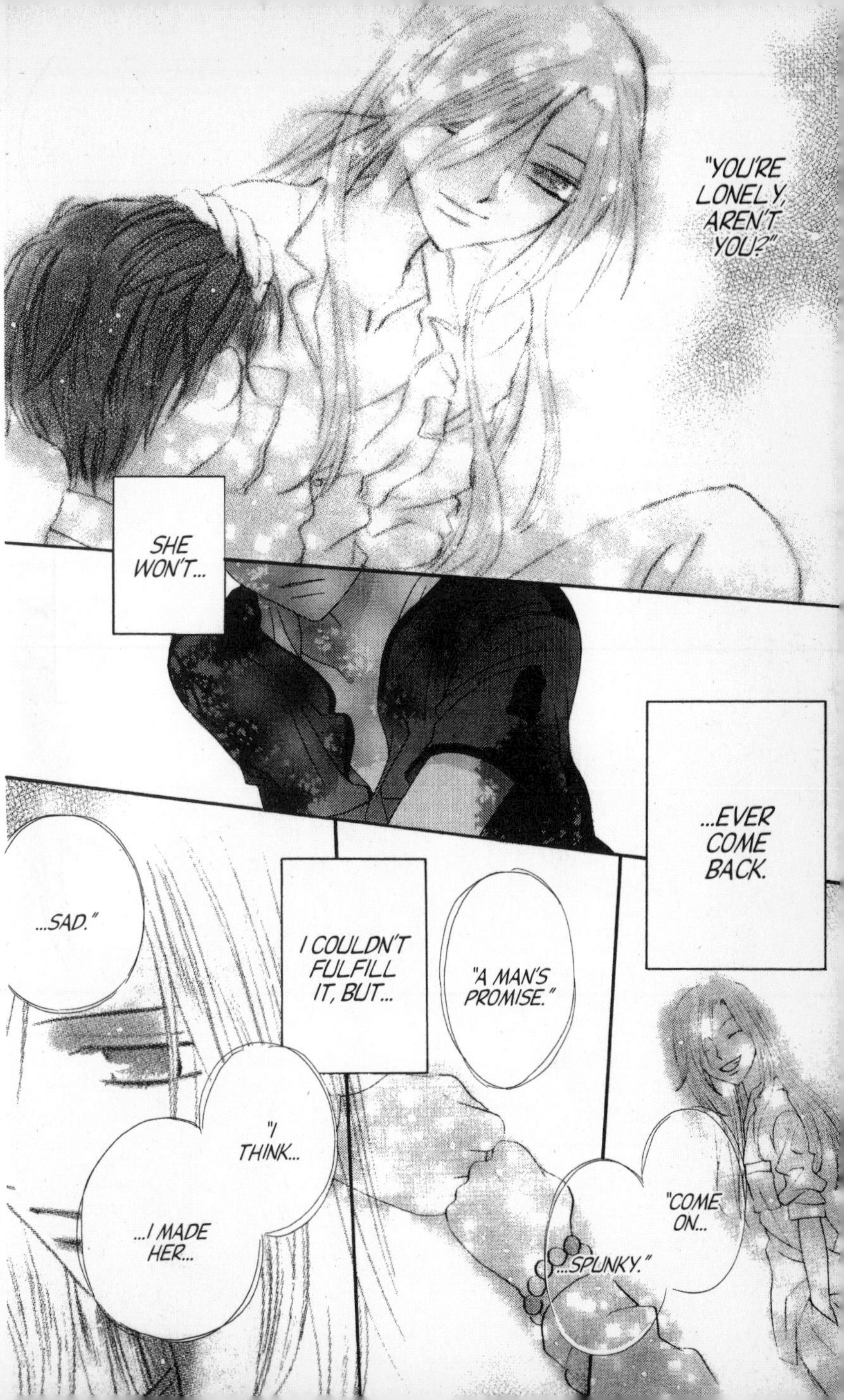
"YOU'RE LONELY, AREN'T YOU?"
SHE WON'T...
...EVER COME BACK.
"COME ON...
...SPUNKY."
"A MAN'S PROMISE."
I COULDN'T FULFILL IT, BUT...
"I THINK...
...I MADE HER...
...SAD."

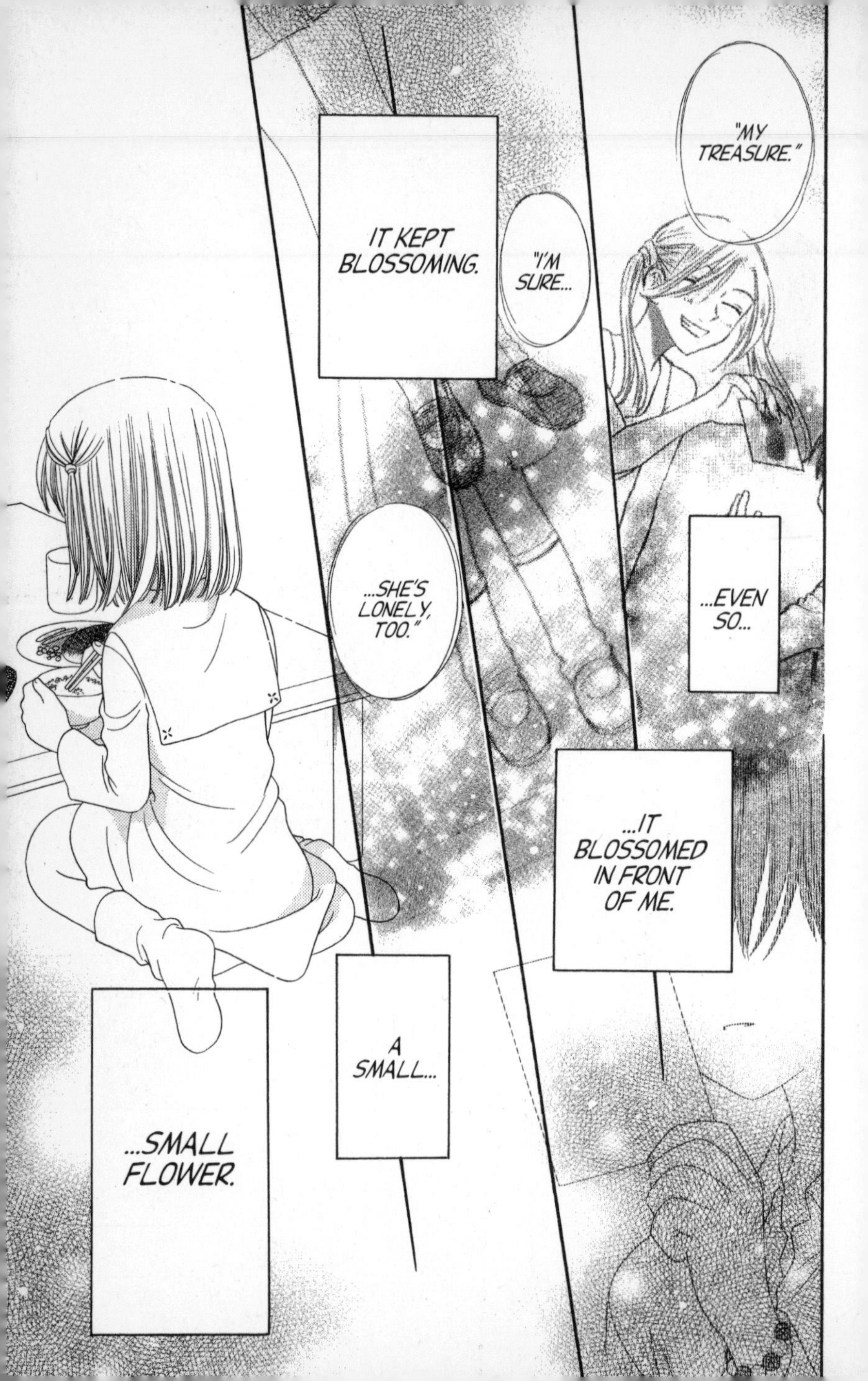
"MY TREASURE."
...EVEN SO...
...IT BLOSSOMED IN FRONT OF ME.
"I'M SURE...
IT KEPT BLOSSOMING.
...SHE'S LONELY, TOO."
A SMALL...
...SMALL FLOWER.

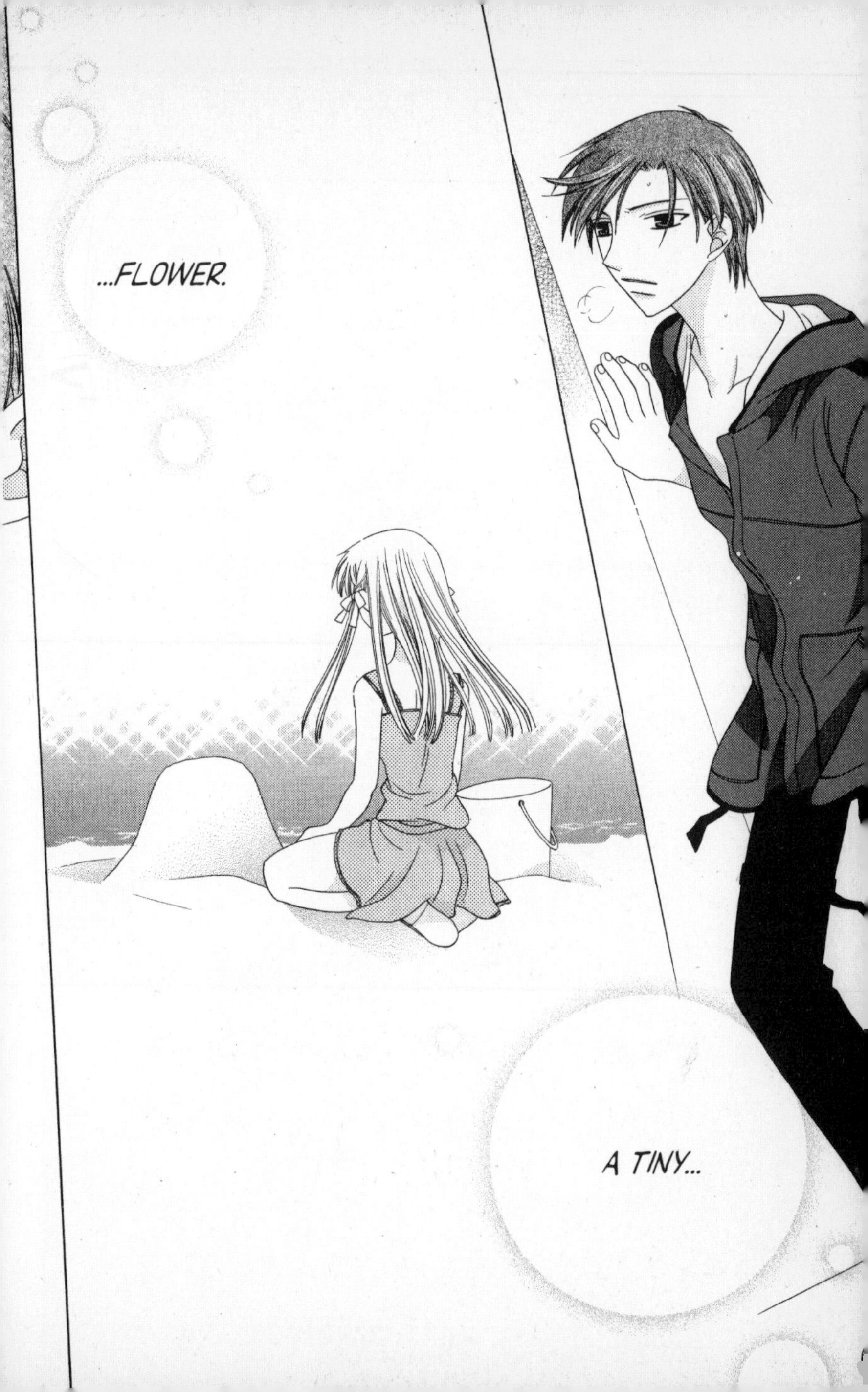
A TINY...
...FLOWER.

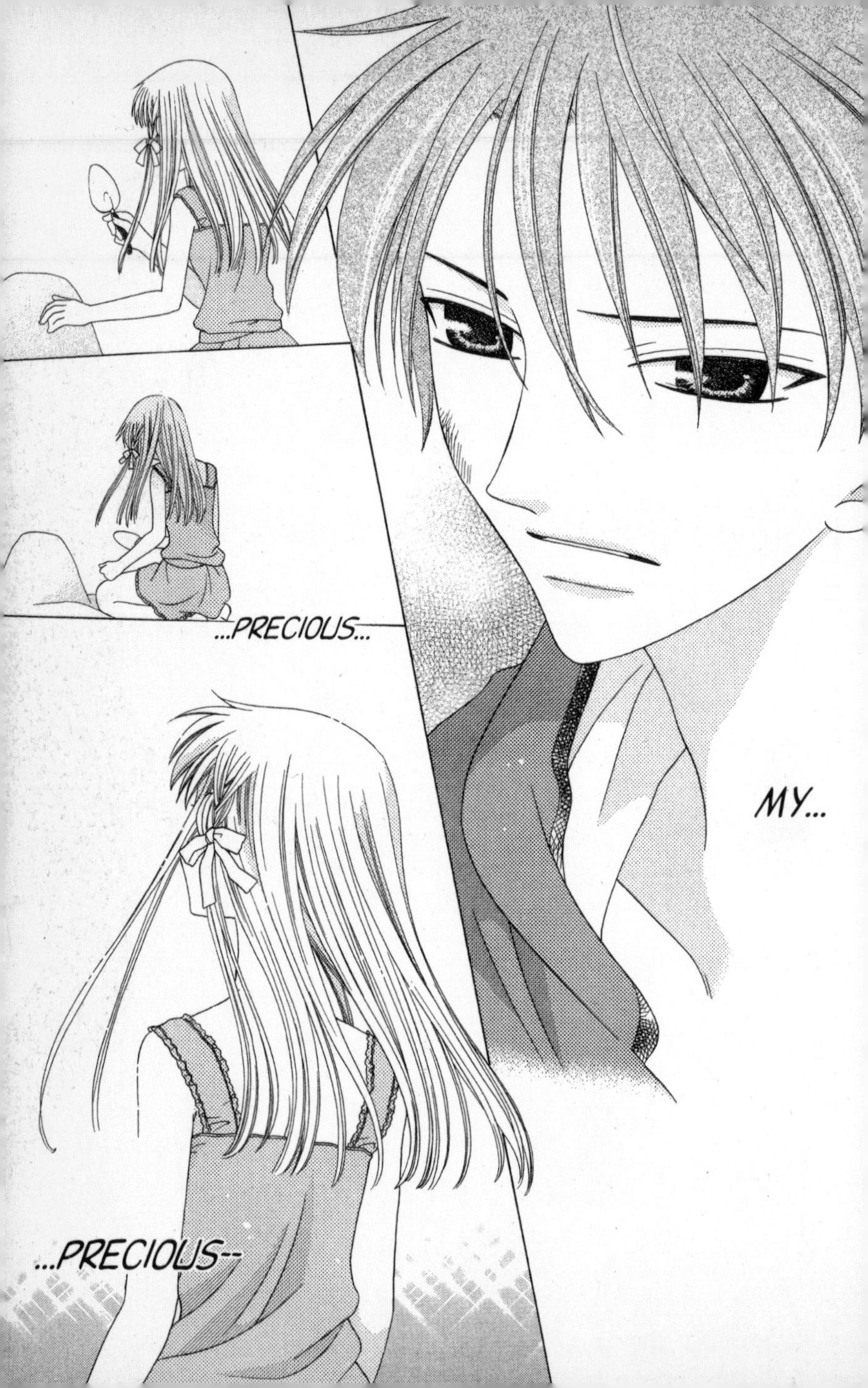
MY...
...PRECIOUS...
...PRECIOUS--

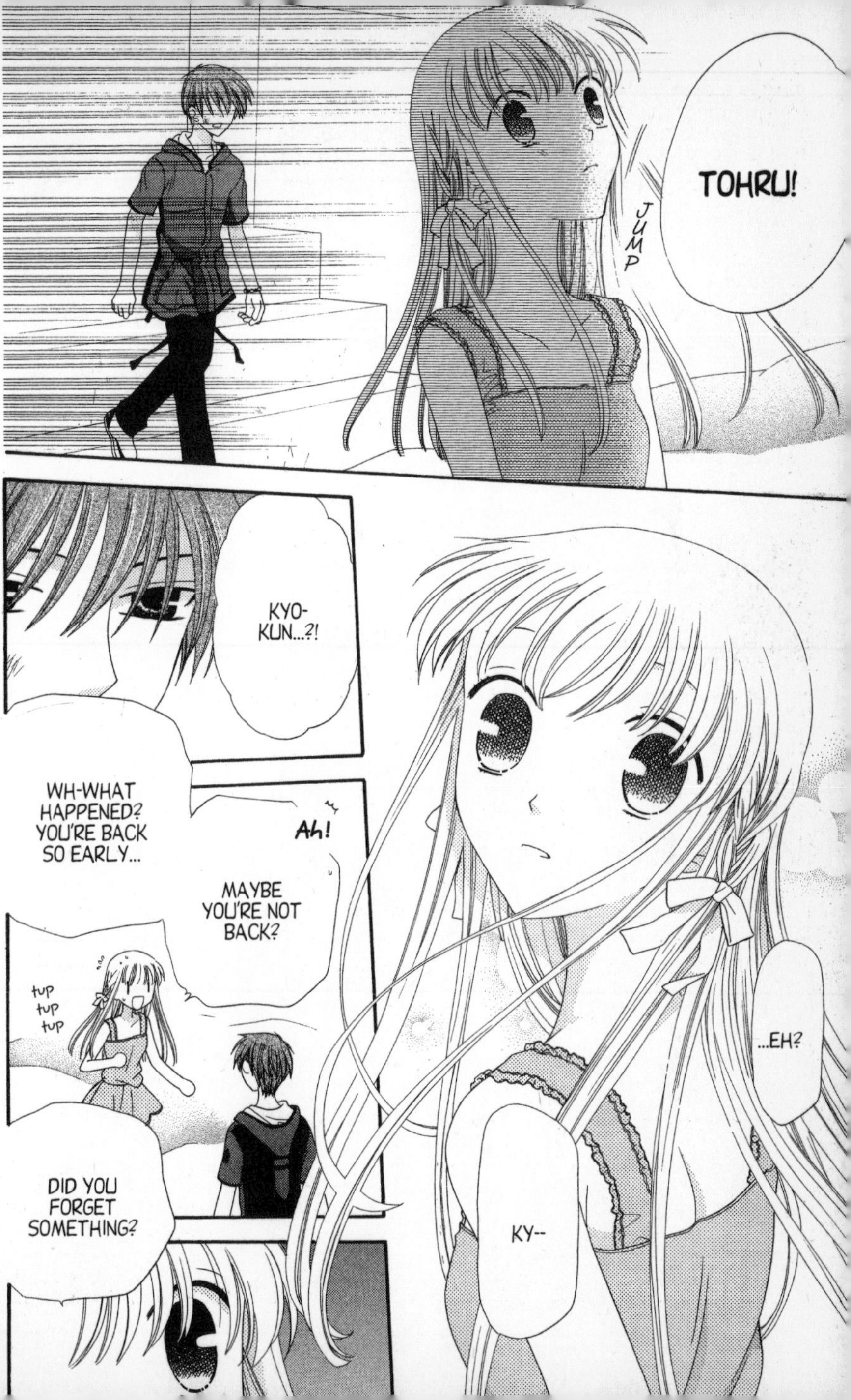
TOHRU!
JUMP
...EH?
KY--
KYO-KUN...?!
WH-WHAT HAPPENED? YOU'RE BACK SO EARLY...
Ah!
MAYBE YOU'RE NOT BACK?
tup tup tup
DID YOU FORGET SOMETHING?

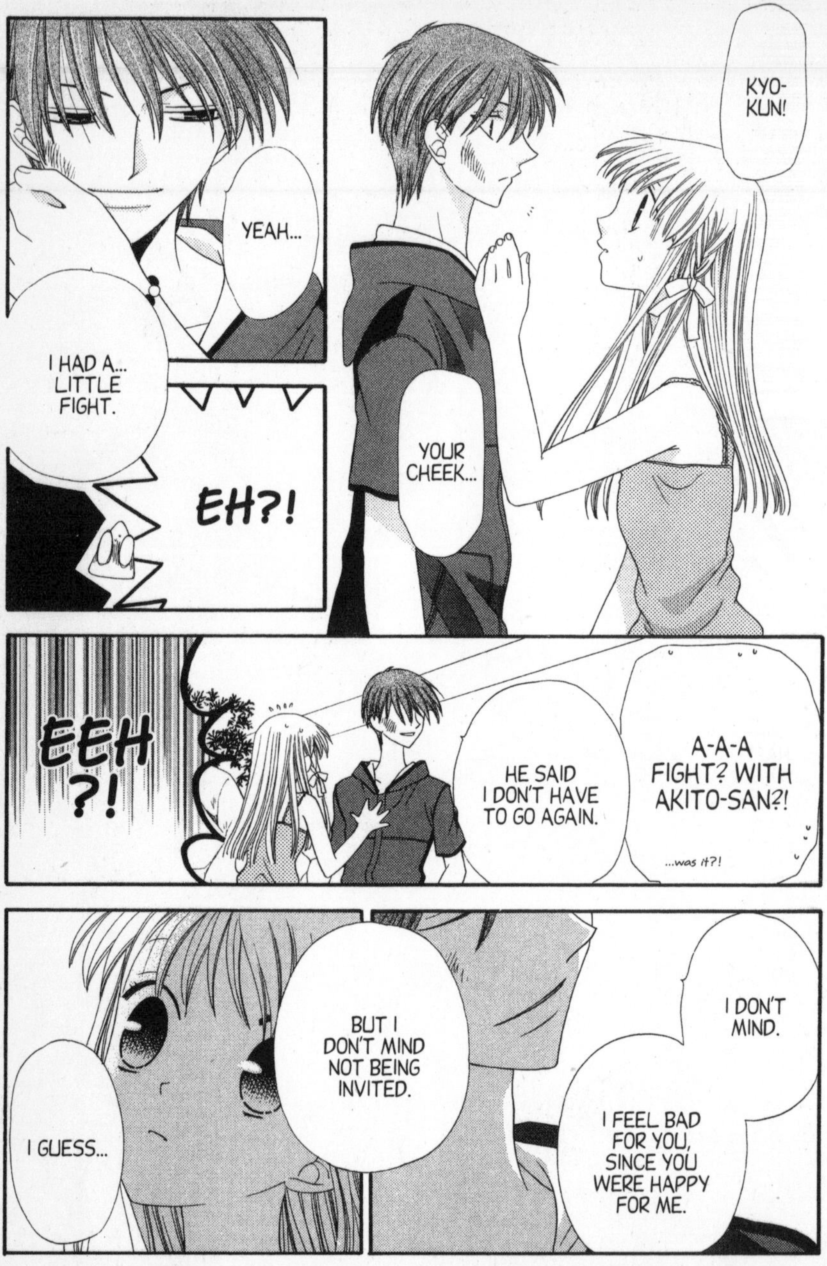
KYO-KUN!
YOUR CHEEK...
YEAH...
I HAD A... LITTLE FIGHT.
EH?!
A-A-A FIGHT? WITH AKITO-SAN?!
...was it?!
HE SAID I DON'T HAVE TO GO AGAIN.
EEH ?!
I DON'T MIND.
I FEEL BAD FOR YOU, SINCE YOU WERE HAPPY FOR ME.
BUT I DON'T MIND NOT BEING INVITED.
I GUESS...

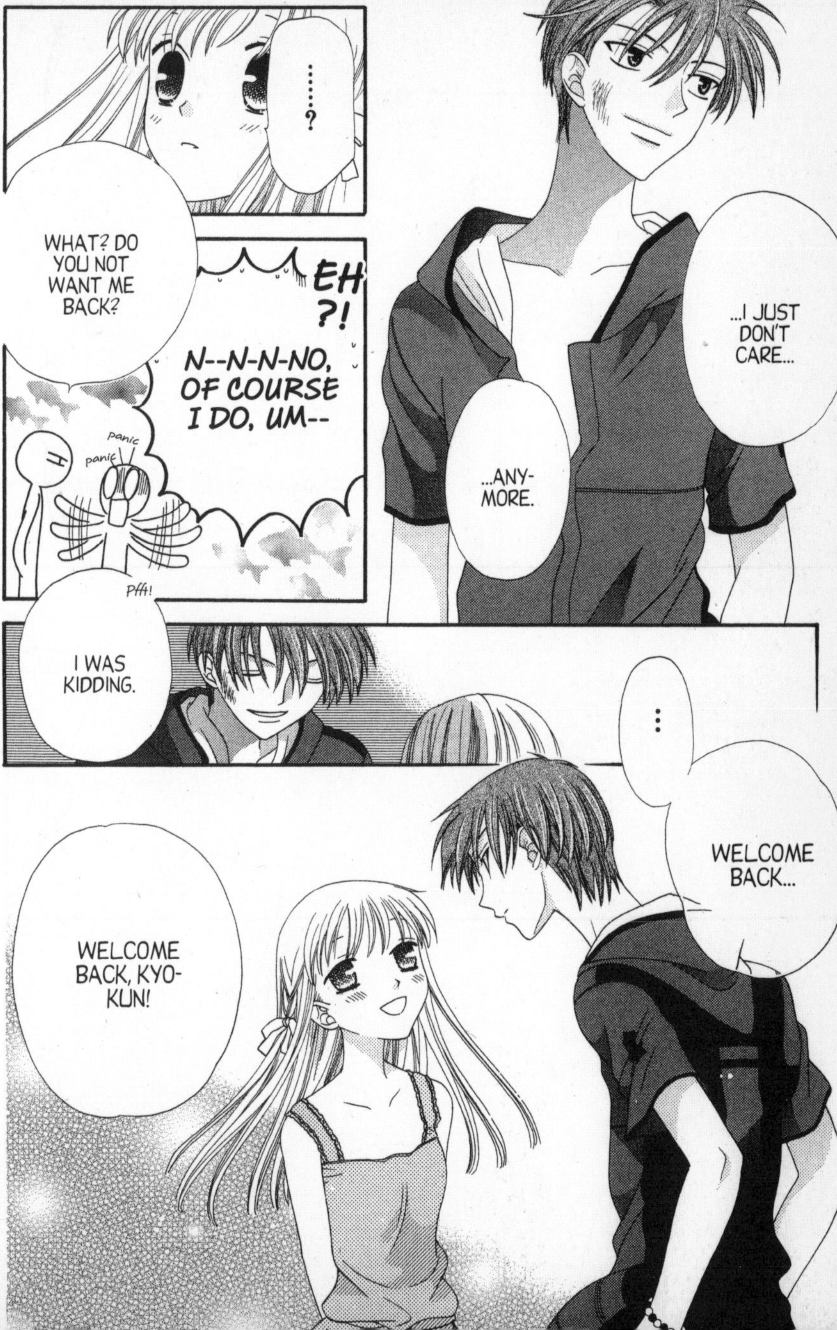
...I JUST DON'T CARE...
...ANY-MORE.
......?
WHAT? DO YOU NOT WANT ME BACK?
EH?!
N--N-N-NO, OF COURSE I DO, UM--
panic
panic
Pfft!
I WAS KIDDING.
...
WELCOME BACK...
WELCOME BACK, KYO-KUN!

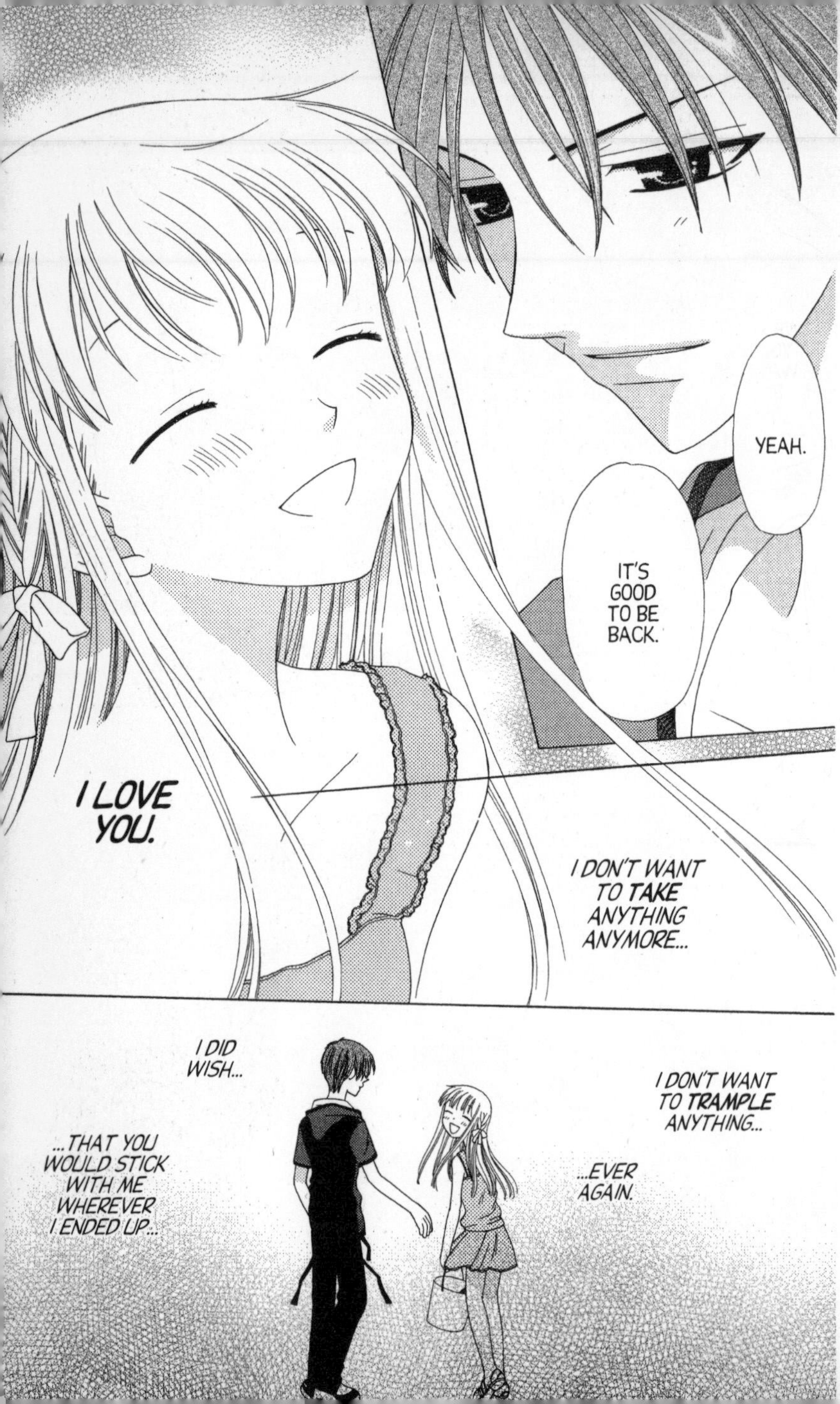
YEAH.
IT'S GOOD TO BE BACK.
I LOVE YOU.
I DON'T WANT TO TAKE ANYTHING ANYMORE...
I DON'T WANT TO TRAMPLE ANYTHING...
...EVER AGAIN.
I DID WISH...
...THAT YOU WOULD STICK WITH ME WHEREVER I ENDED UP...

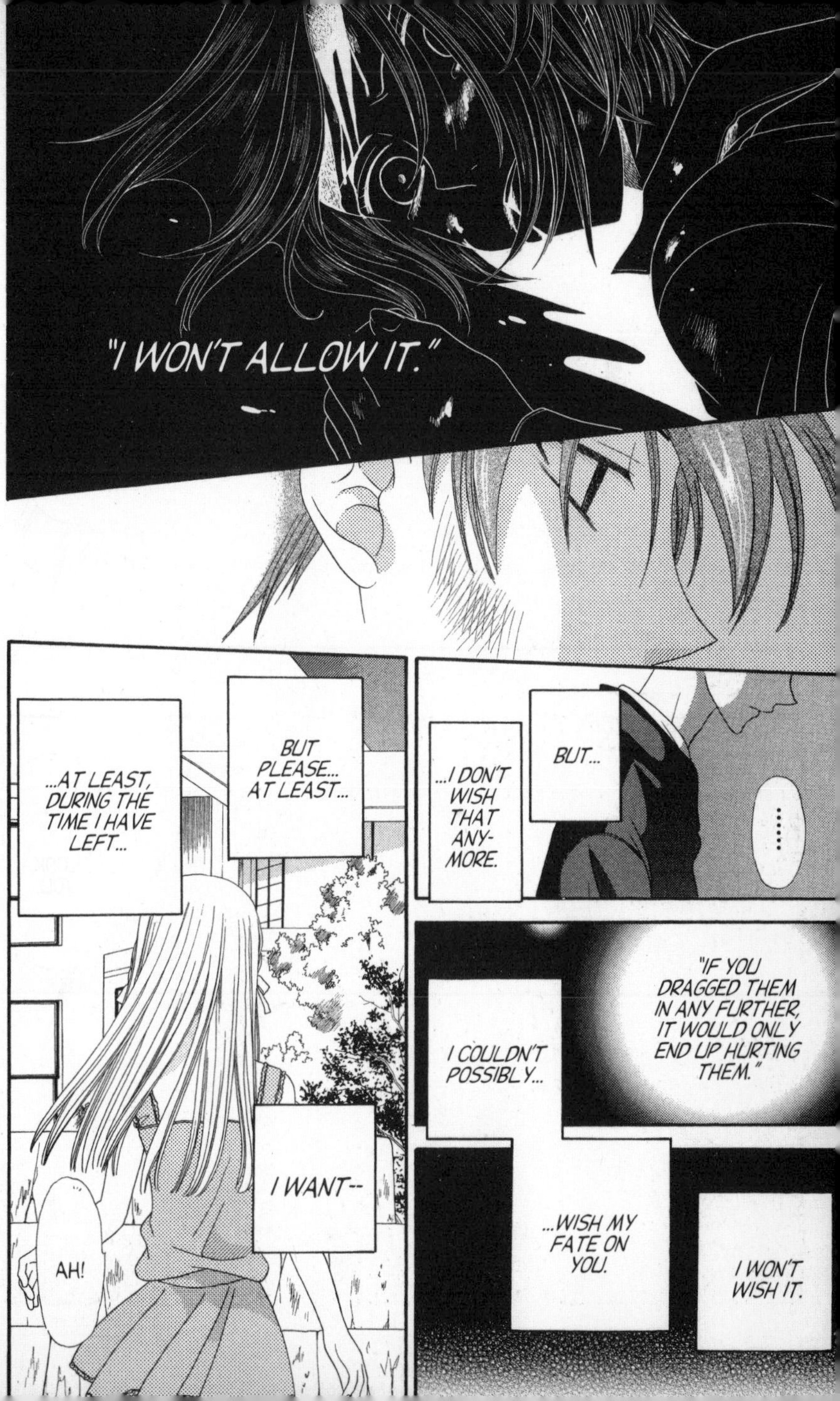

"I WON'T ALLOW IT."
......
BUT...
...I DON'T WISH THAT ANY-MORE.
"IF YOU DRAGGED THEM IN ANY FURTHER, IT WOULD ONLY END UP HURTING THEM."
I COULDN'T POSSIBLY...
...WISH MY FATE ON YOU.
I WON'T WISH IT.
BUT PLEASE... AT LEAST...
...AT LEAST, DURING THE TIME I HAVE LEFT...
I WANT--
AH!

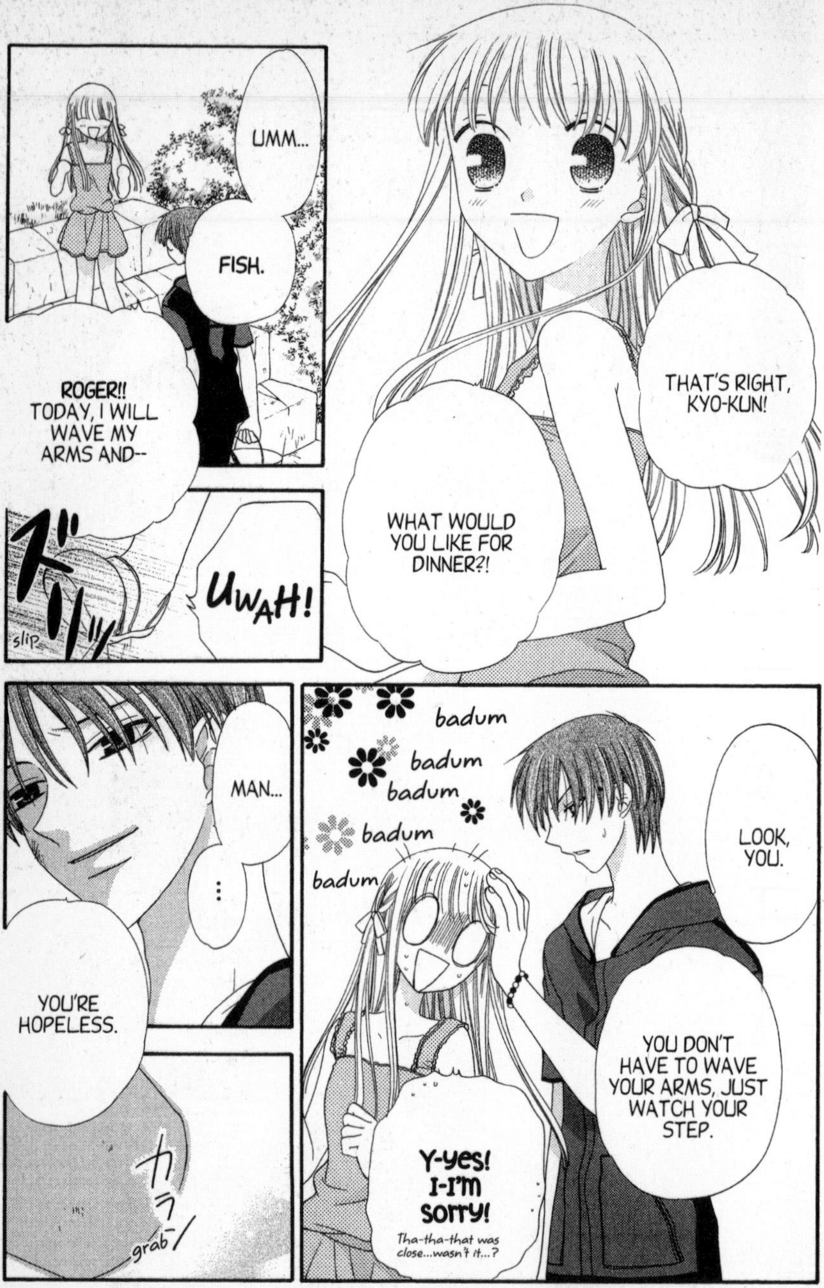
THAT'S RIGHT, KYO-KUN!
WHAT WOULD YOU LIKE FOR DINNER?!
UMM...
FISH.
ROGER!! TODAY, I WILL WAVE MY ARMS AND--
ズリッ
slip
UWAH!
badum
badum
badum
badum
badum
LOOK, YOU.
YOU DON'T HAVE TO WAVE YOUR ARMS, JUST WATCH YOUR STEP.
Y-YES! I-I'M SORRY!
Tha-tha-that was close...wasn't it...?
MAN...
...
YOU'RE HOPELESS.
grab

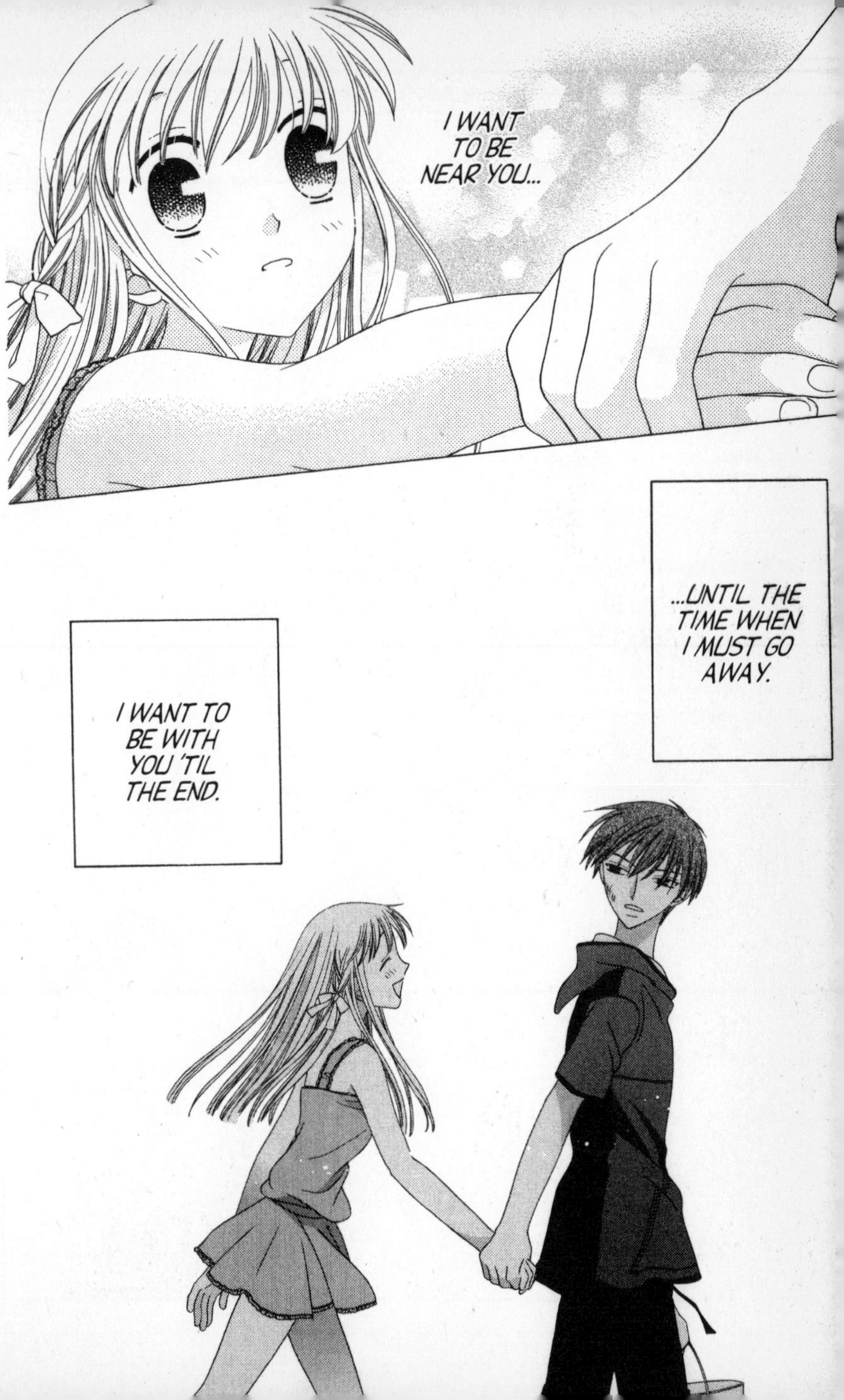
I WANT TO BE NEAR YOU...
...UNTIL THE TIME WHEN I MUST GO AWAY.
I WANT TO BE WITH YOU 'TIL THE END.

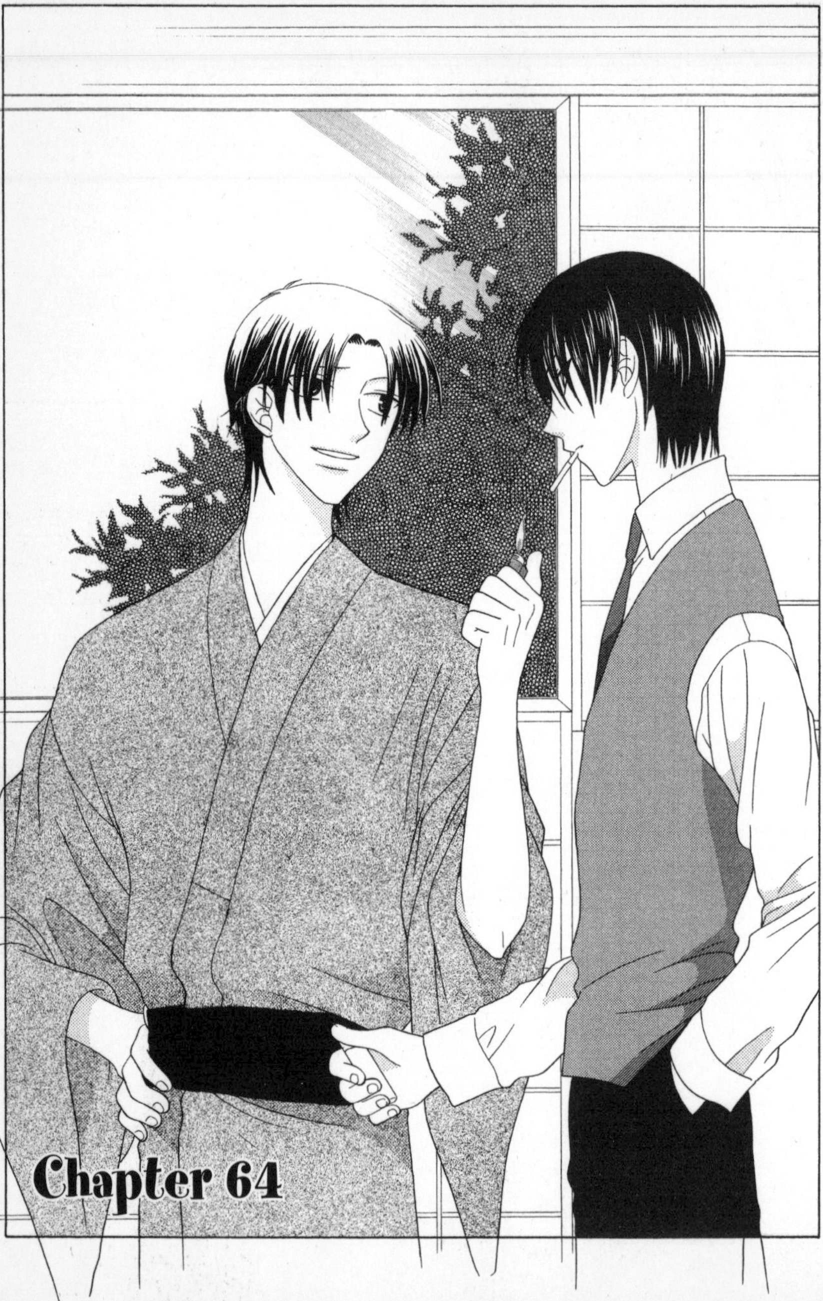
Chapter 64

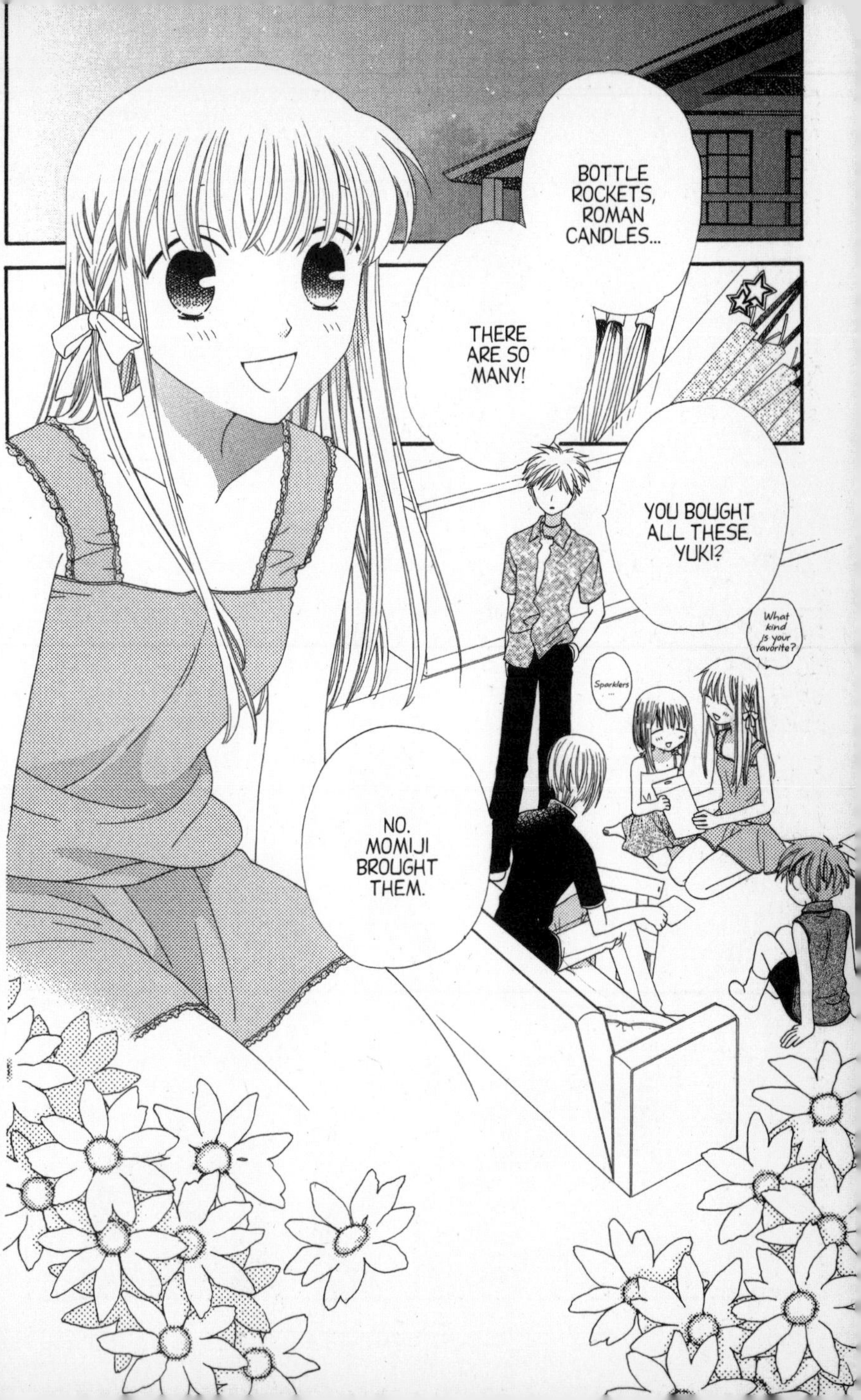
BOTTLE ROCKETS, ROMAN CANDLES...
THERE ARE SO MANY!
YOU BOUGHT ALL THESE, YUKI?
NO. MOMIJI BROUGHT THEM.
What kind is your favorite?
Sparklers ...

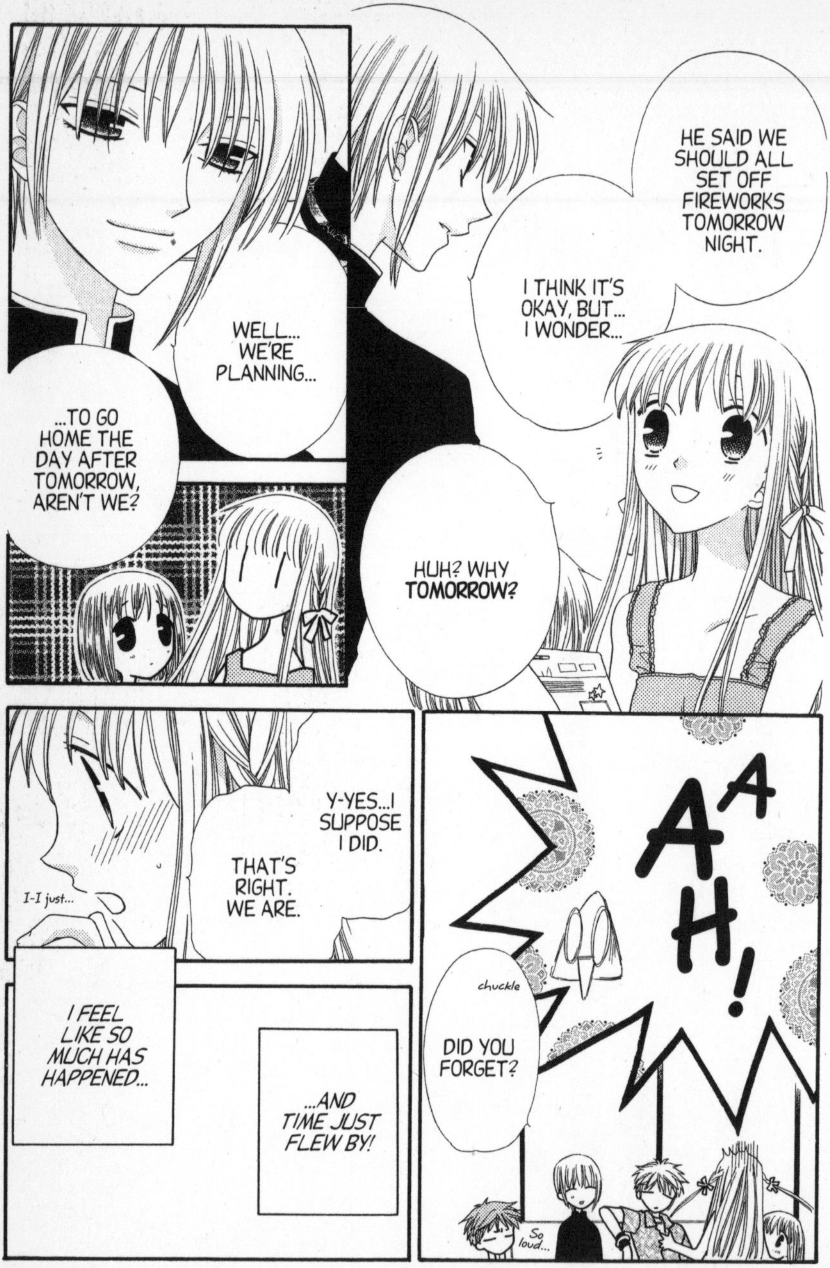

HE SAID WE SHOULD ALL SET OFF FIREWORKS TOMORROW NIGHT.
I THINK IT'S OKAY, BUT... I WONDER...
HUH? WHY TOMORROW?
WELL... WE'RE PLANNING...
...TO GO HOME THE DAY AFTER TOMORROW, AREN'T WE?
AAAH!
chuckle
DID YOU FORGET?
So loud...
Y-YES...I SUPPOSE I DID.
THAT'S RIGHT. WE ARE.
I-I just...
I FEEL LIKE SO MUCH HAS HAPPENED...
...AND TIME JUST FLEW BY!

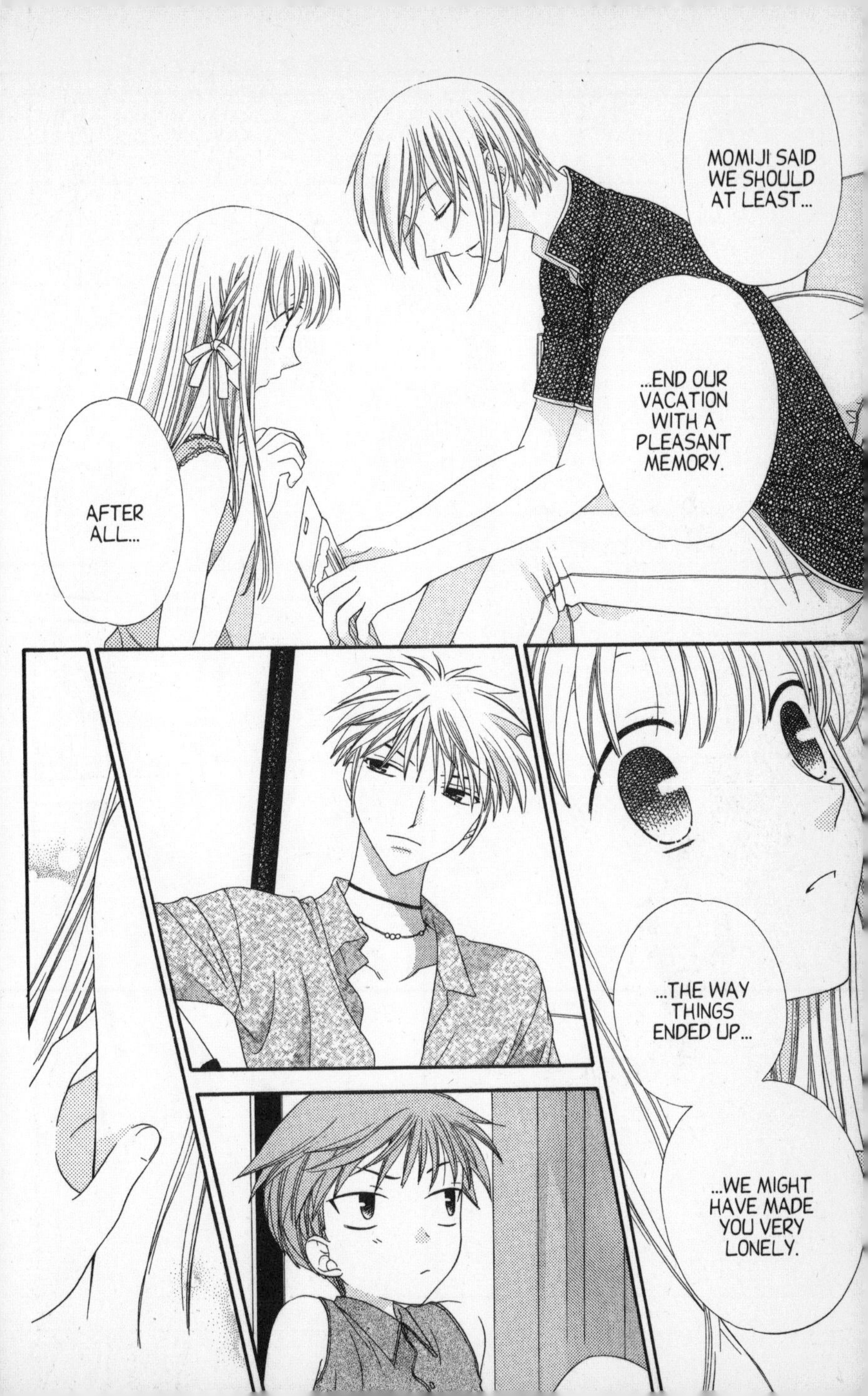
MOMIJI SAID WE SHOULD AT LEAST...
...END OUR VACATION WITH A PLEASANT MEMORY.
AFTER ALL...
...THE WAY THINGS ENDED UP...
...WE MIGHT HAVE MADE YOU VERY LONELY.

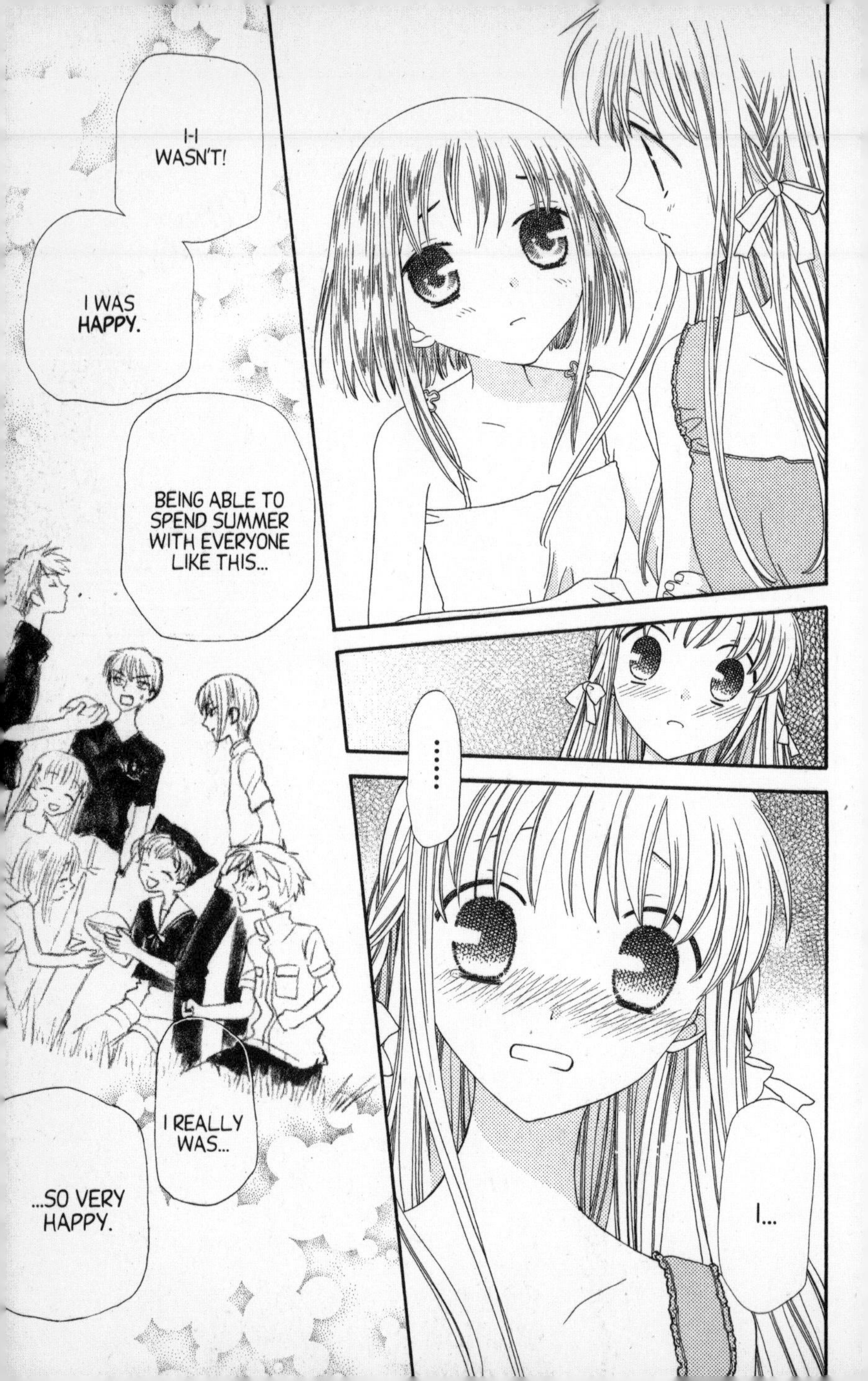
......
I...
I-I WASN'T!
I WAS HAPPY.
BEING ABLE TO SPEND SUMMER WITH EVERYONE LIKE THIS...
I REALLY WAS...
...SO VERY HAPPY.

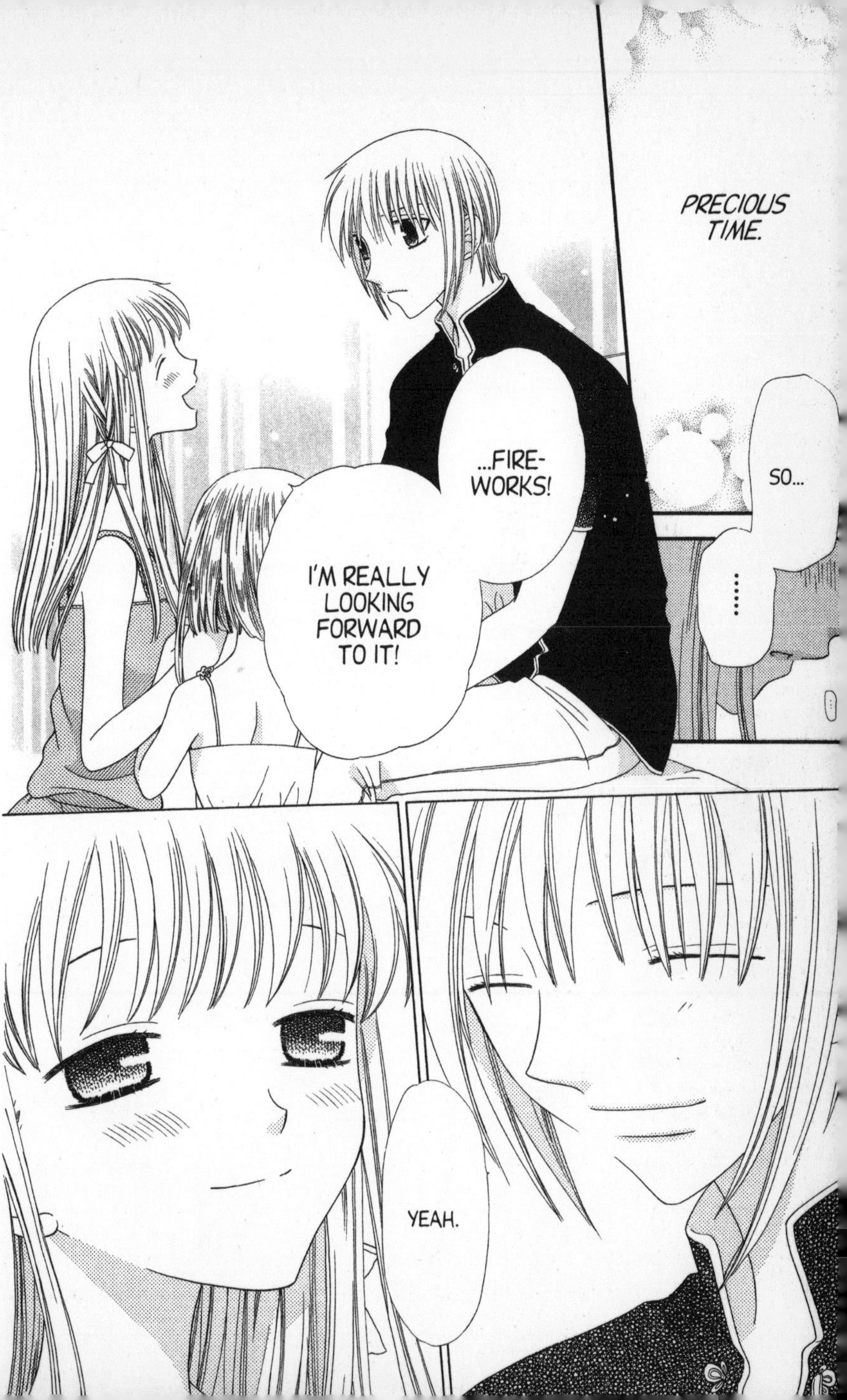
PRECIOUS TIME.
SO...
......
...FIRE-WORKS!
I'M REALLY LOOKING FORWARD TO IT!
YEAH.

Shishou

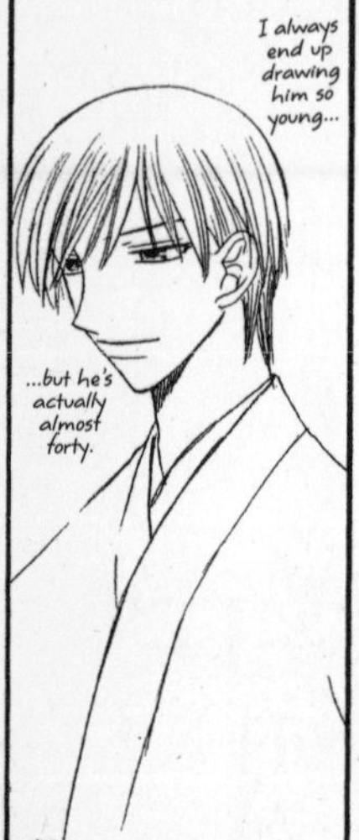
I always end up drawing him so young...
...but he's actually almost forty.

There was a woman he was going out with, but they disagreed on so much that they had to break up. His head is so full with thoughts of his "son" that it seems he's content. Even though they're not close blood relatives, he became Kyo's father because he felt he should, or something. His over-fondness for his child may not surpass Kyoko's, but it's at least on par with hers. Oh, and he's clumsy with his hands and has no sense of flavor.

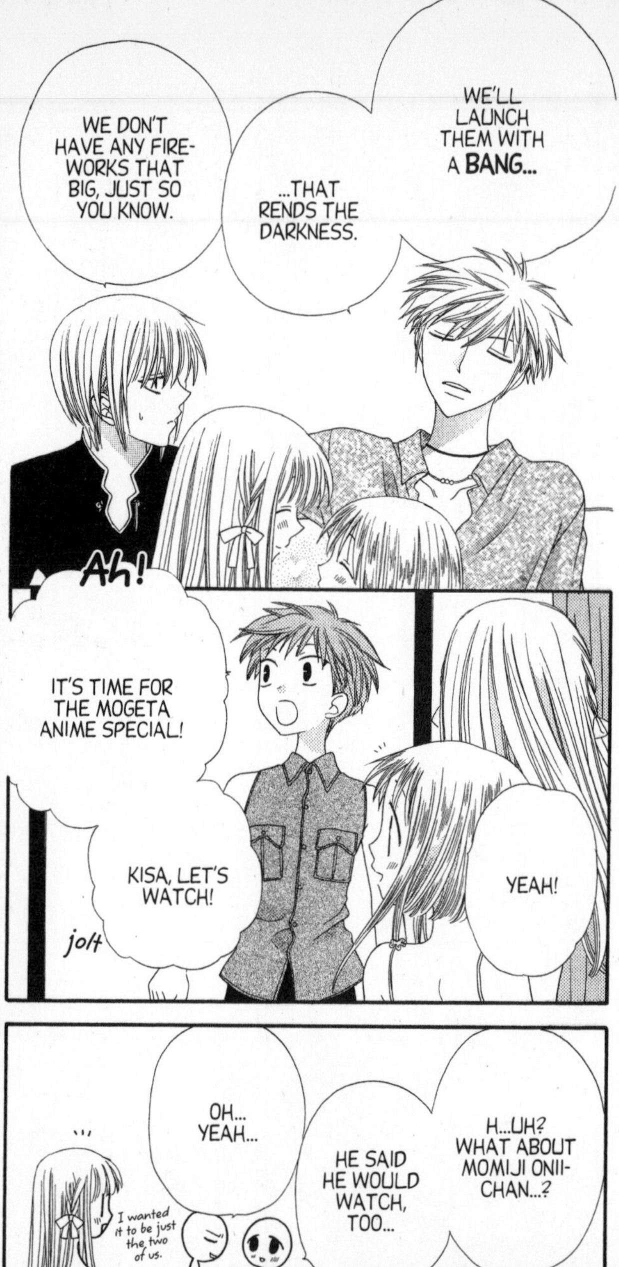
WE'LL LAUNCH THEM WITH A BANG...
...THAT RENDS THE DARKNESS.
WE DON'T HAVE ANY FIRE-WORKS THAT BIG, JUST SO YOU KNOW.
Ah!
IT'S TIME FOR THE MOGETA ANIME SPECIAL!
KISA, LET'S WATCH!
jolt
YEAH!
H...UH? WHAT ABOUT MOMIJI ONII-CHAN...?
HE SAID HE WOULD WATCH, TOO...
OH... YEAH...
I wanted it to be just the two of us.

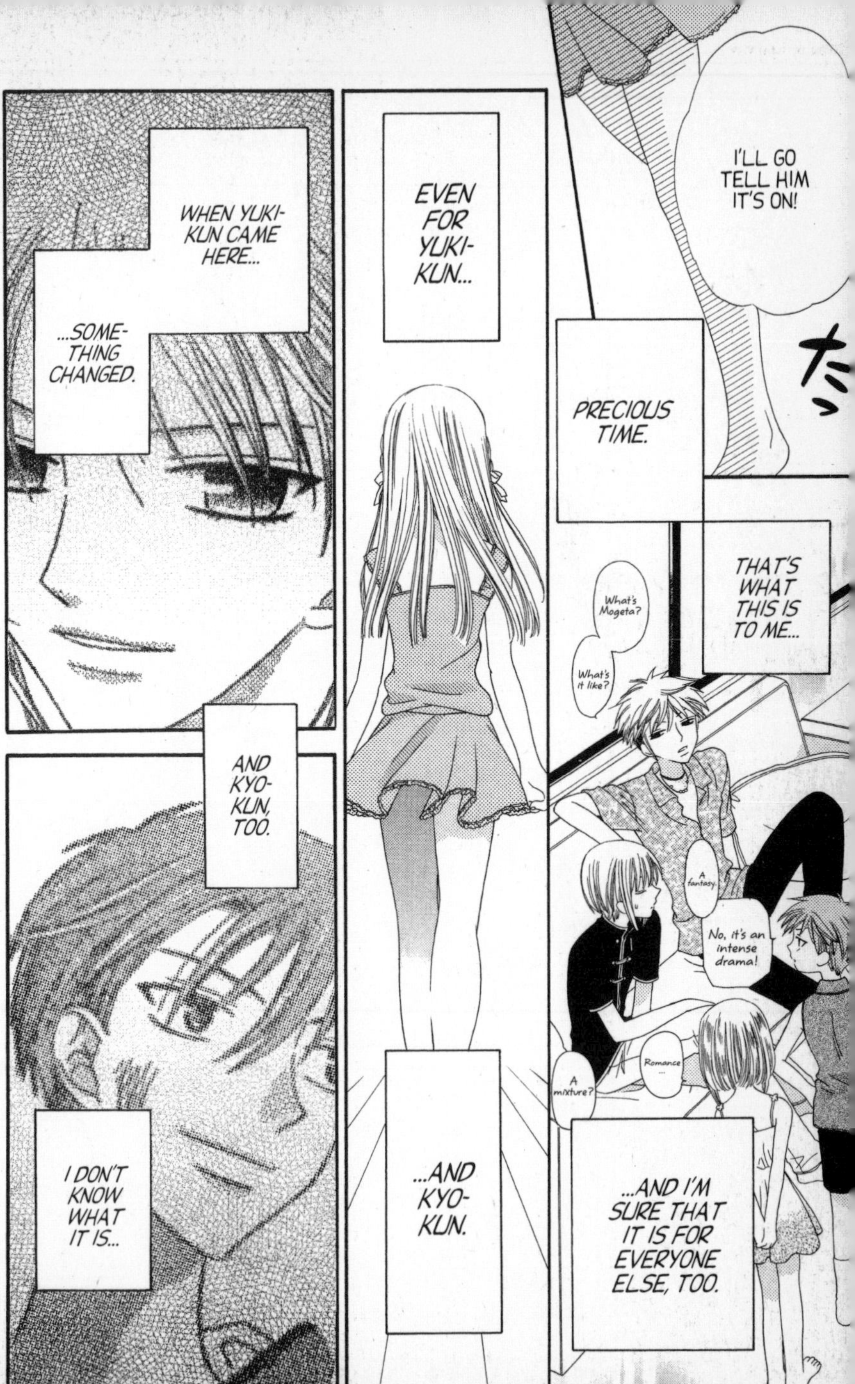
I'LL GO TELL HIM IT'S ON!
たっ
PRECIOUS TIME.
THAT'S WHAT THIS IS TO ME...
What's Mogeta?
What's it like?
A fantasy.
No, it's an intense drama!
Romance...
A mixture?
...AND I'M SURE THAT IT IS FOR EVERYONE ELSE, TOO.
EVEN FOR YUKI-KUN...
...AND KYO-KUN.
WHEN YUKI-KUN CAME HERE...
...SOMETHING CHANGED.
AND KYO-KUN, TOO.
I DON'T KNOW WHAT IT IS...

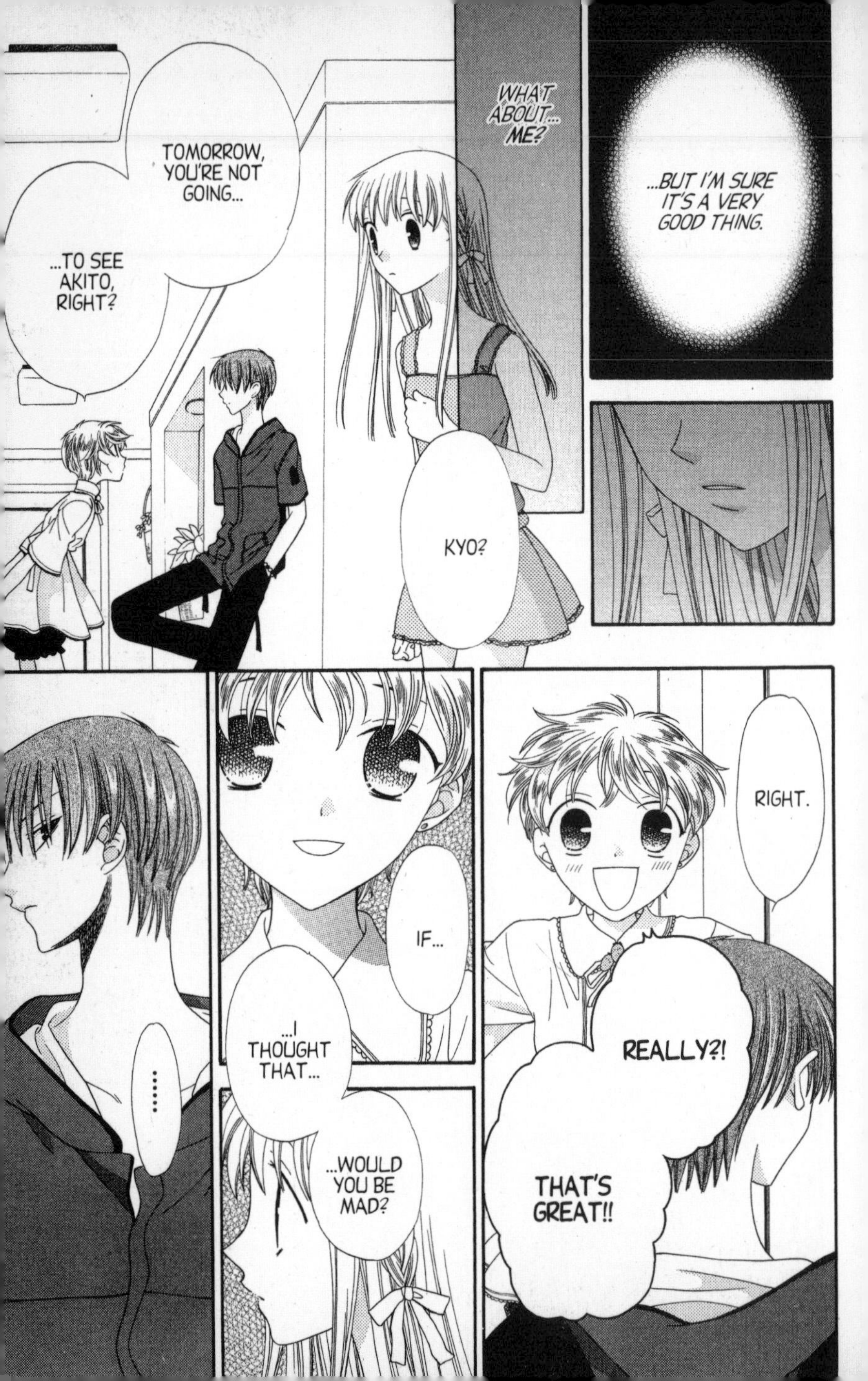
...BUT I'M SURE IT'S A VERY GOOD THING.
WHAT ABOUT... ME?
TOMORROW, YOU'RE NOT GOING...
...TO SEE AKITO, RIGHT?
KYO?
RIGHT.
REALLY?!
THAT'S GREAT!!
IF...
...I THOUGHT THAT...
...WOULD YOU BE MAD?
......

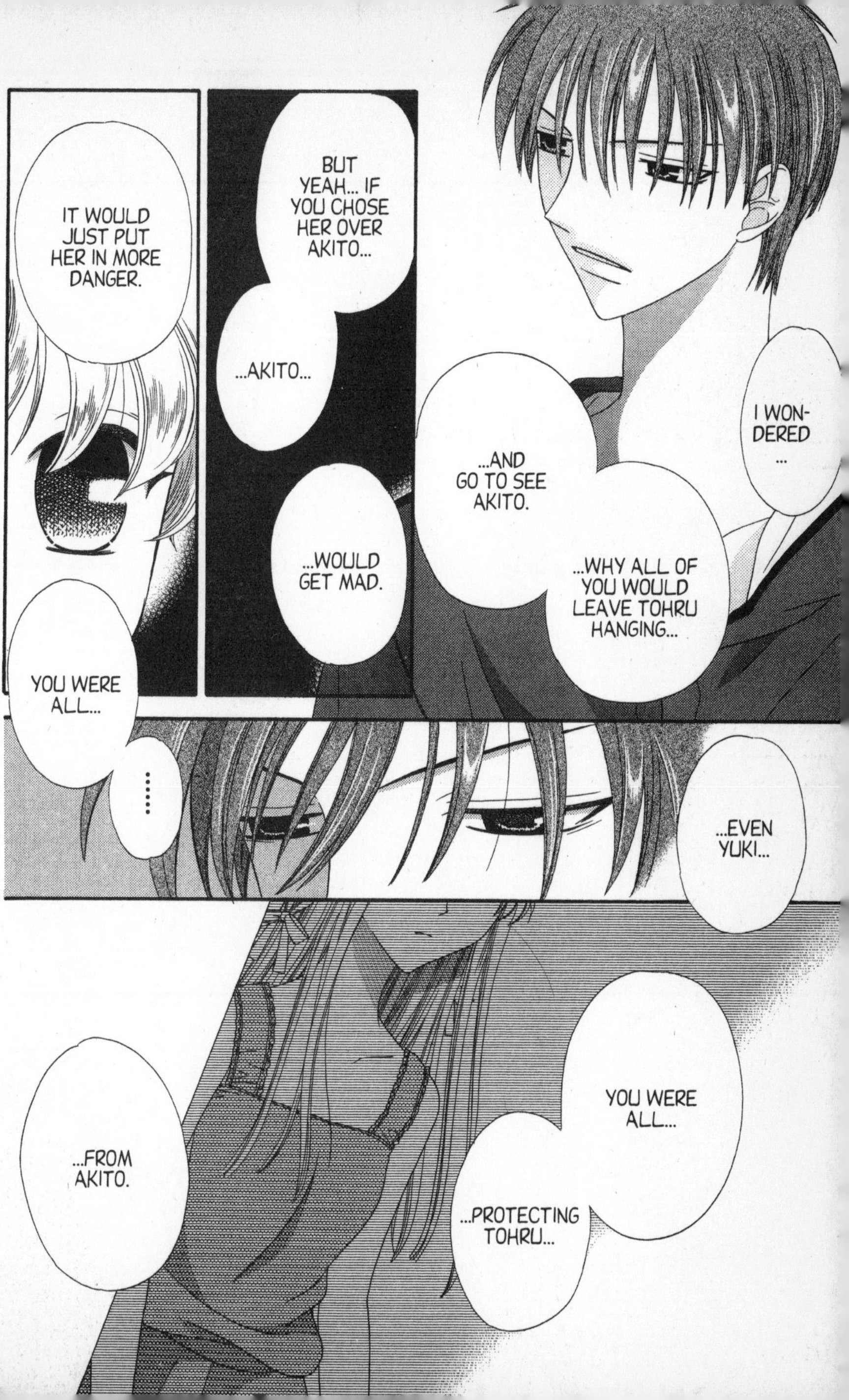
I WONDERED...
...WHY ALL OF YOU WOULD LEAVE TOHRU HANGING...
...AND GO TO SEE AKITO.
BUT YEAH... IF YOU CHOSE HER OVER AKITO...
...AKITO...
...WOULD GET MAD.
IT WOULD JUST PUT HER IN MORE DANGER.
YOU WERE ALL...
......
...EVEN YUKI...
YOU WERE ALL...
...PROTECTING TOHRU...
...FROM AKITO.

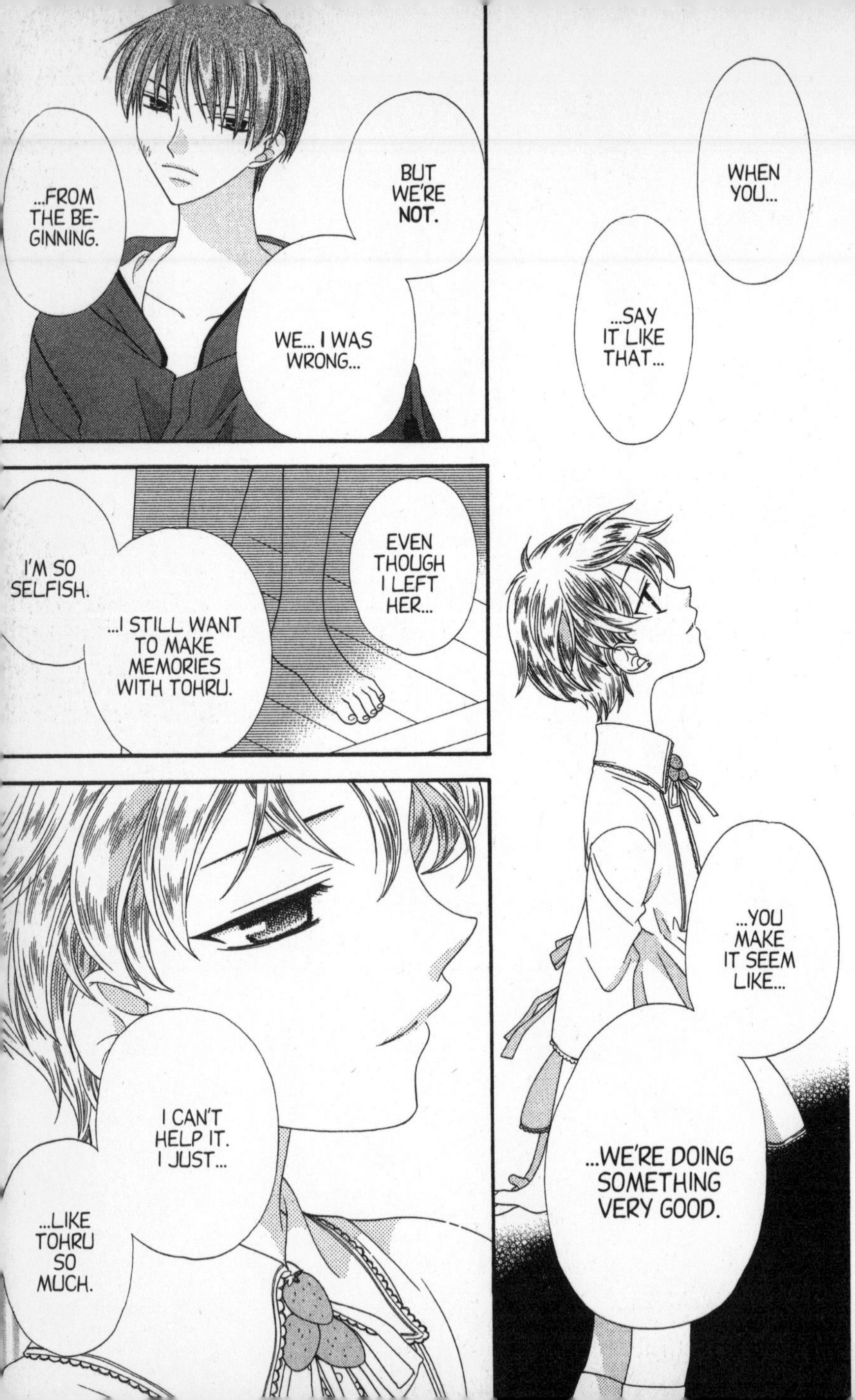
WHEN YOU...
...SAY IT LIKE THAT...
...YOU MAKE IT SEEM LIKE...
...WE'RE DOING SOMETHING VERY GOOD.
BUT WE'RE **NOT.**
...FROM THE BE-GINNING.
WE... I WAS WRONG...
EVEN THOUGH I LEFT HER...
I'M SO SELFISH.
...I STILL WANT TO MAKE MEMORIES WITH TOHRU.
I CAN'T HELP IT. I JUST...
...LIKE TOHRU SO MUCH.

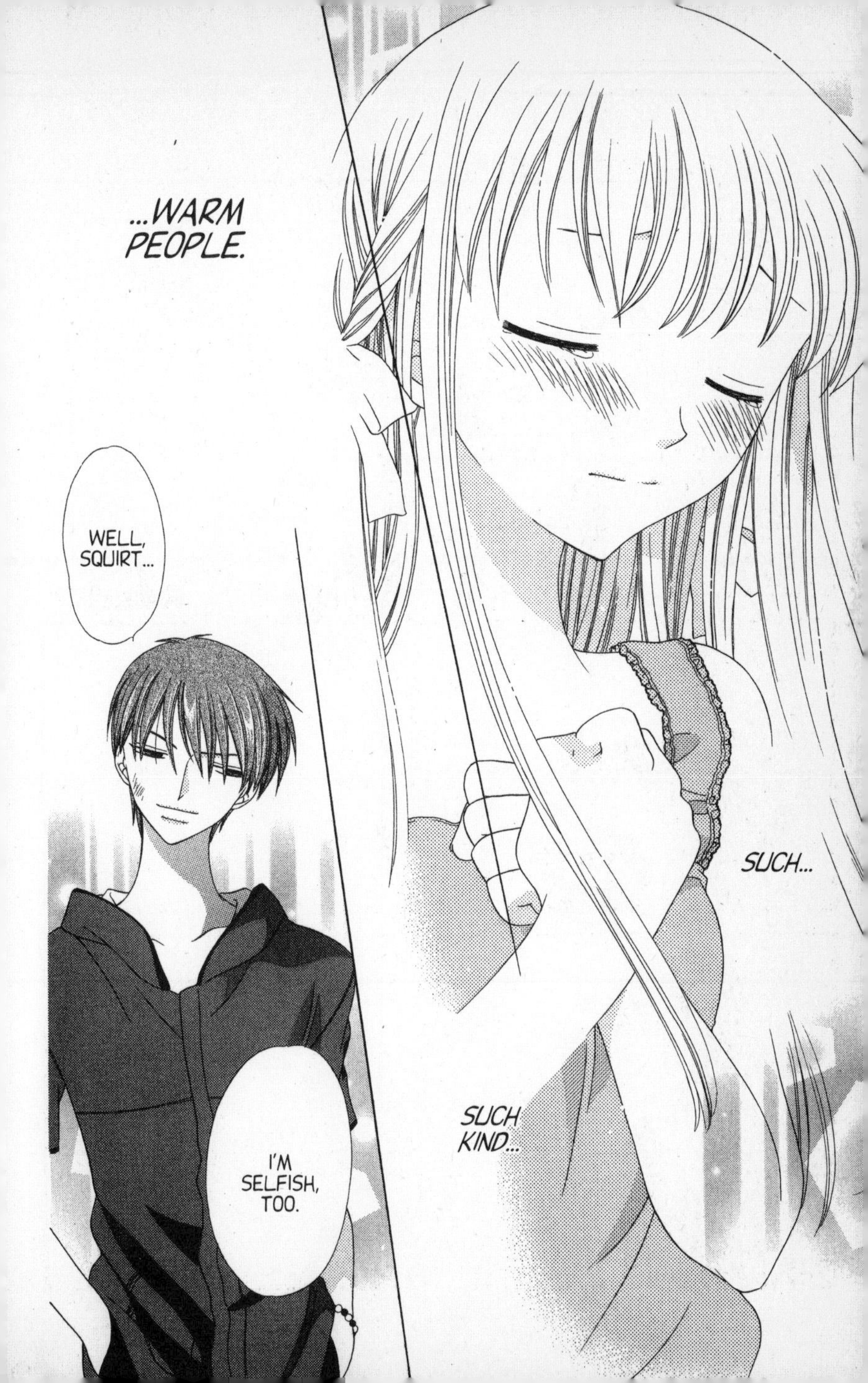
SUCH...
SUCH KIND...
...WARM PEOPLE.
WELL, SQUIRT...
I'M SELFISH, TOO.

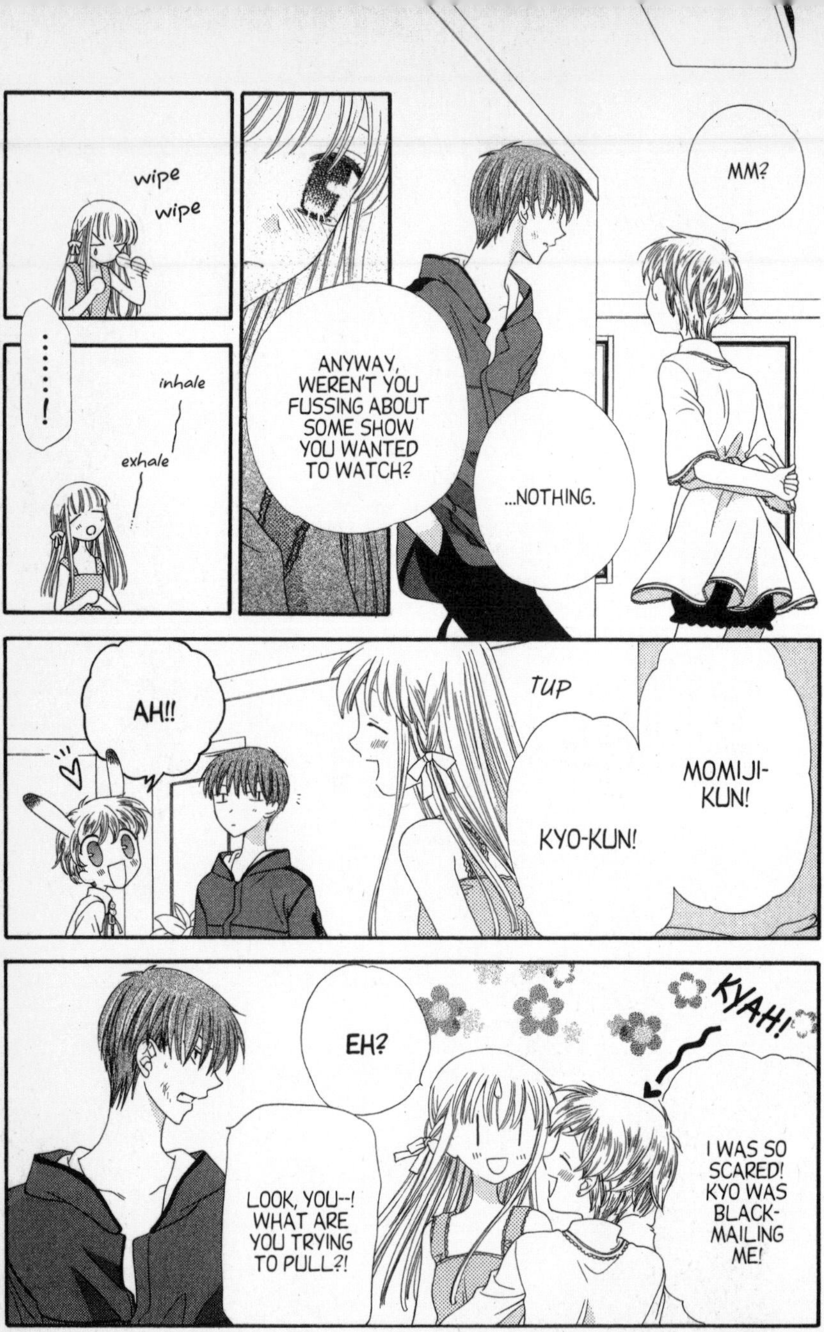

MM?
...NOTHING.
ANYWAY, WEREN'T YOU FUSSING ABOUT SOME SHOW YOU WANTED TO WATCH?
wipe wipe
......!
inhale
exhale
MOMIJI-KUN!
KYO-KUN!
TUP
AH!!
KYAH!
I WAS SO SCARED! KYO WAS BLACK-MAILING ME!
EH?
LOOK, YOU--! WHAT ARE YOU TRYING TO PULL?!

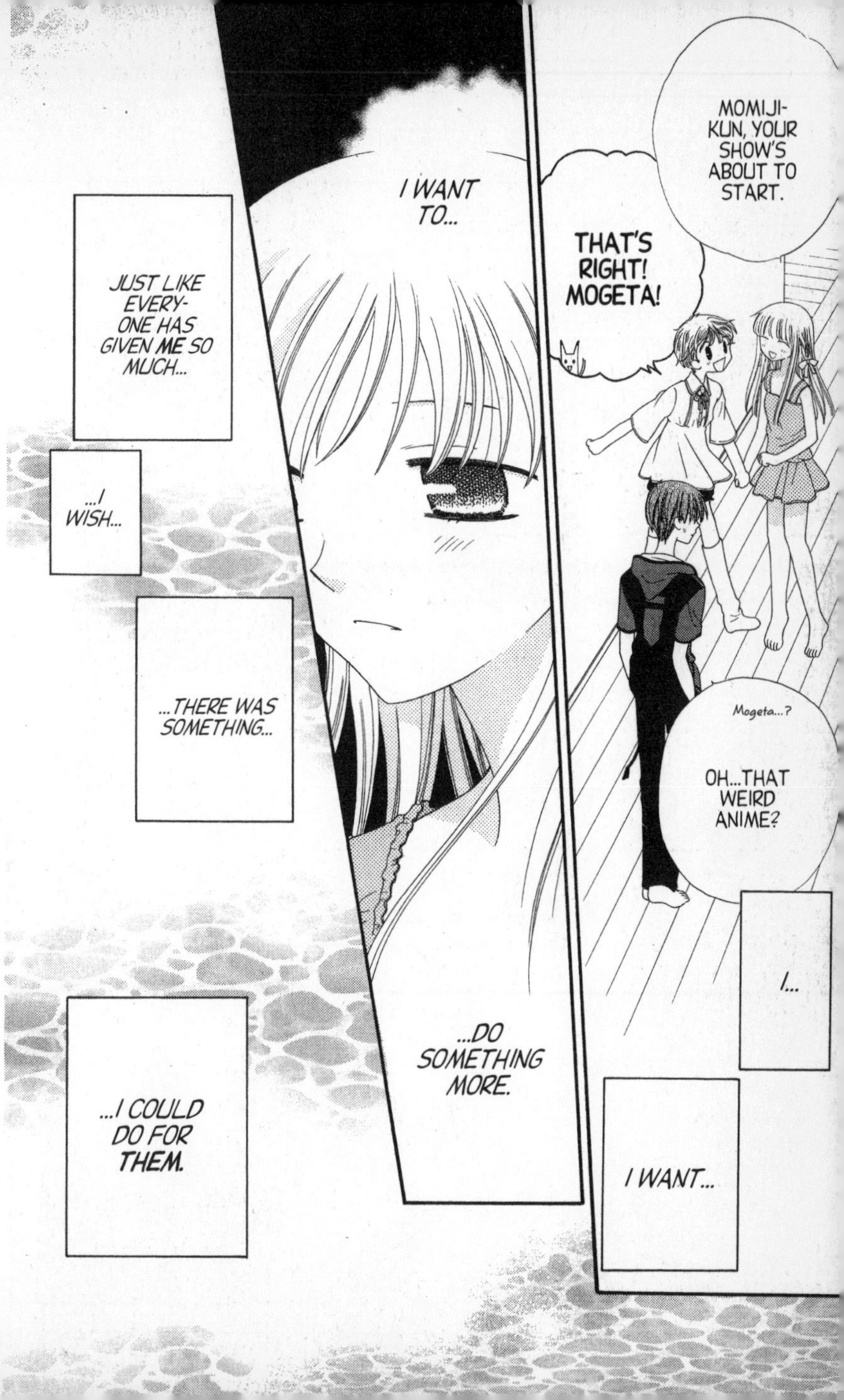
MOMIJI-KUN, YOUR SHOW'S ABOUT TO START.
THAT'S RIGHT! MOGETA!
Mogeta...?
OH...THAT WEIRD ANIME?
I...
I WANT...
I WANT TO...
...DO SOMETHING MORE.
JUST LIKE EVERY-ONE HAS GIVEN ME SO MUCH...
...I WISH...
...THERE WAS SOMETHING...
...I COULD DO FOR THEM.

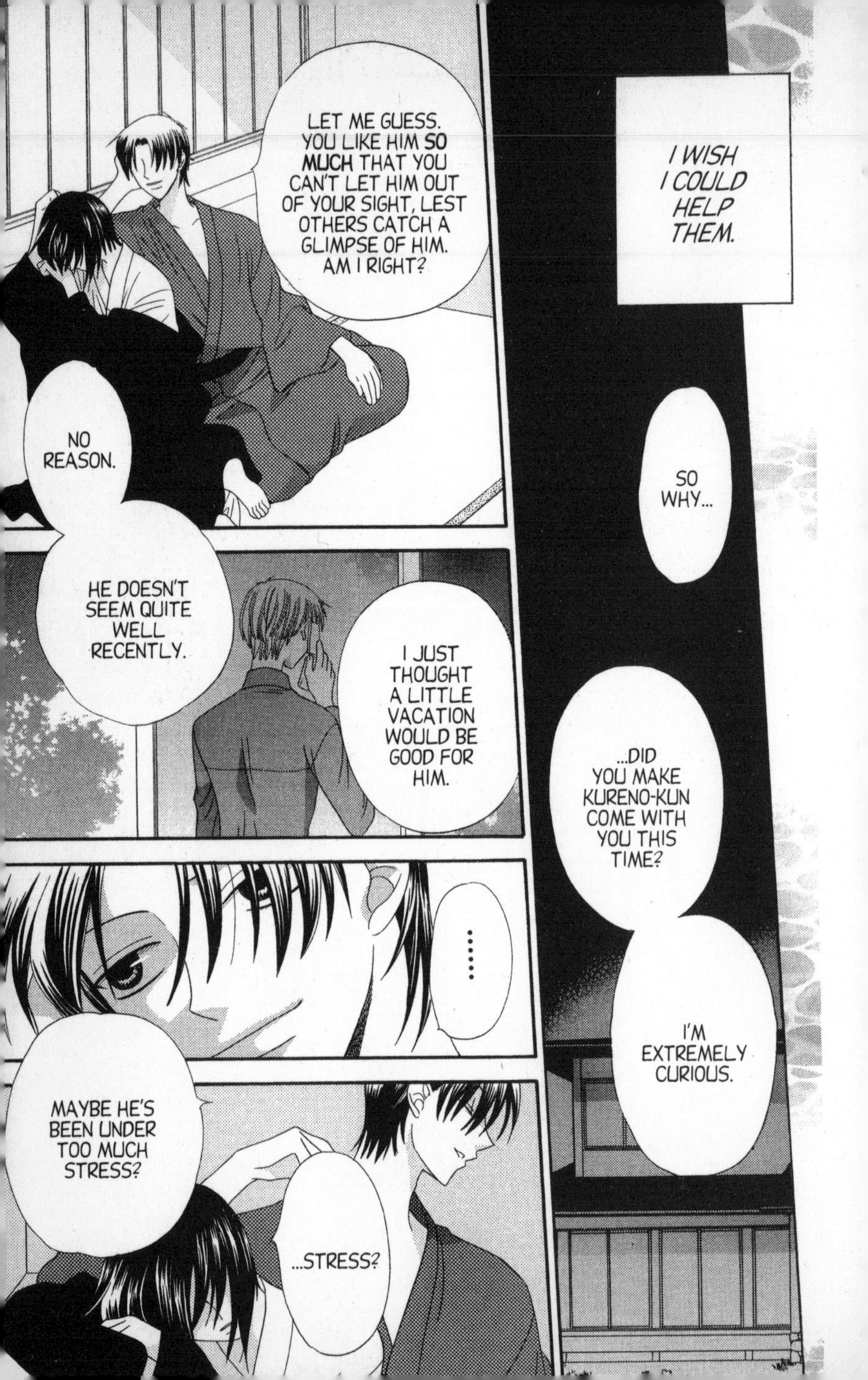
I WISH I COULD HELP THEM.
SO WHY...
...DID YOU MAKE KURENO-KUN COME WITH YOU THIS TIME?
I'M EXTREMELY CURIOUS.
LET ME GUESS. YOU LIKE HIM SO MUCH THAT YOU CAN'T LET HIM OUT OF YOUR SIGHT, LEST OTHERS CATCH A GLIMPSE OF HIM. AM I RIGHT?
NO REASON.
HE DOESN'T SEEM QUITE WELL RECENTLY.
I JUST THOUGHT A LITTLE VACATION WOULD BE GOOD FOR HIM.
......
MAYBE HE'S BEEN UNDER TOO MUCH STRESS?
...STRESS?

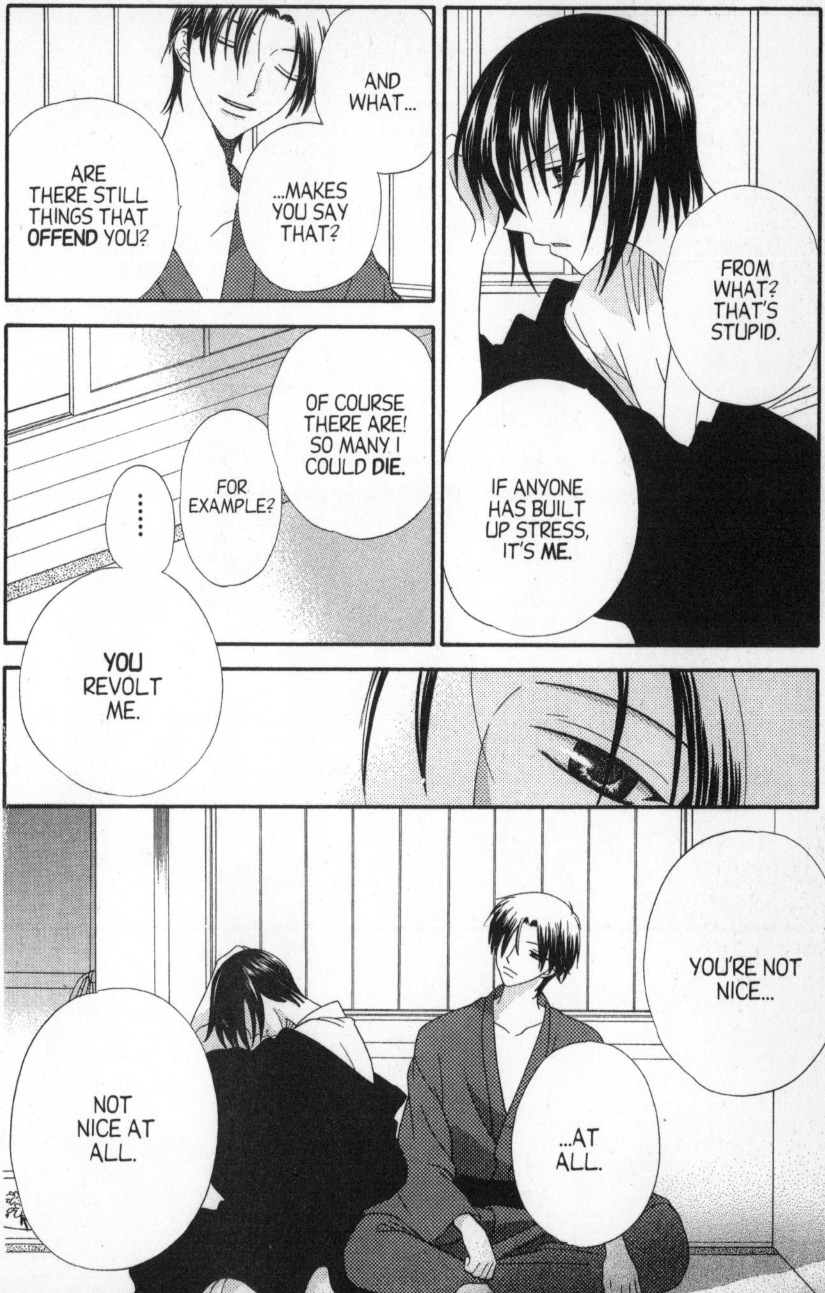
FROM WHAT? THAT'S STUPID.
IF ANYONE HAS BUILT UP STRESS, IT'S ME.
AND WHAT...
...MAKES YOU SAY THAT?
ARE THERE STILL THINGS THAT OFFEND YOU?
OF COURSE THERE ARE! SO MANY I COULD DIE.
FOR EXAMPLE?
......
YOU REVOLT ME.
YOU'RE NOT NICE...
...AT ALL.
NOT NICE AT ALL.

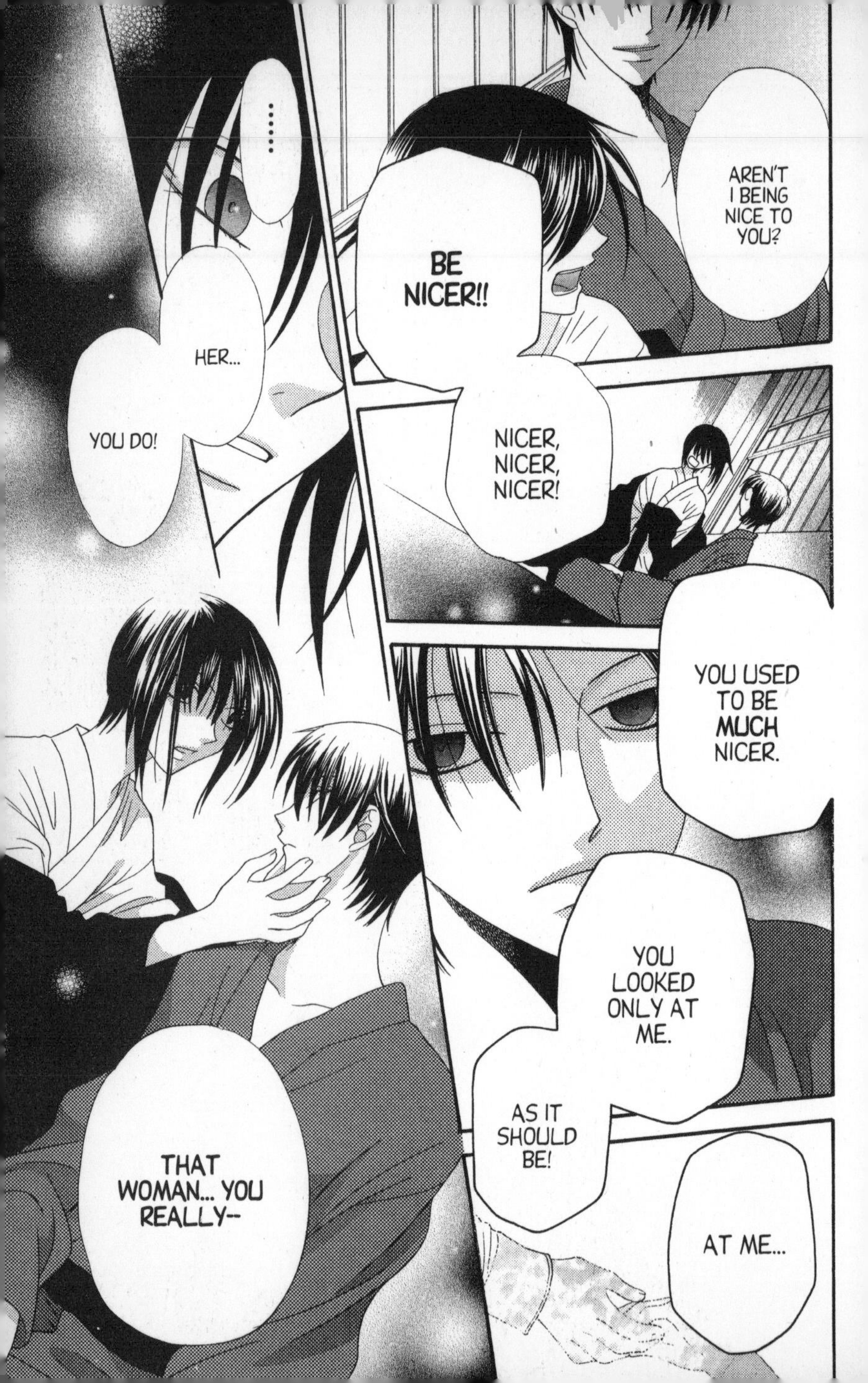
AREN'T I BEING NICE TO YOU?
BE NICER!!
NICER, NICER, NICER!
......
HER...
YOU DO!
YOU USED TO BE MUCH NICER.
YOU LOOKED ONLY AT ME.
AS IT SHOULD BE!
AT ME...
THAT WOMAN... YOU REALLY--

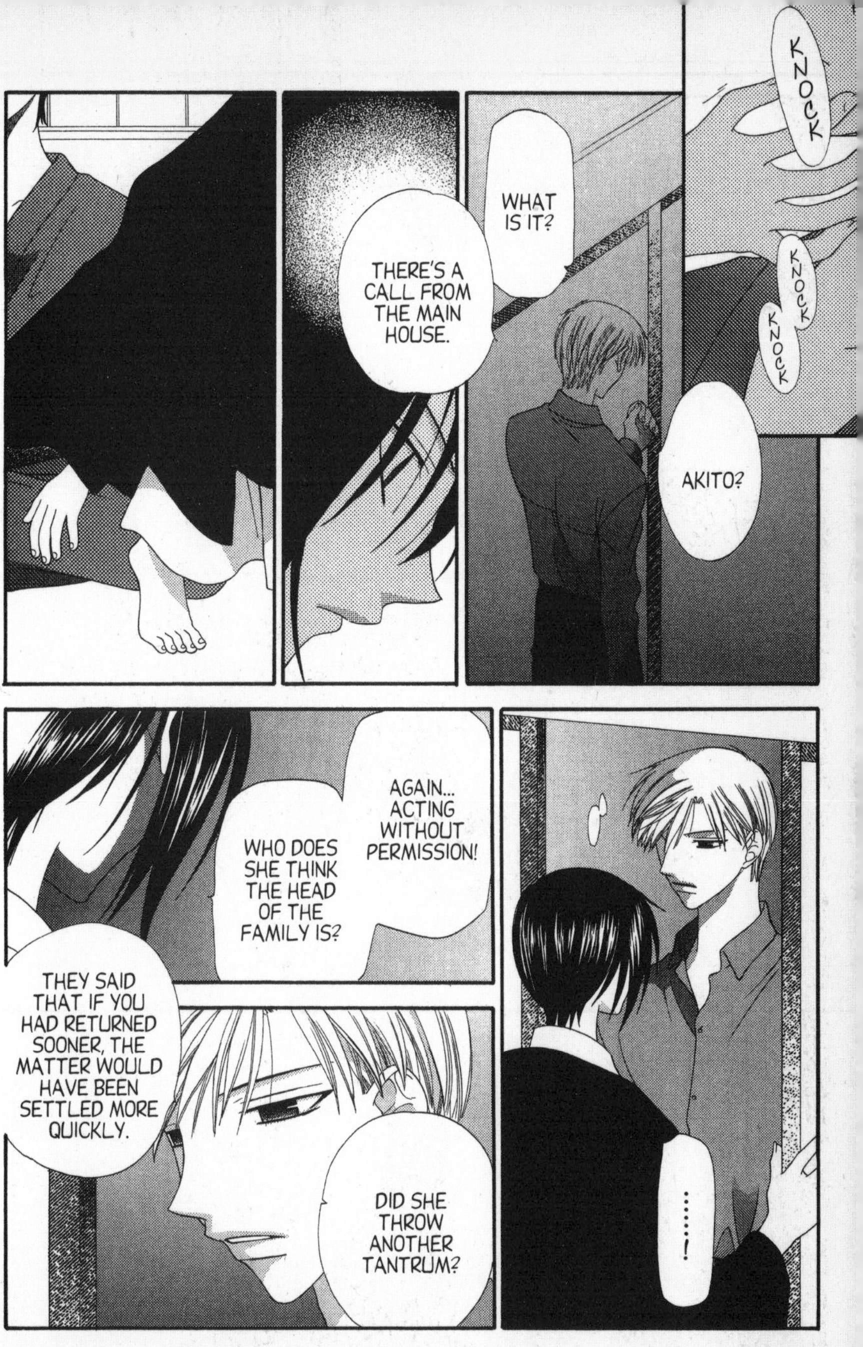
KNOCK
KNOCK KNOCK
AKITO?
WHAT IS IT?
THERE'S A CALL FROM THE MAIN HOUSE.
......!
AGAIN... ACTING WITHOUT PERMISSION!
WHO DOES SHE THINK THE HEAD OF THE FAMILY IS?
THEY SAID THAT IF YOU HAD RETURNED SOONER, THE MATTER WOULD HAVE BEEN SETTLED MORE QUICKLY.
DID SHE THROW ANOTHER TANTRUM?

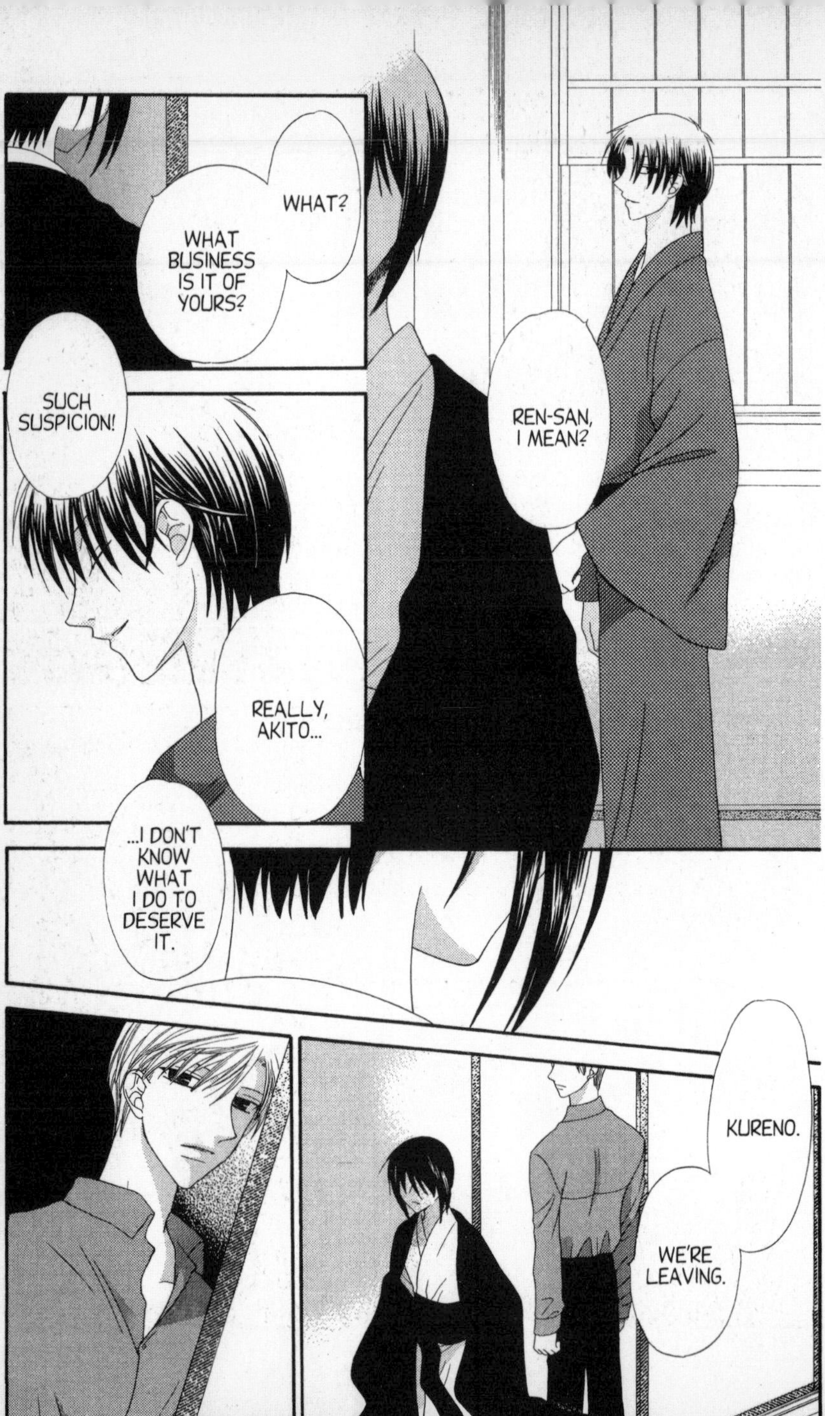
REN-SAN, I MEAN?
WHAT?
WHAT BUSINESS IS IT OF YOURS?
SUCH SUSPICION!
REALLY, AKITO...
...I DON'T KNOW WHAT I DO TO DESERVE IT.
KURENO.
WE'RE LEAVING.

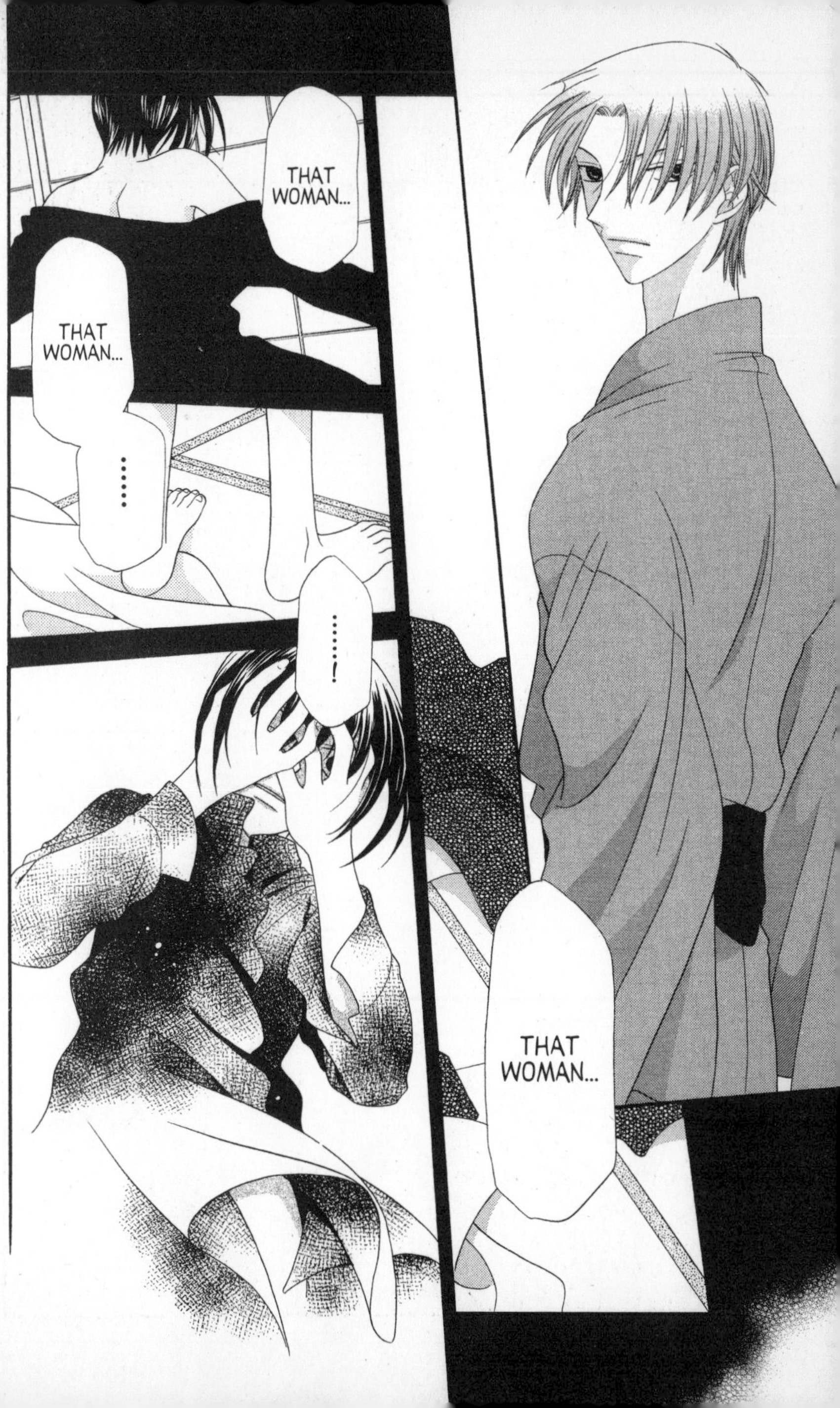
THAT WOMAN...
THAT WOMAN...
THAT WOMAN...
......
......!

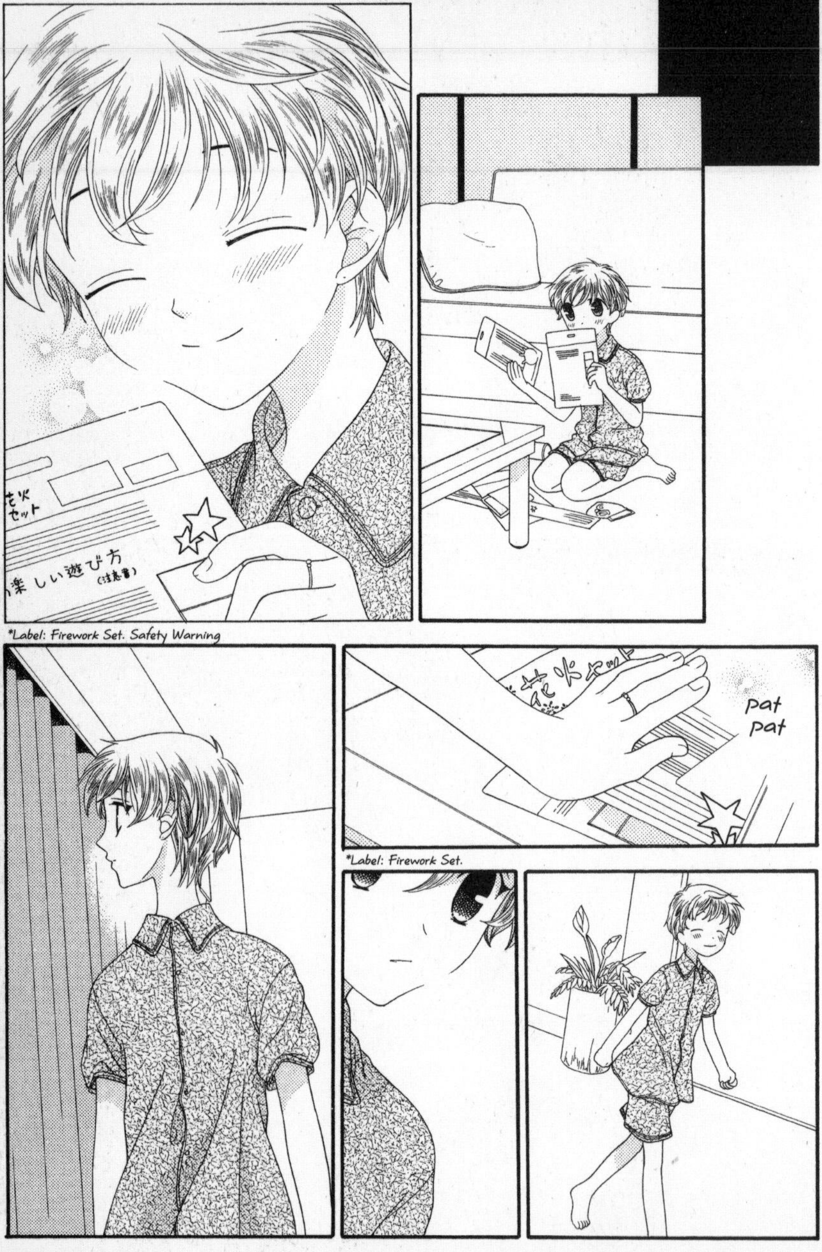
花火セット
楽しい遊び方
(注意書)
*Label: Firework Set. Safety Warning
花火セット
pat
pat
*Label: Firework Set.

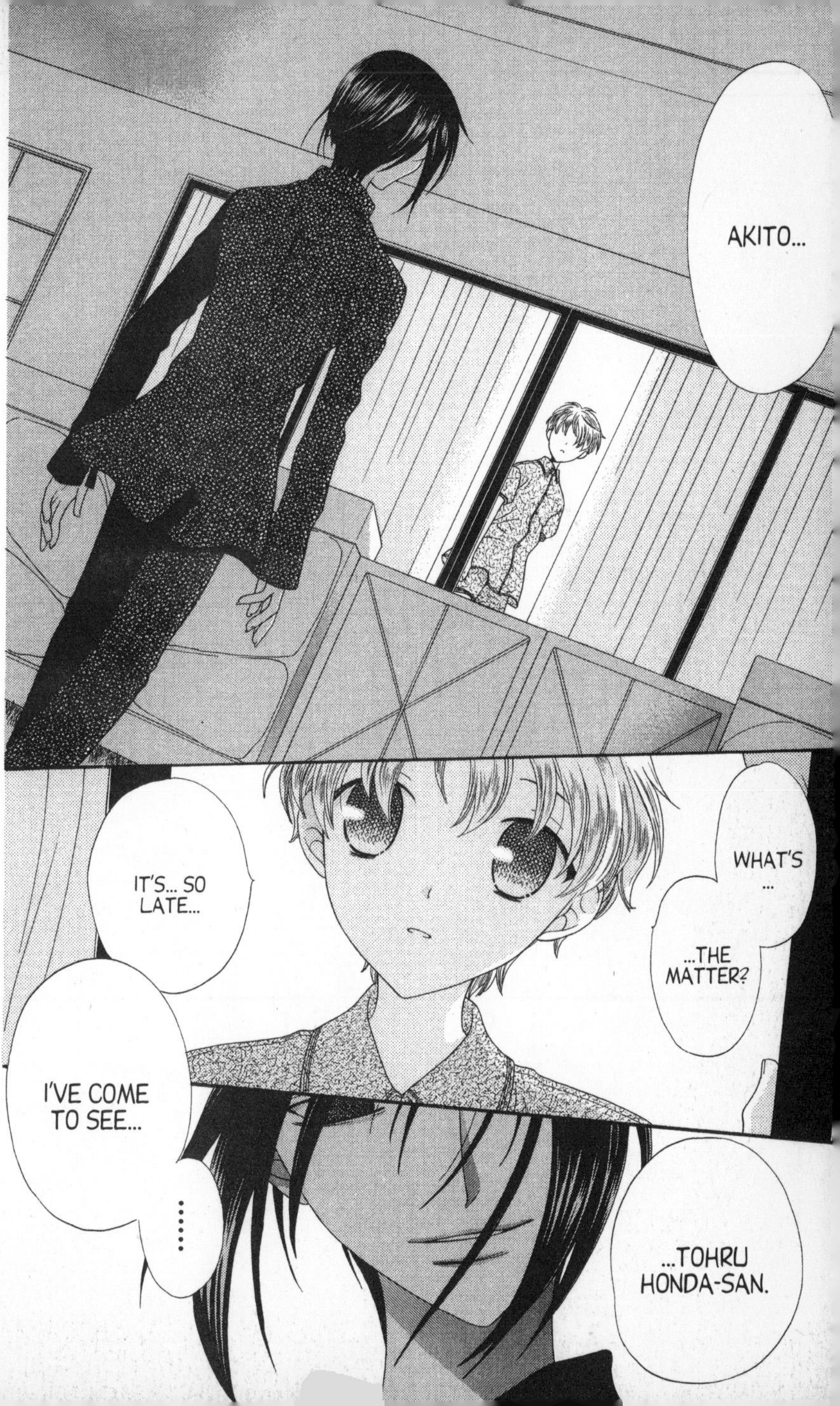
AKITO...
WHAT'S ... ...THE MATTER?
IT'S... SO LATE...
I'VE COME TO SEE...
......
...TOHRU HONDA-SAN.

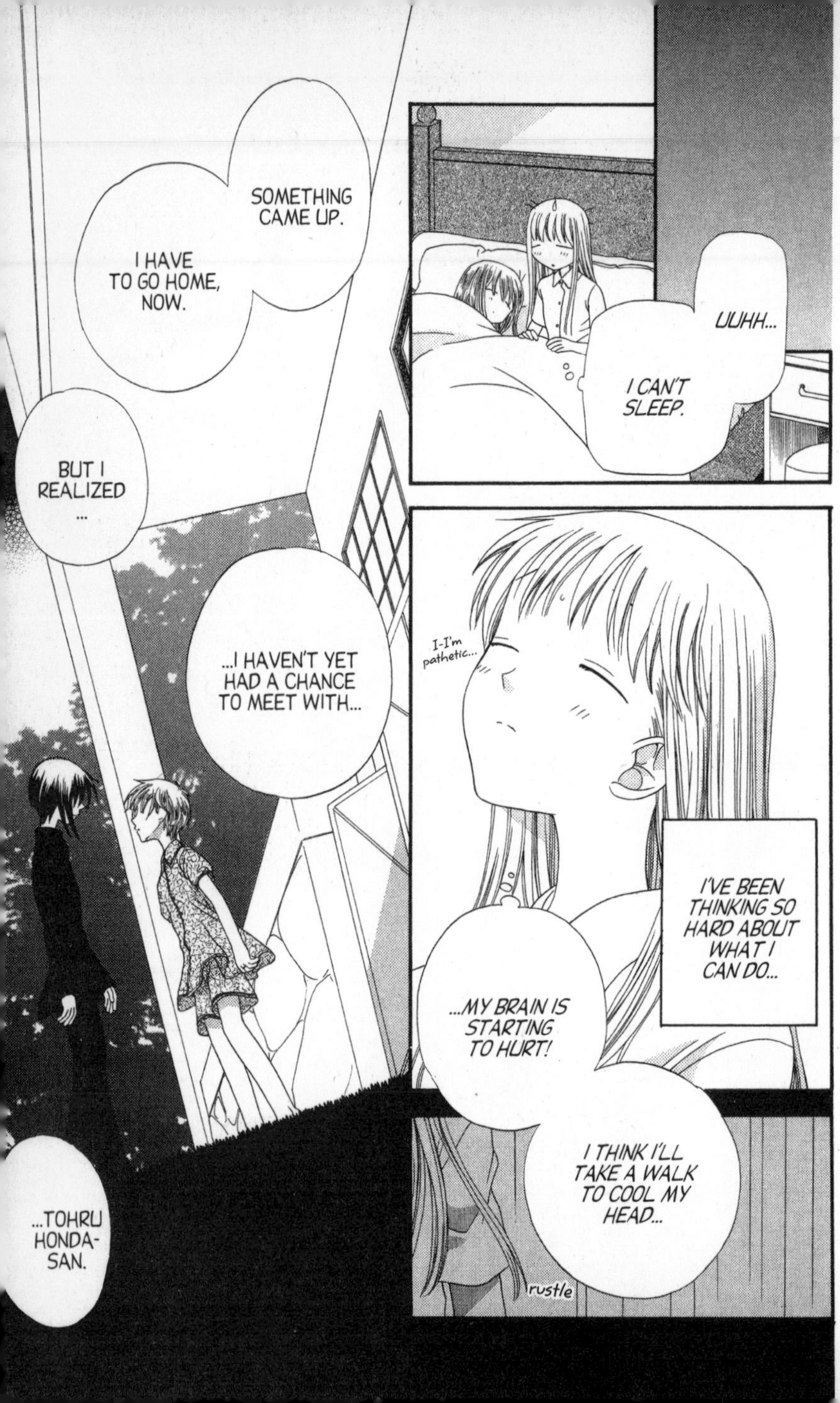
UUHH...
I CAN'T SLEEP.
I-I'm pathetic...
I'VE BEEN THINKING SO HARD ABOUT WHAT I CAN DO...
...MY BRAIN IS STARTING TO HURT!
I THINK I'LL TAKE A WALK TO COOL MY HEAD...
rustle
SOMETHING CAME UP.
I HAVE TO GO HOME, NOW.
BUT I REALIZED ...
...I HAVEN'T YET HAD A CHANCE TO MEET WITH...
...TOHRU HONDA-SAN.

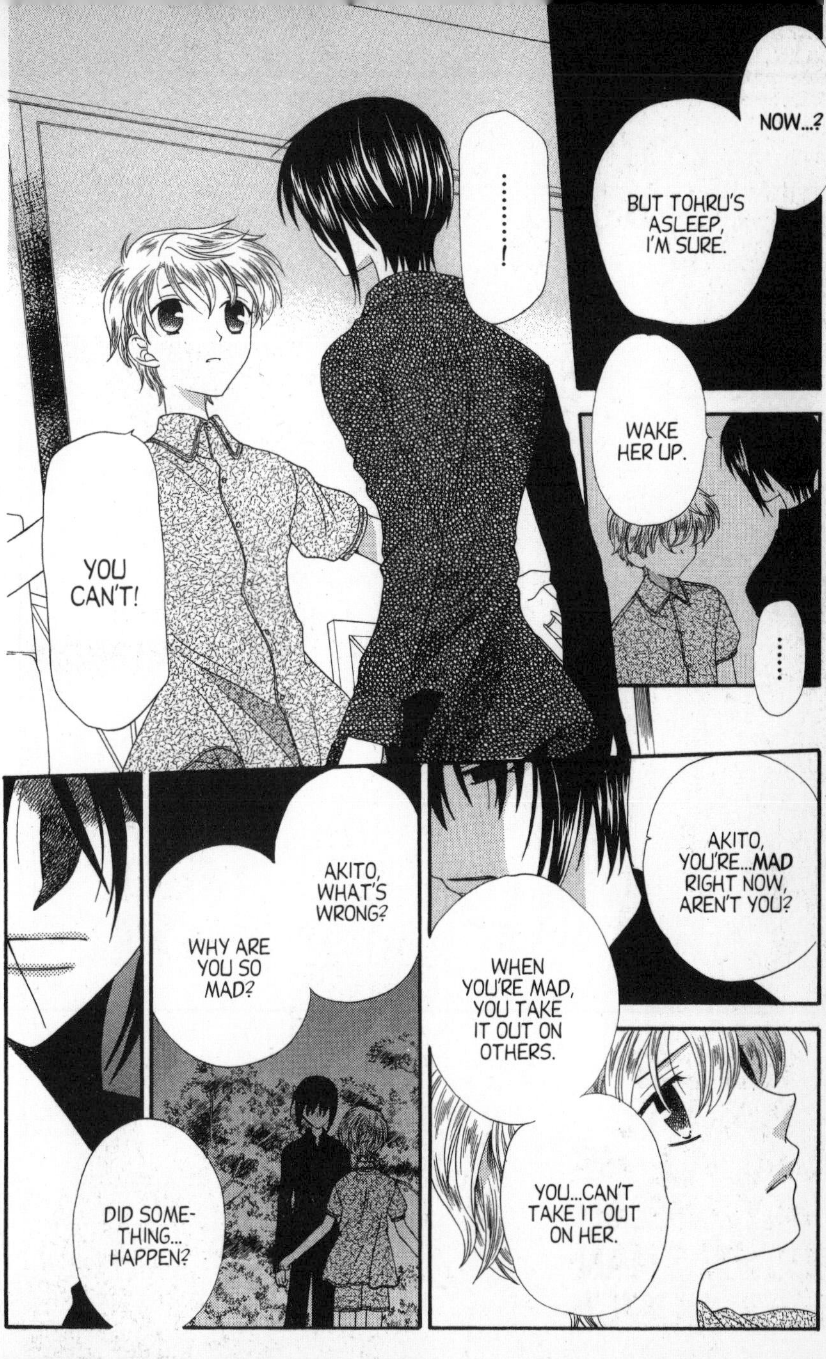
NOW...?
BUT TOHRU'S ASLEEP, I'M SURE.
WAKE HER UP.
......
......!
YOU CAN'T!
AKITO, YOU'RE...**MAD** RIGHT NOW, AREN'T YOU?
WHEN YOU'RE MAD, YOU TAKE IT OUT ON OTHERS.
YOU...CAN'T TAKE IT OUT ON HER.
AKITO, WHAT'S WRONG?
WHY ARE YOU SO MAD?
DID SOME-THING... HAPPEN?

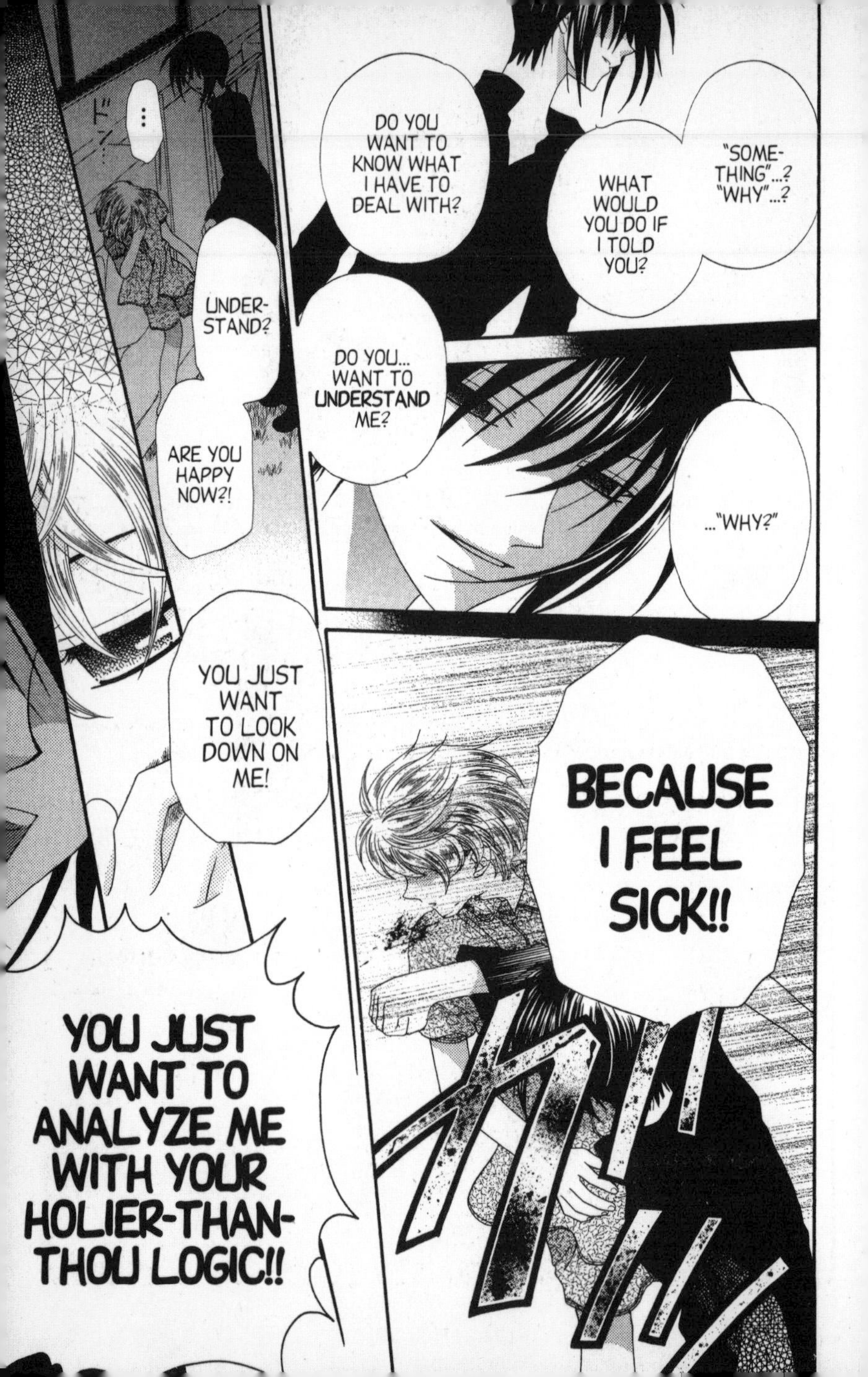
"SOME-THING"...? "WHY"...?
WHAT WOULD YOU DO IF I TOLD YOU?
DO YOU WANT TO KNOW WHAT I HAVE TO DEAL WITH?
DO YOU... WANT TO UNDERSTAND ME?
..."WHY?"
BECAUSE I FEEL SICK!!
...
UNDER-STAND?
ARE YOU HAPPY NOW?!
YOU JUST WANT TO LOOK DOWN ON ME!
YOU JUST WANT TO ANALYZE ME WITH YOUR HOLIER-THAN-THOU LOGIC!!

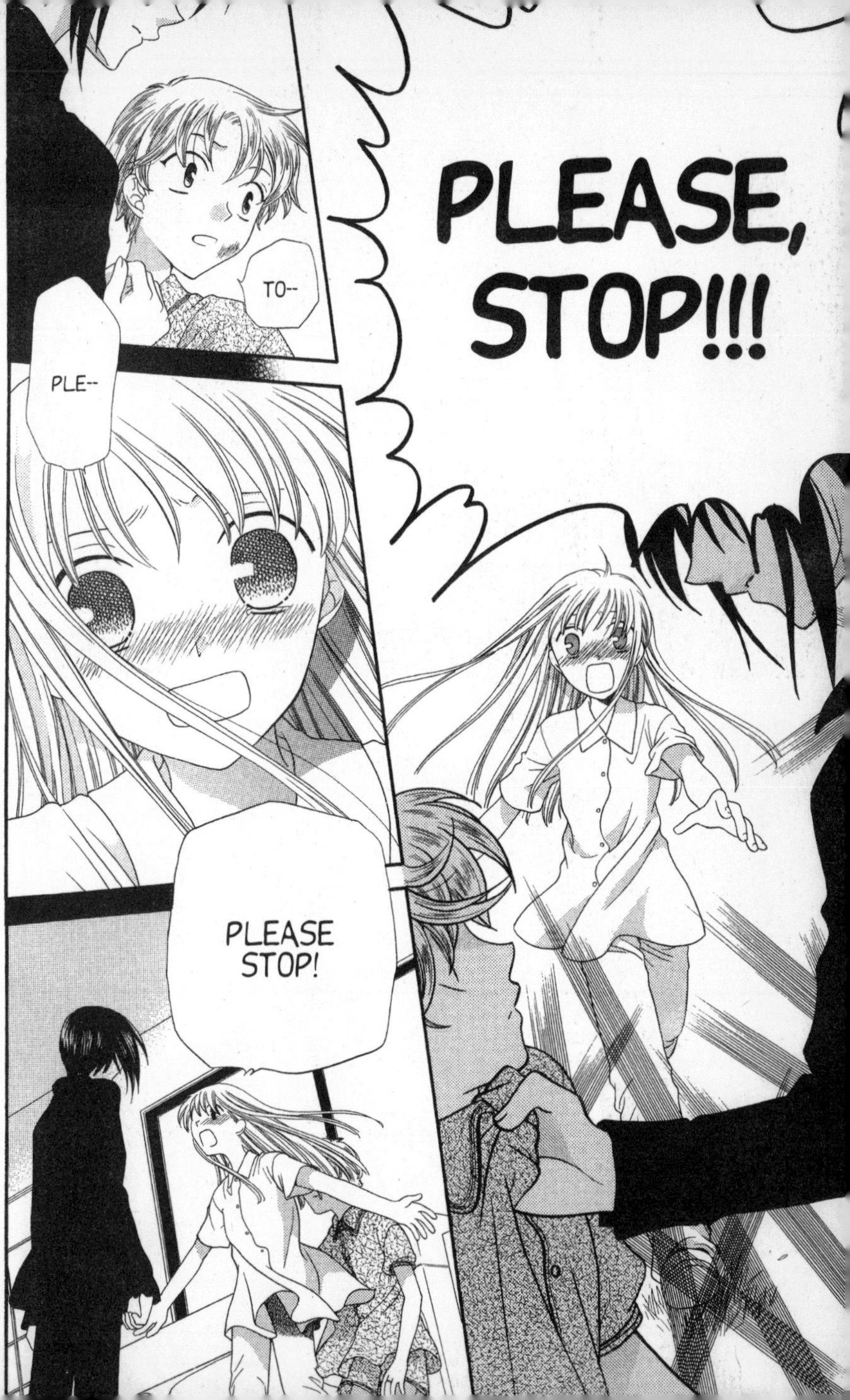
PLEASE, STOP!!!
TO--
PLE--
PLEASE STOP!

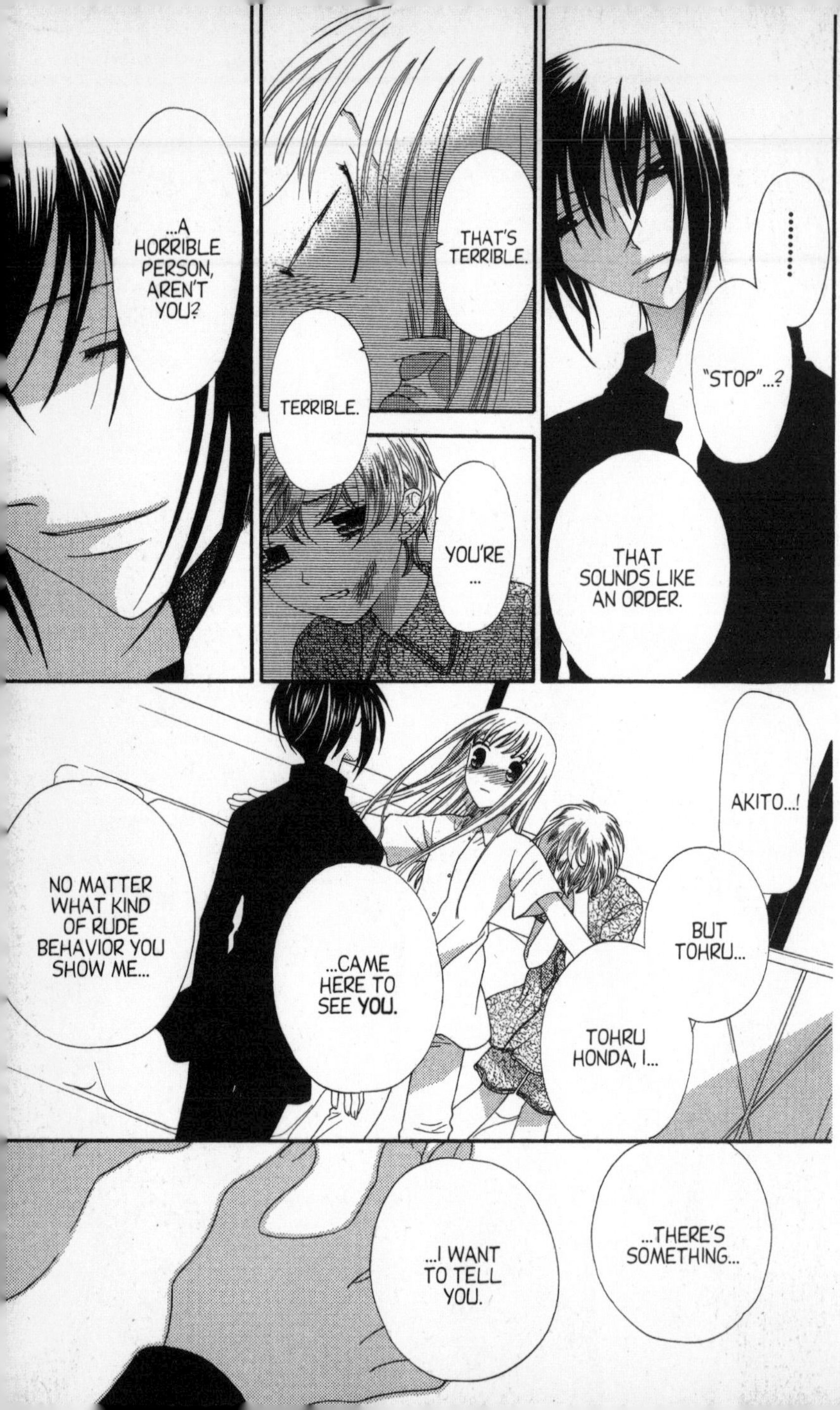
......
"STOP"...?
THAT SOUNDS LIKE AN ORDER.
THAT'S TERRIBLE.
TERRIBLE.
YOU'RE ...
...A HORRIBLE PERSON, AREN'T YOU?
AKITO...!
BUT TOHRU...
TOHRU HONDA, I...
...CAME HERE TO SEE YOU.
NO MATTER WHAT KIND OF RUDE BEHAVIOR YOU SHOW ME...
...THERE'S SOMETHING...
...I WANT TO TELL YOU.

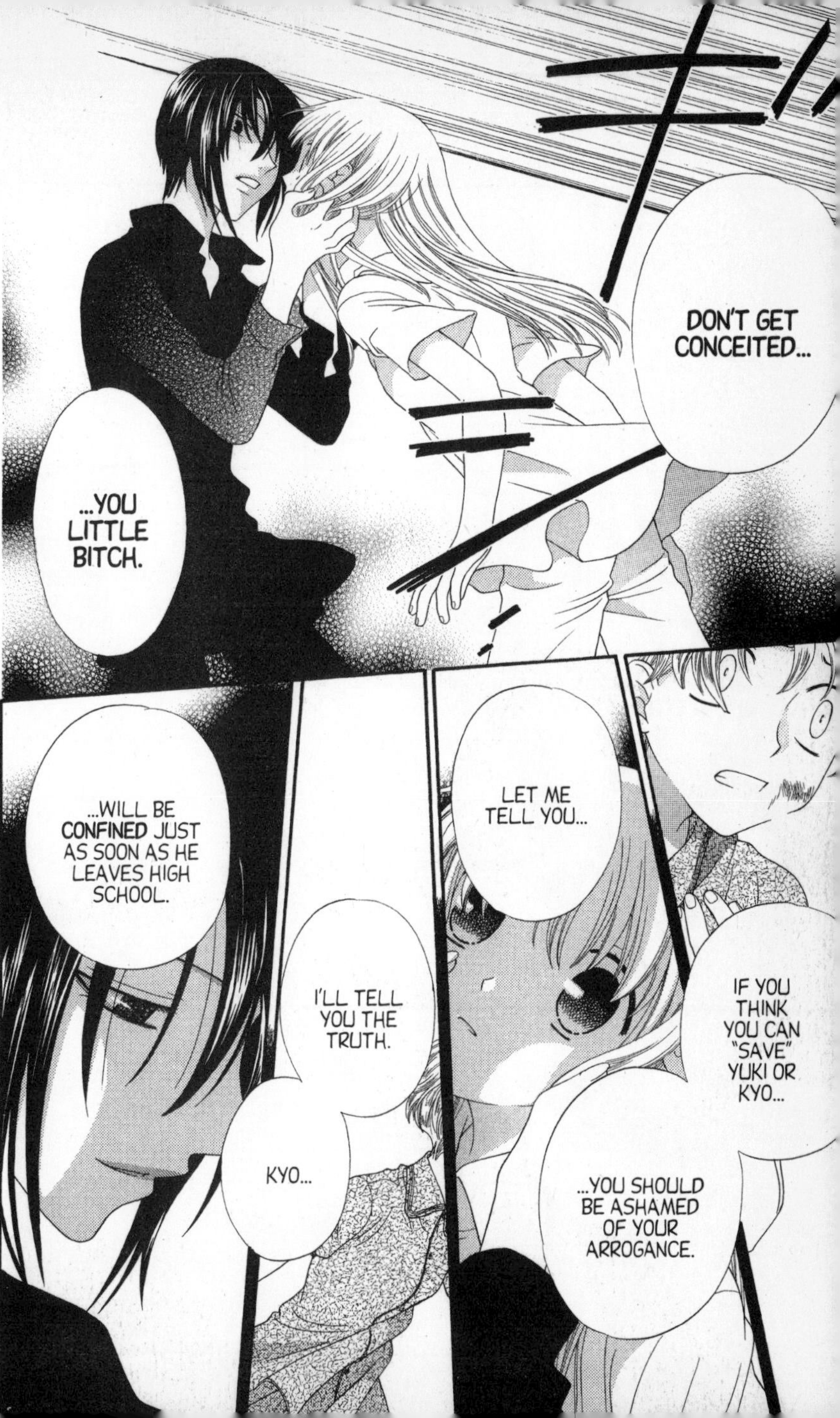
DON'T GET CONCEITED...
...YOU LITTLE BITCH.
IF YOU THINK YOU CAN "SAVE" YUKI OR KYO...
...YOU SHOULD BE ASHAMED OF YOUR ARROGANCE.
LET ME TELL YOU...
I'LL TELL YOU THE TRUTH.
KYO...
...WILL BE CONFINED JUST AS SOON AS HE LEAVES HIGH SCHOOL.

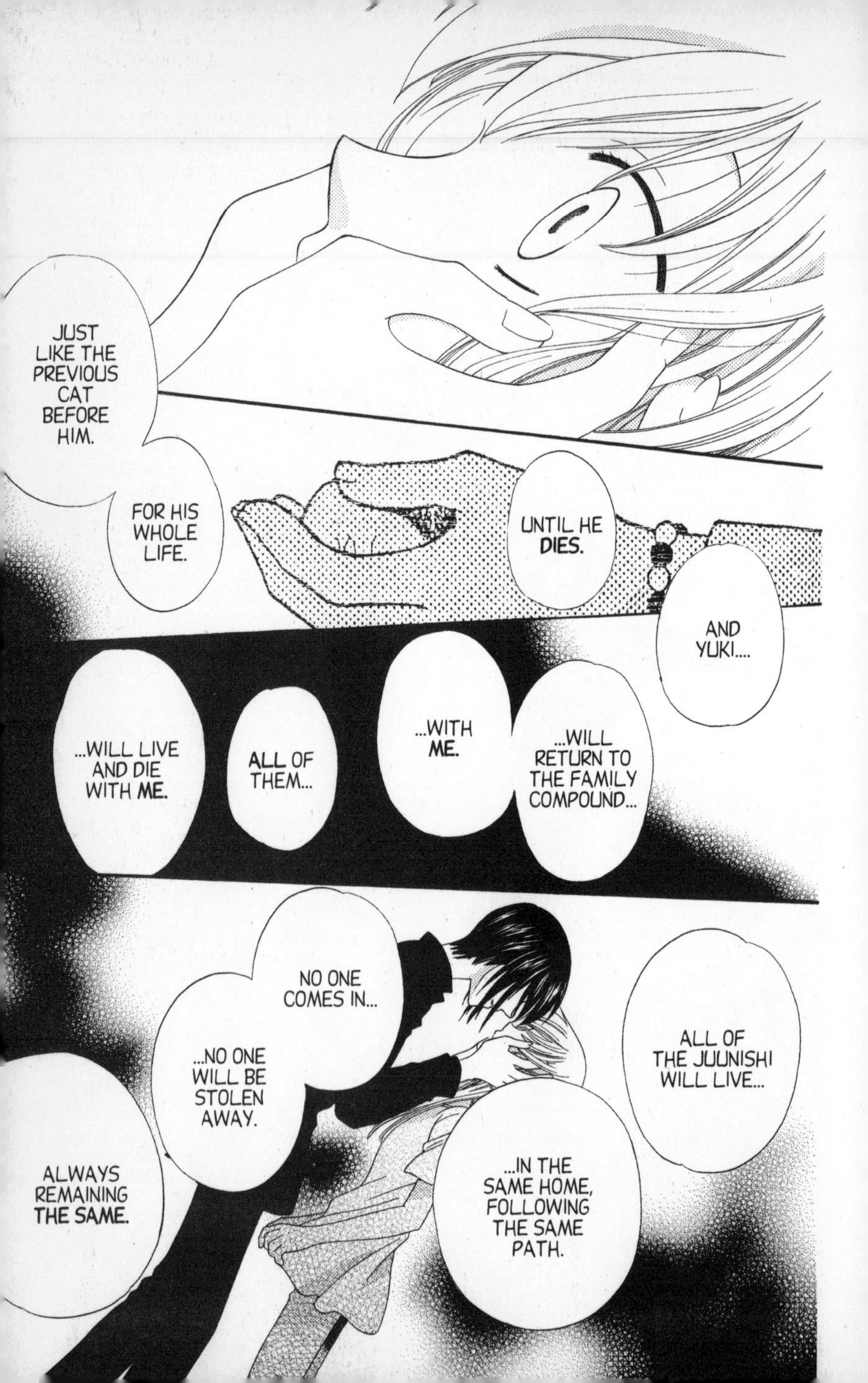
JUST LIKE THE PREVIOUS CAT BEFORE HIM.
FOR HIS WHOLE LIFE.
UNTIL HE **DIES.**
AND YUKI....
...WILL RETURN TO THE FAMILY COMPOUND...
...WITH **ME.**
ALL OF THEM...
...WILL LIVE AND DIE WITH **ME.**
ALL OF THE JUUNISHI WILL LIVE...
...IN THE SAME HOME, FOLLOWING THE SAME PATH.
NO ONE COMES IN...
...NO ONE WILL BE STOLEN AWAY.
ALWAYS REMAINING **THE SAME.**

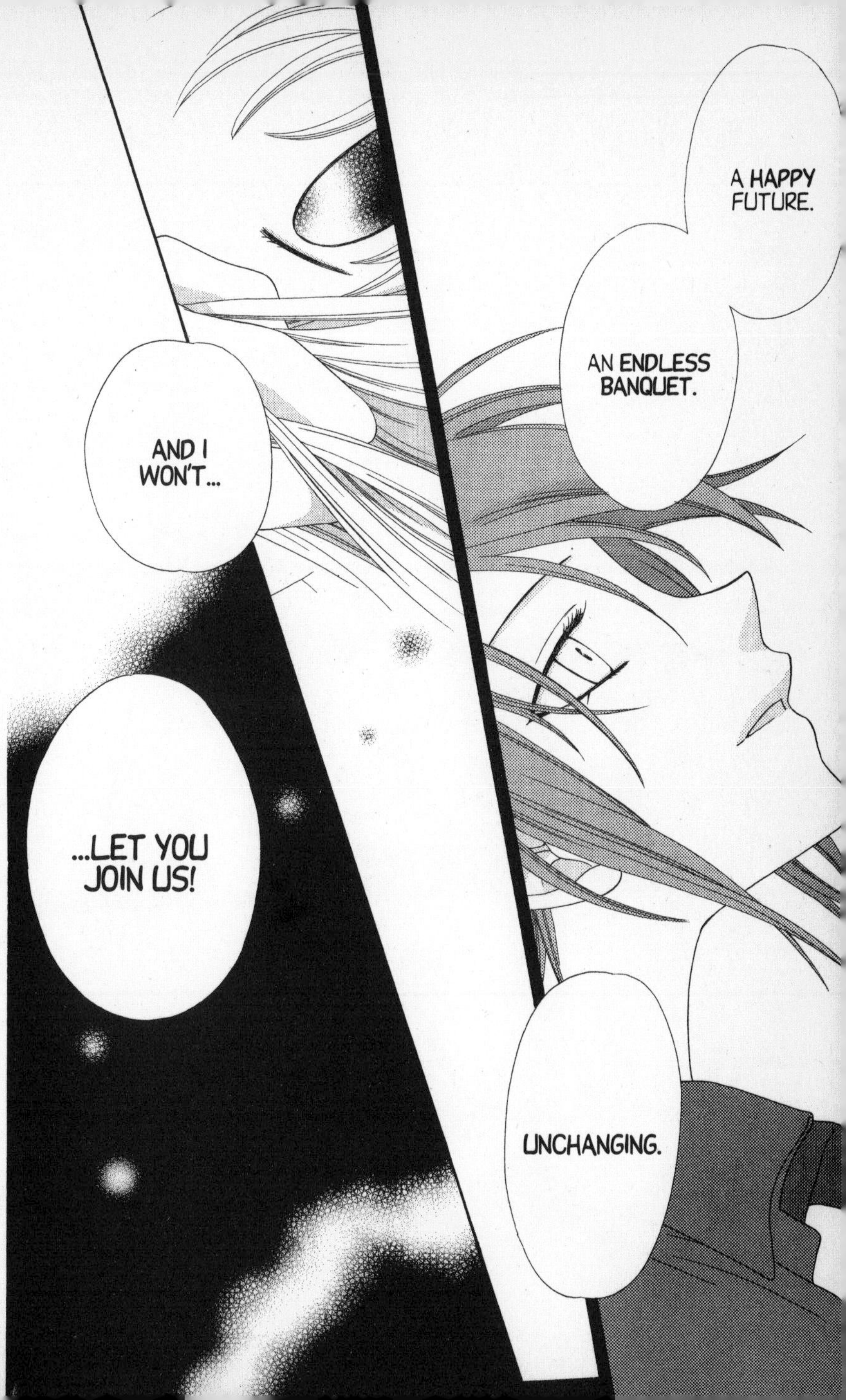
A HAPPY FUTURE.
AN ENDLESS BANQUET.
UNCHANGING.
AND I WON'T...
...LET YOU JOIN US!

Filler
Sketch

This is the rough sketch for the title page for chapter 65.

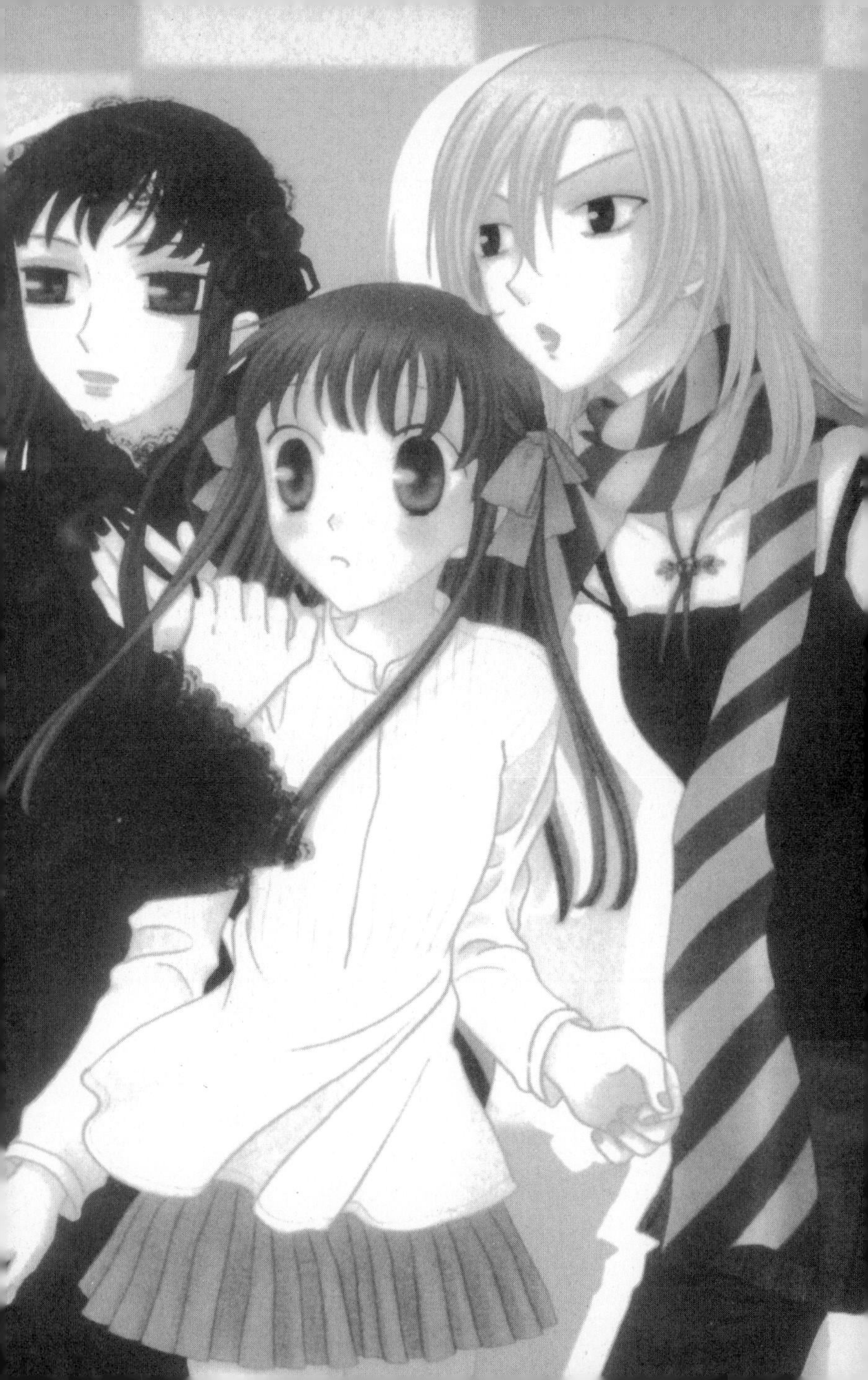

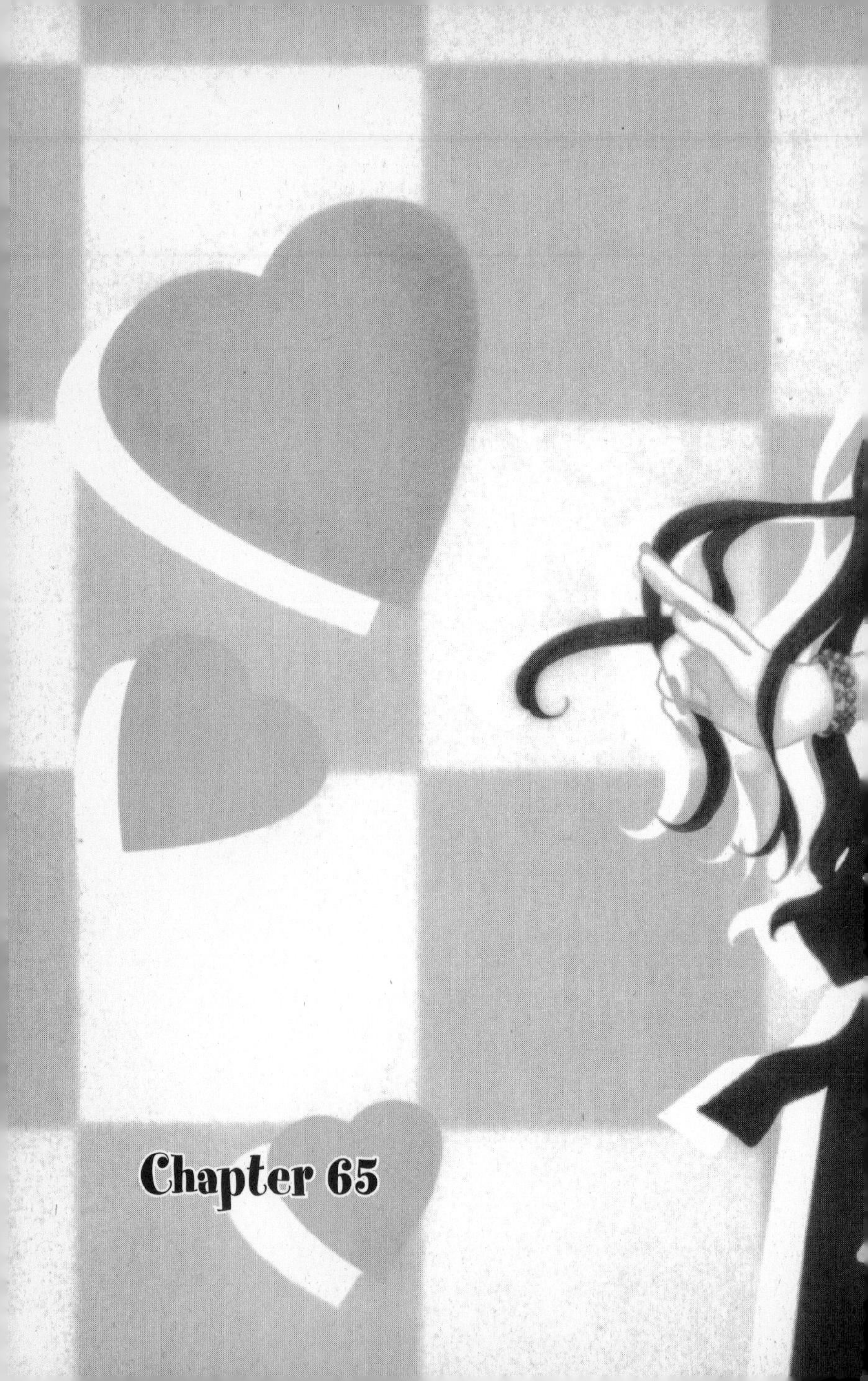
Chapter 65

I feel so grateful!

Sheesh... That's all she ever says...

Harada-sama, Araki-sama, Mom, Dad, and everyone who reads and supports this manga... Thank you so much!

Next is "I... I'm sorry...!" Ritchan!

—Natsuki Takaya

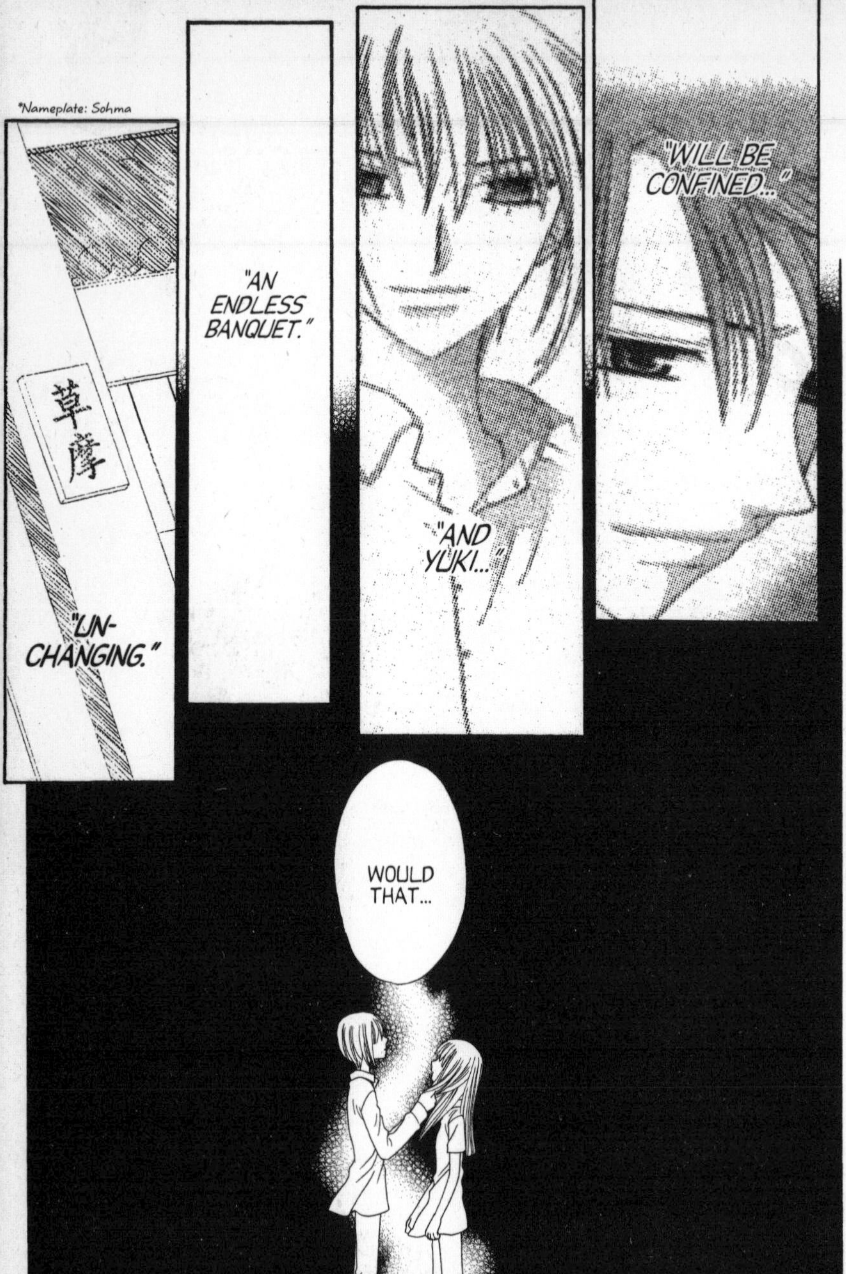
"WILL BE CONFINED..."
"AND YUKI..."
"AN ENDLESS BANQUET."
*Nameplate: Sohma
草摩
"UN-CHANGING."
WOULD THAT...

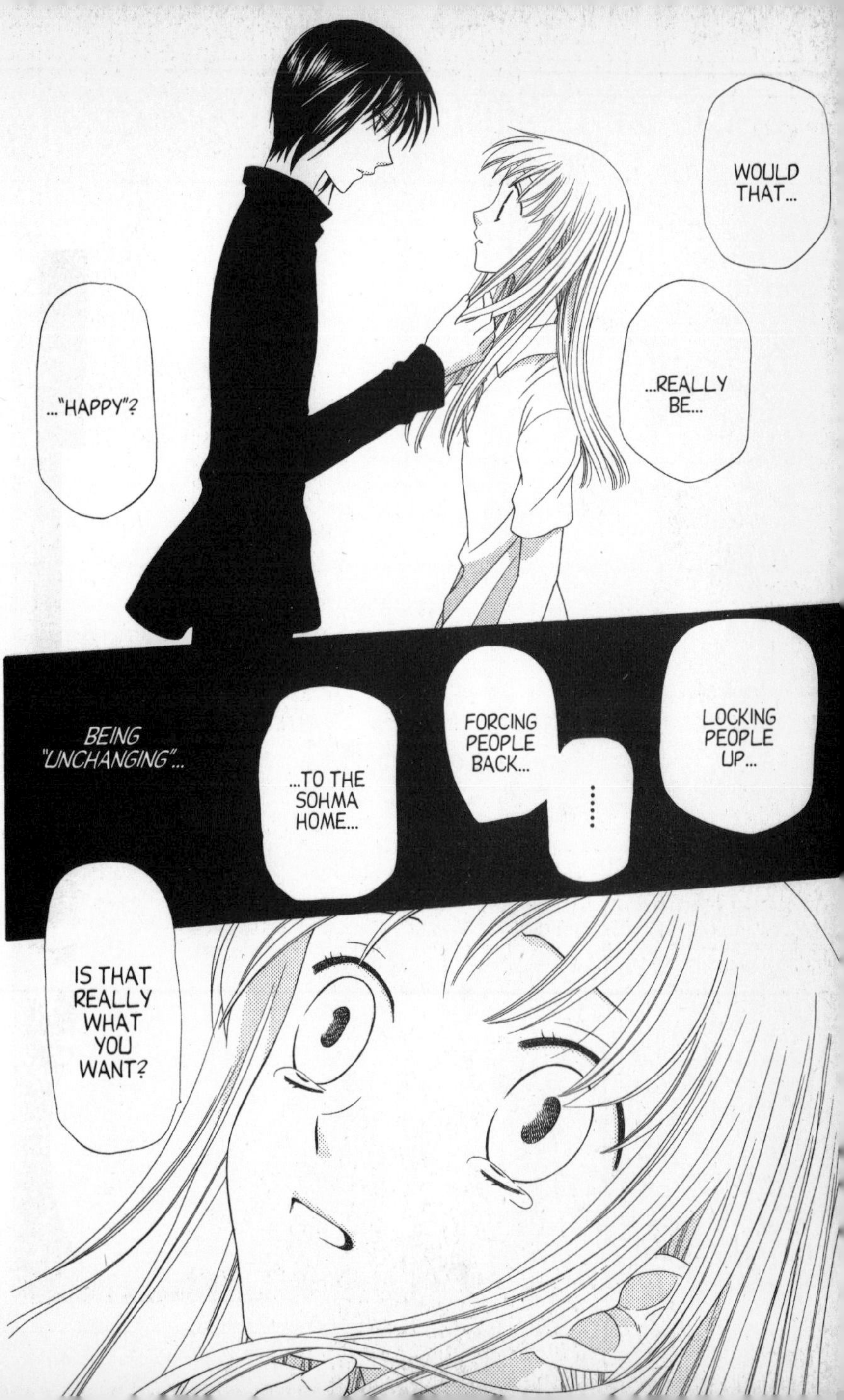
WOULD THAT...
...REALLY BE...
..."HAPPY"?
LOCKING PEOPLE UP...
......
FORCING PEOPLE BACK...
...TO THE SOHMA HOME...
BEING "UNCHANGING"...
IS THAT REALLY WHAT YOU WANT?

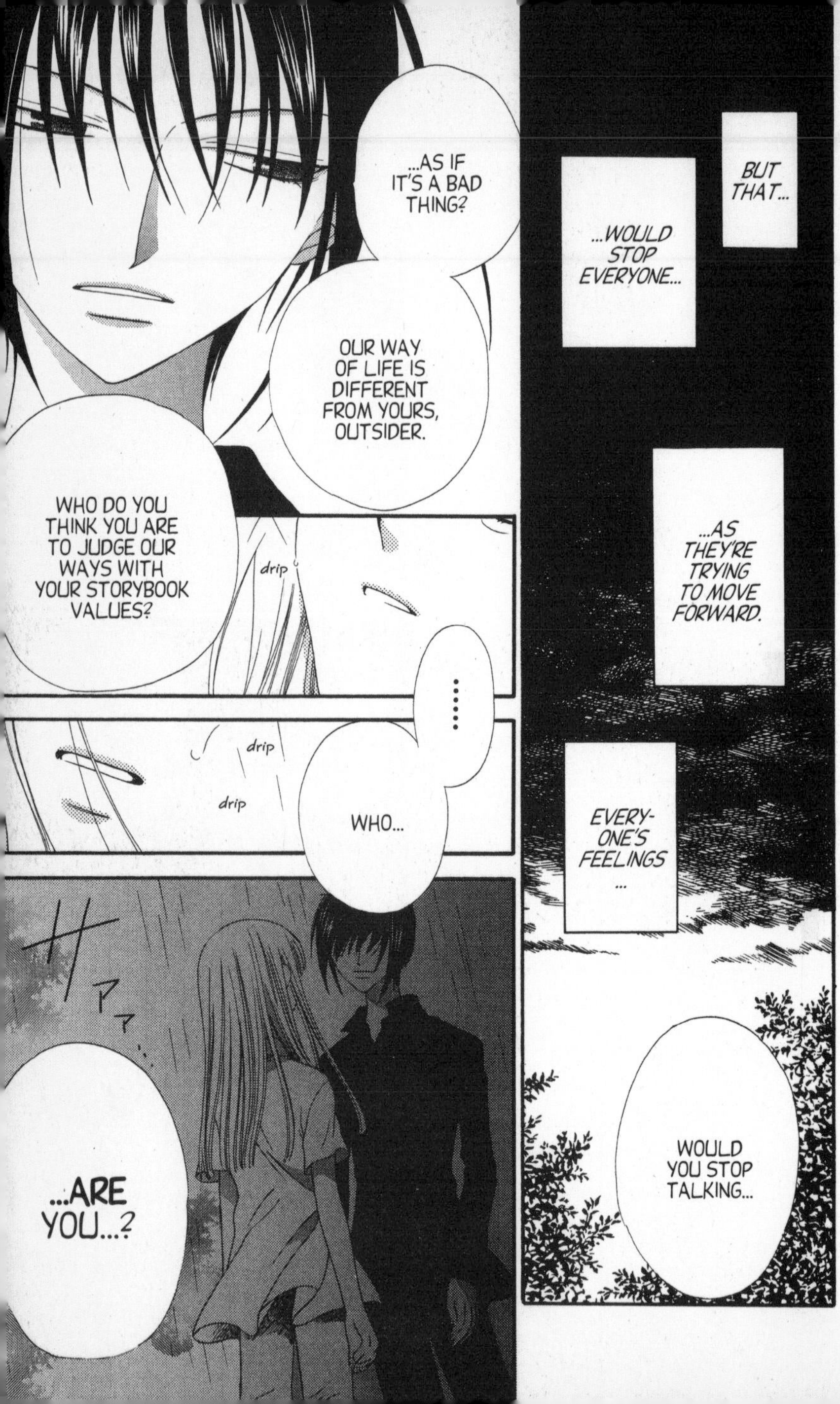
BUT THAT...
...WOULD STOP EVERYONE...
...AS THEY'RE TRYING TO MOVE FORWARD.
EVERY-ONE'S FEELINGS ...
WOULD YOU STOP TALKING...
...AS IF IT'S A BAD THING?
OUR WAY OF LIFE IS DIFFERENT FROM YOURS, OUTSIDER.
WHO DO YOU THINK YOU ARE TO JUDGE OUR WAYS WITH YOUR STORYBOOK VALUES?
drip
......
drip
drip
WHO...
...ARE YOU...?

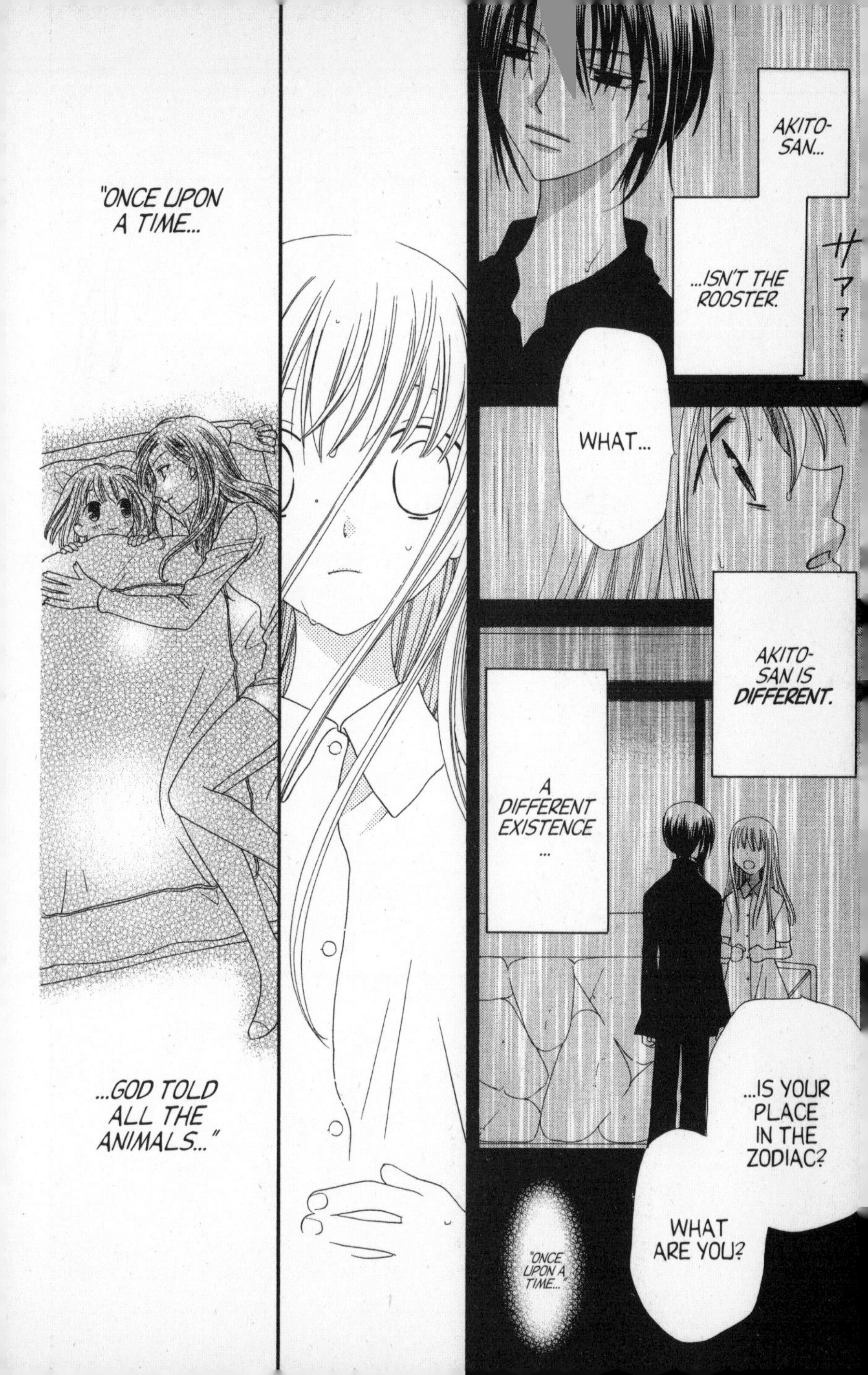
AKITO-SAN...
...ISN'T THE ROOSTER.
サァァ…
WHAT...
AKITO-SAN IS DIFFERENT.
A DIFFERENT EXISTENCE ...
...IS YOUR PLACE IN THE ZODIAC?
WHAT ARE YOU?
"ONCE UPON A TIME..."
"ONCE UPON A TIME...
...GOD TOLD ALL THE ANIMALS..."

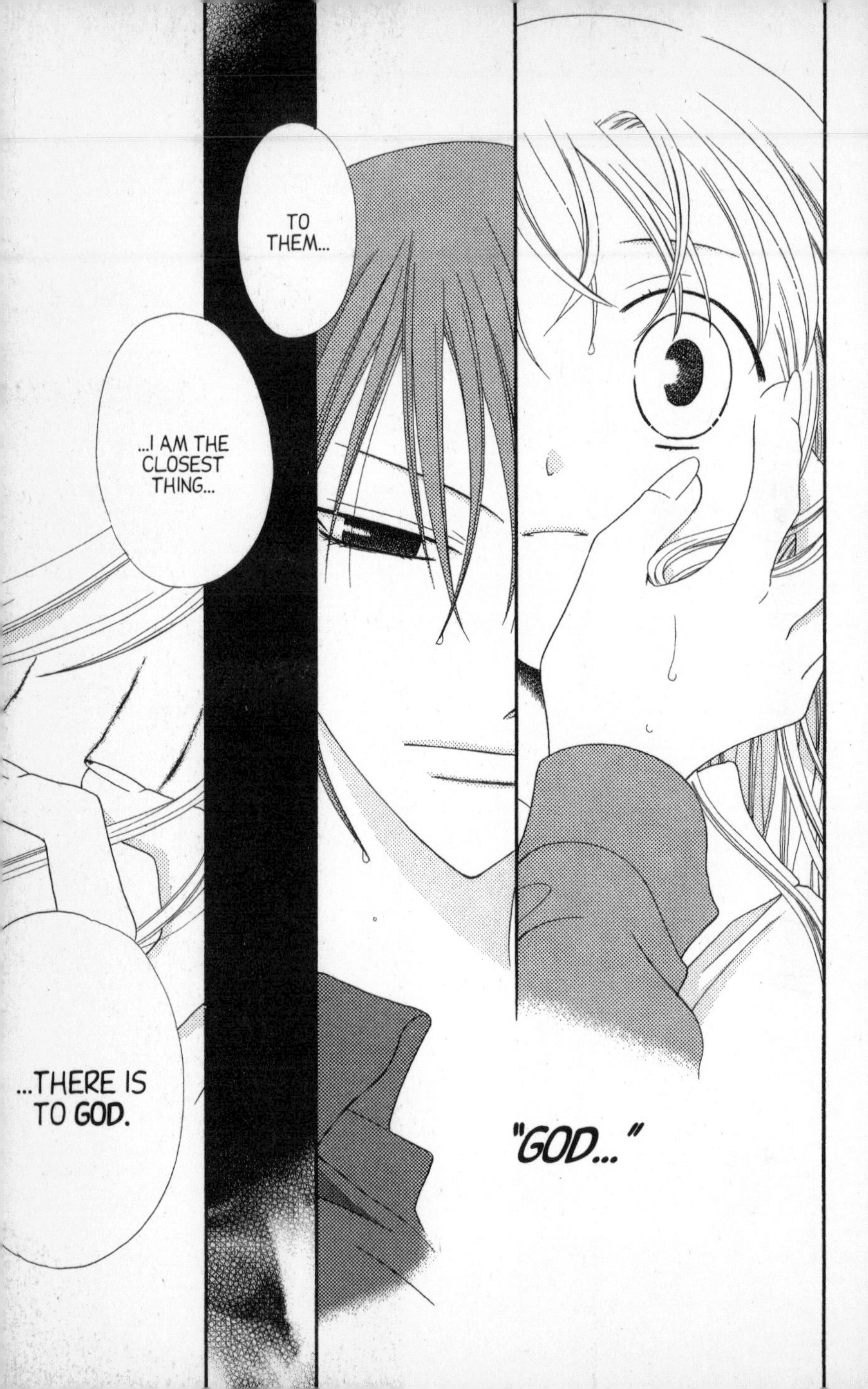
"GOD..."
TO THEM...
...I AM THE CLOSEST THING...
...THERE IS TO GOD.

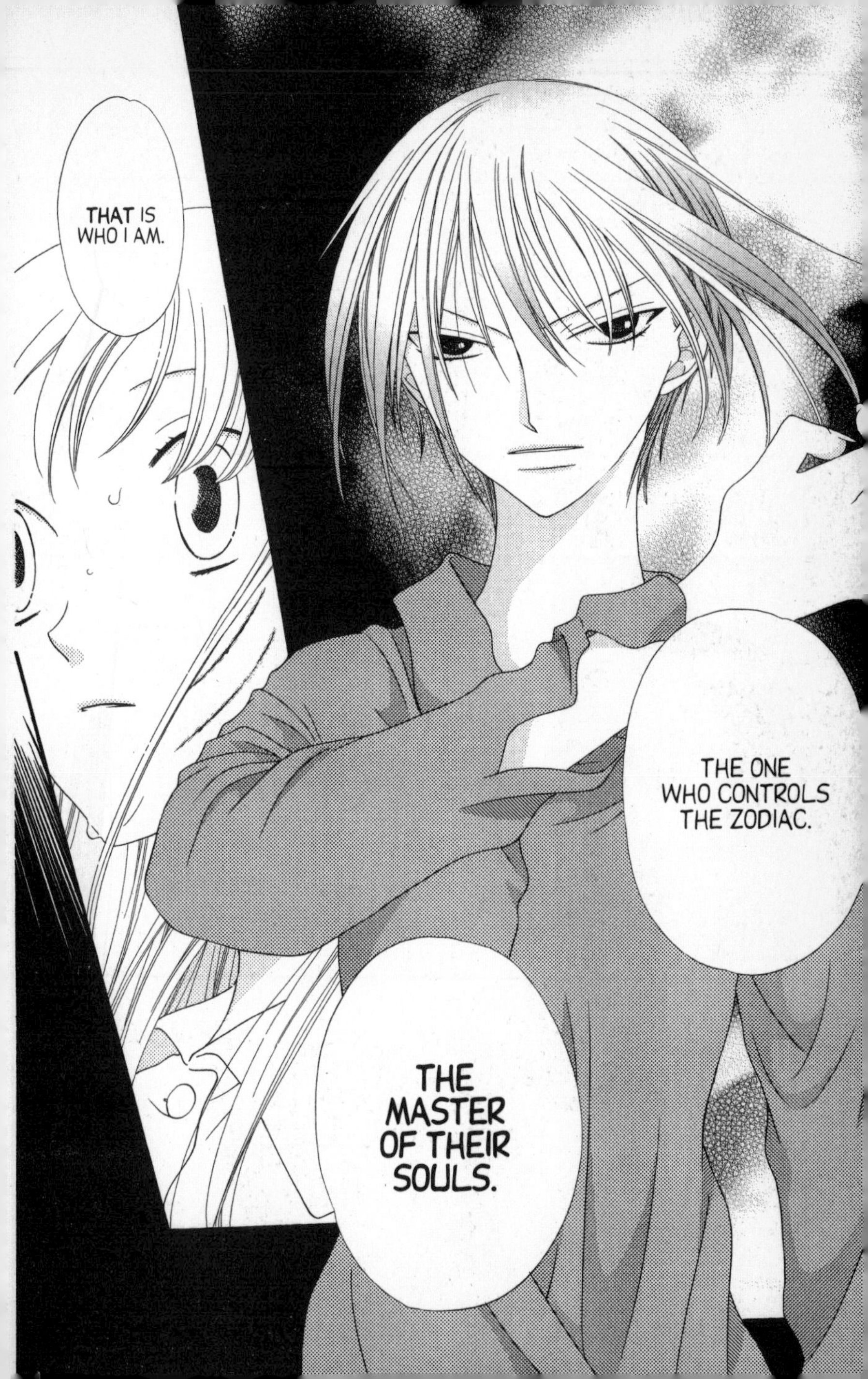
THE ONE WHO CONTROLS THE ZODIAC.
THE MASTER OF THEIR SOULS.
THAT IS WHO I AM.

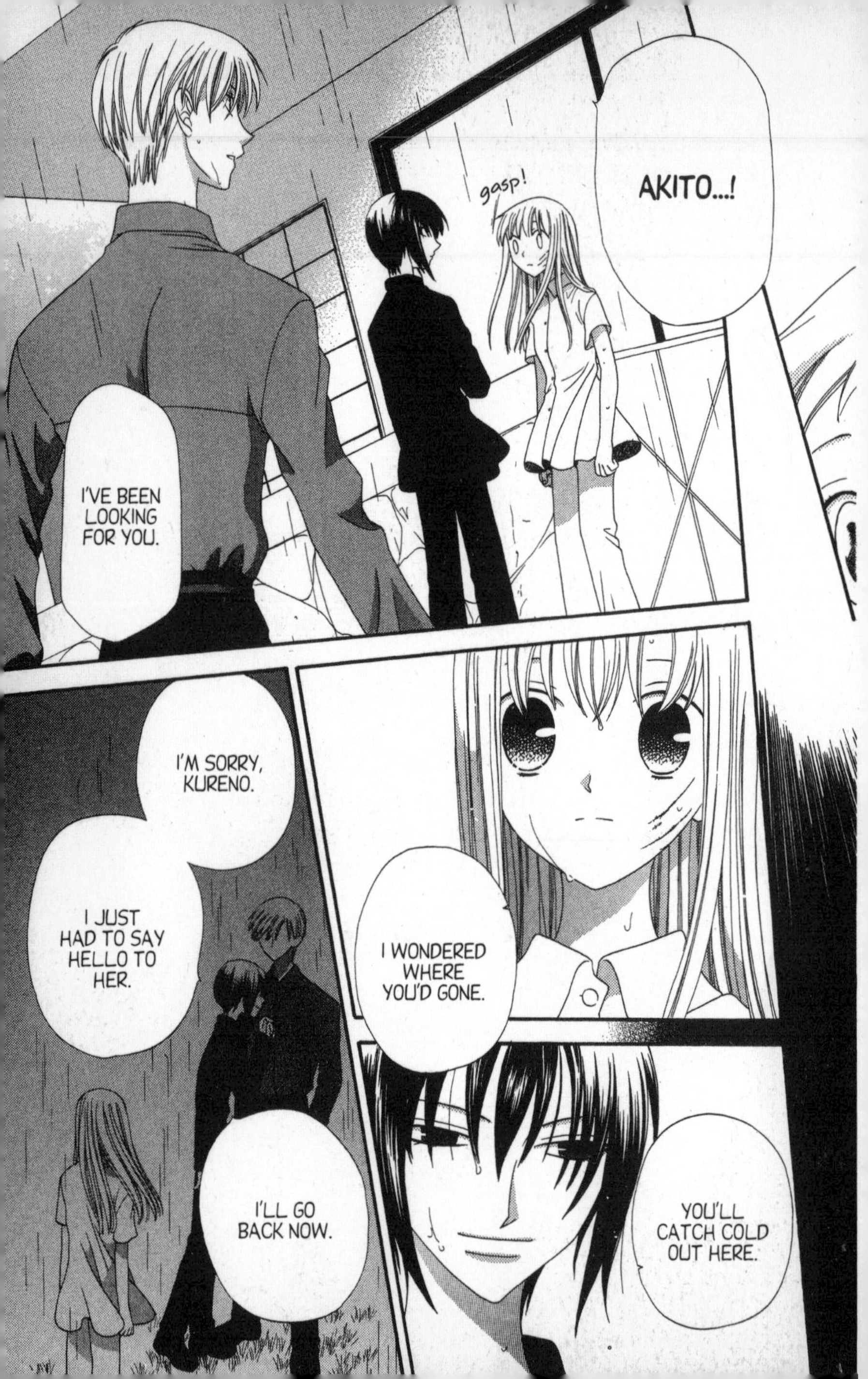
AKITO...!
gasp!
I'VE BEEN LOOKING FOR YOU.
I WONDERED WHERE YOU'D GONE.
YOU'LL CATCH COLD OUT HERE.
I'M SORRY, KURENO.
I JUST HAD TO SAY HELLO TO HER.
I'LL GO BACK NOW.

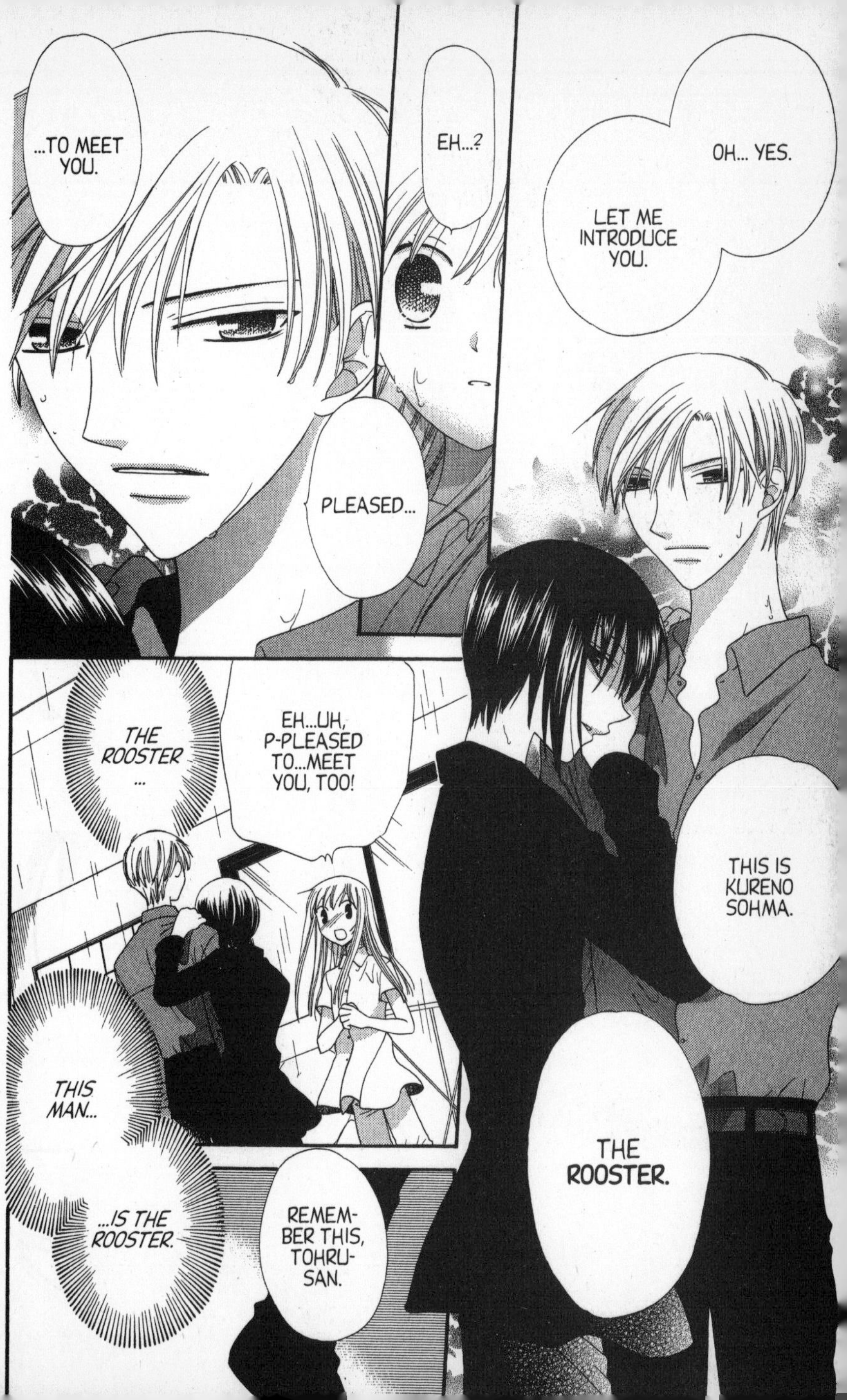
OH... YES.
LET ME INTRODUCE YOU.
THIS IS KURENO SOHMA.
THE ROOSTER.
EH...?
PLEASED...
...TO MEET YOU.
EH...UH, P-PLEASED TO...MEET YOU, TOO!
THE ROOSTER ...
THIS MAN...
...IS THE ROOSTER.
REMEM-BER THIS, TOHRU-SAN.

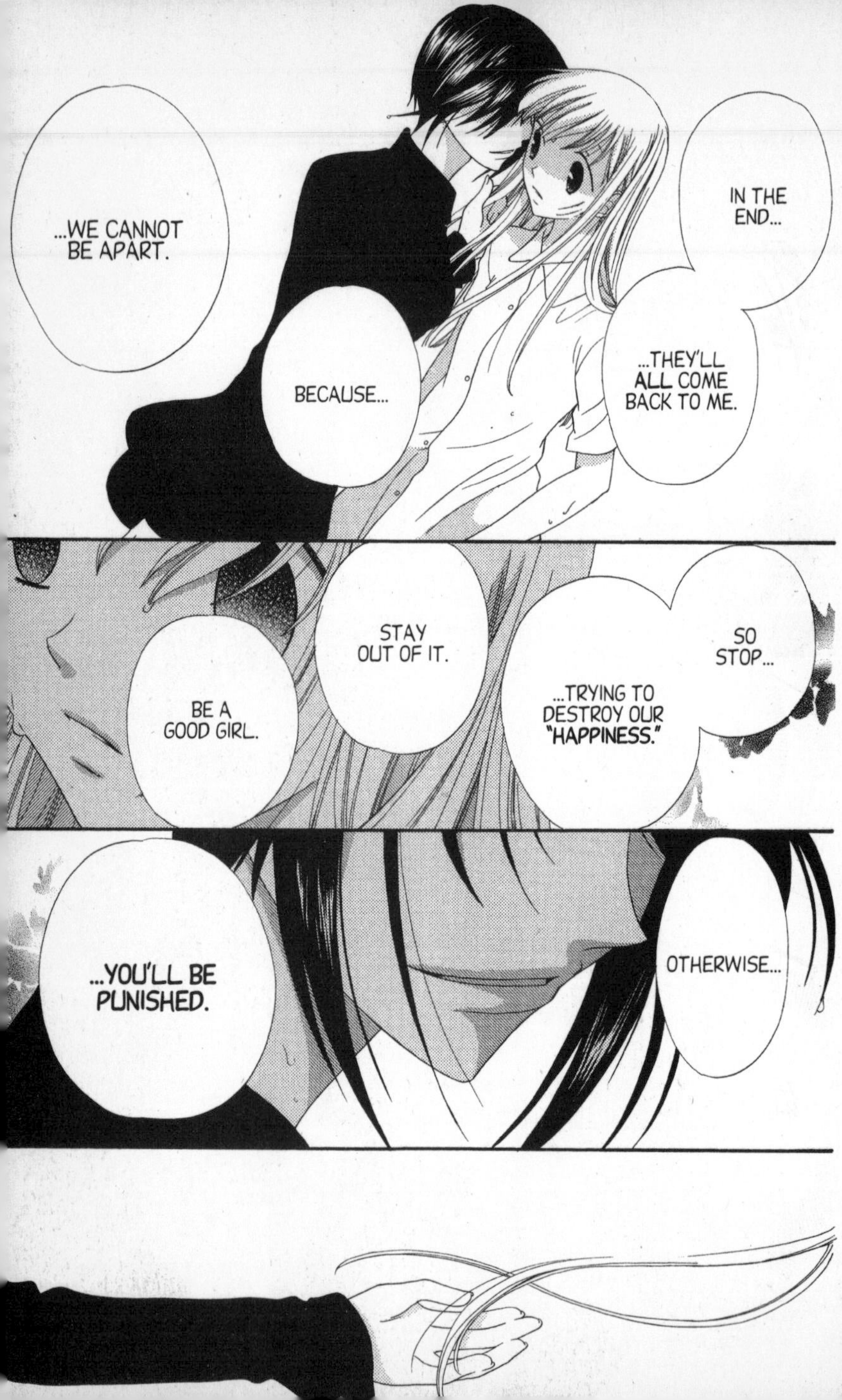
IN THE END...
...THEY'LL ALL COME BACK TO ME.
BECAUSE...
...WE CANNOT BE APART.
SO STOP...
...TRYING TO DESTROY OUR "HAPPINESS."
STAY OUT OF IT.
BE A GOOD GIRL.
OTHERWISE...
...YOU'LL BE PUNISHED.

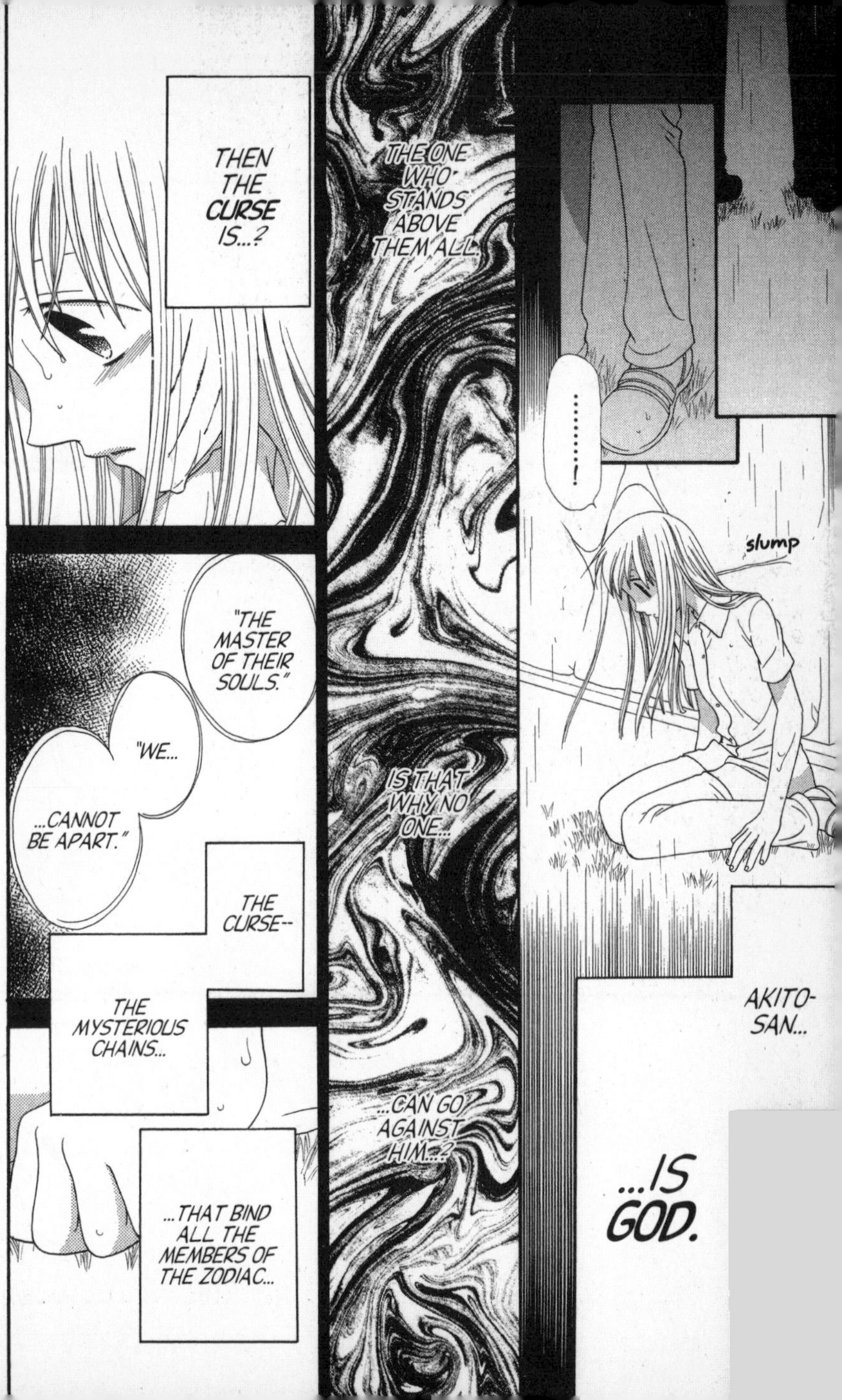
......!
slump
AKITO-SAN...
...IS GOD.
THE ONE WHO STANDS ABOVE THEM ALL.
IS THAT WHY NO ONE...
...CAN GO AGAINST HIM...?
THEN THE CURSE IS...?
"THE MASTER OF THEIR SOULS."
"WE...
...CANNOT BE APART."
THE CURSE--
THE MYSTERIOUS CHAINS...
...THAT BIND ALL THE MEMBERS OF THE ZODIAC...

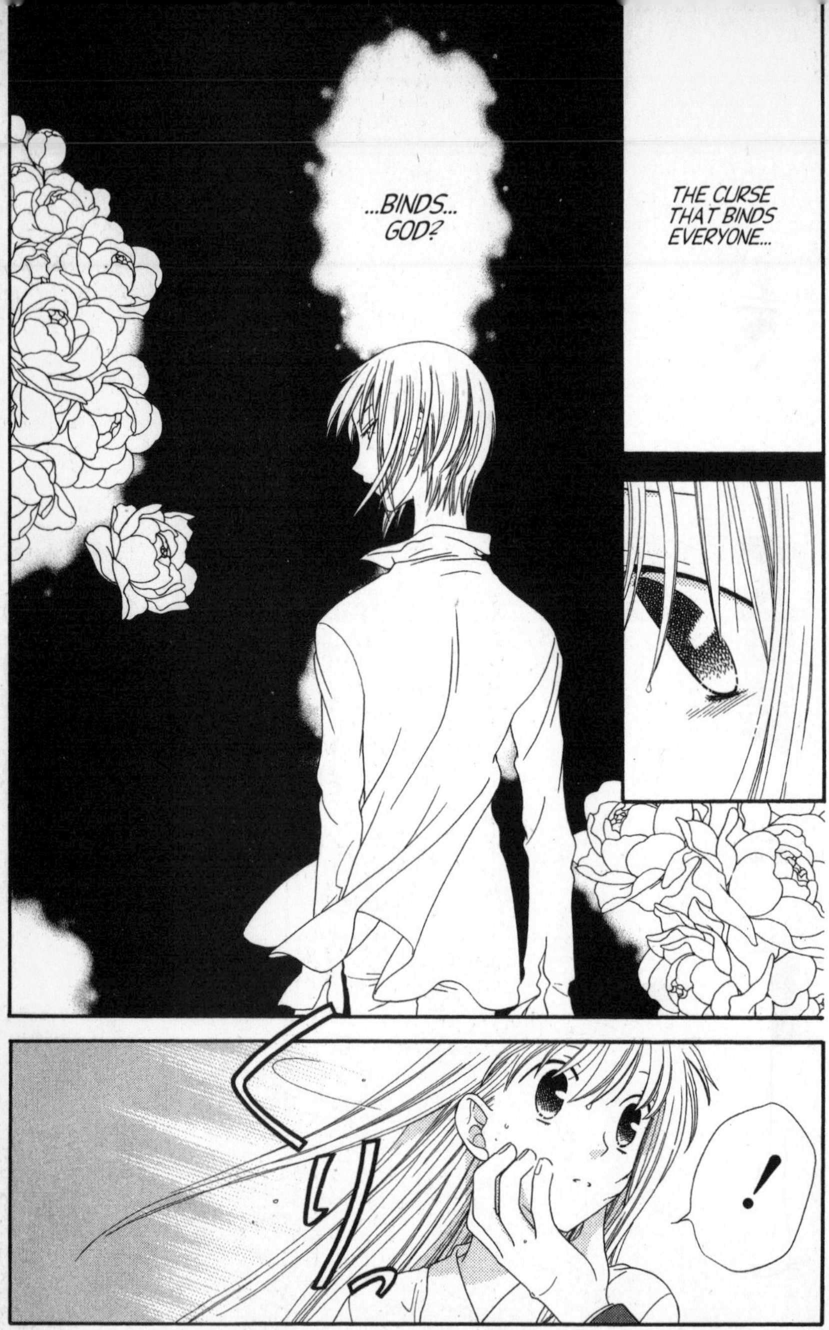
THE CURSE THAT BINDS EVERYONE...
...BINDS... GOD?
!

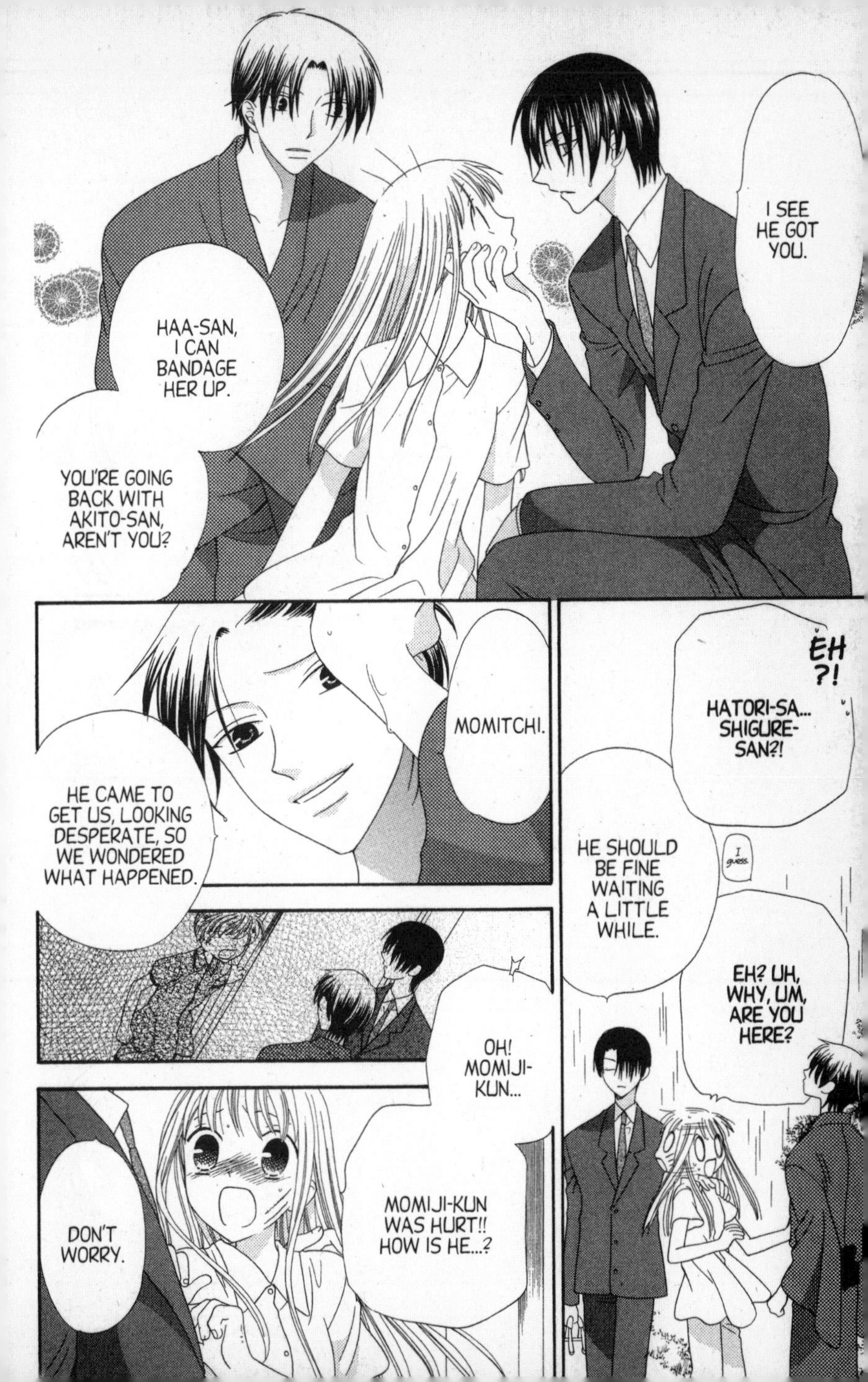
I SEE HE GOT YOU.
HAA-SAN, I CAN BANDAGE HER UP.
YOU'RE GOING BACK WITH AKITO-SAN, AREN'T YOU?
EH ?!
HATORI-SA... SHIGURE-SAN?!
EH? UH, WHY, UM, ARE YOU HERE?
MOMITCHI.
HE CAME TO GET US, LOOKING DESPERATE, SO WE WONDERED WHAT HAPPENED.
HE SHOULD BE FINE WAITING A LITTLE WHILE.
I guess.
OH! MOMIJI-KUN...
MOMIJI-KUN WAS HURT!! HOW IS HE...?
DON'T WORRY.

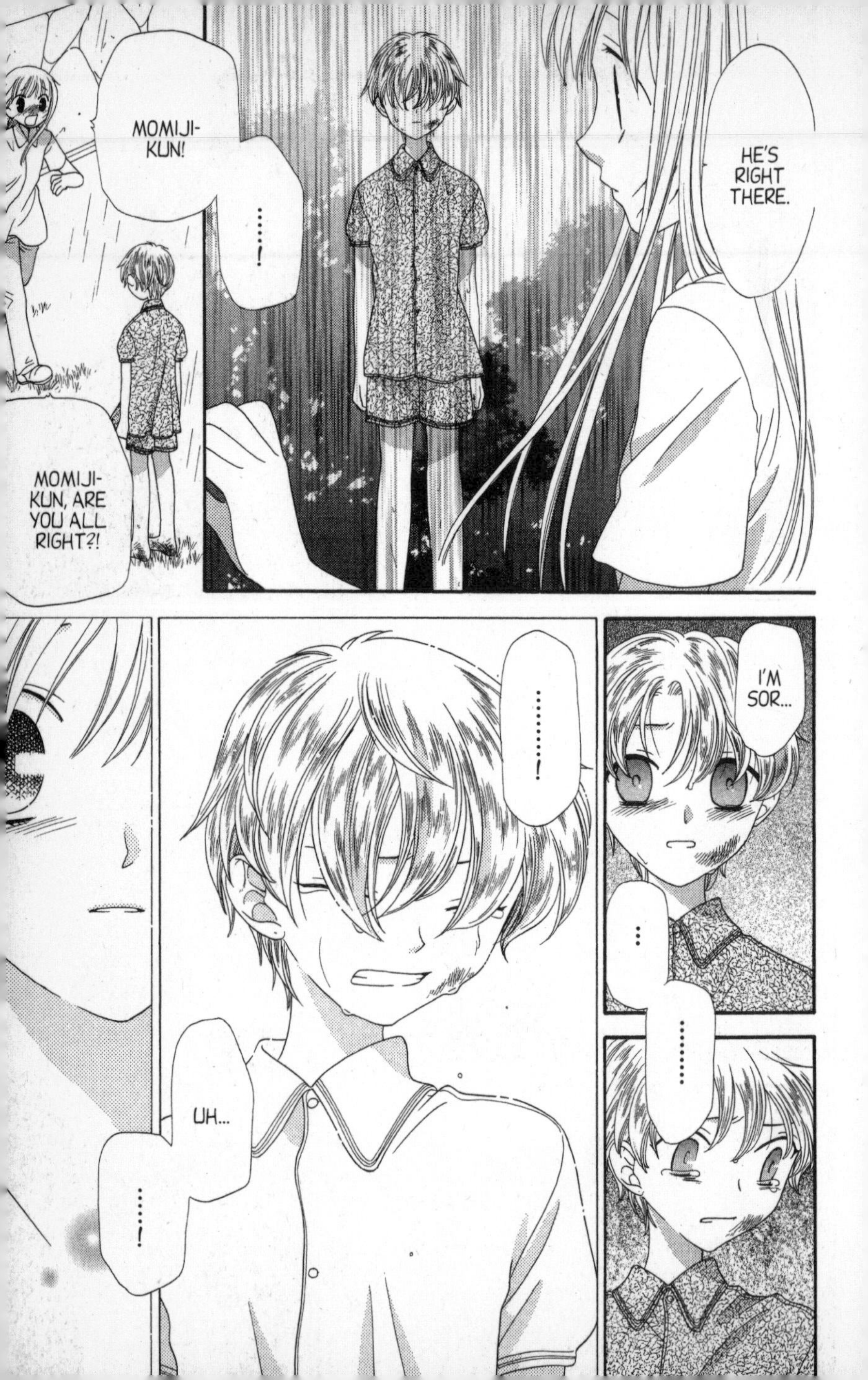
HE'S RIGHT THERE.
MOMIJI-KUN!
.....!
MOMIJI-KUN, ARE YOU ALL RIGHT?!
I'M SOR...
...
....
.........!
UH...
.....!

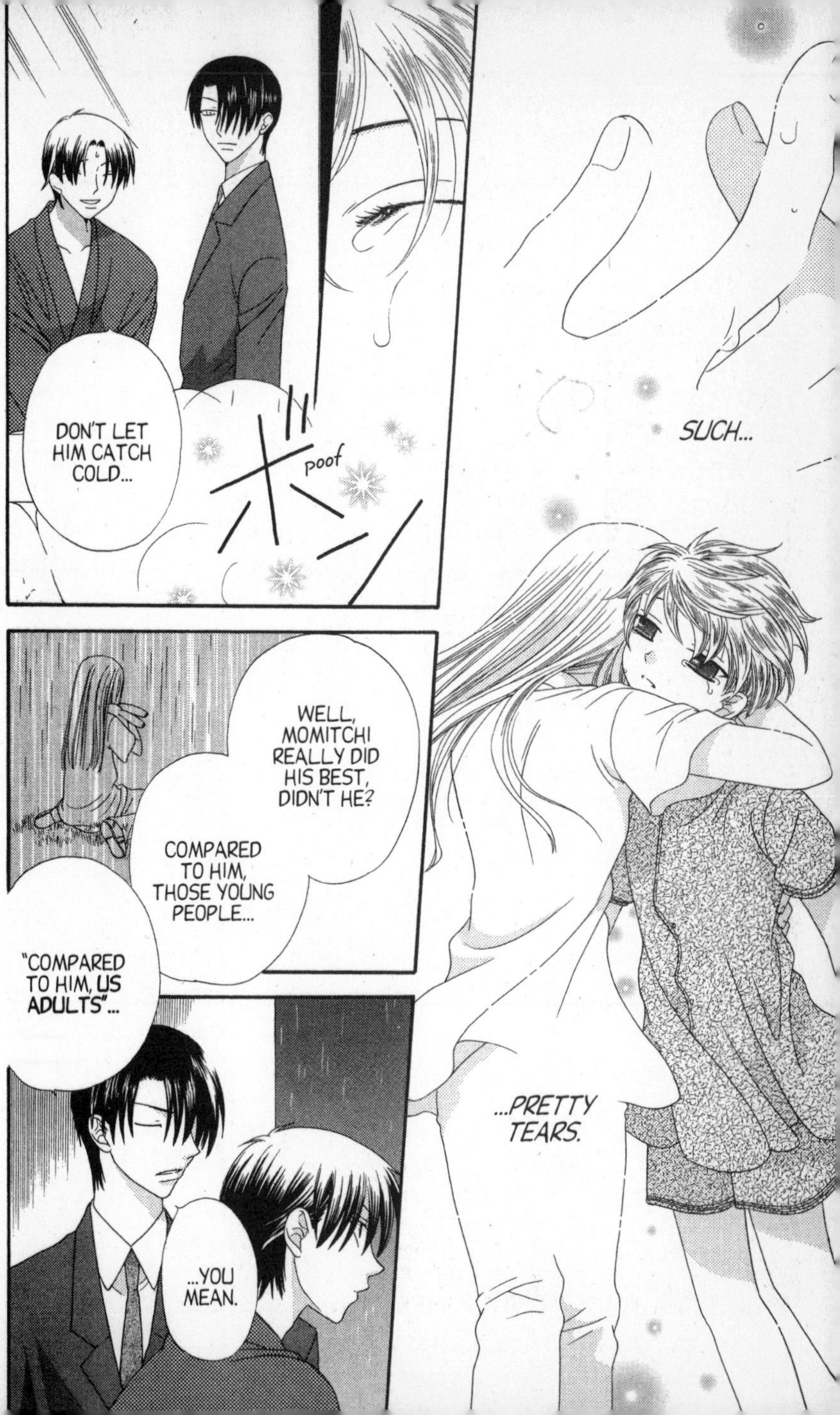
SUCH...
...PRETTY TEARS.
DON'T LET HIM CATCH COLD...
poof
WELL, MOMITCHI REALLY DID HIS BEST, DIDN'T HE?
COMPARED TO HIM, THOSE YOUNG PEOPLE...
"COMPARED TO HIM, US ADULTS"...
...YOU MEAN.

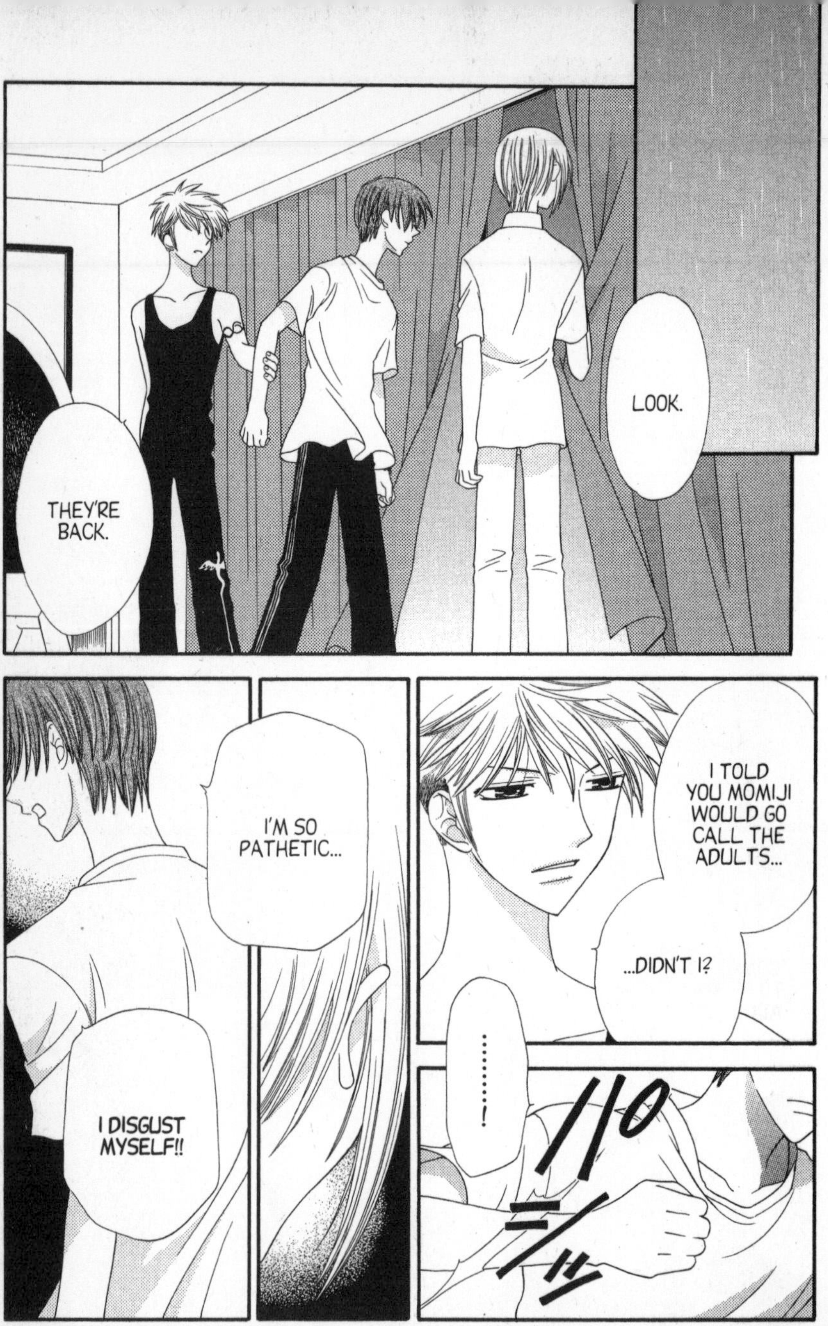

LOOK.
THEY'RE BACK.
I TOLD YOU MOMIJI WOULD GO CALL THE ADULTS...
...DIDN'T I?
......!
I'M SO PATHETIC...
I DISGUST MYSELF!!

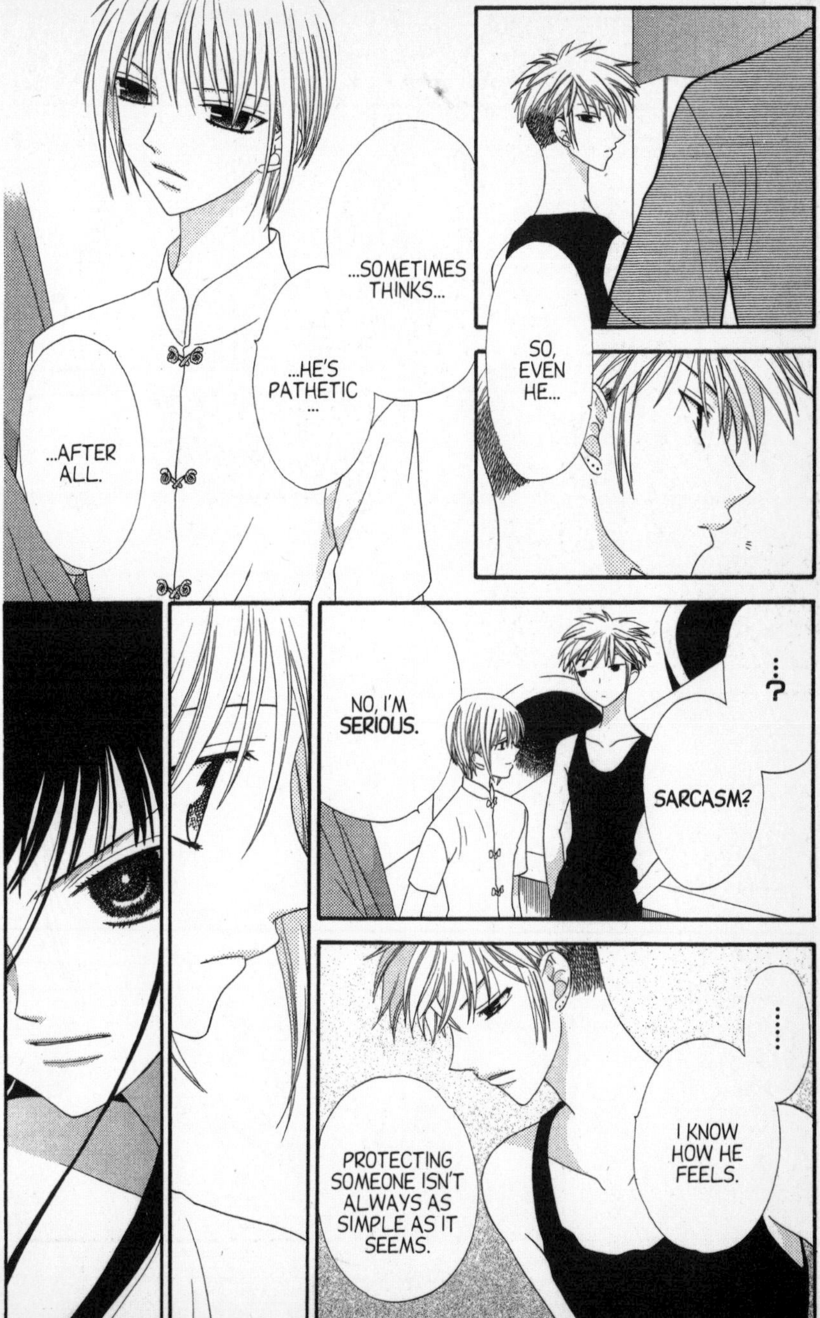
SO, EVEN HE...
...SOMETIMES THINKS...
...HE'S PATHETIC ...
...AFTER ALL.
...?
SARCASM?
NO, I'M **SERIOUS.**
......
I KNOW HOW HE FEELS.
PROTECTING SOMEONE ISN'T ALWAYS AS SIMPLE AS IT SEEMS.

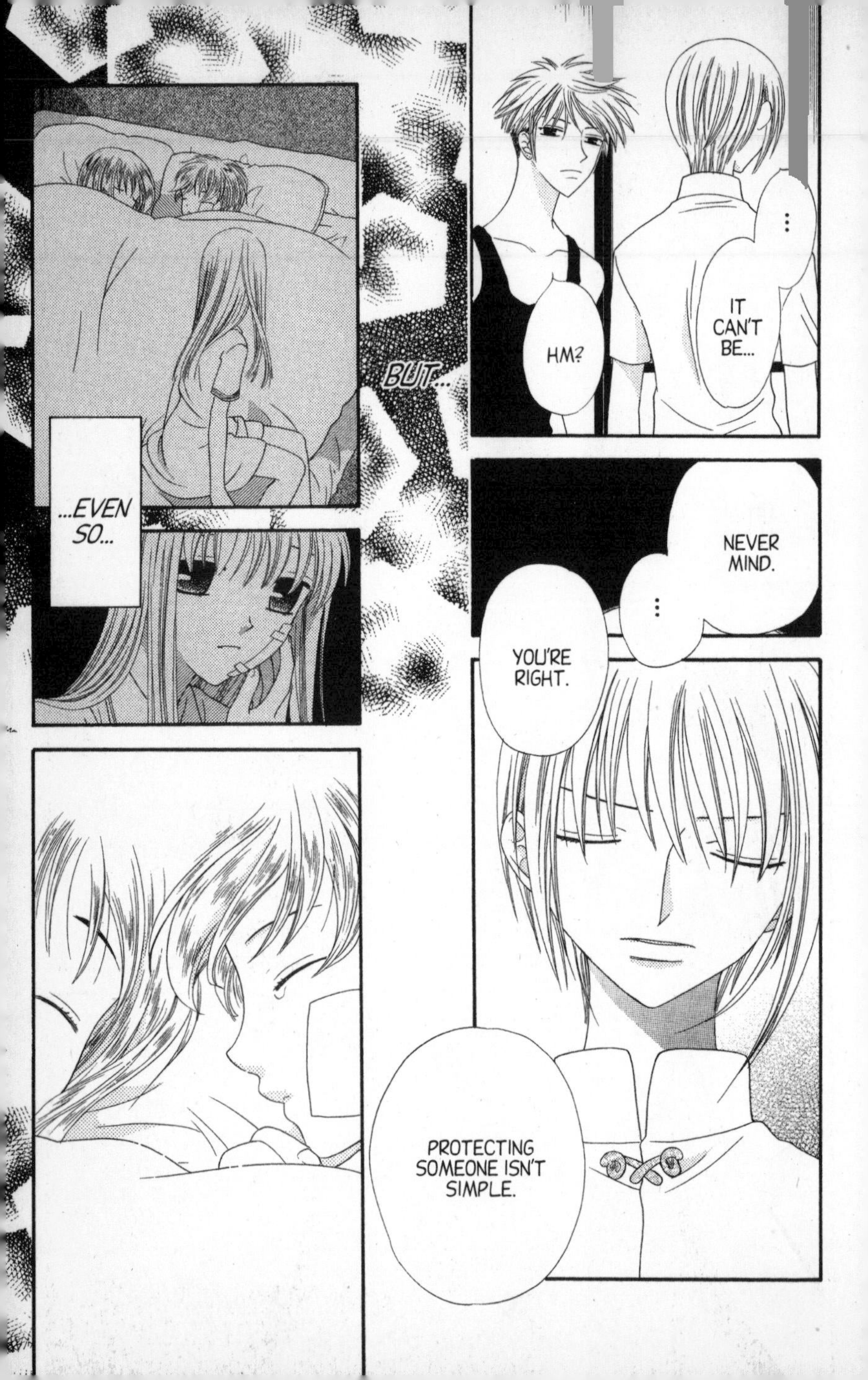
...
IT CAN'T BE...
HM?
BUT...
...EVEN SO...
NEVER MIND.
...
YOU'RE RIGHT.
PROTECTING SOMEONE ISN'T SIMPLE.

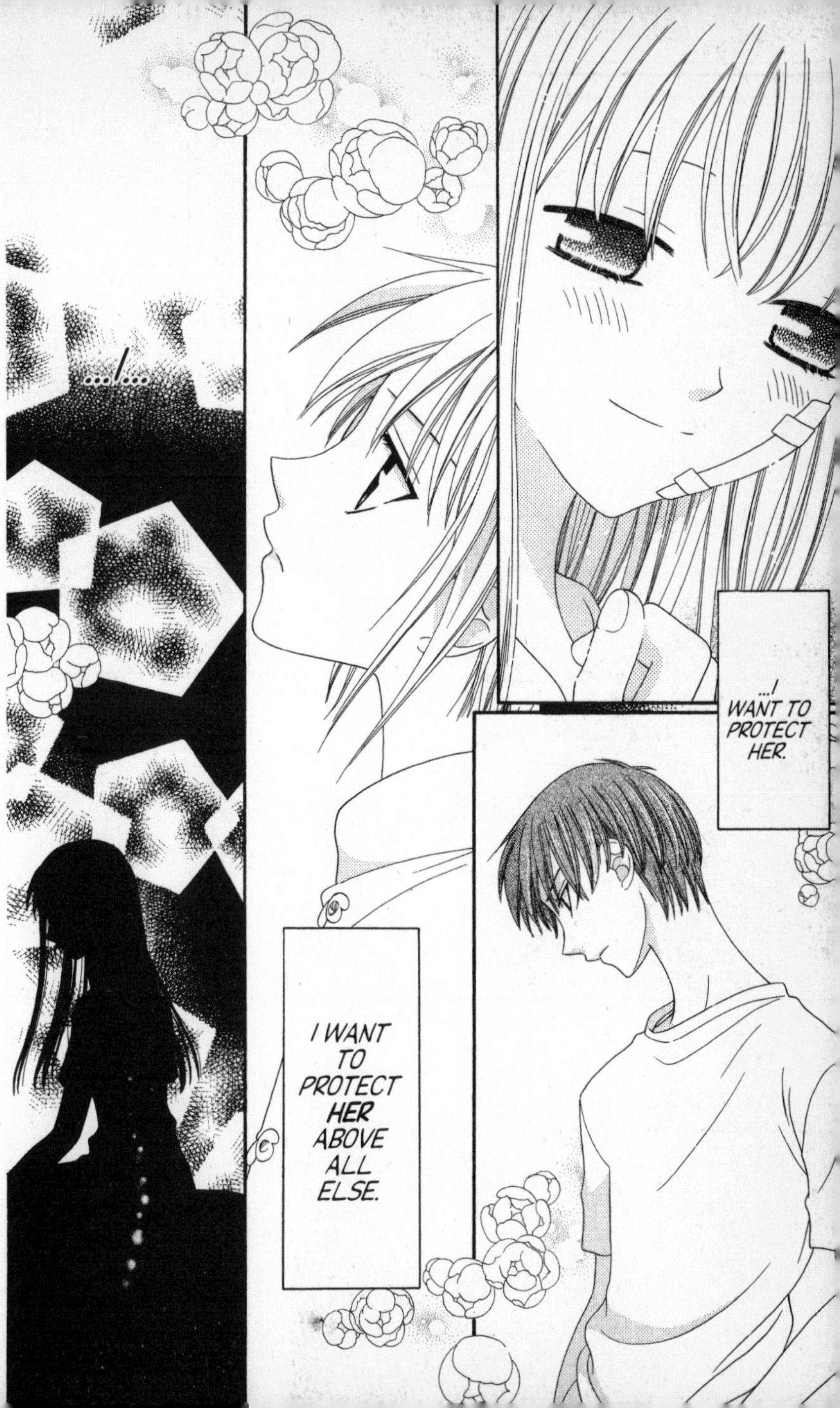
...I WANT TO PROTECT HER.
I WANT TO PROTECT HER ABOVE ALL ELSE.
...!...

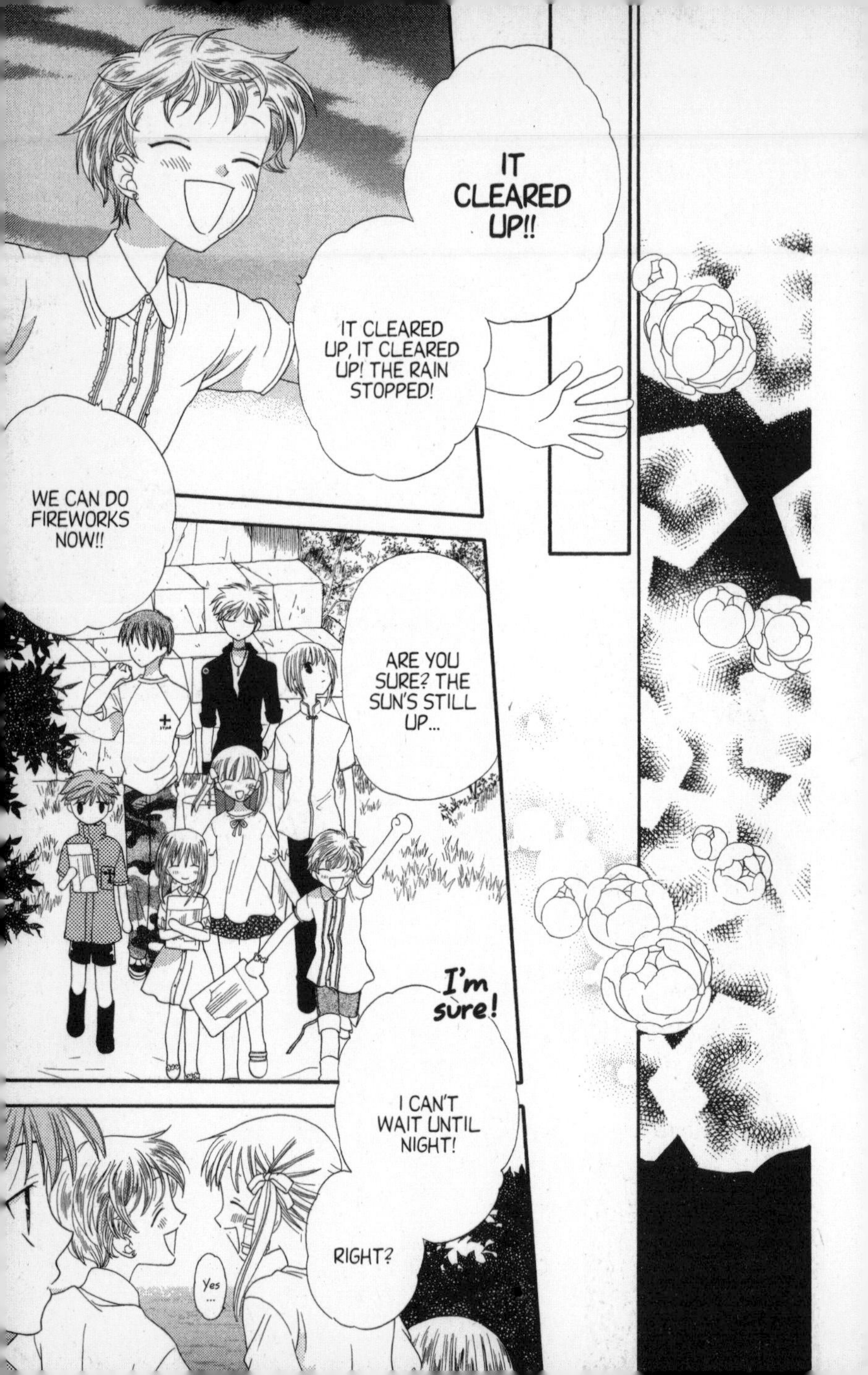
IT CLEARED UP!!
IT CLEARED UP, IT CLEARED UP! THE RAIN STOPPED!
WE CAN DO FIREWORKS NOW!!
ARE YOU SURE? THE SUN'S STILL UP...
I'm sure!
I CAN'T WAIT UNTIL NIGHT!
RIGHT?
Yes ...

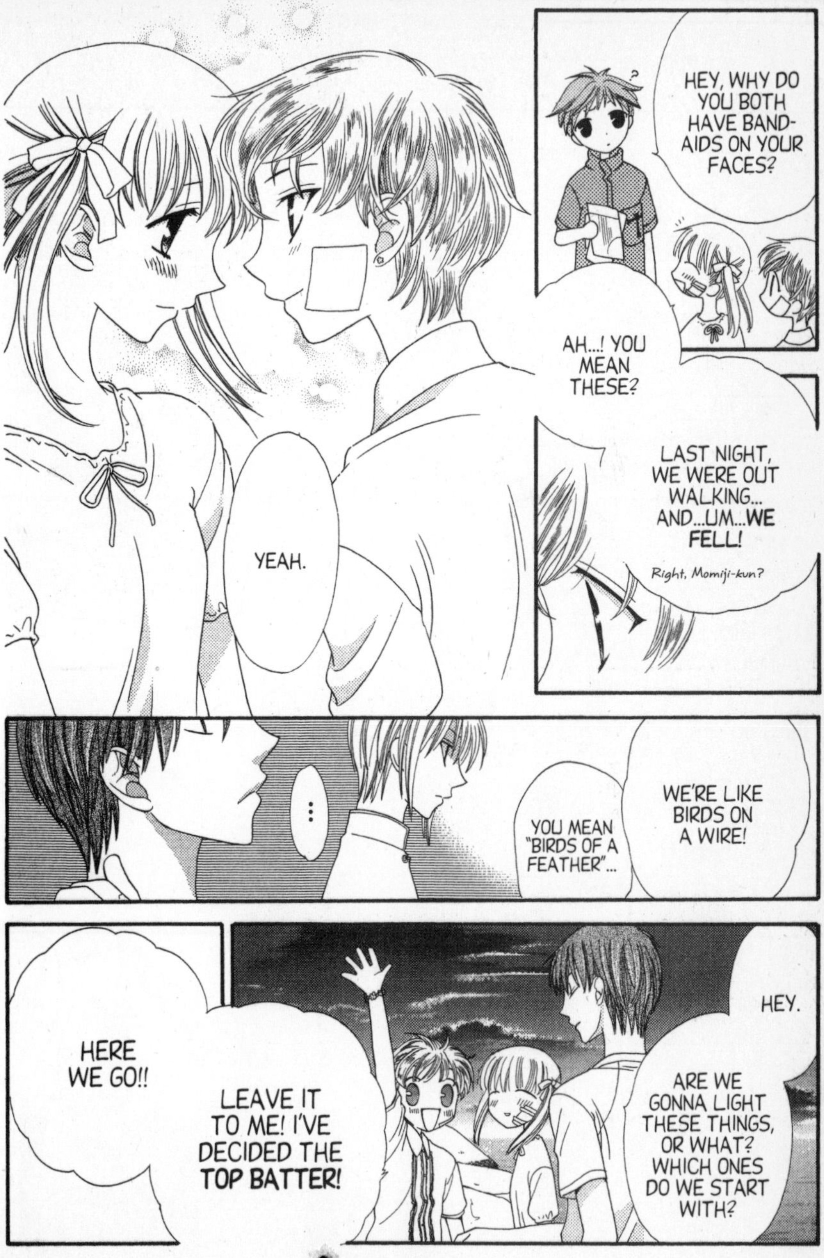
HEY, WHY DO YOU BOTH HAVE BAND-AIDS ON YOUR FACES?
AH...! YOU MEAN THESE?
LAST NIGHT, WE WERE OUT WALKING... AND...UM...**WE FELL!**
Right, Momiji-kun?
YEAH.
WE'RE LIKE BIRDS ON A WIRE!
YOU MEAN "BIRDS OF A FEATHER"...
...
HEY.
ARE WE GONNA LIGHT THESE THINGS, OR WHAT? WHICH ONES DO WE START WITH?
LEAVE IT TO ME! I'VE DECIDED THE **TOP BATTER!**
HERE WE GO!!

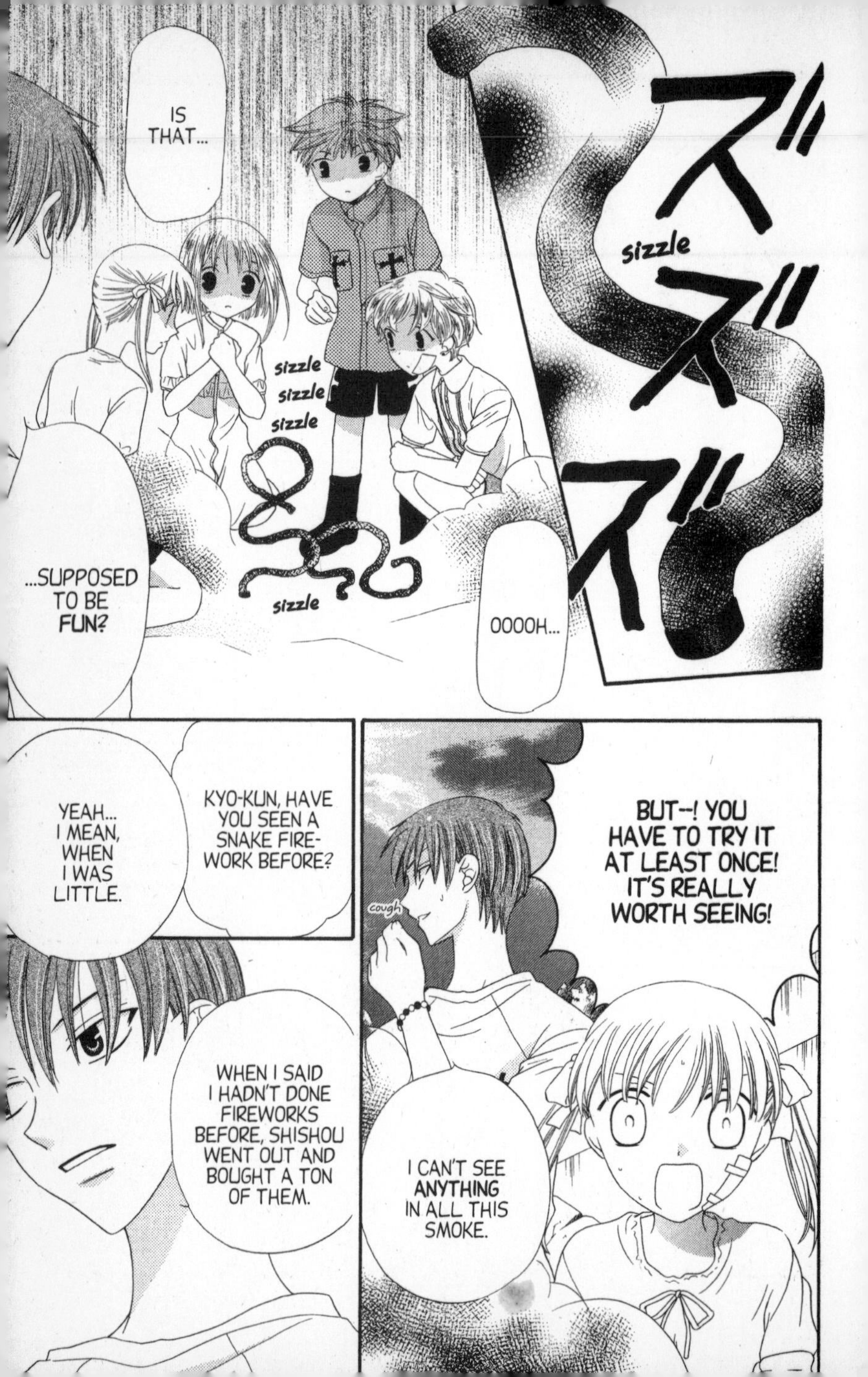
ズズズ
sizzle
OOOOH...
IS THAT...
sizzle
sizzle
sizzle
...SUPPOSED TO BE FUN?
sizzle
BUT--! YOU HAVE TO TRY IT AT LEAST ONCE! IT'S REALLY WORTH SEEING!
cough
I CAN'T SEE ANYTHING IN ALL THIS SMOKE.
KYO-KUN, HAVE YOU SEEN A SNAKE FIRE-WORK BEFORE?
YEAH... I MEAN, WHEN I WAS LITTLE.
WHEN I SAID I HADN'T DONE FIREWORKS BEFORE, SHISHOU WENT OUT AND BOUGHT A TON OF THEM.

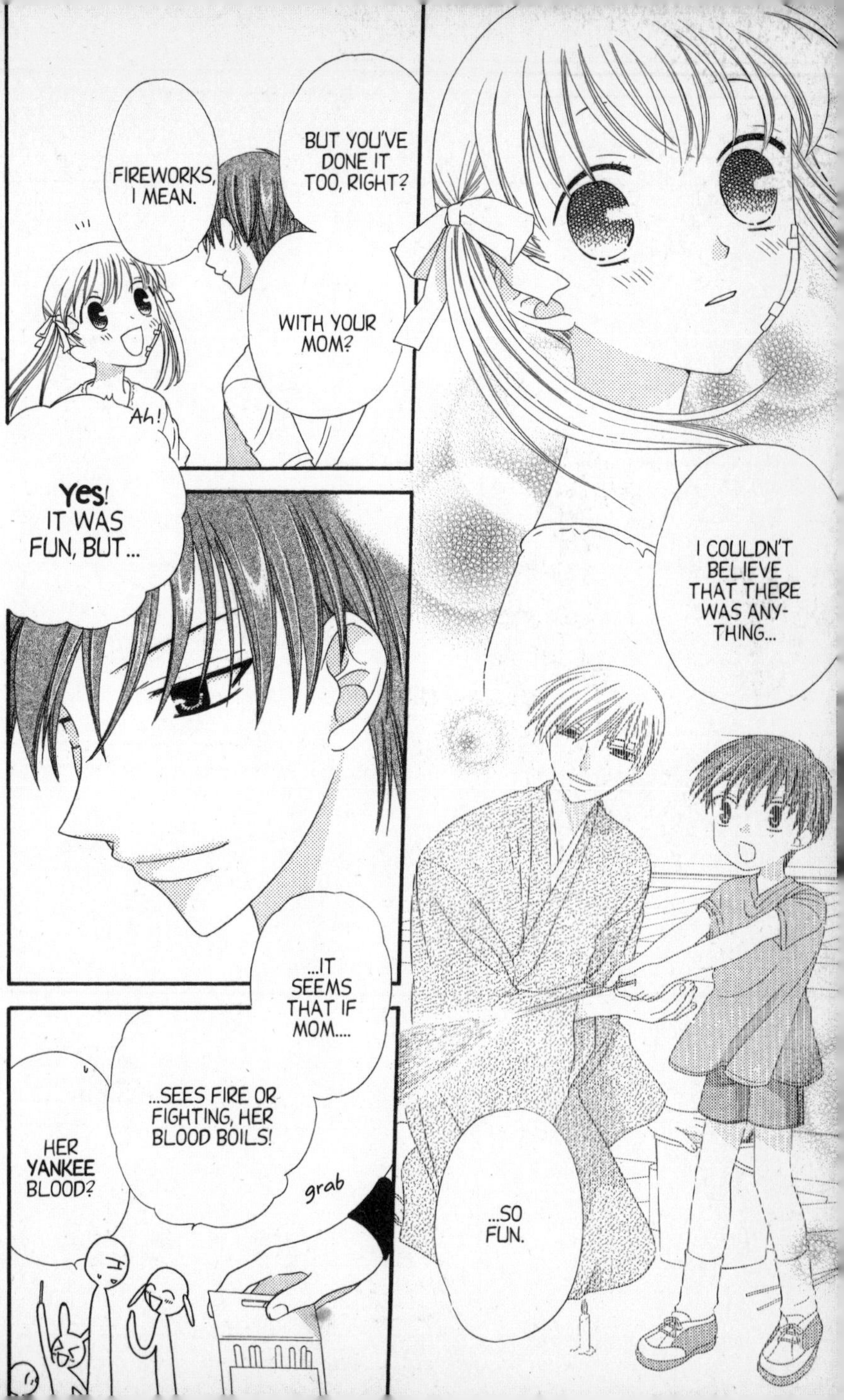

I COULDN'T BELIEVE THAT THERE WAS ANY-THING...
...SO FUN.
BUT YOU'VE DONE IT TOO, RIGHT?
FIREWORKS, I MEAN.
WITH YOUR MOM?
Ah!
Yes! IT WAS FUN, BUT...
...IT SEEMS THAT IF MOM....
...SEES FIRE OR FIGHTING, HER BLOOD BOILS!
HER YANKEE BLOOD?
grab

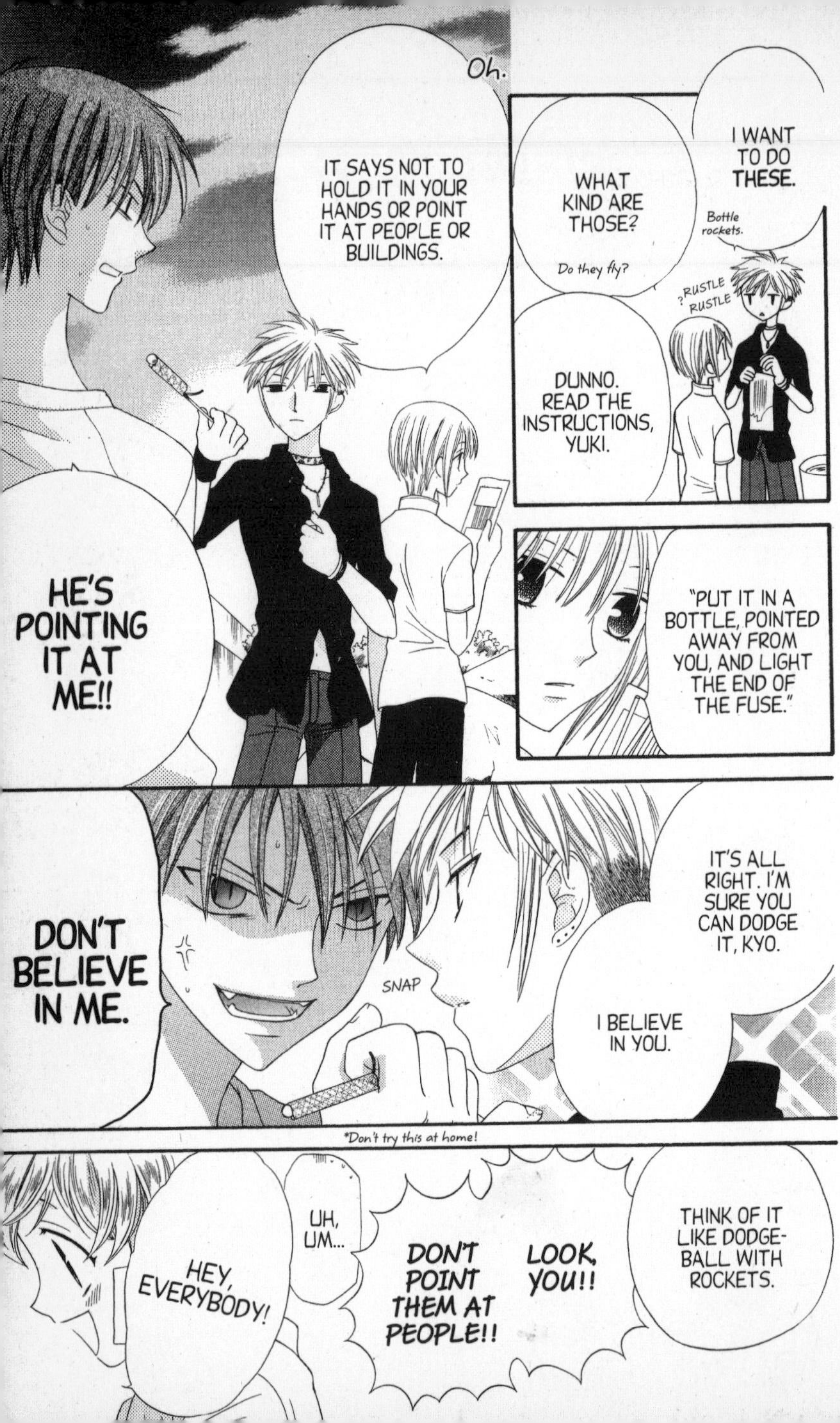
I WANT TO DO THESE.
Bottle rockets.
WHAT KIND ARE THOSE?
Do they fly?
?RUSTLE RUSTLE
DUNNO. READ THE INSTRUCTIONS, YUKI.
"PUT IT IN A BOTTLE, POINTED AWAY FROM YOU, AND LIGHT THE END OF THE FUSE."
Oh.
IT SAYS NOT TO HOLD IT IN YOUR HANDS OR POINT IT AT PEOPLE OR BUILDINGS.
HE'S POINTING IT AT ME!!
IT'S ALL RIGHT. I'M SURE YOU CAN DODGE IT, KYO.
I BELIEVE IN YOU.
SNAP
DON'T BELIEVE IN ME.
*Don't try this at home!
THINK OF IT LIKE DODGE-BALL WITH ROCKETS.
LOOK, YOU!!
DON'T POINT THEM AT PEOPLE!!
UH, UM...
HEY, EVERYBODY!

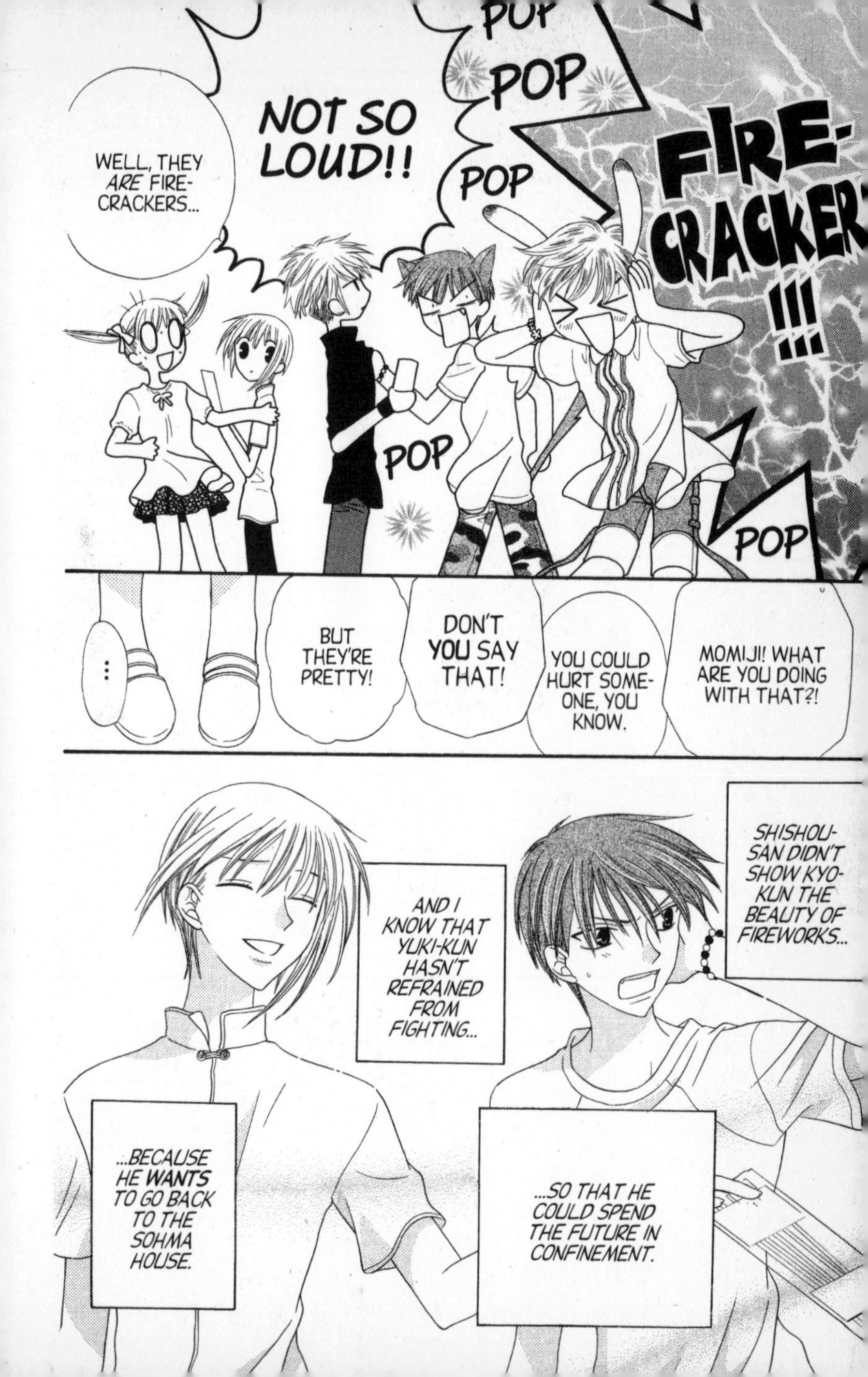
POP
POP
FIRE-CRACKERS!!!
POP
NOT SO LOUD!!
WELL, THEY *ARE* FIRE-CRACKERS...
POP
POP
MOMIJI! WHAT ARE YOU DOING WITH THAT?!
YOU COULD HURT SOME-ONE, YOU KNOW.
DON'T **YOU** SAY THAT!
BUT THEY'RE PRETTY!
...
SHISHOU-SAN DIDN'T SHOW KYO-KUN THE BEAUTY OF FIREWORKS...
AND I KNOW THAT YUKI-KUN HASN'T REFRAINED FROM FIGHTING...
...SO THAT HE COULD SPEND THE FUTURE IN CONFINEMENT.
...BECAUSE HE **WANTS** TO GO BACK TO THE SOHMA HOUSE.

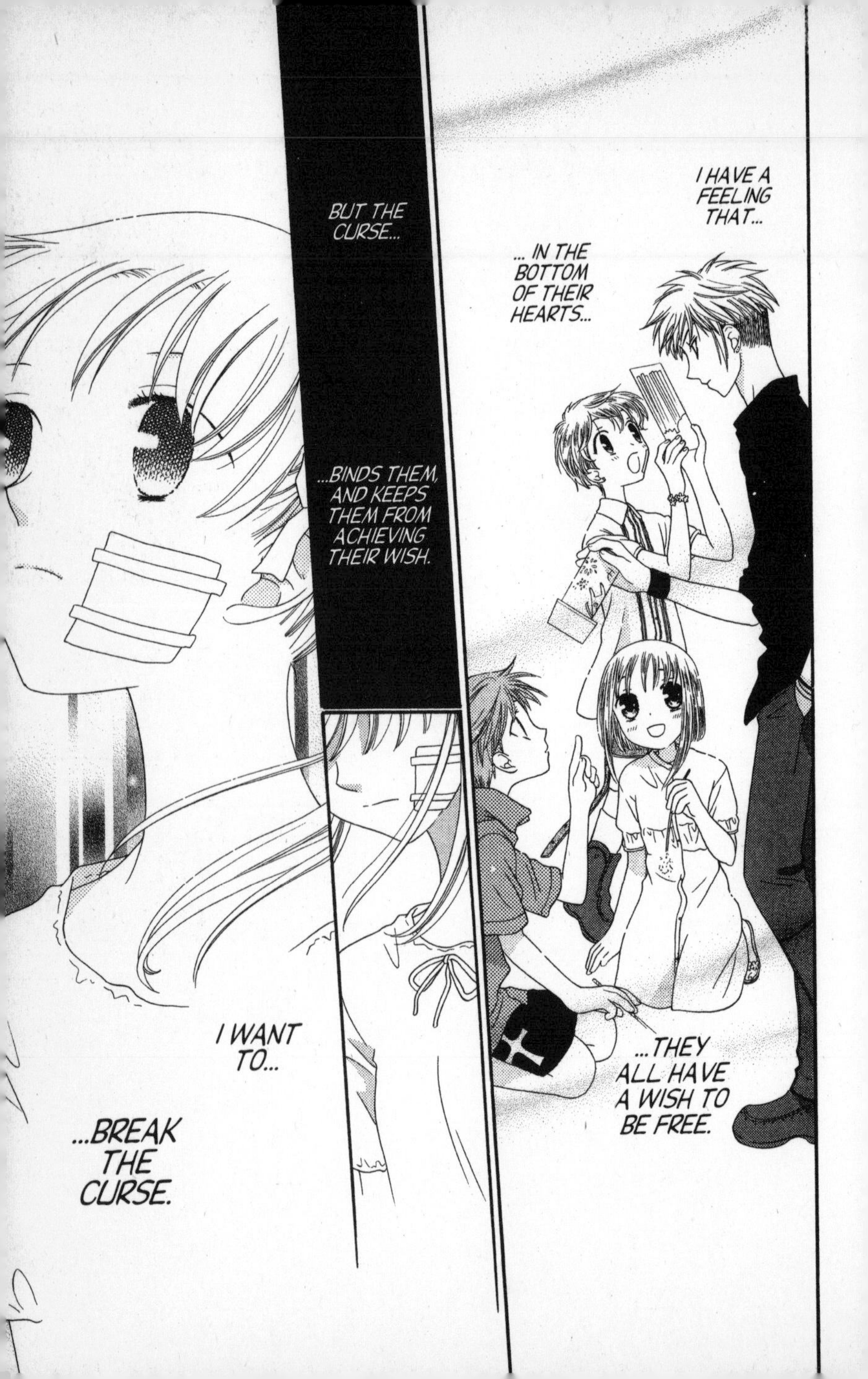
I HAVE A FEELING THAT...
... IN THE BOTTOM OF THEIR HEARTS...
...THEY ALL HAVE A WISH TO BE FREE.
BUT THE CURSE...
...BINDS THEM, AND KEEPS THEM FROM ACHIEVING THEIR WISH.
I WANT TO...
...BREAK THE CURSE.

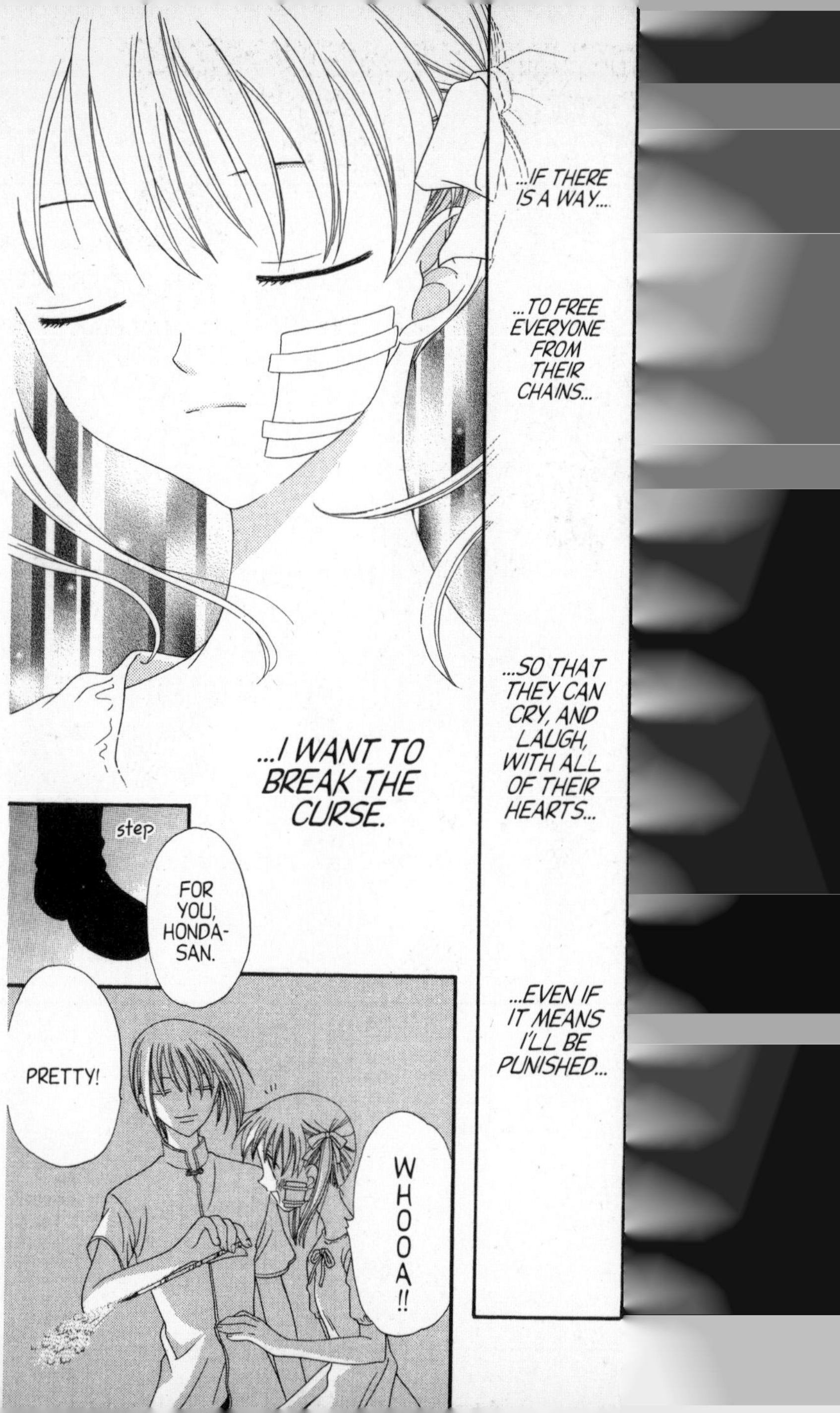
...IF THERE IS A WAY...
...TO FREE EVERYONE FROM THEIR CHAINS...
...SO THAT THEY CAN CRY, AND LAUGH, WITH ALL OF THEIR HEARTS...
...EVEN IF IT MEANS I'LL BE PUNISHED...
...I WANT TO BREAK THE CURSE.
step
FOR YOU, HONDA-SAN.
WHOOA!!
PRETTY!

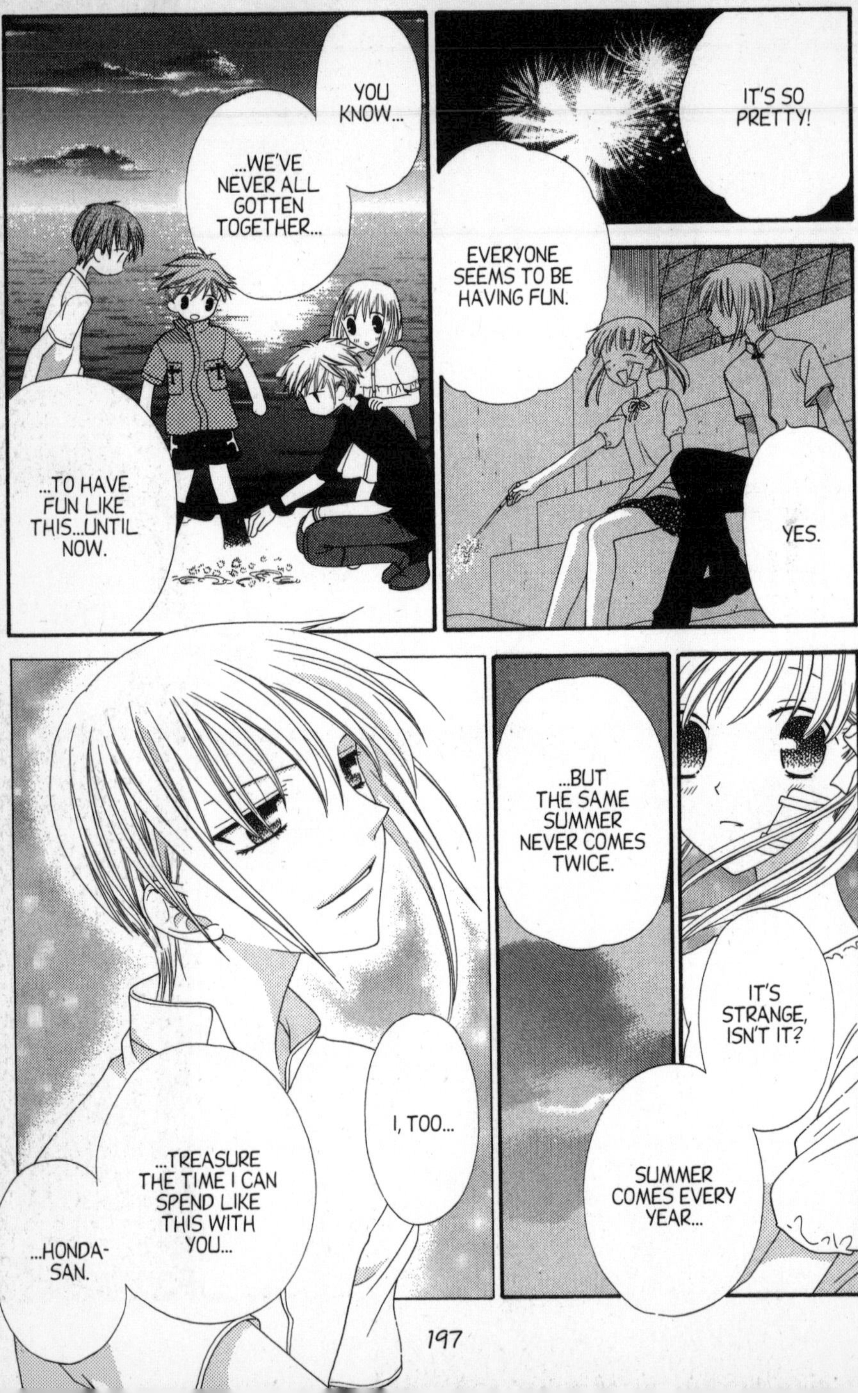
IT'S SO PRETTY!
EVERYONE SEEMS TO BE HAVING FUN.
YES.
YOU KNOW...
...WE'VE NEVER ALL GOTTEN TOGETHER...
...TO HAVE FUN LIKE THIS...UNTIL NOW.
IT'S STRANGE, ISN'T IT?
SUMMER COMES EVERY YEAR...
...BUT THE SAME SUMMER NEVER COMES TWICE.
I, TOO...
...TREASURE THE TIME I CAN SPEND LIKE THIS WITH YOU...
...HONDA-SAN.

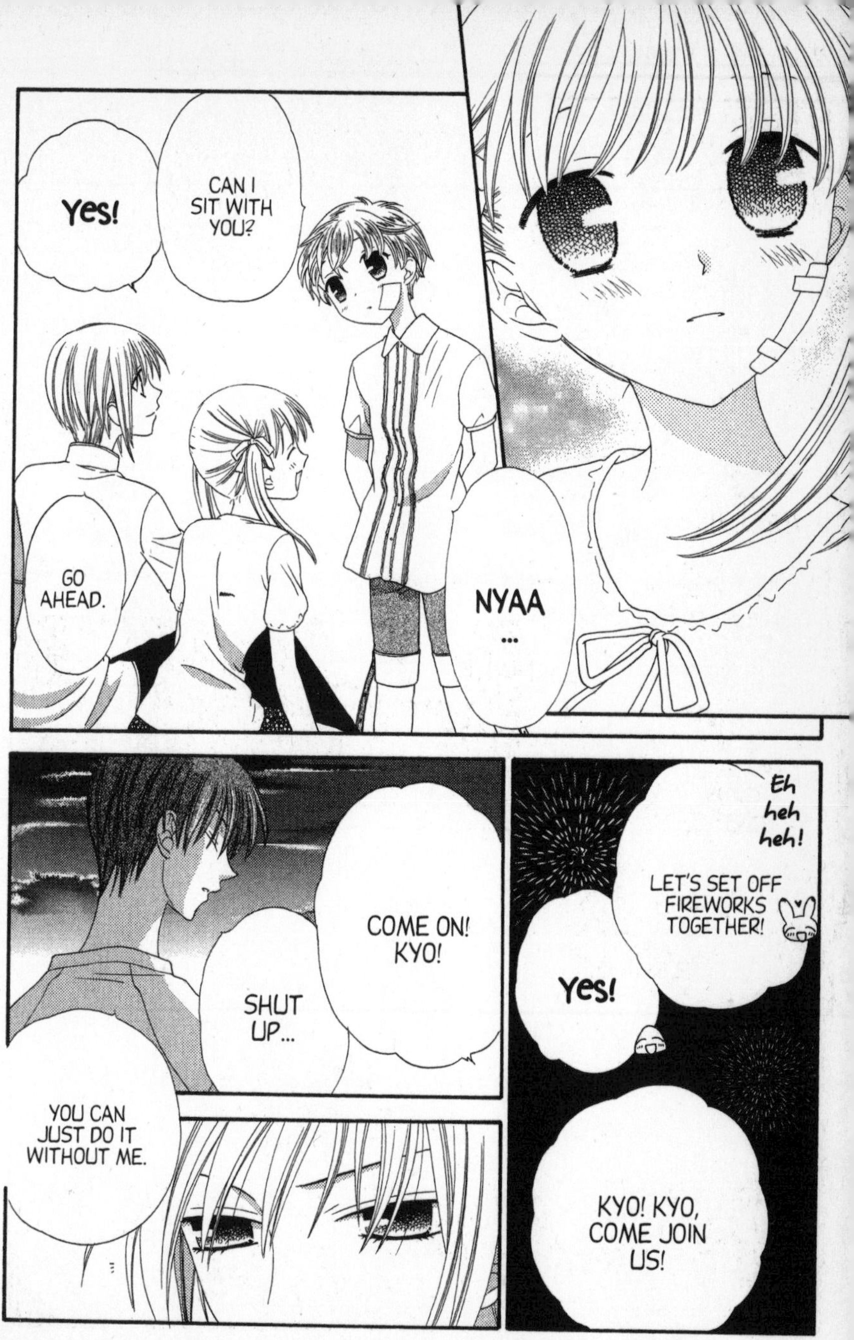
CAN I SIT WITH YOU?
Yes!
GO AHEAD.
NYAA ...
Eh heh heh!
LET'S SET OFF FIREWORKS TOGETHER!
Yes!
KYO! KYO, COME JOIN US!
COME ON! KYO!
SHUT UP...
YOU CAN JUST DO IT WITHOUT ME.

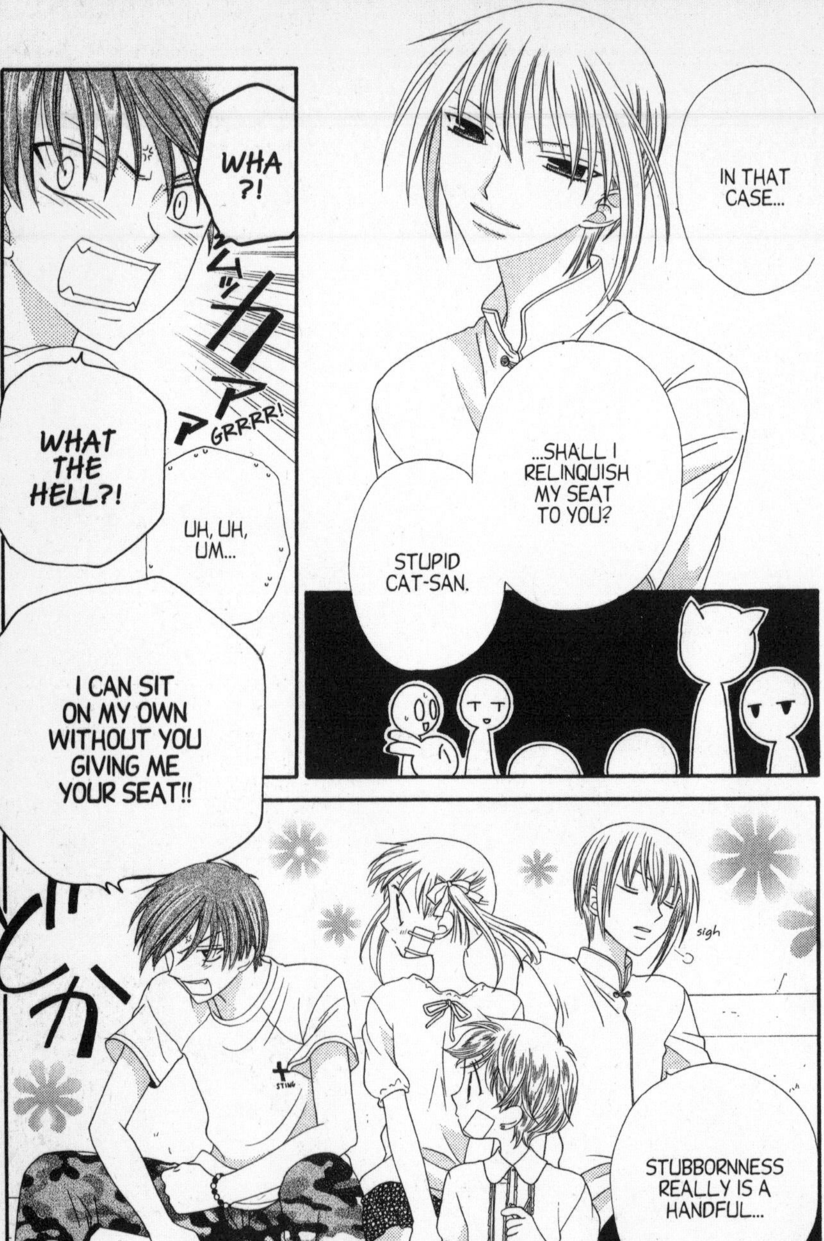
IN THAT CASE...
...SHALL I RELINQUISH MY SEAT TO YOU?
STUPID CAT-SAN.
WHA?!
ムッカァァ
GRRRR!
WHAT THE HELL?!
UH, UH, UM...
I CAN SIT ON MY OWN WITHOUT YOU GIVING ME YOUR SEAT!!
どか
sigh
STUBBORNNESS REALLY IS A HANDFUL...

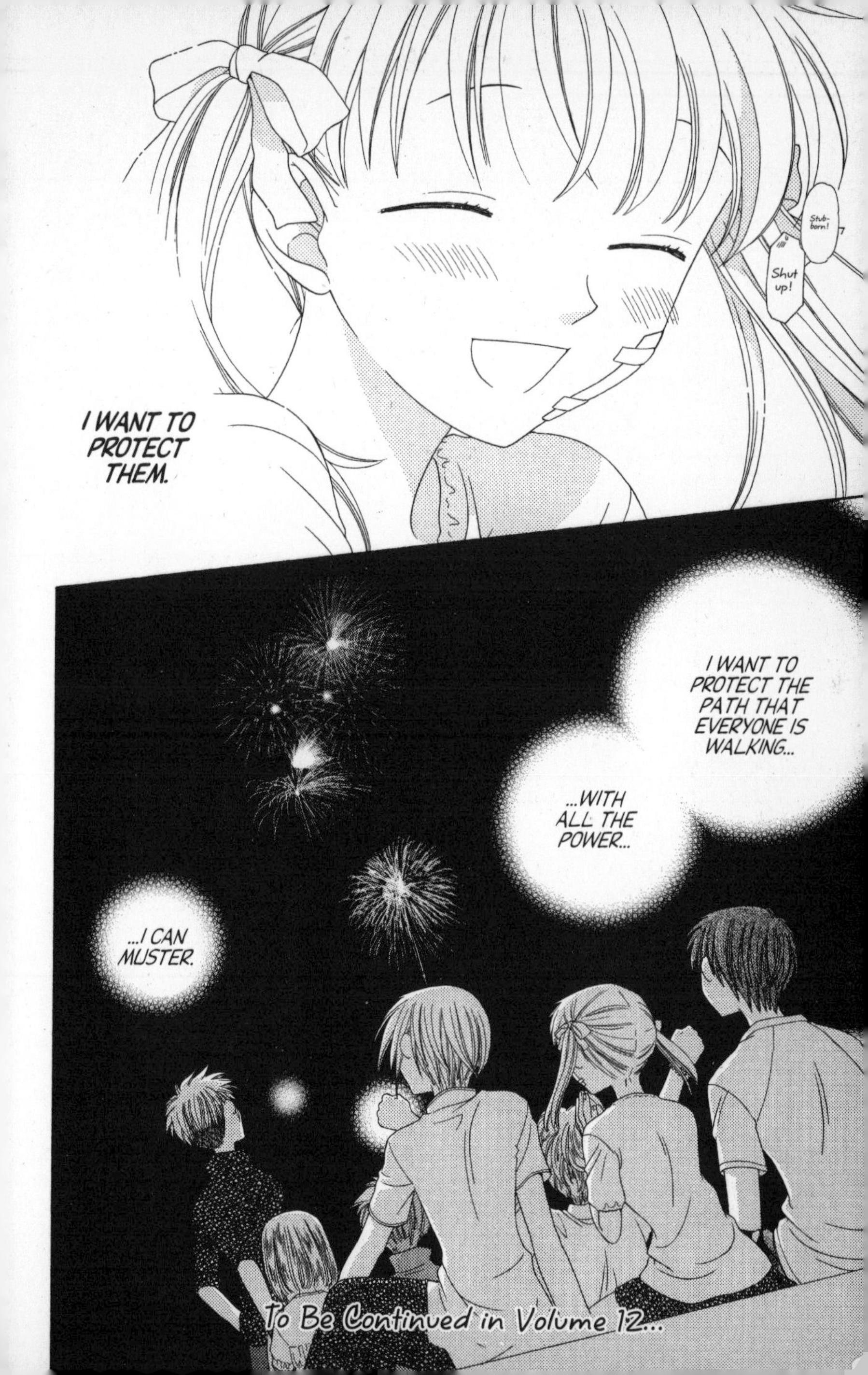
Stub-born!
Shut up!
I WANT TO PROTECT THEM.
I WANT TO PROTECT THE PATH THAT EVERYONE IS WALKING...
...WITH ALL THE POWER...
...I CAN MUSTER.
To Be Continued in Volume 12...

Next time in...

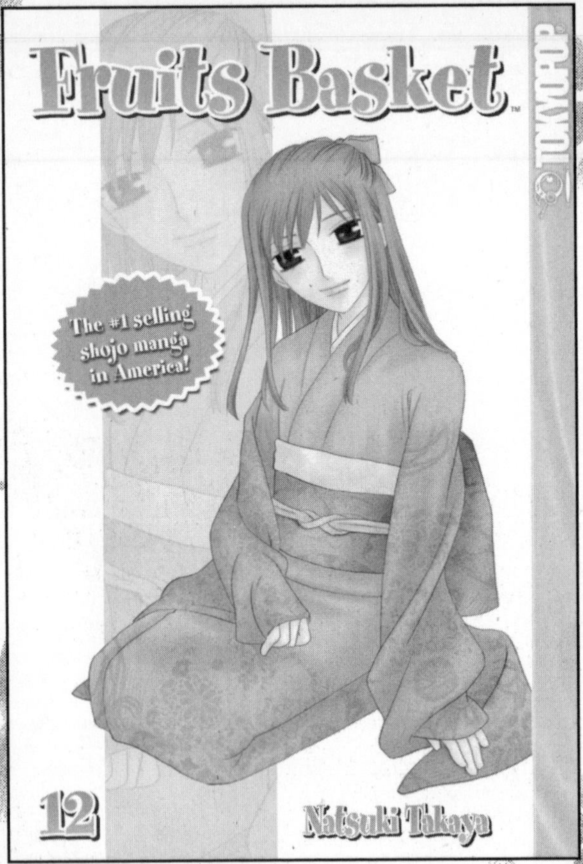
Fruits Basket™
TOKYOPOP
The #1 selling shojo manga in America!
12
Natsuki Takaya

Council Clash and Past Rehash...

Summer vacation comes to a close, and school begins again. Student life, however, is full of strife. A new student council has been assembled, featuring two controversial secretaries: Naohito, who has declared himself Yuki's rival, and Kimi, a devil woman who steals men's hearts. While classmates clash, Tohru becomes convinced that she may have finally discovered a way to break the Sohma's curse. However, Tohru has her own family crisis to deal with--her grandfather has thrown out his back, and while Tohru visits him, he is bent on discussing a painful part of her past.

Fruits Basket Volume 12
Available December 2005

Year of the Sheep: Getting Wooly

Sheep

Years*: 1943, 1955, 1967, 1979, 1991, 2003, 2015, 2027, 2039
Positive Qualities: Creative, Honest, Passionate, Elegant
Grievances: Indecisive, Disorganized, Timid
Suitable Jobs: Actor, Gardener, Chef
Compatible With: Rabbits, Boar, Horses
Must Avoid: Ox
Ruling Hours: 1 PM to 3 PM
Season: Summer
Ruling Month: July
Sign Direction: South-Southwest
Fixed Element: Fire
Corresponding Western Sign: Cancer

Much like the way a Sheep prides its wool coat, women born in the Year of the Sheep have a certain beauty and vigor about them that only adds to their elegance--something cemented by the fact that these ladies spend an exorbitant amount of time dolling themselves up. Their rooms are always filled with nice fragrances and fresh flowers, and they pay great attention to their own hygiene.

While a Sheep's love may be unconditional, their "yes means no" and "no means yes" nature can be a nightmare for any potential partner. Women of this year also have a clever way of getting what they want through pitiful looks and playfully skilled pestering. Sheep are also predisposed to cuddling and, if possible, would love nothing more than to have someone stay with them every second of the day.

Celebrity Sheep:
Pamela Anderson
Jennifer Love Hewitt
Kate Hudson
Norah Jones
Nicole Kidman
Matt LeBlanc
Carrie-Anne Moss
Julia Roberts
Vin Diesel

Also known as the Year of the Ram or Goat, the traits of the Sheep have little in common with those of the astrological sign Aries. Sheep are shy and timid by nature and would prefer to remain anonymous rather than standing out and making a name for themselves--something that tends to happen regardless of their humble intentions.

Nonetheless, Sheep are passionate about their work and everything that they believe in. They are highly religious, but also very materialistic individuals. Sheep are often too dependent on the creature comforts their life brings and end up complaining over the smallest of things--not realizing it may be their own disorganization that they are displeased with. Pessimists by nature and quite vulnerable, Sheep do not respond well to pressure. However, they are quite adept to finding creative and natural solutions to any problems at hand.

* Note: It is important to know on which day Chinese New Year's was held, as that changes what Zodiac animal you are. Example: 1991 actually began on February 15, and anyone born before that date is actually a Horse.

Fans Basket

Once again, another volume of Fruits Basket has come to a close. Naturally, that means you dear readers are going to be treated to some more fan art! I've also thrown in a letter or two in this volume, as well. But let's get the ball rolling with a lovely poem!

- Paul Morrissey, Editor

Tohru's Gift

Within the memory of her mother
Lies Tohru's special gift
To heal the brokenhearted members
And help their Spirits lift.

The Curse encircles dark
Hide away from sight
The Thirteen Members falling
Into the loneliness of night.

But "the flower" holds them back
And shares away the pain
To save Yuki and Kyo,
Until they smile again.

Diana Frances Ferrell
Age 19
El Centro, CA

Thanks, Diana. This poem is melancholy, but it also manages to be hopeful. I think you've captured the tone of *Fruits Basket* extremely well!

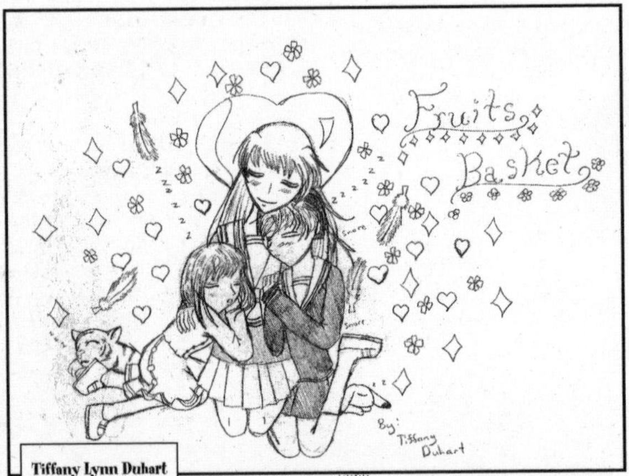
Fruits Basket
By: Tiffany Duhart

Tiffany Lynn Duhart
Age 14
Whites Boro, NJ

Tiffany is finally getting some of her work printed in *Fruits Basket!* Yay! This sketch is by far your best, Tiffany. It really gives a sense of Tohru's caring, maternal nature. It's a very sweet drawing... and I always love seeing Kisa with a tiger!

Hey Furuba,
I am madly in love with Hatori! I had a dream where he was heartbroken because his girlfriend had died. Since I love him, I left a note on his desk. It had my address on it and it said, "I love you, a lot!!" Well, later in my dream, I was rushed into the emergency room for some mysterious reason, and it turned out that Hatori was my doctor! I had a really sharp pain on the left side of my ribs and I wished I would die. While I was in pain, Hatori was sitting right next to me, holding my hand and caressing my hair. I could hear him telling me that he wanted me to open my eyes and that he loved me, too! I felt wet drops falling on my face and Hatori getting closer. I knew he was crying, and he gave me the warmest hug I have ever gotten in my life. I semi-opened my eyes and saw his beautiful pale eyes in front of mine. He got closer and gave me a soft, wet French kiss! When I woke up, I found out that I had passed out in the horse corral! I had fallen off the horse and broke two of my ribs. My dog was the one who "kissed" me. In the ambulance all I could think of was Hatori. Now I'm in bed writing this letter to you all, but I don't regret it! I LOVE Hatori. Well thanks for letting me share this with you all!

Samantha S.
Age 14
Edinburg, TX

Nothing like physical trauma to really get into your favorite Fruits Basket characters! Samantha, you do realize Hatori isn't real, right? Hee hee! Well, I hope your ribs have healed without a hitch! Thanks for writing such a hilarious letter!

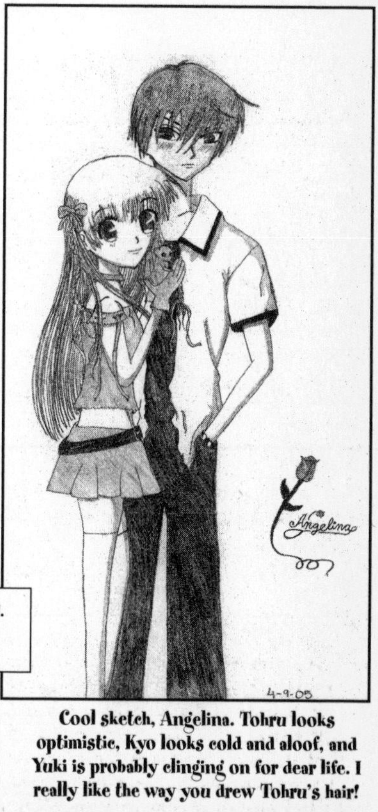
Angelina
4-9-05

Angelina H.
Age 13
Tracy, CA

Cool sketch, Angelina. Tohru looks optimistic, Kyo looks cold and aloof, and Yuki is probably clinging on for dear life. I really like the way you drew Tohru's hair!

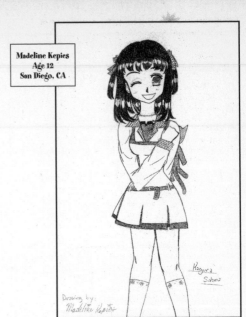

Madeline Kepies
Age 12
San Diego, CA

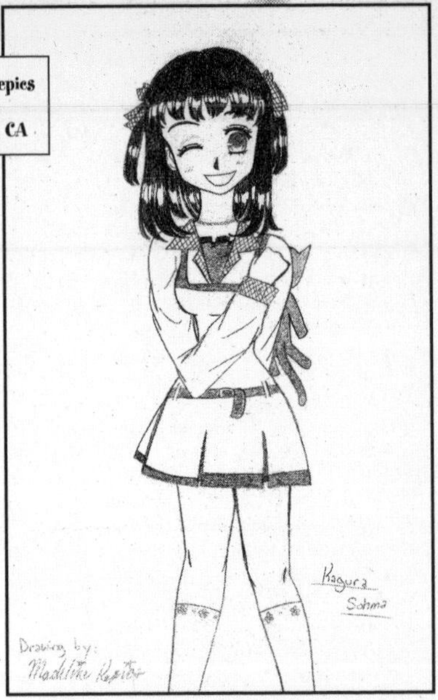
Kagura Sohma
Drawing by:

Fruits Basket **readers, I am continually amazed by your artistic talent! Madeline, you're no exception. It's hard to believe you're only twelve. Keep drawing! I love Kagura's "Kyo backpack" in your sketch! Very clever. Kagura certainly would get Kyo to cling to her...no matter what!**

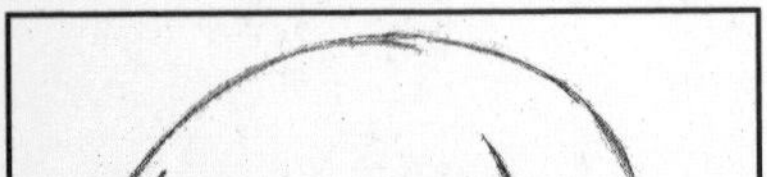

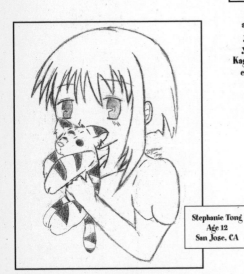

Stephanie Tong
Age 12
San Jose, CA

Another twelve-year-old! Stephanie sent in several pieces of art, but this one was my favorite. I have a soft spot for Kisa. She looks pretty sad in this picture, but she's still manages to be soooo adorably cute. The stuffed tiger is a nice touch, too! Kisa's so shy and insecure, and Stephanie really captured that by having the tiger obscure part of her face.

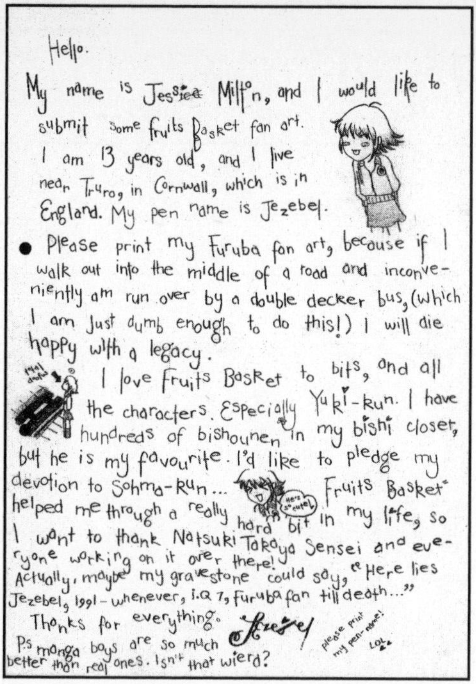

Hello.

My name is Jessica Milton, and I would like to submit some Fruits Basket fan art. I am 13 years old, and I live near Truro, in Cornwall, which is in England. My pen name is Jezebel.

• Please print my Furuba fan art, because if I walk out into the middle of a road and inconveniently am run over by a double decker bus, (which I am just dumb enough to do this!) I will die happy with a legacy.

I love Fruits Basket to bits, and all the characters. Especially Yuki-kun. I have hundreds of bishounen in my bishi closet, but he is my favourite. I'd like to pledge my devotion to Sohma-kun... Fruits Basket helped me through a really hard bit in my life, so I want to thank Natsuki Takaya Sensei and everyone working on it over there!

Actually, maybe my gravestone could say, "Here lies Jezebel, 1991-whenever, I.Q 7, Furuba fan till death..."

Thanks for everything. Jezebel

please print my pen-name! LOL

P.S manga boys are so much better than real ones. Isn't that wierd?

I just had to print Jessica's--er--Jess'--er--Jezebel's wacky letter just as she wrote it. I love the way she printed the text on the page. And I adore her cute drawings even more! You might not think you're very smart, Jezebel, but I think your letter is ingenious!

Jezebel
Age 14
Cornwall, England

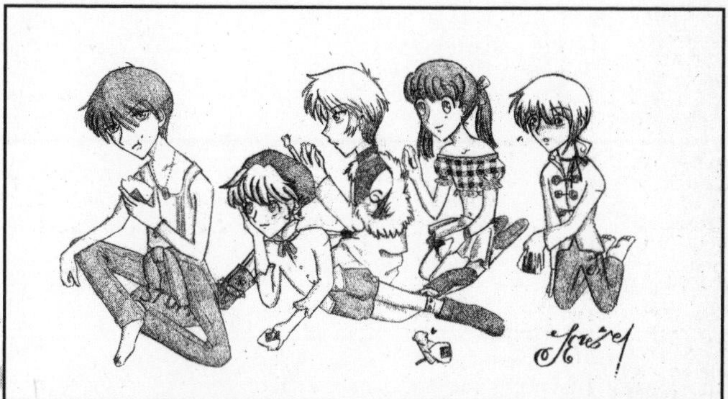

Here's Jezebel's sketch. Just as she has her own letter-writing style, you can see that she has her own art style, too! Thanks for sending this drawing all the way from England!

Do you want to share your love for *Fruits Basket* with fans around the world? "Fans Basket" is taking submissions of fan art, poetry, cosplay photos, or any other Furuba fun you'd like to share!

How to submit:

1) Send your work via regular mail (NOT e-mail) to:

"Fans Basket"
c/o TOKYOPOP
5900 Wilshire Blvd.
Suite 2000
Los Angeles, CA 90036

2) All work should be in black-and-white and no larger than 8.5" x 11". (And try not to fold it too many times!)

3) Anything you send will not be returned. If you want to keep your original, it's fine to send us a copy.

4) Please include your full name, age, city and state for us to print with your work. If you'd rather us use a pen name, please include that, too.

5) IMPORTANT: If you're under the age of 18, you must have your parent's permission in order for us to print your work. Any submissions without a signed note of parental consent cannot be used.

6) For full details, please check out our website: http://www.tokyopop.com/aboutus/fanart.php

Disclaimer: Anything you send to us becomes the exclusive property of TOKYOPOP Inc. and, as we said before, will not be returned to you. We will have the right to print, reproduce, distribute, or modify the artwork for use in future volumes of Fruits Basket or on the web royalty-free.

Joo Hyun Park
Age 13
Ellicott City, MD

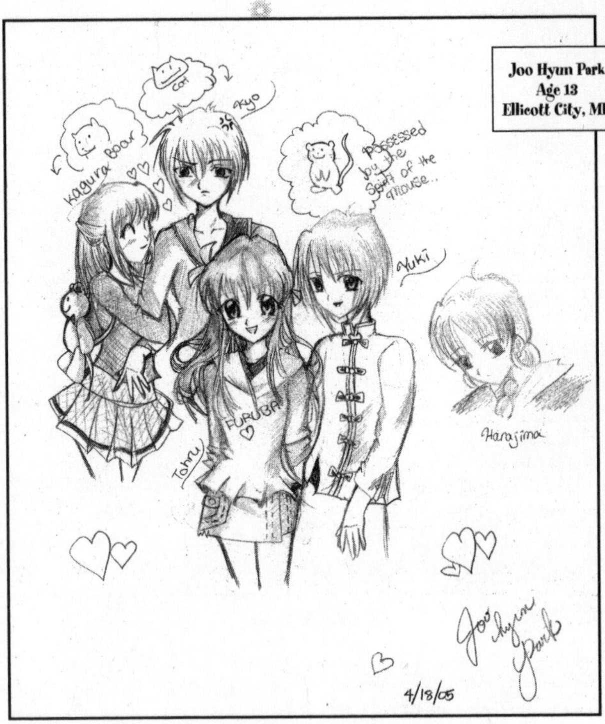

cat
Kyo
Kagura Boar
Possessed by the Spirit of the Mouse..
Yuki
FURUBA
Tohru
Hanajima
Joo Hyun Park
4/18/05

Take a look at Joo Hyun's pencil work. It's very assured, very confident! And she's only 13! This also might be the first piece of fan art I've received that features Hanajima. Nicely done.

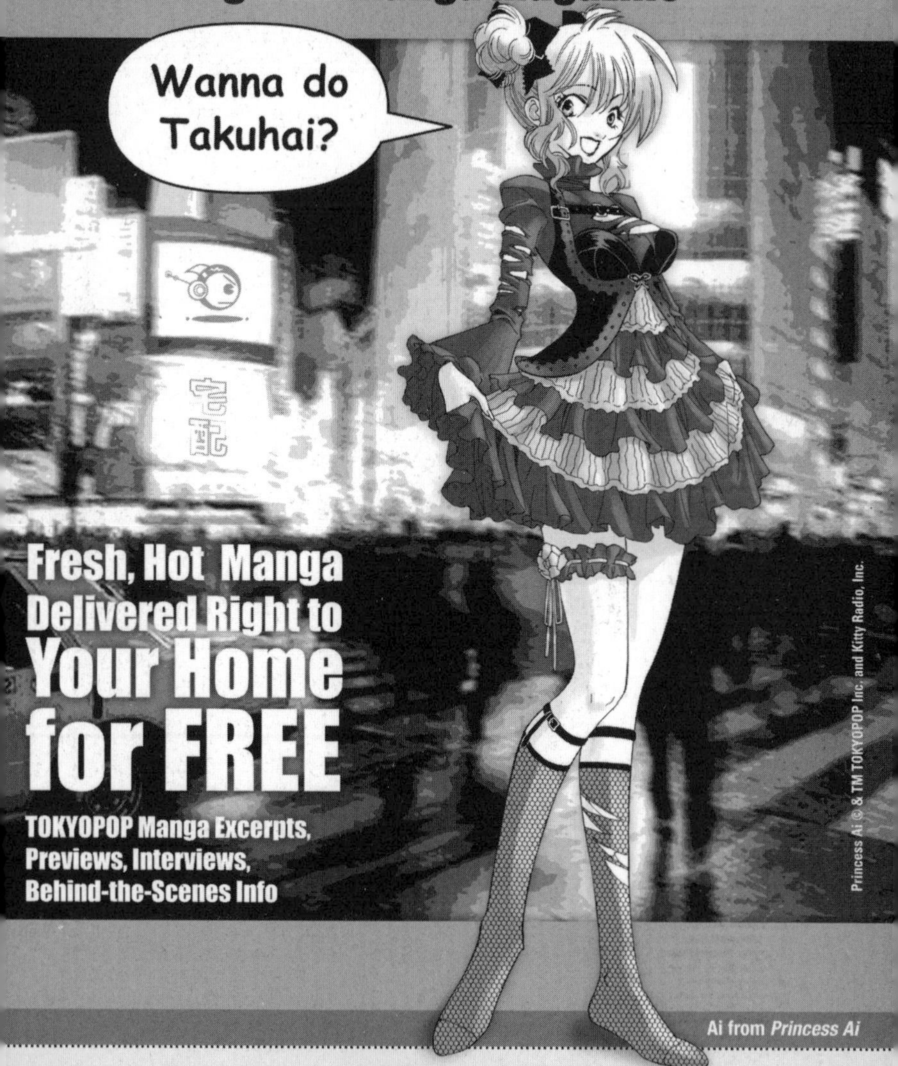
Wanna do Takuhai?
Fresh, Hot Manga Delivered Right to Your Home for FREE
TOKYOPOP Manga Excerpts, Previews, Interviews, Behind-the-Scenes Info
Princess Ai © & TM TOKYOPOP Inc. and Kitty Radio, Inc.
Ai from *Princess Ai*

TOKYOPOP SHOP

OT
OLDER TEEN
AGE 16+

In the deep South, an ancient voodoo curse unleashes the War on Flesh—a hellish plague of voracious Ew Chott hornets that raises an army of the walking dead. This undead army spreads the plague by ripping the hearts out of living creatures to make room for a Black Heart hive, all in preparation for the most awesome incarnation of evil ever imagined… An unlikely group of five mismatched individuals have to put their differences aside to try to destroy the onslaught of evil before it's too late.

VOODOO MAKES A MAN NASTY!

WAR ON FLESH

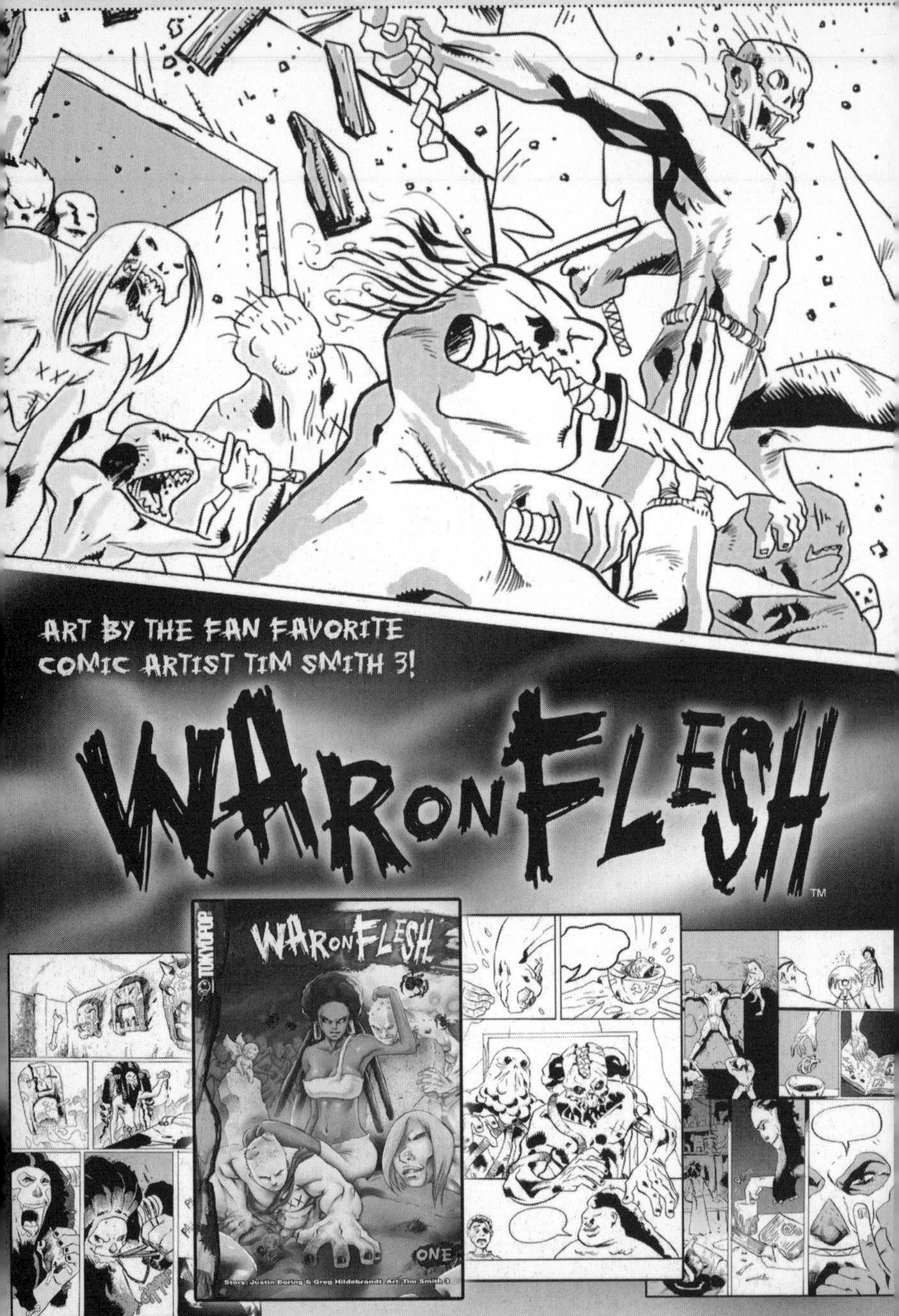
ART BY THE FAN FAVORITE
COMIC ARTIST TIM SMITH 3!
WAR ON FLESH™
TOKYOPOP
WAR ON FLESH
ONE
Story: Justin Boring & Greg Hildebrandt Art: Tim Smith 3

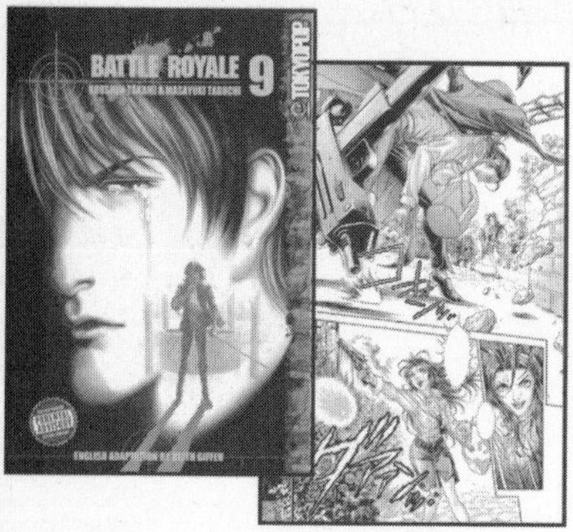
BATTLE ROYALE 9
TOKYOPOP

BY KOUSHUN TAKAMI & MASAYUKI TAGUCHI

BATTLE ROYALE

As far as cautionary tales go, you couldn't get any timelier than *Battle Royale*. Telling the bleak story of a class of middle school students who are forced to fight one another to the death on national television, Koushun Takami and Masayuki Taguchi have created a dark satire that's sickening, yet undeniably exciting as well. And if we have that reaction reading it, it becomes alarmingly clear how the students could be so easily swayed into *doing* it.

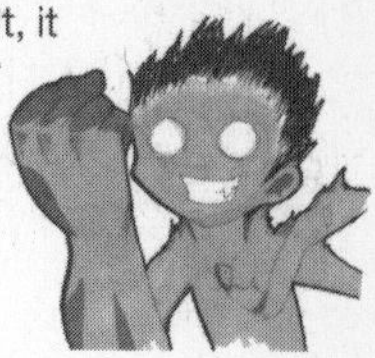

~Tim Beedle, Editor

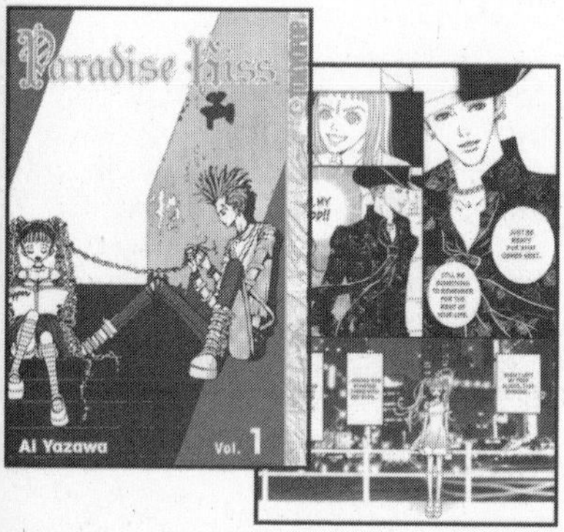
Paradise Kiss
TOKYOPOP
Ai Yazawa
Vol. 1

BY AI YAZAWA

PARADISE KISS

The clothes! The romance! The clothes! The intrigue! And did I mention the clothes?! *Paradise Kiss* is the best fashion manga ever written, from one of the hottest shojo artists in Japan. Ai Yazawa is the coolest. Not only did she create the character designs for *Princess Ai*, which were amazing, but she also produced five fab volumes of *Paradise Kiss*, a manga series bursting with fashion and passion. Read it and be inspired.

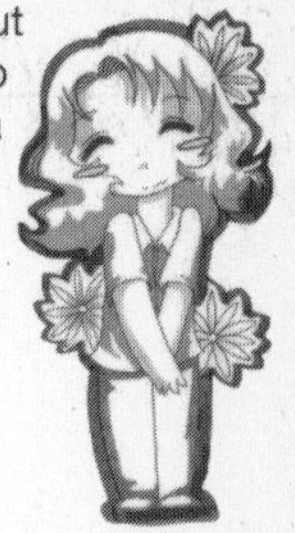

~Julie Taylor, Sr. Editor

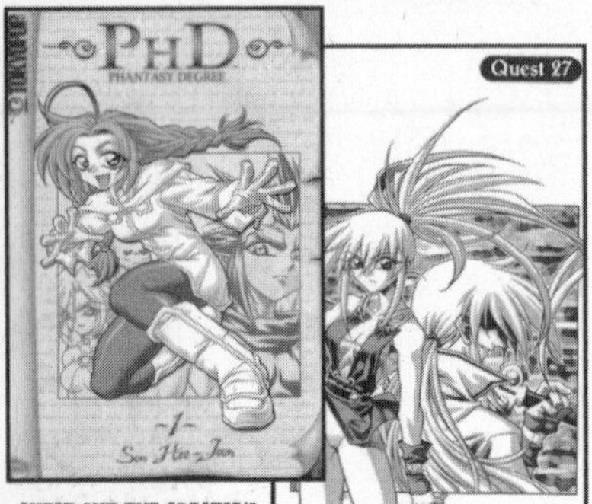
PhD
PHANTASY DEGREE
Quest 27

CHECK OUT THE CREATOR'S *iD_eNTITY*

BY SON HEE-JOON

PhD: PHANTASY DEGREE

So you think you've got it rough at *your* school? Try attending classes at Demon School Hades! When sassy, young Sang makes her monster matriculation to this arcane academy, all hell breaks loose—literally! But what would you expect when the graduating class consists of a werewolf, a mummy and demons by the score? Son Hee-Joon's underworld adventure is pure escapist fun. Always packed with action and often silly in the best sense, *PhD* never takes itself too seriously or lets the reader stop to catch his breath.

~Bryce P. Coleman, Editor

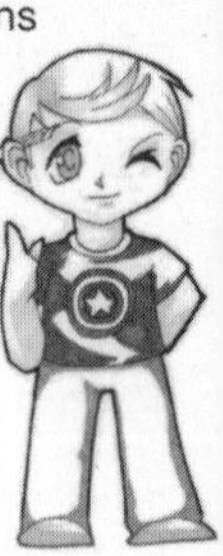

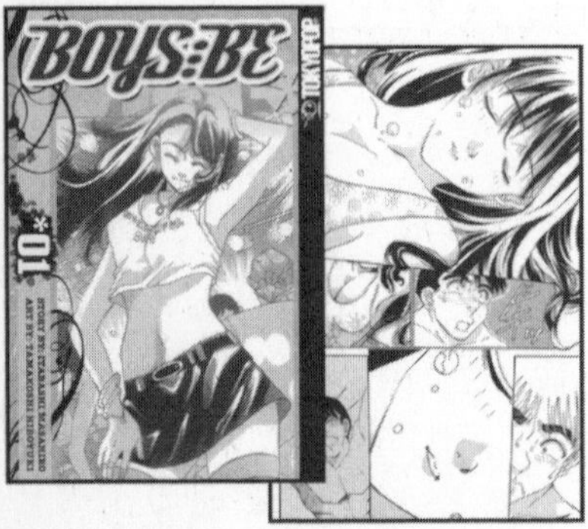
BOYS:BE
TOKYOPOP

BY MASAHIRO ITABASHI & HIROYUKI TAMAKOSHI

BOYS BE...

Boys Be... is a series of short stories. But although the hero's name changes from tale to tale, he remains Everyboy—that dorky high school guy who'll do anything to score with the girl of his dreams. You know him. Perhaps you *are* him. He is a dirty mind with the soul of a poet, a stumblebum with a heart of sterling. We follow this guy on quest after quest to woo his lady loves. We savor his victory; we reel with his defeat...and the experience is touching, funny and above all human.

Still not convinced? I have two words for you: fan service.

~Carol Fox, Editor

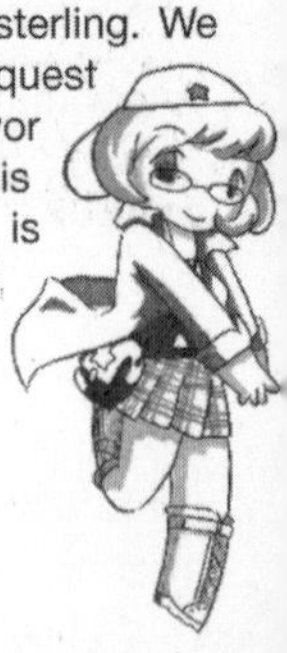

RIZELMINE
BY YUKIRU SUGISAKI

Tomonori Iwaki is a hapless fifteen-year-old whose life is turned upside down when the government announces that he's a married man! His blushing bride is Rizel, apparently the adorable product of an experiment. She does her best to win her new man's heart in this wacky romantic comedy from the creator of *D•N•Angel*!

Inspiration for the hit anime!

T TEEN AGE 13+

© YUKIRU SUGISAKI / KADOKAWA SHOTEN.

HONEY MUSTARD
BY HO-KYUNG YEO

When Ara works up the nerve to ask out the guy she has a crush on, she ends up kissing the wrong boy! The juicy smooch is witnessed by the school's puritanical chaperone, who tells their strict families. With everyone in an uproar, the only way everyone will be appeased is if the two get married—and have kids!

T TEEN AGE 13+

© Ho-Kyung Yeo, HAKSAN PUBLISHING CO., LTD.

HEAT GUY J
BY CHIAKI OGISHIMA, KAZUKI AKANE, NOBUTERU YUKI & SATELIGHT

Daisuke Aurora and his android partner, Heat Guy J, work with a special division of peacekeepers to keep anything illegal off the streets. However, that doesn't sit too well with the new ruthless and well-armed mob leader. In the city that never sleeps, will Daisuke and Heat Guy J end up sleeping with the fishes?

The anime favorite as seen on MTV is now an action-packed manga!

T TEEN AGE 13+

© Satelight/Heatguy-J Project.

STOP!

This is the back of the book.
You wouldn't want to spoil a great ending!

This book is printed "manga-style," in the authentic Japanese right-to-left format. Since none of the artwork has been flipped or altered, readers get to experience the story just as the creator intended. You've been asking for it, so TOKYOPOP® delivered: authentic, hot-off-the-press, and far more fun!

DIRECTIONS

If this is your first time reading manga-style, here's a quick guide to help you understand how it works.

It's easy... just start in the top right panel and follow the numbers. Have fun, and look for more 100% authentic manga from TOKYOPOP®!